Beauvoir

and Western Thought

from Plato to Butler

Beauvoir

and Western Thought from Plato to Butler

edited by SHANNON M. MUSSETT
and WILLIAM S. WILKERSON

Published by
STATE UNIVERSITY OF NEW YORK PRESS
Albany

© 2012 State University of New York

All rights reserved

Printed in the United States of America

No part of this book may be used or reproduced in any manner whatsoever without written permission. No part of this book may be stored in a retrieval system or transmitted in any form or by any means including electronic, electrostatic, magnetic tape, mechanical, photocopying, recording, or otherwise without the prior permission in writing of the publisher.

For information, contact
State University of New York Press
www.sunypress.edu

Production and book design, Laurie Searl
Marketing, Michael Campochiaro

Library of Congress Cataloging-in-Publication Data

Beauvoir and Western thought from Plato to Butler / edited by Shannon M. Mussett and William S. Wilkerson.
   p. cm.
  Includes bibliographical references and index.
  ISBN 978-1-4384-4454-3 (paperback : alk. paper)
  ISBN 978-1-4384-4455-0 (hardcover : alk. paper) 1. Beauvoir, Simone de, 1908–1986. 2. Philosophy. I. Mussett, Shannon M. II. Wilkerson, William S., 1968–
  B2430.B344B44 2012
  194—dc23
                              2011053328

10 9 8 7 6 5 4 3 2 1

To my father in thanks, William S. Wilkerson

To my parents for all of their encouragement, Shannon M. Mussett

Contents

Acknowledgments — ix

Editors' Introduction — 1

The Literary Grounding of Metaphysics: Beauvoir and Plato on Philosophical Fiction — 15
   Shannon M. Mussett

Existence, Freedom, and the Festival: Rousseau and Beauvoir — 35
   Sally J. Scholz

A Different Kind of Universality: Beauvoir and Kant on Universal Ethics — 55
   William S. Wilkerson

Simone de Beauvoir and the Marquis de Sade: Contesting the Logic of Sovereignty and the Politics of Terror and Rape — 75
   Debra Bergoffen

Beauvoir and Marx — 91
   William L. McBride

Saving Time: Temporality, Recurrence, and Transcendence in Beauvoir's Nietzschean Cycles — 103
   Elaine P. Miller

Beauvoir and Husserl: An Unorthodox Approach to The Second Sex — 125
   Sara Heinämaa

Beauvoir and Bergson: A Question of Influence 153
    MARGARET A. SIMONS

Beauvoir and Merleau-Ponty: Philosophers of Ambiguity 171
    GAIL WEISS

From Beauvoir to Irigaray: Making Meaning out of Maternity 191
    ERIN MCCARTHY

Ambiguity and Precarious Life: Tracing Beauvoir's Legacy in the
Work of Judith Butler 211
    ANN V. MURPHY

True Philosophers: Beauvoir and bell 227
    BELL HOOKS

Contributors 237

Index 241

Acknowledgments

As is only fitting, my first thank you is to Bill Wilkerson, who instantly took up this project from my first pitch to a table of Beauvoireans many years ago. Working with him has been nothing short of ideal. He is generous, intelligent, hardworking, and philosophically imaginative. He is also a dear friend. I would also like to thank all of the contributors to this collection. Your work has inspired me deeply and will affect future scholars in profound ways. Further, I want to thank Kris McLain for her help with researching and indexing this volume, Peg Simons for everything she does for Beauvoir scholarship, and Sheila Malovany-Chevallier and Constance Borde for their devotion and work on the new translation of *The Second Sex*. My own essay benefited tremendously from input received from Daniel Graham, Bill Wilkerson, and Michael Shaw. Finally, I would like to thank my family: Mike, Cleo, and Milo, for their love and support over the years as we saw this project through to completion. *Shannon M. Mussett*

First, I must say more than thanks to Shannon, who thought up the idea for this anthology. I just happened to be in a bar at the right time and felt lucky to see a brilliant idea when it appeared before me. Since then, I've been fortunate to work with somebody who is so smart, so hard working, and so funny, and who I now call a dear friend—thanks, buddy. Next, I'd like to thank our contributors: as I read these essays again and again, I never cease to feel privileged to have such excellent and inspiring scholarship collected together; thank you all for bringing your best work to show the continuing power of Beauvoir's thought. My thanks also go to numerous friends and colleagues, among them, Brian Martine, Peg Simons, Sarah LaChance Adams, Debra Bergoffen, Gail Weiss, and Linda Martín Alcoff; and to the editors at SUNY, who supported us without qualification from the start. Finally, gratitude goes to my partner Keith, who sat by my side, earning his graduate degree while I worked on this collection—forever this collection and your success will be intertwined in my mind. *William S. Wilkerson*

Editor's Introduction

More than twenty years after her death, the magnetism and authority of Simone de Beauvoir's writings continue to inspire new theories and connections in philosophical thinking. The resulting explosion of interest and scholarship treats her as a fully independent thinker, expressing her own views on ethics, politics, sexuality, literature, existentialism, and phenomenology. Although she now stands on her own as one the most far-reaching and innovative minds of the last century, one significant indicator of her importance has been neglected. True philosophers are extensively discussed in relation to other canonical figures in the philosophical tradition. To that end, our collection places Beauvoir in an engagement with the full spectrum of the philosophical tradition by bringing her into one-on-one conversation with individual thinkers from Plato to Irigaray. This volume thus presents Beauvoir's intellectual relationship to a remarkably wide array of thinkers: her influences, her contemporaries, and her successors, written by scholars whose expertise centers not only on Beauvoir, but also each thinker with whom they put her in direct conversation.

Thus far, scholars have demonstrated Beauvoir's independence from the circle of Sartre by showing that she either originated some of his ideas or that her ideas differ from his. Rather than address either of these approaches, our collection offers a third way to view her as a philosopher in her own right. By showing how she dialogued with a variety of thinkers and intellectuals of her own choosing, the essays in this volume show that Beauvoir sought to offer her voice as a unique response to the philosophical canon. Additionally, Beauvoir's writings inspired the works of a number of contemporary feminist thinkers, thus broadening the very definition of what constitutes the Western "canon" and offering a trajectory into future thinking that is intimately tied to the traditional sense of the history of Western philosophy. Each chapter reveals how Beauvoir's engagement with philosophers and intellectuals is remarkable in its breadth—including meditations on philosophers with approaches as different as Bergson and Kant, political thinkers like Rousseau and Marx, unexpected connections with philosophers such as Plato, important but marginal voices like Sade, as well as current philosophers such as Butler and hooks. In fact, *Beauvoir and Western Thought from Plato to Butler* has no article on the relationship to Sartre, in order to highlight the richness of her unique philosophical background and the independence with which she chose philosophical interlocutors apart from her association with Sartre.

BEAUVOIR IS NOT A PHILOSOPHER

What does it mean to call oneself a philosopher? What does it mean to take a position of theoretical engagement with prominent figures in the history of Western philosophy while remaining critical of the overall project and methodology of truth formulation at play in this history? That Beauvoir was never comfortable with the mantle of philosopher is well known. Yet, equally clear is her impact on philosophical thought in the twentieth and twenty-first centuries, as well as her thorough knowledge of and dialogue with thinkers ranging from the Greeks to the phenomenologists. As in most matters, Beauvoir's simultaneous unease with being a "philosopher" and advocacy of philosophical theory illustrates her notion of ambiguity as the core fact of human existence.

As some of the authors in this collection point out, when Beauvoir objects to the position of the philosopher, she is largely criticizing the omniscient and atemporal claims of systematic and scientific truth. The scope of his systematicity is part of why Beauvoir abdicated to Sartre—a thinker deliberately absent from the present collection—in matters philosophical. Much debate has taken place over the status of Beauvoir as a philosopher and how far we are to believe her own self-proclamations as to her philosophical inferiority.

Toril Moi, guided by Michèle Le Doeuff, points to an important event in the young Beauvoir's development as a thinker and a philosopher. As Beauvoir recounts in *Memoirs of a Dutiful Daughter*, she confronted Sartre in 1929 at the age of twenty-one for the first time with her own philosophy. She writes that,

> Day after day, and all day long I set myself up against Sartre, and in our discussions I was simply not in his class. One morning in the Luxembourg Gardens, near the Medici fountain, I outlined for him that pluralist ethics which I had cobbled together to vindicate the people I liked but whom I didn't want to resemble: he took it apart. *I clung to my system*, because it authorized me to look upon my heart as the arbiter of good and evil. (Moi 1994, 15–16; emphasis added)[1]

Sartre challenged Beauvoir for three hours and she eventually gave up her burgeoning philosophical system. According to Moi, this pivotal account "consciously or unconsciously, demonstrates the way in which the philosophical initiative now belongs to Sartre" (Moi 1994, 17). On Moi's read, Beauvoir accepts (at an early stage in her intellectual development) that Sartre is the leader in philosophical ability. Similarly, in her work on this passage, Le Doeuff argues that Beauvoir's self-effacement regarding her own abilities and her admiration for Sartre and his "gang" is a "sad" state of affairs. Le Doeuff laments, "All her life she kept repeating that she 'left the philosophy to Sartre,' as though there were room for only one person" (Le Doeuff 1991, 136–139).

Although the readings offered by Moi and Le Doeuff regarding Beauvoir's abnegation of philosophy are legitimate and in many ways accurate, they do not fully address what it is about *philosophy* that Beauvoir renounces. Educated in philosophy from a young age, pursuing philosophical studies all through her most formative years, Beauvoir was certainly interested in advanced studies in philosophy as more than just a component of her overall education.[2] In the above passage, the young Beauvoir argues for three hours to protect the *system* that she has developed. As she debates with Sartre during this episode, she experiences not only the insecurities she has regarding her own understanding, but more importantly, the *limits* of philosophical systems in general. She continues the above passage from *Memoirs of a Dutiful Daughter* saying, "I had realized, in the course of our discussion, that many of my opinions were based only on prejudice, dishonesty, or hastily formed concepts, that my reasoning was at fault and that my ideas were in a muddle" (Beauvoir 1959, 344; Moi 1991, 16). Beauvoir realizes that the system that she had developed was in fact no system at all, but rather a hodgepodge of ideas, prejudices, and personal opinions. In other words, her system was not *scientific*—it did not offer a unified and systematic interpretation of the world. By her own self-evaluation, Beauvoir was too enmeshed in the personal and the prejudicial to offer Sartre an ahistorical, atemporal, and universally valid philosophical position. Even at an early age, Beauvoir displayed an admiration for the systematicity of philosophy as evinced by her admiration of Sartre and her captivation with many of the great philosophers,[3] while still maintaining a healthy skepticism and suspicion as to its ability to address the human condition in all of its complexity.

In the *Prime of Life* we find the famous assertion made by Beauvoir that she is not a philosopher because she does not build systems. In an extensive passage she claims,

> I did not regard myself as a philosopher: I was well aware that the ease with which I penetrated to the heart of a text stemmed, precisely, from my lack of originality. In this field a genuinely creative talent is so rare that queries as to why I did not attempt to join the elite are surely otiose: it would be more useful to explain *how* certain individuals are capable of getting results from that conscious venture into lunacy known as a "philosophical system," from which they derive that obsessional attitude which endows their tentative patterns with universal insight and applicability. (Beauvoir 1960, 265)

Beauvoir says two important things in this elusive passage. On the one hand, she acknowledges that she can penetrate philosophical texts with great ease, yet curiously she attributes this ability to a "lack of originality" on her part. It seems strange that she would associate understanding philosophy with unoriginal thinking, especially when it is precisely her highly original appropriation and reconfiguration of other philosophers that makes her their equal. On the other hand, this passage shows her association of "philosophy" with "system" and her distaste for the "lunacy" of systematicity and the obsessional character one must possess to engage in such an enterprise. She goes on to claim, almost with flippancy, that this stubbornness is all but absent in women because "women are not by nature prone to obsessions of this type" (Beauvoir 1960, 266). Partially self-revelatory, but said more in jest, Beauvoir mocks the professional philosopher while admitting that her feminine conditioning did not orient her to such studies.

But perhaps taking Beauvoir at her own words in an entirely literal fashion ignores the ambiguity to which she struggled so desperately to give voice. She clearly associates philosophy with the systematicity for which she has little patience. Problematically, Moi argues that in the above passage, Beauvoir shows that she suffers from an "excessive ambition" such that "if she cannot produce an original philosophical system of her own, become the master philosopher *par excellence*, she would rather not do philosophy at all" (Moi 1991, 33). Although clearly there is an element of competitiveness to Beauvoir, to write off her wariness of the philosophical endeavor as merely indicative of her overzealous ambition ignores a deeper insight. Such suspicion on Beauvoir's part, attests to her general mistrust of the philosophical project of unifying all reality under a set of logical principles that are universal and ahistorical, that is, *scientific* in a deeply Hegelian sense. For Beauvoir, to make philosophy scientific is to speak from the perspective of the absolute, which is the standpoint of perfect truth where all doubt is removed. Such a perspective is not only impossible from the position of a finite individual, it is also dangerous and potentially tyrannical.

By focusing on contingency and individual experience, Beauvoir altogether avoids the teleological drive that plagues systems from Plato to Marx. To counter the problematic absolutism of so many thinkers in the history of philosophy, Beauvoir avers that the philosopher is always involved in her philosophy. One could argue that this is why she devoted so much of her energy to chronicling her own autobiography as she came to the awareness of her theories. One cannot eliminate the personal for Beauvoir, and this is why she begins her greatest philosophical text with the assertion: "*I* hesitated a long time before writing a book on woman," thereby showing us that it is *her* doing the analysis, not some depersonalized *philosopher* (Beauvoir 2010, 3; emphasis added). The fact that she is a woman will have everything to do with what is questioned and how it is questioned.

At the conclusion of *The Ethics of Ambiguity*, Beauvoir offers a sensitive and personal account of why she chooses existentialism, with its emphasis on the finite individual and the fundamental absurdity of existence, over the grand justifications of systematic philosophy. She writes,

> As soon as one considers a system abstractly and theoretically, one puts himself, in effect, on the plane of the universal, thus, of the infinite. That

is why reading the Hegelian system is so comforting. I remember having experienced a great feeling of calm on reading Hegel in the impersonal framework of the Bibliothèque Nationale in August 1940. But once I got into the street again, into my life, out of the system, beneath a real sky, the system was no longer of any use to me: what it had offered me, under a show of the infinite, was the consolations of death; and I again wanted to live in the midst of living men. (Beauvoir 1976, 158)

To live among human beings is to live among a plurality of contingent, factical, and absurd situations, deeds, and beliefs. Beauvoir here rejects the validation of all contingency and sacrifice in a final, grand culmination of history. She emphasizes the role of the individual not only in ethical action, but in the very investigation of philosophically understanding the human condition. Beauvoir's approach, which preserves the thickness of individual experience, makes all the difference in coming to terms with the complexities and realities of oppression, authoritarianism, alienation, and exclusion. Her rejection of strict systematicity grants her a sensitivity to those people who are silenced by the universal, those institutions that demand unquestioned allegiance, and those practices that rob the existent of the joy and struggle of living in the infinitely expansive moment.

BEAUVOIR IS A PHILOSOPHER

Yet, if Beauvoir rejects systematic philosophy and its pretensions, she nonetheless remains a philosopher. Indeed, in her century, rejection of systematic philosophy was a badge of honor for philosophers ranging from Wittgenstein to Deleuze and Guattari. In this respect, Beauvoir was always ahead of Sartre, the system builder. What is more, her rejection of system is neither haphazard nor due to any lack of ability: her autobiographical claims about inabilities hold little validity when one looks at her incisive discussions of figures in the tradition. She shows considerable knowledge of and insight into the systematic practice of philosophy. Thus, we must say that she rejects system for thoroughly principled, one might even add, *philosophical* reasons. System kills the living ambiguity that forms the ground of all philosophical thought, and it is this ground that Beauvoir seeks to think about, understand, and display.

Her philosophy thus consists precisely in the attempt to articulate this ground without falsifying it. On the one hand, this produced some discussions that any would recognize as philosophy, since, one philosophical issue above all others runs through her work: the problem of the self and the Other. Her first novel, *L'invitée*, portrayed the unsuccessful attempt of one woman, Françoise, to preserve her individuality at the cost of all other people. Yet, Beauvoir had already abandoned Françoise's ideal by the time the novel went to press. Subsequently, her philosophico-moral essays of the 1940s, *Pyrrhus and Cineas* and *Ethics of Ambiguity* begin with an individual's freedom, but in these works the individual's freedom cannot be fully realized unless the freedom of the Other is acknowledged and included in one's own project. If Beauvoir's ethical thinking comprises her most famous contribution to the school of existentialism, and the most "typically" philosophical aspect of all her writing, this probably results from her most abiding interest in the need an individual freedom has for another freedom. Such an interest cannot but result in something that will resemble modern ethics in at least one important sense: it concerns the form of the relationship the individual has with other people.

On the other hand, this interest in ethics and the relation of the self to Other can only be seen as an attempt to understand the living ground of all human existence. As two or more individual freedoms will always be indeterminate and unpredictable, there can be no way ultimately to describe or theorize their relationship in advance. Individual freedoms disclose the world to themselves and to Others in unique and individual ways. This practical fact means that no ultimate standard for living, no single way of disclosing the world, can establish itself as ultimate or universal without engaging in a kind of tyranny or false totalization. Beauvoir, although committed to human individual freedom, rejects any form of humanism that would establish a nature or *telos* in human affairs, and she equally rejects religious standards, not because they are simply false, but because even they would be understood on human terms and offer no help. Yet, even though she encourages us to reject all of these "foreign absolutes" (Beauvoir 1976, 14), Beauvoir also stops short of the negative notion of absurdity. The world we live in, according to Beauvoir, is not and can never be devoid of meaning: "human spontaneity always projects itself towards something. The psychoanalyst discovers a meaning even in abortive acts and attacks of hysteria" (Beauvoir, 1976, 25). Human beings populate the world with meaning, and this meaning is passed on from generation to generation through the process of childhood and socialization, both of which assume paramount importance in her mature thought. It is the task of each individual to take up his or her place in this social nexus of meanings, and to do so in ways that reflect an individual's own unique brilliance at living. In this respect, her ethics is also classical: Beauvoir offers practical guidance on living a "good life"—but here *eudaemonia* is replaced with a struggle to attain a justification that can never be complete, and which again comes from Others as much as it comes from oneself. And she cannot honestly offer any abstract principles or ideals for living this free life; she can at best illustrate it with concrete examples.

Beauvoir's specifically philosophical work on self and Other thus ends up leading away from "typical" philosophical approaches. She criticized her own philosophical writings often and for the same reasons that she criticized philosophical systems—for being too abstract and for leading away from the real ground of thought. Literature and autobiography were more able to show the genuine human existence, as were her more "specific" analyses of such experiences as gender and old age.

Her analyses of these phenomena arise out of her belief that individual freedoms living in a world devoid of absolutes will produce conflict and the denial of the freedom of some by others. Indeed, she shares with Sartre and Heidegger some notion of inauthentic living or bad faith. In her scheme, people fall into bad faith or dishonesty when they try to hold onto a particular way of living or value as absolute, typically out of fear or anxiety. The tendency toward this kind of life builds itself into the very structure of human consciousness and freedom: as beings without a determinate nature, the struggle to maintain meaning and justification falls into a degenerated state of allowing an external absolute to determine our existence.[4] Only individual human effort, supported by the freedom of others, can prevent this, but that means we can look only to ourselves and to others for success. It also means that, paradoxically, failure is the very condition necessitating success and for this reason Beauvoir eschews any utopian ideals: complete harmonizing of wills is neither possible nor desirable.

The perspective she opens up thus finds that oppression is the greatest evil that can be named—the denial of one's freedom by another:

> Only man can be an enemy for man; only he can rob him of the meaning of his acts and his life because it also belongs to him alone to confirm it in its existence, to recognize it in actual fact as freedom. . . . . if [other men] keep me below the level which they have conquered and on the basis of which new conquests will be achieved, then they are cutting me off from the future; they are changing me into a thing. (Beauvoir 1976, 82)

Beauvoir's concern with this particular human evil stretches across the entirety of her career. From her young worries about the ill effects of the repressive structures of the Catholic Church, through her ethics, and on to her mature discussions of gender, race, class, and age as social locations fraught with oppression and inequality.

This work on oppression, particularly the groundbreaking discussion of gender in her chef d'oeuvre, *The Second Sex,* is among her most famous, but it is important to see the deep connections between this work and her overall philosophical project. We must see just *how* it is also philosophy, in other words. Beauvoir's view that any individual's freedom can only be realized in relation to another means that the distorted structures of socialization, like those of gender, consign much of humanity to an imperfect realization of their freedom and their own selves. While this is obvious for women or racial minorities who live under the yoke of domination, Beauvoir maintains that oppressive structures require bad faith on the part of the oppressors as well, and so distort all human living. The initially abstract discussions of bad faith and the lack of genuine human freedom in the earlier work becomes explicit, concrete explanations of how humans refuse the freedom that defines them, and refuse it in ways that produce inequalities and deformations across all of society.

Some might brand this later work as "less philosophical" because it is less "universal," but Beauvoir, in fact, turns this criticism around. Just as she rejects the pretensions of system builders for freezing the fluidity of living experience, so she deliberately turns away from the idea that a universal human knowledge can be found and that a universal human condition is the object philosophers seek to describe. Even the most basic descriptions of human experience, discovered by her phenomenologically trained companions, contain unacknowledged distortions and blind spots because they neglect to see human existence as *gendered*. Since there could be no real universal human experience or knowledge, philosophy begins with concrete particularity and must stay at this level if it is not to falsify itself. Although not a system builder, Beauvoir's methods and subject matter remain remarkably consistent and consonant, and also a testament to doing philosophy in a way that never denies ambiguity but allows it to appear irreducibly.

BEAUVOIR AND WESTERN THOUGHT

True to the stated desire to place Beauvoir in a dialogue with the rich traditions of Western philosophy from her past, present, and future, this collection presents twelve original essays. The authors trace a historical trajectory of Beauvoir's engagement with philosophers from the past, her dialogue with her contemporary milieu and her impact on later thinkers.

Beginning with Beauvoir's relationship to ancient Greek philosophy is a fitting place to open up any historical treatment of Beauvoir's thought. Exploring an unexpected connection between Beauvoir and Plato, in "The Literary Grounding of Metaphysics: Beauvoir and Plato on Philosophical Fiction," Shannon M. Mussett writes on the theme of metaphysical fiction. Providing an in-depth analysis of Beauvoir's essay, "Literature and Metaphysics," Mussett applies Beauvoir's study of philosophy and literature to Plato's *Phaedrus*. Teasing out a number of key elements of the metaphysical novel—such as the emphasis on the ambiguous nature of experience, the *activity* of system building over the presentation of a completed system, and a focus on lived embodiment as the ground for systematic and scientific truth—Mussett finds Plato to be a model of the kind of philosophical fiction that Beauvoir advocates as the highest expression of both metaphysics *and* literature. Mussett argues that: "Given the significance of philosophical literature to Beauvoir's corpus, Plato becomes a central figure in understanding what her existentialism seeks to accomplish in its stated aim to disclose the singular and finite texture of existence." The interpretative approach provided by Mussett's treatment of Beauvoir opens up a reading not only of the *Phaedrus*, but also of any Platonic dialogue depicting robust descriptions of character, setting, plot, and myth.

Sally J. Scholz presents an intriguing connection between Beauvoir and Rousseau on the role of festivals in their respective philosophies. In "Existence, Freedom, and the Festival: Rousseau and Beauvoir," Scholz investigates the commitments between the individual and his or her community as revealed in these temporary yet recurrent events. Not only do Rousseau and Beauvoir share a belief in the significance of the festival in understanding the relationship between the members of the community to each other and to the whole, both philosophers share the belief that the festival embodies freedom. Scholz demonstrates how for Rousseau and Beauvoir, "festivals illustrate our most vibrant human characteristics—those we embrace as well as those we scorn—while also simply providing a space for communal celebration." As rare sites of exuberant merriment and social self-reflection, festivals honor our freedom as well as serve as vehicles to uncover and even remedy social inequities according to the philosophies of both Beauvoir and Rousseau.

William S. Wilkerson's "A Different Kind of Universality: Beauvoir and Kant on Universal Ethics," traces out the complex relationship between Kantian ethics and Beauvoir's own ethics. While Beauvoir disavowed the Kantian aspects of her own thought, they nonetheless both articulate an ethic of autonomy that sees obligation arising from the very fact of human freedom. Yet, they differ significantly: Kant argues that this human freedom is inherently rational; Beauvoir sees human freedom originating in our very lack of a predetermined nature. As a consequence, no singular moral principle can guide human living, and her ethics thus turns out to be explicitly anti-universal. Wilkerson writes that "Beauvoir does not solve the problem of conflicting freedoms in a higher universality; she only shows how it arises and offers practical advice for living with it." However, Beauvoir can still be said to have a kind of universality; rather than the "spatial" universal that Kant portrays in which all individuals are equally and always already obligated, Beauvoir describes a temporal universality that requires individuals to continually will their own ambiguity as a positive fact about themselves.

In "Simone de Beauvoir and the Marquis de Sade: Contesting the Logic of Sovereignty and the Politics of Terror and Rape," Debra Bergoffen portrays the ambiguity of Beauvoir's thought with respect to the person and thought of the Marquis de Sade. On the one hand, Beauvoir sees in Sade an authentic recognition of the difficulties of intersubjectivity; on the other hand, she is repelled by Sade's own view of sovereignty which denies a fully human and free status to individuals (despite Sade's own protestations about the illegitimate sovereignty of the state). Bergoffen writes, "the logic which circumscribes the possibility of being an individual in Sade's world by making it a matter of class privilege or terrorist power operates today when certain peoples claim the right and use their power to expel others from the sphere of the human." With this, she masterfully connects the discussion of Sade with Beauvoir's later writing on the Boupacha case and the current use of terror and rape as tools of war and conquest. Bergoffen shows how Beauvoir's reading of Sade remains relevant today by providing us with an embodied standard for condemning sovereignty, terror, and rape.

The chapter by William L. McBride, "Beauvoir and Marx," considers the relationship of Beauvoir's thought to that of Marx. Noting that there are relatively few references to Marx and Marxism in her published writings, McBride nevertheless shows that Beauvoir's understanding of Marx was deep and accurate. More importantly, McBride shows the curious contradiction in her relationship with Marx. Her thought in *The Second Sex* is indebted to Marx's democratic idea of a society of equals, and she sees Marx as sympathetic to the oppression of women. Typically, as McBride shows, Beauvoir defends Marx, even if she retains a critical distance. Conversely, the very thought and direction of *The Second Sex* ends up radically transforming and resituating Marxist thought. By showing both the validity of the existential-phenomenological approach for understanding oppression, and also the necessity of thinking about gender as a world-historical fact on the same level as class, Beauvoir's work shows the limits of a Marxist approach that thinks only in terms of class and what emerges "from *The Second Sex* and the vast intellectual movement that it ultimately generated was in fact no longer the Marxism of Marx."

In "Saving Time: Temporality, Recurrence, and Transcendence in Beauvoir's Nietzschean Cycles," Elaine P. Miller unearths a deep association between Beauvoir and Nietzsche on the centrality of willing. Specifically, Miller focuses on the way that Beauvoir utilizes a Nietzschean conception of willing through time as a way to both critique the confinement of women to immanence as well as to show the possibilities of escaping the cyclic time of housework and domestic life in general. The repetitive and alienating time of labor in Marx reappears in Beauvoir's analysis of woman's confinement to mostly uncreative work. Avoiding the pitfalls of indifference and fanaticism, Nietzsche's conception of the eternal return provides Beauvoir with a positive model of repetition and a way out of this cycle of immanence. This view of transcendence, Miller argues, "is a self-surpassing that takes place firmly within this existence, and one that will always give rise to further self-overcomings." As such, Beauvoir reiterates the fundamental insight of Zarathustra by transforming all "it was" into "thus I willed it" through the artful transformation out of immanence and into transcendence.

"Beauvoir and Husserl: An Unorthodox Approach to *The Second Sex*," by Sara Heinämaa, takes up the question of the body in Beauvoir's thought in relation to both Husserl and the phenomenological tradition more generally. Heinämaa shows that Beauvoir's approach to the body and gender in *The Second Sex* is more radical than might be thought. Beauvoir does not just reject masculine standards for understanding women; she shows instead that there are no gender-neutral understandings or standards that could be used to think about human existence. Hence, Beauvoir's contributions to the phenomenology of human existence consist not just in "adding" the perspective of women but most importantly in showing how both men's and women's existence is misunderstood because of gender bias. Beauvoir's "discourse on feminine experience implies fundamental claims about human existence," and, Heinämaa argues, "by developing this discourse further we can question certain dominant ideas of 20th century phenomenology of embodiment." She concludes by showing how pregnant embodiment causes us to rethink many of the common understandings of how the body is lived.

Margaret A. Simons provides striking evidence of the influence that Henri Bergson had on Beauvoir's early philosophical development in the paper, "Beauvoir and Bergson: A Question of Influence." Continuing her work on the recently compiled and translated student diaries, Simons shows that despite Beauvoir's autobiographical protestations against being a kind of "female Bergson," she was in fact quite captivated by Bergsonian philosophy long before her introduction to thinkers such as Hegel, Marx, Sartre, or Husserl. As a result, her theories of intersubjectivity, freedom, and bad faith were initially developed in communication with the Bergsonian ideas of the social self and the deep self, intuition, and the importance of literature to philosophy. Simons notes, "Beauvoir's autobiographical erasure of her early enthusiasm for Bergson's philosophy is part of a wider autobiographical erasure of her work in philosophy," which has been a consistent problem in Beauvoir scholarship. Even though Beauvoir later distances herself from Bergson, his obvious influence, as discovered in Simons' work in the diaries, allows us to contextualize this erasure within the larger question of Beauvoir as a philosopher. With this in mind, Simons concludes with an analysis Beauvoir's early fiction, *When Things of the Spirit Come First* and *She Came to Stay*, reading them through the lens of key Bergsonian ideas.

In "Beauvoir and Merleau-Ponty: Philosophers of Ambiguity," Gail Weiss discusses the centrality of ambiguity to both of these philosophers. Although Weiss notes that both consider ambiguity to be among their central concepts, she nicely displays the different use each thinker made of ambiguity. For Merleau-Ponty, ambiguity fundamentally names the indeterminacy in the field of our perception. Since perception is our most basic and primary hold on the world, this ambiguity ramifies throughout the whole of our existence, into or conceptual understandings and even our freedom. As Weiss shows, Beauvoir acknowledges this ambiguity by focusing her discussion on the ambiguity of our desire to exist and to be. We are always caught, Beauvoir argues, between a desire to disclose a world in all its ambiguity, and a desire to trap being in a singular project that denies ambiguity. Yet, this does not mean that we can escape the desire to avoid ambiguity; rather it is "in affirming the competing desires that produce the failure, that I succeed existentially and ethically in assuming the ambiguity of my existence."

Erin McCarthy's chapter, "From Beauvoir to Irigaray: Making Meaning out of Maternity," explores the connection between Beauvoir and Irigaray on the issue reproduction. Noting the bind feminists face in discussing maternity because of the historical weight of women's confinement to their biological bodies, McCarthy finds that both Beauvoir and Irigaray offer us a way to approach maternity as liberatory—even if a woman does not bear any biological children—and worthy of celebration. Although both feminists offer views to support maternity as a positive experience of embodiment, McCarthy argues that Irigaray takes us further than Beauvoir, who found the myth of maternity to be a particularly virulent force in women's oppression. Thus, as McCarthy informs us, "where Beauvoir seeks to escape the myth of maternity through first exposing and then rejecting it, Irigaray embraces the maternal as a metaphor" insofar as woman's becoming is always in flux and full of the possibilities of creative movement. As such, a characterization of women that has long served as a site of historical oppression gives way to a positive form of embodiment and transcendence.

Ann V. Murphy's chapter, "Ambiguity and Precarious Life: Tracing Beauvoir's Legacy in the Work of Judith Butler," begins by addressing Beauvoir's often troubled acceptance in philosophical circles and popular culture. Briefly acknowledging

Beauvoir's influence on Butler's theory of gender performativity, the main focus of Murphy's article surrounds Butler's more recent theory of corporeal vulnerability. Murphy argues "that Butler's recent philosophy of vulnerability—couched in the language of dispossession and precariousness—is deeply resonant with Beauvoir's own thinking on the ambiguity that accompanies all human action to the degree that it is haunted, permanently, by the possibility of violence." Murphy expands our understanding of Beauvoir's influence on Butler in the latter's development of not only the notions of vulnerability, but also precariousness, interdependency, and their social and ethical implications. Carefully studying Beauvoir's formulation of ambiguity alongside Butler's notion of precariousness, Murphy discovers many previously unexplored correlations between these two thinkers along the lines of violence, responsibility, and the obfuscation of the fragility of the human condition.

The final chapter of the collection, "True Philosophers: Beauvoir and bell" illuminates not only Beauvoir's importance to contemporary philosophy but the way in which philosophers speak to each other across time and space. As a contemporary feminist who continues to impact culture in profound ways, bell hooks provides an essay which serves as both an extension of the historical treatment of Beauvoir's thought, as well as a disruption of the very notion of canonical thinking. Unsettling the boundaries of thinking generally, hooks works both within and outside of traditional Western philosophy in her corpus and this essay is no different. In many ways, hooks's own strategy to write on the margins illuminates how Beauvoir, too, was a part the Western philosophical tradition, as well one of its greatest twentieth-century critics. In her only sustained treatment of Beauvoir's philosophy to date, hooks writes of the profound impact that Beauvoir's philosophy and autobiography had on her as she moved from the segregated South of her childhood, through her college education, and into her status as independent thinker and writer. As hooks notes, Beauvoir's "life, her work, was vital to my survival and personal growth for she was the one female intellectual, thinker/writer who had lived fully the life of the mind as I longed to live it." Regardless of the fact that hooks and Beauvoir offer fundamentally opposed positions on gender, their shared dedication to the philosophical life and feminist movement unite them in surprising and moving ways. hooks's writing stands as a testament to the profound impact that Beauvoir has on contemporary philosophy as well as confirms the continued relevance and power of contemporary feminist scholarship.

This collection reveals the complexity and depth of Beauvoir's relationship to Western philosophy. Not only was Beauvoir a revolutionary thinker on the issues of gender, age, and oppression, she was deeply committed to dialoguing with the rich traditions that educated her throughout her life. Her work is a testament to the achievements of the kind of philosophy that relentlessly challenges itself and in so doing, opens up radically new pathways of thinking. As every author in this collection illustrates, Beauvoir is a force that remains relevant not only to the study of the history of philosophy, but also to contemporary and future advances in philosophical discovery.

NOTES

1. This passage can also be found in Beauvoir 1959, 344. See also Le Doeuff 1991, 136.
2. See Simons 1999 for one of many rich discussions of Beauvoir's philosophical development as a student.
3. With the recent publication of Beauvoir's student diaries (Beauvoir 2006), her profound understanding and admiration of a surprising number of philosophers has been made all the more apparent.
4. Beauvoir's fascination with the allure of the absolute is a central theme not only of her philosophical work, but her literary writings as well. See Mussett 2005.

WORKS CITED

Beauvoir, Simone de. 2010. *The Second Sex*. Trans. Sheila Malovany Chevallier, Constance Borde. New York: Knopf Doubleday.

———. 2006. *Diary of a Philosophy Student: Volume 1, 1926–27*. Ed. Barbara Klaw, Sylvie Le Bon de Beauvoir, and Margaret A. Simons with Marybeth Timmermann. Trans. Barbara Klaw. Urbana: University of Illinois Press.

———. 2004. Pyrrhus and Cineas. In *Philosophical Writings*, 77–150. Ed. Margaret A. Simons and Sylvie Le Bon de Beauvoir. Trans. Marybeth Timmermann and Mary Beth Mader. Urbana: University of Illinois Press.

———. 1976. *The Ethics of Ambiguity*. Trans. Bernard Frechtman. New York: Citadel Press.

———. 1960. *The Prime of Life*. Trans. Peter Green. New York: Lancer Books.

———. 1959. *Memoires of a Dutiful Daughter*. Trans. James Kirkup. New York: Viking Penguin.

Le Doeuff, Michèle. 1991. *Hipparchia's Choice: An Essay Concerning Women, Philosophy, Etc.* Trans. Trista Selous. Oxford: Blackwell Publishers.

Moi, Toril. 1994. *Simone de Beauvoir: The Making of an Intellectual Woman*. Oxford: Blackwell Publishers.

Mussett, Shannon M. 2005. "Personal Choice and the Seduction of the Absolute in *The Mandarins*." In *The Contradictions of Freedom: Philosophical Essays on Simone de Beauvoir's* The Mandarins. Ed. Sally J. Scholz and Shannon M. Mussett. Albany: State University of New York Press.

Simons, Margaret A. 1999. "Beauvoir's Early Philosophy: The 1927 Diary." In *Beauvoir and the Second Sex: Feminism, Race, and the Origins of Existentialism*. Lanham, MD: Rowman & Littlefield.

The Literary Grounding of Metaphysics

Beauvoir and Plato on Philosophical Fiction

SHANNON M. MUSSETT

> Indeed, Plato has given to all posterity the model of a new art form, the model of the *novel.*
> —Nietzsche, *The Birth of Tragedy*

INTRODUCTION

Simone de Beauvoir's essay, "Literature and Metaphysics" (1946) advocates for the metaphysical novel on the grounds that it provides a rich dialogue between lived experience, artistic creation, and philosophical practice. Outright rejecting the possibility of philosophers like Aristotle, Spinoza, or Leibniz writing novels because of the absence of subjectivity and temporality in their works, Beauvoir finds the case of Plato to be more ambiguous. In a revealing passage, she discusses the connection between literature and metaphysics that motivates her own writing and that unites her, somewhat surprisingly, to the Greek giant. She explains:

> As long as Plato asserts the supreme reality of the Forms, which this world only mirrors in a deceptive, debased way, he has no use for poets; he banishes them from his republic. But when he describes the dialectical movement that carries man toward the Forms, when he integrates man and the sensible world into reality, then Plato feels the need to make himself a poet. He situates his dialogues that show a path to an intelligible heaven amidst blooming fields, around a table, at a deathbed, that is, on earth. (Beauvoir 2004, 274)[1]

Such allusions to Plato often indicate the necessity of art for meaningful existence and the rejection of philosophical abstraction as the ultimate truth; however, few of them so poignantly praise Plato's writing as an example of philosophical fiction.

I propose that Beauvoir's understanding of the metaphysical novel places her in direct communion with the Platonic dialogue.[2] With this in mind, I read Beauvoir's essay alongside Plato's masterpiece, the *Phaedrus*, in order to highlight the aesthetic connection between these two thinkers. The *Phaedrus* illustrates the exact tension that Beauvoir explicates above as it struggles between the poetry of embodiment and the rejection of it as overly problematic and confusing to philosophical practice. As indicated by the above quotation, Beauvoir has in mind Plato's dialogues of the so-called middle period (the *Republic, Phaedo, Symposium*, and particularly the *Phaedrus*[3]). Such focus is not surprising, given the richness not only of Platonic doctrine in these works but also of the carnal presence of the characters and settings, and the proliferation of myths which are themselves philosophical fictions. Of all of Plato's dialogues, the *Phaedrus*, with the combination of its dramatic setting, the erotic (and therefore deeply personal) nature of its subject matter and the abundant myths, offers a most illuminating illustration of Beauvoir's idea of the metaphysical novel.

To do justice to the richness of the connection between Beauvoir and Plato, this paper is divided into three sections. In the first section, I place the question of the metaphysical novel in a historical trajectory that is framed specifically by Nietzsche's rejection of the Platonic style as novelistic. Following this, I discuss Beauvoir's denunciation of systematic philosophy and her embracing of the metaphysical novel as superior in disclosing living reality. Finally, I turn to the *Phaedrus* to show that, Nietzsche's criticisms notwithstanding, Plato provides a model for the metaphysical work of fiction as outlined by Beauvoir. Given the significance of philosophical literature to Beauvoir's corpus, Plato becomes a central figure in understanding what her existentialism seeks to accomplish in its stated aim to disclose the singular and finite texture of existence. This paper thus offers a Beauvoirean reading of a single Platonic text in order to demonstrate how—despite their myriad differences—both are engaged in writing metaphysical literature.

HISTORICAL CONFIGURATION OF THE WORK

Nietzsche's reading of the Platonic dialogue in *The Birth of Tragedy* is far from eulogistic. Observing the way in which it supplants the earlier forms of tragedy and poetry, he claims "the Platonic dialogue . . . hovers between narrative, lyric, and drama, between prose and poetry" (Nietzsche 1967, 90). With its somewhat sloppy mixture of artistic forms, he famously notes that the Platonic dialogue is the barge on which ancient poetry survived with all of her children. Nietzsche argues that Plato offers the world the first form of the novel, which places dialectical philosophy and poetry into an unequal relationship. With the ascendency of systematic thought, philosophy gains mastery over poetic art and forces the latter to serve its needs as the condition of its survival. With the advent of Plato's literary form, "poetry holds the same rank in relation to dialectical philosophy as this same philosophy held for many centuries in relation to theology: namely, the rank of *ancilla*. This was the new position into which Plato, under the pressure of the demonic Socrates, forced poetry" (Nietzsche 1967, 91). In short, Plato's genius is not to be found in his brilliant blending of philosophy and literature, but rather, in the crafty way that he subjects literature to the domination of scientific thought.[4] With the death of tragedy, the new philosophical hero is born who oversees the process wherein "philosophical thought overgrows art and compels it to cling close to the trunk of dialectic" (Nietzsche 1967, 91).

Nietzsche's scathing criticisms of Plato somewhat belies the German's own relationship to philosophy and literature. The charge against the Platonic dialectic as the first form of the novel is more complicated than Nietzsche lets on initially in *The Birth of Tragedy*. Nietzsche was himself a voracious reader of novels by authors such as Cervantes, Dostoyevsky, Flaubert, and many others.[5] And of course, *Thus Spoke Zarathustra* stands as one of the quintessential philosophical novels of the Western tradition. Despite his vilification of Plato as novelistic in *The Birth of Tragedy*, he also shows gratitude to the Greek for saving poetry for posterity. Because of Plato, we have a historical lineage connecting the tragic age and modernity. Nietzsche's views on the relationship between philosophy and literature influenced modern existentialism, and particularly, modern existentialist novels.[6] Given Nietzsche's derisive evaluation of Plato as the one who brought to an end the tragic age of Greek art and engendered the form of the modern novel, Beauvoir's voice emerges as one artistically beholden to the influence of both Plato and Nietzsche. In the essay, "Literature and Metaphysics," the connections become particularly apparent.

Deirdre Bair tells us that Beauvoir's essay "Literature and Metaphysics" was born out of a lecture Beauvoir gave in February 1945, to Gabriel Marcel's students in which she defended existentialism against unsympathetic attacks.[7] As Bair notes, "this essay is her only sustained example of literary criticism," even if it doesn't stick strictly to the standard definition of that style (Bair 1990, 320).[8] Read in this light, we can see Beauvoir attempting to defend Existentialism on *artistic* grounds. She accordingly proposes not only a new way to understand the relationship between philosophy and literature, but like Nietzsche before her, a way to comprehend philosophy *as* literature, or at least as thoroughly indebted to the artistic, rather than the theoretical, impulse. From this vantage point, Beauvoir's clear ranking of literature over abstract metaphysics makes perfect sense.

Toward the end of "Literature and Metaphysics," Beauvoir warns that we should be wary of those who try to cover over dead essences with the living veneer of experience. She assures us, though, that "this fear is well founded only in regard to philosophers who, separating essence from existence, disdain appearance in favor of the hidden reality; fortunately, *they are not tempted to write novels*" (Beauvoir 2004, 275; emphasis mine). In one stroke, Beauvoir banishes the philosophers of abstract concepts who attempt to make their theories speak by adding lived experience to dead theories. But who then is Plato through this Beauvoirean lens? Is he, as Nietzsche argues, a philosopher who has pillaged art and made it the handmaiden of philosophy through the form of the novel? Would Plato as an artist thus be guilty of those same crimes of which Beauvoir herself was accused—writing *romans à thèse* with characters who are little more than "incarnated ideas"?[9] Or, is Plato, in fact, the originator of the philosophical novel that Beauvoir so fervently believes in and to which existentialist writing so often aspires? This last possibility allows us to view the modern existentialist project as a massive arc returning to the style and project of Plato. Rather than outright rejecting the Platonic project on Nietzschean grounds, we can take Plato as the form of a philosophical aesthetic that both discloses truth and yet denies the notion that truth could ever be totally divulged.

Despite the correlation I propose, Beauvoir urges that we see the artistic inclination of existentialism as an expression of the core ambiguity of existence, a theme we can hardly attribute at first glance to Plato. She writes: "It is not by chance if existentialist thought today attempts to express itself sometimes by theoretical treatises and sometimes by fiction; it is because it is an effort to reconcile the objective and the subjective, the absolute and the relative, the timeless and the historical" (Beauvoir 2004, 274). If we downplay the emphasis on truth and highlight instead the aporetic nature of the Platonic dialogue, then the connection between these two thinkers becomes more apparent. Despite the fact that the goal of the dialogue most often centers on seeking formal essences, Beauvoir is right to point out the myriad ways in which such a goal is sought through the same reconciliations attempted by existentialist thought.[10] Seen from this perspective, modern existentialism overtly (but more often covertly) pays homage to the iconic presentation of the Platonic dialogue, which never fully answers the questions it proposes. Plato's skill focuses on the *method* of questioning, which is besieged by ambiguities of all kinds; a central component to Beauvoir's philosophy similarly emphasizes the expression and celebration of ambiguity as the very condition of our existence.

Clearly, the Western tradition harbors its fair share of philosophers who seek to cure, decipher, or deny ambiguity. For this reason, Beauvoir opens the *Ethics of Ambiguity* by observing that "as long as there have been men and they have lived, they have all felt this tragic ambiguity of their condition, but as long as there have been philosophers and they have thought, most of them have tried to mask it" (Beauvoir 1997, 7). There is something deeply dishonest in most philosophical endeavors—including Plato's—which attempt to "solve" the ambiguity of existence. However, those endeavors—including Plato's—that seek to *disclose* this ambiguity are in many ways the most authentic forms of philosophical expression. When Plato's theories emerge from the living, embodied, and experiential ground of existence—that is, when they emerge out of *life as art*—they embody the ideal of metaphysical literature or, for Beauvoir, philosophy in its highest form.[11]

BEAUVOIR AND SYSTEMATIC PHILOSOPHY

If we are to grasp the crucial point that Beauvoir argues in "Literature and Metaphysics," namely, that "philosophical concerns are far from finding themselves incompatible with the requirements of the novel" (Beauvoir 2004, 275), then it behooves us to look at her first from the perspective of a philosopher and then as a writer (even as she eschews this kind of artificial separation). Beauvoir criticizes the uses and abuses of systematic thinking in two ways. First, she takes issue with the position of the philosopher as a depersonalized, universalized, and unbiased mouthpiece of truth, and second, she disparages the promotion of unified systems of reality accessible to intellection and abstraction alone.[12] This systematic thinking allows the supposed voice of truth to abstract from the individual, removing the concreteness of subjective experience. These two poles of abstraction lead to her famous and controversial rejection of the moniker "philosopher."[13]

Despite her mistrust of abstraction, it is crucial to realize that Beauvoir draws a sharp distinction between "systematic" and "metaphysical" in her essay. She explains:

> Metaphysics is, first of all, not a system; one does not "do metaphysics as one "does" mathematics or physics. In reality, "to do" metaphysics is "to be" metaphysical; it is to realize in oneself the metaphysical attitude, which consists in positing oneself in one's totality before the totality of the world. Every human event possesses a metaphysical signification beyond its psychological and social elements, since through each event, man is always entirely engaged in the entire world. (Beauvoir 2004, 273)

In this remarkably profound and rich claim, Beauvoir denies the systematic nature of metaphysics itself. Metaphysics is actually an attitude—an attunement to world—wherein (much like Kierkegaard would assert) we posit ourselves as singular totalities in a relationship with the totality of the world. Although we can never grasp the limits of this relationship, the metaphysical attitude takes the position of the radically individualized subject wholly connected to the vastness of the world at each moment. Given the impossibility of systematizing this relationship, Beauvoir forces us to understand it more as an *experience* or an overall *metaphysical attitude*.

Beauvoir zeroes in on the shortcomings of systematic philosophy to capture this metaphysical attitude:

> There is an original grasping of metaphysical reality . . . We can strive to elucidate its universal meaning in an abstract language, thus developing theories where metaphysical experience will be described, and more or less systematized in its essential character, thus as timeless and objective. If, moreover, the system so constituted affirms that *this aspect alone is real,* and, if it posits the subjectivity and historicity of experience as negligible, *it obviously excludes any other manifestation of the truth.* (Beauvoir 2004, 273–274; emphasis mine)

In short, much systematic thought, although a viable and valuable explication of metaphysical reality, virtually annihilates the ambiguity of experience. As such, it is both seductive—in that it provides clarity, univocity, and authority—but also myopic. One need only recall that very soon after this essay, Beauvoir writes not only of her own admiration of the Hegelian system, with its promises of eternity, immortality, and escape from ambiguity but also of its ultimate failure to deliver a concrete presentation of lived experience. Existentialism, she writes in *The Ethics of Ambiguity*, "does not offer to the reader the consolations of an abstract evasion: existentialism proposes no evasion. On the contrary, its ethics is experienced in the truth of life" (Beauvoir 1997, 158–159). When viewed from the Absolute, Hegel's system (like Plato's) removes us from the vicissitudes of time by showing us the perspective of timeless truth, unaffected by change. This is certainly *a* perspective one can take on finite existence, but in no way is it *the* perspective.

It is no accident that Plato and Hegel figure prominently in Beauvoir's discussion of systematic philosophy in "Literature and Metaphysics" as exemplars of philosophical abstraction. But even these great theoreticians owe a debt to lived experience that is more or less evident in their works. When viewed from the standpoint of the actors and settings of their grand narratives, truth becomes a literary expression of the idiomatic encounters of individual existents. Despite the fact that Hegel's actors are all too easily swept up in the grand historical march of spirit, Beauvoir notes that "when spirit [*l'esprit*] has not accomplished itself but is only in the process of accomplishing itself, Hegel must confer on it a certain carnal thickness in order to recount adequately its adventures" (Beauvoir 2004, 274). Indeed, in order to prove her point all the more, she acknowledges that Hegel resorts to *literary myths* such as *Don Juan* and *Faust* (and certainly this list could go on) in order to illustrate the debt his system owes to the "concrete and historical world" (ibid.). Plato, no doubt, serves as the origin of this technique that Beauvoir highlights in both of their philosophies; myths play central roles in the Platonic dialogue in a way that clearly indicates Beauvoir's point about concrete indebtedness. Plato, even more than Hegel, manages to display the living soil of experience from which abstraction springs in that most of his dialogues so clearly blend art and science. Even if something like Hegel's *Phenomenology of Spirit* is a kind of bildungsroman, the poetic superiority of the Platonic dialogue brings it much closer to the existentialist fiction of which Beauvoir speaks. Such a style—although anathema to Nietzsche's tastes—allows us to read Plato as a proto-existential novelist.

For Beauvoir, not to take into consideration the historical situation of the philosopher and the questions asked misconstrues the nature of "truth." In the event that a systematic thinker determined that such insight into the timeless nature of truth would be an effective starting point for a novel, Beauvoir is quick to chastise: "Certainly, if one imagines that through the colorful and living paste of things he sees only desiccated essences, one can fear that the author will hand over to us a dead universe, as foreign to the one we breathe in as an X-ray picture is different from a fleshed body" (Beauvoir 2004, 275). In other words, if one is too philosophical in one's art, then the work will be dishonest. If the author only pastes colors over monochromatic essences, then the author will have failed before she has even begun. The question becomes then, how can one write a *philosophical* novel? The danger appears to be either that the final product will smack too much of abstract metaphysics or be too closely aligned with what she calls the "psychological novel." As opposed to the abstract universalism of systematic philosophy, Beauvoir argues that the philosophical novel's superiority is found in its ability to show the mind *in action* as it builds systems, rather than in the explication of a perfected science.

THE METAPHYSICAL NOVEL

In a prefiguration of Derrida's insight into the infinite proliferation of meaning in a work of literature, Beauvoir writes: "A true novel, therefore, allows itself neither to be reduced to formulas nor even to be retold . . . Although made of words, it exists as objects in the world do, which exceed anything that can be said about them in words" (Beauvoir, 2004, 270). The excessive quality of fiction is due to its grounding in immediate experience, which is always phenomenologically incomplete and thus exceeds all attempts we make at totalizing it. The metaphysical novel will therefore in some ways be *more* true to lived experience than a psychological novel or a metaphysical system. As Eleanore Holveck explains, the metaphysical novel is a fictional expression that "is prior to, and necessary for, the creation of a philosophical system" (Holveck 1999, 3). So if the philosophical novel does not give us abstract truth and yet somehow audaciously claims to precede and ground it, what exactly does it give us?

In some ways, Beauvoir falls prey to the very problems she indicates plague traditional metaphysics. In "Literature and Metaphysics" she explains to us that "Existentialist thought claims to grasp the essence at the heart of existence" (Beauvoir 2004, 274), as if somehow there were *an* essence there to be grasped. And yet, as she continues, it becomes clear that what she has in mind is not the abstract universal but the truth of the concrete individual. The novel, unique in its literary approach, is able to "evoke the original upspringing (*jaillissement*) of existence in its complete, singular, and temporal truth" (ibid.). In fact, the writer is able to do what the philosopher cannot: elucidate the distinctiveness of singular experience in the universality of language. There is a dramatic and elusive character to living in the world that philosophy must necessarily leave behind if it desires systematicity. This is not to say that there isn't something of profound value in metaphysics proper, but that the profundity rests on a more original experience that grounds and sustains it—and some philosophers are able to pay homage to this ground better than others. Being-in-the-world is most readily accessed through artistic—specifically literary—approaches because of the inherently subjective nature of novel writing and reading. In fact, the metaphysical novel "provides a disclosure of existence in a way *unequaled by any other mode of expression*" (Beauvoir 2004, 276; emphasis mine). While this is certainly a self-serving claim proffered by Beauvoir, who desired to be an author most of all, this grandiose language draws us into the inherently artistic nature of lived existence as such. Borrowing from Nietzsche, Beauvoir's philosophy of literature rests on the understanding not that art imitates life, but that life is art. As Nietzsche so eloquently phrases it, "it is only as an *aesthetic phenomenon* that existence and the world are eternally *justified*" (Nietzsche 1967, 52). Beauvoir's own take on the aesthetics of life and work argues similarly in that the best philosophy will be an artistic, specifically literary, production. Put differently, the best philosophy will be closest to lived experience, which is itself aesthetic.

If the work of literature is successful, it provides a "living discovery" of freedom for both author and reader.[14] Any work of art that is heavy-handed in its philosophical message will ultimately fail at establishing a communicative bond between reader and writer. While the skeleton of the project preexists its writing, the author who has the entirety of the work planned out from the beginning will be unsuccessful:

> Certainly the demands of the novelistic experiment are not satisfied if one limits oneself to disguising a preconstructed ideological framework in a fictional, more or less shimmering garment. One renounces the philosophical novel if one defines philosophy as a fully constituted, self-sufficient system. Indeed, *the adventure of the mind is lived out in the course of the building of the system.* (Beauvoir 2004, 272; emphasis mine)

Thus we are left with a rather ambiguous claim on the part of Beauvoir. To have a system entirely worked out in advance is a kind of failure philosophically *and* literarily. Such a system will invariably fall short of capturing the drama and singularity of an individual reader's lived experience, which, by definition, is impossible to universalize. Yet, the most successful philosophical novel will appeal to the inviolable *freedom* of the reader and writer in an irreducible form of communication (Beauvoir 2004, 271). This latter claim then sets up a kind of existential truth that must remain a constant throughout the work if it is to be successful: Why else would an author write and a reader read if there were not some sort of shared freedom from which both form a communicative bond? Thus, on the one hand, freedom remains universally shared and appears to function as an idea worked out in advance; while on the other hand, a system (or novel) built on any philosophical constant is discarded as lifeless and inert. Such a claim appears at worst sloppy and at best contradictory. And yet, Beauvoir's point is precisely that both poles of the argument must be maintained; the rejection of universals and the adherence to freedom as universal encapsulates her notion of ambiguity as well as illustrates the superiority of the metaphysical novel to all other art forms in disclosing this very tension. Put another way, Beauvoir wants to uphold the position that experience grounds philosophical truth in a singular way and which is more closely aligned with the literary form. Yet, she clearly approaches her understanding of the work of literature with a well-formulated philosophical position based in freedom. This tension is in many ways unsurpassable in her approach to the link between philosophy and literature; yet, such a tension sets the stage for an analysis of the Platonic dialogue, which presents a similar—if not inverted—strain between the literary and the philosophical.[15]

PLATO'S PHAEDRUS AS READ THROUGH BEAUVOIR

Although the "freedom of the existent" is hardly a conspicuous theme in Platonic philosophy, the dialectic (especially as Beauvoir conceives it) relies on the careful, deliberate, and in many ways artistic give and take between sovereign interlocutors. Whereas Beauvoir argues for the literary and experiential source of all philosophy (systematic and otherwise), Plato's theories most often point to a truth preceding any individual experience of the world. Recollection, for example, requires lived experience as a trigger, but what is triggered is an insight into a truth that precedes and exceeds the experience that gave rise to it. Yet, Plato is himself trapped in a kind of Beauvoirean dilemma in reverse. Whatever the contours and limits of the truth his theories attempt to grasp, he so often undertakes his search through literary and poetical devises. The completed system he strives after is thus destabilized by the openness of the literary approach he employs. Like Beauvoir, there is a tension between the literary and the philosophical that cannot simply be resolved by the removal or subsumption of one over the other.

Despite her more nuanced approach to Plato as an artist in "Literature and Metaphysics," Beauvoir maintains her distrust of Plato as metaphysician in *The Ethics of Ambiguity*. In this work, she presents a more one-dimensional view of the Platonic aesthetic as one that banishes the poets from the city, since "art reveals the transitory as absolute" (Beauvoir 1997, 80). Because of the transitoriness and flux of our finite existence, Plato "wanted to wrest man away from the earth and assign him to the heaven of Ideas" (ibid.). Out of fear of finitude, he built eternal systems to keep out the corrupting forces of time, transformation, and decay. Art can only deceive for Plato, or, as Beauvoir writes, "art is mystification because there is the heaven of Ideas" (Beauvoir 1997, 157). Although this critique remains central to Beauvoir's overall interpretation, her treatment of Plato in "Literature and Metaphysics" avoids this gross oversimplification. I propose that a careful reading of the *Phaedrus* encourages an application of Beauvoir's views on both philosophy and literature and their point of contact, while opening up an entirely new way to understand Beauvoir's relationship to Plato. When we read Plato as a writer of philosophical fiction, he becomes so much more than simply the philosopher who banished the poets from the city. Instead, he becomes the model for the kind of writing Beauvoir advocates so passionately for in "Literature and Metaphysics."

While much of "Literature and Metaphysics" engages Platonism, seldom does she address Plato by name; yet, he haunts the text from beginning to end. Beauvoir openly rejects the ability to grasp truth solely through noetic illumination, and argues that, rather, meaning is *disclosed* through a living engagement with the concrete environment. As opposed to Platonic essentialism, "the meaning of an object is not a concept graspable by pure understanding" (Beauvoir 2004, 270). The object's meaning arises in the overall relation we sustain with it, which includes not only our conceptual minds, but also our emotions, our surroundings, our societies, and our interpersonal relations. In Plato's *Phaedrus*, all of these experiential (and consequently literary) elements are present and vital to the philosophical message of the work. Plato and Phaedrus take a beautifully described journey where setting, character, and plot are integral to the ideas that are disclosed through the ensuing conversation. As described above, what interests Beauvoir is not the intelligible divorced from the experiential, but rather the integration of the latter in the *movement* toward the former. This means that Beauvoir takes literary devices very seriously in the expression of philosophical truths. Let us now engage in a Beauvoirean analysis of the dialogue in order to tease out the ways in which we can read it as a work of metaphysical fiction as propounded by Beauvoir.

In the *Phaedrus*, Phaedrus seduces Socrates outside the city walls, "amidst [the] blooming fields" of Athens to recite and compose speeches on love. The dramatic setting and character development of the interlocutors are radiant—all the more so because Plato manages to set the stage in so few words. Immediately we find two men joking, flirting, and exhibiting the familiarity of a well-established friendship. We are directly drawn into the singularity of the two characters, their unique friendship, and the exclusivity of the ensuing conversation. When the two meet outside of the city walls, Phaedrus quickly informs Socrates that he's "just the right person to hear the speech" (Plato 1995, 227c)[16] that he has brought with him to the countryside.

Both men are barefoot, walking in the heat of the day across the river to the plane tree where they lie down in the grass to enjoy a speech written by Lysias (227a–229b). The setting is so rich that Socrates spends a good deal of time describing it:

> It really is a beautiful resting place. The plane tree is tall and very broad; the chaste-tree, high as it is, is wonderfully shady, and since it is in full bloom, the whole place is filled with its fragrance. From under the plane tree the loveliest spring runs with very cool water—our feet can testify to that . . . Feel the freshness of the air; how pretty and pleasant it is; how it echoes with the summery, sweet song of the cicadas' chorus! The most exquisite thing of all, of course, is the grassy slope: it rises so gently that you can rest your head perfectly when you lie down on it. (230b–c)

In this palpable and lush background, which invokes nearly all of the senses, Socrates will first hear a speech of Lysias and then construct two of his own in an effort to guide Phaedrus away from the *eros* of the physical to the *eros* of the metaphysical.[17] However, for our purposes, we should pause at the poetic description Plato provides for us. With one effusive proclamation by Socrates we are transported to the unusual and surprising place where the conversation transpires. This location, rather than standing as a mere decoration for the conversation, serves as its very condition of possibility. In fact, the next words of Phaedrus keep us focused on the specifics of the location: "And you, my remarkable friend, appear to be totally out of place . . . Not only do you never travel abroad—as far as I can tell, you never even set foot beyond the city walls" (230c–d). Indeed, Socrates has been transported out of the *agora* in order to direct our attention to the uniqueness of this particular dialogue and to provide a sketch of Socrates's character as one who normally acts otherwise. As Socrates explains to Phaedrus: "Forgive me, my friend. I am devoted to learning; landscapes and trees have nothing to teach me—only the people in the city can do that" (230d). This is a somewhat peculiar claim from the man who just waxed poetic in his description specifically of the landscape and trees. Subtly, Plato indicates how the setting, rather than merely providing the stage for what is to come philosophically, actually becomes the necessary soil out of which the theoretical investigation grows.

What follows, of course, is the presentation of the three speeches on love that clearly illustrate the Beauvoirean *movement* toward the truth—the building of the philosophical system—rather than its completion.[18] If, as I argue, the fertile description of the location, the characters' relationship to it and to each other in fact gives rise to the philosophical exchange that follows, then we would expect to find a clear link between the literary elements and the ensuing speeches. And we are not disappointed in our search. As Socrates proceeds to offer a corrective speech to that of Lysias, we are brought back the physicality of the two men engaged in conversation. Given the nature of the speeches that follow—centered on the effects of love and desire on both the lover and the beloved—it is no surprise to find such carnal elements in the men themselves.

For example, when Phaedrus finishes his reading of Lysias's poorly written speech, Socrates claims to be in ecstasy. This moment of ecstasy does not result from the speech, but from the physiognomic transformation of Phaedrus as he reads it: "It's a miracle, my friend; I'm in ecstasy. And it's all your doing, Phaedrus: I was looking at you while you were reading and it seemed to me the speech had made you radiant with delight; and since I believe you understand these matters better than I do, I followed your lead, and following you I shared your Bacchic frenzy" (234d). Phaedrus, thinking that Socrates mocks him, chastises Socrates's flowery language. Socrates, playing coy, forces Phaedrus to beg him to give his own speech. Such depictions fill out each man's character and enriches their unique interpersonal relationship. On the one hand, we can read this exchange as a momentary break between speeches. Plato needs a way to dramatically split Lysias's original speech from the consequent curative that Socrates provides. However, from a Beauvoirean perspective, we can see that this moment is much more than that. In fact, with the upsurging of the physicality and personality of the two men, we are provided with a literary glimpse into the existential reality that subtends the investigation at hand. They are two friends, reclining under a tree on the soft grass in the heat of the day. Plato even goes so far as to remind us of the setting once again when Phaedrus pleads, "I swear in all truth that, if you don't make your speech right next to this tree here, I shall never, never again recite another speech for you" (236e). We can actually see Phaedrus patting the tree and hear his frustrated voice as he begs Socrates to instruct him on the proper manner of speech giving. Clearly this break between speeches provides a necessary pause, but more significantly, it unveils the living ground that serves as the condition for the philosophical inquiry at hand. One might say that this is one of many examples of Beauvoir's distinction between the metaphysical attitude and the philosophical system. Both interlocutors are individualized in their experience but yet placed in a deep connection to the totality of the world—both physically (through the setting) and philosophically (through the content of the conversation). The living ground becomes visible when the work of philosophy pauses for a breath as it does here.

As Socrates brings his first speech to a conclusion, he tells Phaedrus that he is in the grip of the godly and notes that there is "something really divine about this place" (238c–d). The divinity of the location (so richly described by Socrates in the opening pages) and the close nature of the friendship (so vividly portrayed in the exchanges between the interlocutors) allows for the speech to grow almost organically. Interestingly, in this speech, Socrates's supposed vindication of the nonlover is defended on the ground that the lover pursues the very kinds of sensuousness mirrored in Plato's vibrant description of the setting and the bond between the two friends.

In preparation for the "Great Speech," Plato once again situates us in the concrete setting of the dialogue. Socrates, promising he will not utter another word and, planning to cross the river and return home, is countered by Phaedrus who tells him, "Not yet, Socrates, not until this heat is over. Don't you see that it is almost exactly noon 'straight-up' as they say? Let's wait and discuss the speeches, and go as soon as it turns cooler" (242a). Immediately we are given over to the promising coolness of the flowing river and the weighty heat of the day. The purifying promise of the river echoes in Socrates's call for purification after his first speech. Feeling he has offended the gods with his words against the lover, Socrates informs Phaedrus that his *daimon* has called to him, "forbidding me to leave until I made atonement for some offense against the gods" (242c). The place holds Socrates. He cannot cross the literal cooling and purifying waters until he has made his Palinode to Love. The river thus serves as a physical barrier preventing a premature end to the dialogue, just as the heat of the day increases their physical agitation. Both the discomfort and the promise of alleviation emerge prominently in the final speech.

The physicality of the Greet Speech is at once obvious and surprising. The body appears everywhere and clearly tethers itself to the lofty discussion of winged lovers and gods on chariots; pain, frustration, madness, fear, desire, and joy permeate the telling of the journey of the good soul. Plato writes of the recent initiate into love who gazes on Beauty in face or form and thus experiences the growth of his wings:

> First he shudders and a fever comes over him like those he felt at the earlier time; then he gazes at him with the reverence due a god, and if he weren't afraid people would think him completely mad, he'd even sacrifice to his boy as if he were the image of a god. Once he has looked at him, his chill gives way to sweating and a high fever, because the stream of beauty that

pours into him through his eyes warms him up and waters the growth of his wings. (251a–b)

As indicated above, the Great Speech occurs at noon, in the sweltering heat of the day. That the suffering lover in Socrates's Palinode himself suffers from "a high fever" illustrates a clear link between the content of the story and the physical location in which Socrates tells it. The promising stream of beauty offers itself as a relief to the agitated lover just as the cool stream promises to both end and cure the heat of the day for Phaedrus and Socrates. The burning, uncomfortable day and the cooling waters of the stream arise literally in the story of the distressed lover and the beautiful boy he pursues, thus building a clear bridge between the characters giving *and* appearing in the speech.

Up to this point, the ties between lived experience and theory are clear. The setting and characters connect irrefutably to the three speeches on love. However, the entire second half of the dialogue poses a more complicated problem with its discussion of rhetoric. To claim that the setting and subject matter seduces Phaedrus (and us along with him) to the upward path of philosophical truth is one thing, but how does the living literary ground maintain its connection to the pedantic and abstract lesson in speech writing and giving that follows? Recalling Beauvoir's earlier distinction between metaphysics and system, must we reject the discussion of rhetoric on literary grounds since it explicitly seeks systematicity? (270c–d). "Literature and Metaphysics" provides two possible ways to read this turn in the dialogue. On the one hand, we could view the second half of the dialogue as an illustration of what happens when Plato (as Beauvoir accuses him not only in this essay but also in the *Ethics of Ambiguity*) debases this world in the movement toward perfect and timeless truth. From this position, Phaedrus's education through the speeches is merely preparatory for their subsumption into the *real* point of the journey, which is solely to teach him about rhetoric. Although strong support for this interpretation traverses the dialogue, it doesn't do justice to the connection to the "subjective, singular, and dramatic aspect of experience" (Beauvoir 2004, 274) that has been so thoroughly connected to the philosophical content thus far. In light of Beauvoir's essay, we see that the discussion of rhetoric is tied completely to the three speeches that came before, and consequently to the descriptive richness of the story set forth from the opening pages. Not only is this a stronger reading of the dialogue as a whole—insofar as it joins the two seemingly disparate halves—but such an interpretation is backed by the fact that the dogmatic lesson which follows is introduced by and concluded with two literary myths.

The singing of the cicadas ushers in the break between the speeches and the lesson on speech giving. Those cicadas, "who are singing and carrying on conversations with one another in the heat of the day above our heads" (Plato 1995, 258e–259a) are themselves incorporated into a story. Once again the setting erupts into the foreground of the dialogue. It is still hot, the cicadas are making a beautiful ruckus around the two men, and there is a danger of becoming "sluggish of mind, nodding off," and falling asleep in the grass like two slaves (259a). The return of the heat and the song of the insects underscores the physicality of the dialogue through an appeal to our skin and ears. This moment significantly gives rise to a poetical story about those human beings who were so overwhelmed by the song of the muses that they unreflectively died from lack of personal (physical) care. This living ground—accessible to anyone who has spent a hot day outdoors in the summertime—awakens in us the unique taste of existence and relaxes us into the following lessons on rhetoric.

After Plato has completed the discussion on oratory, he closes with yet another myth—the myth of Thoth and Theuth and the ambiguous gift of the written word. Although much can be (and has been) said about the concluding myth on writing, one thing is abundantly clear in its role in the dialogue: it is for Phaedrus. The man who is aflutter with excitement over a speech on love and who has, somewhat unwittingly, been lead into a discussion on the method of collection and division, is rewarded by a beautiful and complex myth on the nature of writing (274c–275b). Thus, the man who brought Socrates out of the city to read a written speech on love, will leave the conversation as one who has been carefully lead through a dialogue that will cause him to question the very origin of the literary endeavor itself.

Clearly the soul in question is the soul of Phaedrus, yet this insight emerges from the surroundings of the dialogue itself. Recalling that great sycamore tree that serves as the *omphalos* of the discussion, we are drawn into a comparison between this tree and the eager student of speeches. In the heat of the day, at the apex of the discussion on living speech and writing, Socrates asks Phaedrus:

> Would a sensible farmer, who cared about his seeds and wanted them to yield fruit, plant them in all seriousness in the gardens of Adonis in the middle of the summer and enjoy watching them bear fruit within seven days? . . . Wouldn't he [instead] use his knowledge of farming to plant the seeds he cared for when it was appropriate and be content if they bore fruit seven months later? (276b)

In other words, philosophical work must continue well past the heated conversation in which Socrates and Phaedrus are currently engaged. To think that the training of the soul could be accomplished in such a short time—even under the auspices of love so brilliantly hinted at with the mention of Aphrodite's beautiful lover, Adonis—fails at properly educating the soul. Such a task takes far longer than the time the two friends share together under the tree. In fact the tree, which took time to grow into something large enough to shade the two men, stands as the silent representative of Phaedrus whose soul requires the same kind of patient growth if there is any chance of successfully educating him.

It is certainly no accident that the dialogue, which opens with the rich descriptions of the location—the trees, the grass, the cicadas, the river, and so on—, ends with an organic metaphor as well. Socrates warns that Phaedrus must be serious-minded in his philosophical endeavors: "The dialectician chooses a proper soul and plants and sows within it discourse accompanied by knowledge—discourse capable of helping itself as well as the man who planted it, which is not barren but produces a seed from which more discourse grows in the character of others" (276e–277a). Despite the fact that Plato has cultivated the wild nature in which the two men began their discussion—effectively enclosing the wildness of the speeches on love within the garden of the dialectic—the link between the two is nonetheless critically preserved. Again the reference to the natural setting forms the soil of the philosophical lesson: to become as great as this tree, the student must be properly and patiently cultivated into philosophical maturity.[19]

At the risk of grossly oversimplifying the complexity of the dialogue, we can certainly assert that in many ways, the three speeches are given in order to "prepare" Phaedrus for the lessons on dialectical logic. However, if the lesson in dialectic was the ultimate goal of Plato's project, why not provide a treatise on the matter and be done with it? Quite simply, because the truth disclosed by Plato is *not* to be found only in the discussion on rhetoric. No, the truth, from the perspective of the Beauvoirean interpretive framework, is that the integration of the literary elements in the quest for the truth reveals something of which all of the previous discoveries are vital components. One could say that the discussion on rhetoric could not exist without the previous speeches on love. The proof for the immortality of the soul (245c–e), the description of what the soul is like, the components of rhetoric (266e–272c), and even the method of collection and division (266b) are all building blocks to the disclosure of the truth emerging between Phaedrus and Socrates as the protagonists of this philosophical story.

CONCLUSION

If Nietzsche is right, and Plato has in fact given the form of the novel to posterity, then perhaps we should revisit this and see it as a true gift, rather than a diminishment or confusion of forms. Certainly Beauvoir's analysis opens up this possibility for our own reading of Plato. As I have argued in this paper, if we examine Plato's *Phaedrus* from the viewpoint of "Literature and Metaphysics" we have all of the elements for the metaphysical novel present: we find the mind seeking to build systems rather than reflecting on them in completion, literarily we experience the proliferation of perspectives on truth (rather than the diminution of them), and finally, we discover the very thing Beauvoir most admired in Plato—the integration of the sensible world into reality itself. I also believe that the results of this inquiry places one final demand on us: we should return to Beauvoir's fiction with new eyes—rejecting the original criticisms that she subsumed literature under a philosophical project and entertaining the possibility that a much more authentic disclosure is at work.

According to Beauvoir's description of a metaphysical novel, it becomes clear that Plato's *Phaedrus* stands as a model, not in the least because of the burden it puts on us as readers to engage the work actively. At the conclusion of "Literature and Metaphysics" Beauvoir admonishes readers who fail to take risks in the activity of reading. Those of us who approach a work with the notion that it has a specific meaning that only requires the right key to unlock it, fall into the task of *translating* a work, rather than being taken in by it. To those readers Beauvoir's appeal is most significant: "He should not forget that his collaboration is necessary, since the novel's distinctive feature is, precisely, to appeal to his freedom" (Beauvoir 2004, 276). Indeed, Plato's dialogues are filled with esoteric systems that beckon to the philosophical mind. However, there no doubt also exists an open-endedness and lack of finality in almost all of his works. Plato invites not only his fictional interlocutors, but also the readers of the dialogues to continue the indefinite work of making meaning of the themes under discussion. Phaedrus—and we as well—leaves the discussion not with an answer, but with what essentially entails a lifelong commitment to understanding the nature of reading, writing, and speaking.

Given the naive excitement Phaedrus has for the original speech by Lysias and the sensitive and romantic soul that such exuberance reveals, Socrates must be careful to take his friend on a unique and poetic journey toward the truth. Just as the musician would gently inform a novice that he has the components of harmony without harmony itself (Plato 1995, 268d–e), so Socrates must incorporate nature, seduction, and mythology into the conversation on the nature of speaking and writing because he is speaking with Phaedrus and no other. Certainly the three speeches incorporate numerous literary elements in their construction, but even the pedantic discussion of rhetoric is framed by the myths of the cicadas and the gift of writing. When Socrates asserts that the rhetorician must know how many kinds of souls there are, what kind of soul(s) he is speaking to, and how best to persuade the souls in question, this only makes sense because of the unique setting, characters, and plot of the dialogue itself (271d–272b). All of these fictional elements reveal (what philosophical theory cannot do adequately) that the soul in question is the soul of Phaedrus; by extension, the inquiry broadens to incorporate the souls of the readers who have also been seduced into the narrative. This seduction is accomplished through the enticing setting, character development, and story told by Plato in his desire to provide a metaphysical education.

In the moments where the concrete "thickness" of the interlocutors and the space they occupy come to the foreground, we are provided a glimpse into the thoroughly subjective and finite nature of experience that gives rise to the grandest theories. Perhaps we now have a partial answer to the question as to why Plato did not simply provide a philosophical treatise on the nature of the method of collection and division. One standard reading is that in the *Phaedrus*, Plato struggles with his earlier theory of the forms and the precise nature of philosophical methodology. Beauvoir's analysis of the metaphysical novel gives us yet another interpretation. The discussions on rhetoric, collection, and division, and philosophical dialectic are only possible *because* of their grounding in and emergence from a poetic and literary fiction. As such, the *Phaedrus* is an invitation to continue "the adventure of the mind" as it builds systems, rather than providing the last word on anything. All of this has been accomplished through the blending of philosophy and literature, rather than through the sacrifice of the latter to the former.

NOTES

1. "Literature and Metaphysics" was originally published as "Littérature et métaphysique," in *Les Temps modernes* 1(7), avril 1946, 1153–1163.
2. Very little has been written explicitly about the direct connection between Plato and Beauvoir. One notable exception to this is Fullbrook and Fullbrook 2001. In their essay, "Beauvoir and Plato: The Clinic and the Cave," the Fullbrooks take very seriously the influence of Plato (in this case, his allegory of the cave) on Beauvoir's development of embodied consciousness. It is certainly critical that they discover this Platonic metaphor in the convalescence of the character of Françoise in the novel, *L'Invitée* and not in Beauvoir's strictly philosophical works. Wherever we find Plato in Beauvoir, he is most often linked to the borders between philosophy and art.
3. In fact, one could almost map out the dialogues according to Beauvoir's characterization above: the "blooming fields" of the *Phaedrus*, interlocutors gathered around a table of sorts in the *Symposium* and the "deathbed" of the *Phaedo*.
4. From one perspective, the organization of the *Phaedrus*, wherein the discussion of rhetoric trumps the beauty of the Great Speech is a perfect illustration Nietzsche's very point.
5. Yi-Ping Ong provides us with a detailed catalog of the works Nietzsche read in his life and at the time of writing many of his most important works in "A View of Life: Nietzsche, Kierkegaard, and the Novel" (Yi-Ping Ong 2009).
6. In her article, "Nietzsche's Existential Signatures," Debra Bergoffen provides a convincing argument of the pervasive influence of Nietzsche's thinking not only on Sartre but on Beauvoir's thought as well. Although she focuses primarily on the critical analysis of myth operative in *The Second Sex*, it is also clear, as I argue here, that Nietzsche's aesthetics play a role in Beauvoir's general views on philosophy and art (Bergoffen 2002).
7. Although, Margaret Simons points out that there are at least three conflicting stories about the origin of this particular piece by Beauvoir in her Introduction to "Literature and Metaphysics" (Simons 2004, 267).
8. Bair oversimplifies the essay with her emphasis on the writer seeking self-discovery rather than disclosure of the world, but her contextualization of the essay within Beauvoir's role of public defender of existentialism helps to shed light on the importance of the essay to her overall philosophical position.

9. These characterizations are taken from Maurice Blanchot's criticisms of *The Blood of Others* in his essay "Les romans de Sartre," found in *L'arche* 10 (October 1945) written one year before "Literature and Metaphysics," as cited by Simons 2004, 267. Elizabeth Fallaize also tackles this problematic in Beauvoir in *The Novels of Simone de Beauvoir* (Fallaize 1990, 51–52).
10. To add weight to my claim that the Platonic dialogue engages in the same kinds of reconciliations between the temporal and eternal that existentialist literature does (and why I have focused particularly on the *Phaedrus*), it is noteworthy that this dialogue is anachronistic. As Alexander Nehamas and Paul Woodruff inform us in their Introduction to the *Phaedrus*, despite the supposedly historical (and therefore temporal) nature of the conversation between Socrates and Phaedrus, "there doesn't seem to have been a time when this meeting between Phaedrus and Socrates could have occurred" (Nehamas and Woodruff 1995, xiii). The anachronistic component allows the two interlocutors to seek eternal truths without having to be tied down to a historical time and place. Yet, clearly Plato utilizes finite existing individuals in a particular time and space in the philosophical pursuit, thus allowing for a great deal more ambiguity in the dialogue than a superficial reading allows for.
11. Beauvoir's adherence to the significance of philosophy and literature is highlighted by Karen Vintges's conception of Beauvoir's "art of living" in her book, *Philosophy as Passion: The Thinking of Simone de Beauvoir* (Vintges 1996).
12. Sara Heinamäa produces a persuasive argument that much of Beauvoir's rejection of systematic philosophy has its roots in the Kierkegaardian rejection of Hegelianism and the Husserlian emphasis on lived experience in her article, "The Background of Simone de Beauvoir's Metaphysical Novel: Kierkegaard and Husserl" (Heinamäa 2006).
13. See, for example, Beauvoir's *The Prime of Life* (Beauvoir 1966, 265).
14. Sartre argues a similar claim one year later (1947) in the essays compiled in *What Is Literature?* (Sartre 1988). Given the literary and philosophical interest of all of those working on *Les Temps Modernes* together, it is not surprising to find Beauvoir and Sartre engaged in their own conversation on the relationship between philosophy and literature at this time.
15. I would like to thank William Wilkerson for his insights into this dilemma.
16. For clarity and ease of reading, I will adopt the marginal numbers alone for all further citations from the *Phaedrus*.
17. Notably, the sense of taste is absent. Yet, this taste emerges later after Socrates concludes the first speech. Noting his dissatisfaction with his rhetoric, Socrates cries, "I want to wash the bitterness of what we've heard with a more tasteful speech" (243d).
18. First, Phaedrus presents the speech by Lysias, which is poorly constructed and devoid of a concern for the truth of its subject matter. Socrates then "corrects" the speech by giving one of his own that exhibits a better-crafted form, but still remains unconcerned with the truth about love. Finally, Socrates presents his

Palinode and argues against the two earlier speeches' misdirected emphasis on the evils of love in favor of the truth that love reveals to us. Of course, this is not the final word on the matter as the second half of the dialogue is devoted to a lengthy discussion on speech writing and rhetoric.

19. It almost seems as if Nietzsche's earlier claim from the *Birth of Tragedy*— "philosophical thought overgrows art and compels it to cling close to the trunk of dialectic" is directed precisely at Plato's point here.

WORKS CITED

Bair, Deidre. 1990. *Simone de Beauvoir: A Biography*. New York: Summit Books.
Beauvoir, Simone de. 1966. *The Prime of Life*. Trans. Peter Green. New York: Lancer Books.
———. 1997. *The Ethics of Ambiguity*. Trans. Bernard Frechtman Seacaucus, NJ: Carol Publishing.
———. 2004. Literature and Metaphysics. In *Philosophical Writings*, 269–277. Ed. Margaret A. Simons and Sylvie Le Bon de Beauvoir. Trans. Veronique Zaytzeff and Frederick M. Morrison. Urbana: University of Illinois Press.
Bergoffen, Debra. 2002. Nietzsche's Existential Signatures. *International Studies in Philosophy* 34(3):83–93.
Fallaize, Elizabeth. 1998. *The Novels of Simone de Beauvoir*. New York: Routledge.
Fullbrook, Edward and Kate. 2001. Beauvoir and Plato: The Clinic and the Cave. In *The Existential Phenomenology of Simone de Beauvoir*, 53–65. Ed. Wendy O'Brien. Dordrecht, Holland: Kluwer Academic Publishers.
Heinämaa, Sara. 2006. The Background of Simone de Beauvoir's Metaphysical Novel; Kierkegaard and Husserl. *Acta philosophica Fennica* 79, 175–190.
Holveck, Eleanor. 1999. *The Blood of Others*: A Novel Approach to the *Ethics of Ambiguity*. *Hypatia* 14(4):3–3.
Nehamas, Alexander and Paul Woodruff. 1995. Introduction to the *Phaedrus*. Indianapolis: Hackett Publishing Company.
Nietzsche, Friedrich. 1967. *The Birth of Tragedy*. Translated by Walter Kaufmann. New York: Vintage Books.
Ong, Yi-Ping. 2009. A View of Life: Nietzsche, Kierkegaard, and the Novel. *Philosophy and Literature* 33(1):167–183.
Plato. 1995. *Phaedrus*. Translated by Alexander Nehamas and Paul Woodruff. Indianapolis: Hackett Publishing Company.
Sartre, Jean-Paul. 1988. *What Is Literature?* Trans. Bernard Frechtman. Cambridge: Harvard University Press.
Simons, Margaret. 2004. Introduction to Literature and Metaphysics. In *Philosophical Writings*, 263–268. Ed. Margaret A. Simons and Sylvie Le Bon de Beauvoir. Urbana: University of Illinois Press.
Vintges, Karen. 1996. *Philosophy as Passion: The Thinking of Simone de Beauvoir*. Trans. Anne Lavelle. Bloomington: Indiana University Press.

Existence, Freedom, and the Festival

Rousseau and Beauvoir

SALLY J. SCHOLZ

> Existence attempts in the festival to confirm itself positively as existence.
> —Beauvoir, *Ethics of Ambiguity*

Festivals, those often creative, frequently spontaneous, and always exuberant celebrations, hold us captive only for a short time, perhaps in spite of our efforts to forestall their demise. But the importance of festivals is not just in the revelry. As Simone de Beauvoir reminds us, they also exhibit aspects of the relation between the self and the Other that have implications for ontology, ethics, and politics. As a celebration shared among members of a community, festivals offer a snapshot into social relations. In many ways, festivals are the counterpoint to wars. Both tell us about ourselves by presenting an intense moment of the life of the community. Wars reveal our commitments by highlighting those things for which we willingly risk our lives; festivals reveal our commitments by celebrating those things we hold dear, such as freedom, community, or just leisure time. Somewhat ironically, pivotal moments in human history are often articulated through the wars that mark or force a change in course, but pivotal moments in individual history are delineated through the celebrations shared with others that mark the moment and announce a new stage: birth, graduation, marriage, and even death. Those somewhat rarer large communal festivals, like the Fête de la Fédération on the first anniversary of the storming of the Bastille or the celebration at the liberation of Paris at the end of World War II, might also be seen as marking a change in course of human history. While philosophers have plumbed the depths of war searching for insights into humanity for centuries, festivals have received comparatively little attention. Beauvoir and Jean-Jacques Rousseau are notable among the few who turn to the festival to unmask philosophical wisdom.

Beauvoir rather famously criticizes Rousseau's portrayal of women. He claims for nature what she argues is really socially determined strictures of femininity. This criticism, and the contrast between their positions, is brought into sharp relief in Beauvoir's discussion of adornment for a celebration or festival. Yet there are elements of her discussion of festivals that are striking in their similarity to Rousseau. In this paper, I argue that Beauvoir's discussion of festivals is in the tradition of Jean-Jacques Rousseau's and offers an informative glimpse into revolutionary social changes, the effects of social construction, and freedom. Festivals offer a site of freedom where socially constructed roles are tossed aside and individuals revel in a libratory moment. Collectively, festivals are experienced as the creation of the community itself, the celebration of a project completed, or the announcement of a new era. Both Rousseau and Beauvoir recognize these philosophically important components of festivals even while they also express their appreciation for the simplicity of the spontaneous, lively, carefree displays of collectivity.

After a brief discussion of Rousseau's influence on Beauvoir, I look at the context in which their respective discussions of the festival appear. I then turn to examine the festival as marking a revolutionary change in social conditions, as both inspiring and challenging social constructions at the foundation of inequalities, and as demonstrating the integral collective at the heart of freedom. The penultimate section looks at two of the most important aspects of their shared philosophical interests—women and work—to demonstrate the practical revelatory functions of festivals and to punctuate Beauvoir's critique of a philosopher she also clearly admired.

Beauvoir directly appropriates from Rousseau's account of freedom and that impacts her understanding of the festival. Throughout this examination, we see how Beauvoir expanded the Rousseauian notion that freedom is circumscribed by the community. In its negative manifestation, social expectations or social construction limits freedom. But in the positive sense exhibited by the festival, freedom finds its clearest—if also most transitory—expression with the freedom of others.

ROUSSEAU'S INFLUENCE ON BEAUVOIR

Rousseau is not often among the thinkers identified as influential to Beauvoir's thinking. Hegel, Marx, Freud, Husserl, Heidegger, Merleau-Ponty, and, of course, Sartre receive the lion's share of attention among scholars. Nevertheless, there is ample evidence of Beauvoir's Rousseauian intellectual heritage.

During their first year together, when Beauvoir joined Sartre's friends at the École *Normale* to study for their exams, Sartre would talk about Rousseau while Beauvoir presented Leibniz (the subject of her thesis).[1] Rousseau was an important part of her education in philosophy and, like him, she distanced herself from philosophy per se and claimed not to be articulating a system like the philosophers. In addition, Beauvoir cites a wide variety of Rousseau's texts throughout her corpus, thereby showing that she read rather extensively from his work. One of the clearest impacts Rousseau made on Beauvoir is in her analysis of women's situation and in the model of autobiographical literature. For example, *The Second Sex* refers frequently to Mme de Warens, the woman who so captivated the Young Rousseau. Mme de Warens is a model of women whose artificial "maternal tenderness" seeks "identity in their lovers" (2009, 633); the dominating woman in love (707); and even the independent woman who selects her lover so as best to display generosity (729). Rousseau is also presented as an example of the Oedipus complex in his relation with Mme de Warens (2009, 427). Clearly, Beauvoir read Rousseau's *Confessions* carefully, as Mme de Warens is virtually absent from history except for this infamous relationship with Rousseau. Rousseau's *Confessions*, which transformed the genre of autobiography and set the stage for the development of the field of psychoanalysis (Damrosch 2005, 437), thereby indirectly influencing Beauvoir's understanding of a self, also directly influenced her own autobiographies. Beauvoir found in the *Confessions* inspiration or exemplification for many of the ideas she was developing. She followed his style of self-scrutiny and revelation and, as Karen Vintges notes, she sought to discover in both Rousseau and herself (and other autobiographers) "'the link between the daily life of a writer (a link so different for each) and the books in which he expresses himself'" (1996, 129, citing *All Said and Done*, 161).

Beauvoir does not confine her interest in Rousseau to his *Confessions*, however. *The Ethics of Ambiguity* favorably discusses the system of education Rousseau devises in his treatise on education, *Emile* (1948, 141–142); and *Must We Burn Sade* (1962) makes reference to *Confessions* (32, 58), *Julie* (55), and *The Social Contract* (63). Finally, although worthy of a separate study, in both the *First Discourse* and *Emile* (1997, 8, 13–14; 1993, 244), Rousseau discusses Pyrrhus and Cineas, historical figures whom Beauvoir used to frame her first philosophical essay on ethics aptly named after them.[2]

Recovering Rousseau's influence on a thinker as well-versed in philosophy as Simone de Beauvoir is no easy task. Beauvoir's use of the festival does not clearly or directly refer to Rousseau or any of his works, but their accounts of the festival emphasize many of the same themes. In particular, a study of festivals in Rousseau and Beauvoir reveals the nature and development of social construction, the social imposition of class and gender roles, and the obscuring of the existent from him or herself, thereby dramatically impacting the ability to assume freedom. Festivals lay bare the arbitrariness of social construction and, at least momentarily, liberate the self from social mores. In that sense, festivals are used by both Beauvoir and Rousseau to talk about the problems and prospects for freedom.

CONTEXT: CRITIQUING THE ENLIGHTENMENT

Just prior to discussing festivals in part IV of *The Ethics of Ambiguity*, Beauvoir offers a critique of Enlightenment science. She explains that the eighteenth and nineteenth centuries were marked by "the dream of a universal science," wherein the individual "instead of accepting his limits, he tries to do away with them" (Beauvoir 1948, 121). The folly of this dream is that it destroys the meaning of action: "For a scientist who would aspire to know everything about a phenomenon would dissolve it within the totality; and a man who would aspire to act upon the totality of the Universe would see the meaning of all action vanish" (1948, 121).

The significance of this context for festivals is twofold. First, festivals, as we shall see, are themselves actions and may also mark the end of actions. This is in sharp contrast with acting "upon the totality of the Universe." Rather than make the meaning of action disappear, festivals celebrate a project completed and hence might be said to punctuate the meaning of action. Second, situating her discussion of festivals within the context of a critique of the Enlightenment echoes Rousseau's formula and extends his social and ethical critique of Enlightenment into the existential.

In the essay that launched his career, Rousseau argues against Enlightenment progress in the sciences and arts. He holds that by progressing unchecked, Enlightenment progress in the sciences and the arts are responsible for social inequality and moral degradation. Rousseau disparaged his former colleagues for their desire to catalog knowledge in *L'Encyclopédie*. In his critique of Enlightenment science, he claims that our drive for perfection in science has led to depravity. Much like the fine arts, science brings with it vanity and luxury. It is out of vanity that we pursue science in the way we have, often at the expense of morality according to Rousseau. In the *Second Discourse*, it is precisely the festival that marks the jumping off point toward the depravity exhibited by Enlightenment attempts to totalize. That is, the festival is born from the early instances of progress that create leisure time. In that festival, as we shall see, humans plant the seeds of progress that eventually result in the Enlightenment attempts to totalize knowledge that in turn stifles natural virtue.

Both Beauvoir and Rousseau situate their discussions of festivals within a wider argument against the Enlightenment's totalizing tendency. In that sense, the festival is a lively contrast. The free, spontaneous, particular, and unique character of festivals serves as an illustrative challenge to attempts to catalog, encapsulate, and master humanity.

BREAKING WITH THE PAST: REVOLUTIONARY SOCIAL CHANGE

Rousseau discusses festivals in many of his works; they are a form of social entertainment, a representation of the communal feelings of a people, and a potential site for destructive social comparisons.[3] Perhaps the most basic account of the festival is in his posthumously published essay *On the Origin of Language*. Rousseau suggests that the "original festival" arises out of daily activities, such as fetching water for one's household or animals. As he explains, these original festivals served as meeting places or mingling places for the sexes: "Little by little, they become less shy with each other. In trying to make oneself understood, one learns to explain oneself" (Rousseau 1966, 45), and the "first discourses [around the fountain] were the first songs" (1966, 50). Perhaps even more interesting than this primitive courtship is that Rousseau also indicates that from the festival at the fountain springs a nation: "Feet skipped with joy, earnest gestures no longer sufficed, being accompanied by an impassioned voice; pleasure and desire mingled and were felt together. There at last was the true cradle of nations: from the pure crystal of the fountains flow the first fires of love" (1966, 45). Rousseau calls this first gathering a festival to mark it as distinct from work. Festivals mark a beginning of social life and collective projects. That is a dramatic change from the previous existence which was characterized by isolated wanderers tending to their immediate needs. In Rousseau's terminology, the first festival marks a revolution; societies formed, uniting families into peoples. In addition to this monumental transformation in human history, Rousseau emphasizes the ardor with which those first festival participants engaged each other. Their desires and pleasures merged in the moment of coming together. In short, festivals indicate a break from the past—announcing a new era—while they celebrate the present.

Beauvoir similarly sees festivals as a moment in time breaking with the past and engaging the present in the opening of her discussion of festival in *The Ethics of Ambiguity*. She states, "if it is true that men seek in the future a guarantee of their success, a negation of their failures, it is true that they also feel the need of denying the indefinite flight of time and of holding their present between their hands" (Beauvoir 1948, 125). Her example is even more revealing. The festival she has in mind follows the liberation of Paris:[4] "The hours following the liberation of Paris, for example were an immense collective festival exalting the happy and absolute end of that particular history which was precisely the occupation of Paris" (1948, 125). The festival is an event that announces the end of a particular history. Like Rousseau's festival participants, Beauvoir's seek the pleasure of the moment even while human history undergoes a dramatic—revolutionary—change. The festival is, after all, fleeting. Kimberly Hutchings suggests that there is something false in the festival as Beauvoir describes it. In her view, Beauvoir points out "how the experience of the pure affirmation of existence in the festival is illusory, 'the joy becomes exhausted, drunkenness subsides into fatigue.' It is illusory because the absolute assertion of existence is an impossibility, a denial of the undeniability of death" (Hutchings 2003, 60). The passage from which Hutchings quotes is worth further scrutiny:

> But the tension of existence realized as a pure negativity can not [*sic*] maintain itself for long; it must be immediately engaged in a new undertaking, it must dash off toward the future. The moment of detachment, the pure affirmation of the subjective present are only abstractions; the joy becomes exhausted, drunkenness subsides into fatigue, and one finds himself with his hands empty because one can never possess the present. (Beauvoir 1948, 126–127)

There is, in other words, more to the passage that actually belies the conclusion that the affirmation of existence in festivals is merely an abstraction. Beauvoir's point is about grasping the present. She recognizes that the festival is temporary.

The work that one invests in such projects as liberation of the oppressed and cessation of injustice gives the celebration at their accomplishment its meaning, but the celebration or festival also reveals freedom as an absolute insofar as through the festival existence "seeks to confirm itself positively as existence" (Beauvoir 1948, 127). Beauvoir extends her discussion of festivals into the future in a way that Rousseau only hints at. Even during the liberation of Paris, she argues, there were some few people whose focus was on the future and what new problems it would bring. Nevertheless, the majority of people in a festival regard the present moment as a confirmation of sorts—the end of a war or the end of an era. The festival suspends "the indefinite flight of time" temporarily so that freedom may be experienced without the weight of the future, and so that the break from the past may be collectively celebrated.

SOCIAL CONSTRUCTION AND INEQUALITY

The Discourse on the Origin of Inequality Among Mankind or *Second Discourse* (1755) offers a very different assessment of festivals but also demonstrates how festivals mark a break with the past. Rousseau offers an account of humanity's start in nature as consisting of isolated wanderers dependent only their own abilities. In the *Second Discourse*, Rousseau argues that changes in social relations followed a series of "revolutions"; his aim is to describe how such free, content beings like natural humans accepted various "yokes" and "chains" that made us into the enslaved social beings we are. Social propriety replaced natural virtue and made us subject to the opinions of others. A key moment in this development—or rather this fall—is the festival or the gathering around a tree for amusement and entertainment.[5]

One of the most important and earliest revolutions was the creation and use of tools. By making the process of work more efficient, tools aided in the creation of leisure time. Leisure time invites other pursuits like entertainment and, in this context, Rousseau warns that the likely result will be pernicious forms of entertainment that serve as the origins of inequality. As he explains, some will have more leisure time than others, which is itself a form of inequality. This leisure time is then used to create "yokes" for oneself in the form of "conveniences"; a nascent form of keeping up with the Joneses begins. In addition, Rousseau describes the transitions from simple tools and conveniences to more permanent dwelling places that thereby establish relations among families. As more social interaction and more leisure time develop, "the head and the heart become active." Primitive humans had little use for reason and emotion, but these new social humans find all sorts of outlets for feelings and ideas. The progression of development then takes us to the festival. With leisure time and affective interest in others, peoples begin to "assemble round a great tree: singing and dancing" (Rousseau 1967, 218). Far from being the idealized festival we read about elsewhere in Rousseau's writings, this festival is considered the "first step towards inequality" because it is here that individuals turn toward public opinion and away from nature and virtue. Rousseau describes the singers and dancers comparing themselves to each other and through that comparison developing social values (vices) that cemented inequality. As he explains:

> In proportion as ideas and feelings succeed each other, and the head and the heart become active, men continue to shake off their original wildness, and their connections become more intimate and extensive. They now began to assemble round a great tree: singing and dancing, the genuine offspring of love and leisure, became the amusement or rather the occupation of the men and women, free from care, thus gathered together. Everyone began to notice the rest, and wished to be noticed himself; and public esteem acquired a value. He who sang or danced best; the handsomest, the strongest, the most dexterous, or the most eloquent, came to be the most respected: this was the first step towards inequality, and at the same time toward vice. From these first distinctions there arose on one side vanity and contempt, on the other envy and shame; and the fermentation raised by these new leavens at length produced combinations fatal to happiness and innocence. (1967, 218; see also Cladis 2003, 92–93)

Festivals are the original source of the valuing of public opinion rather than natural virtue, but they are also "genuine" occurrences.[6] Rousseau uses the festival as a way to show how we create the social codes by which we measure ourselves and others. Oppression and social inequality originate from humans; in order to combat them or obviate their influence in our lives, we ought to look toward nature.

Nancy Bauer provocatively suggests that Rousseau's *Discourse on the Origin of Inequality Among Mankind* provides something of a template for the history section of *The Second Sex* (2001, 2).[7] Beauvoir's discussion of history features a celebration similar to Rousseau's festival of the *Second Discourse*, and while the social inequality based on class is not evident, that based on gender is. As Beauvoir explains, by creating tools and conquering waterways, man "tests his own power: he posits ends and projects paths to them: he realizes himself as existent. To maintain himself, he creates; he spills over the present and opens up the future. This is the reason fishing and hunting expeditions have a sacred quality. Their success is greeted by celebration and triumph; man recognizes his humanity in them" (Beauvoir 2009, 73). Women, having a different role, celebrate men's accomplishments in festivals (74). For Beauvoir, this festival recognizes men as transcendent but women merely see their social role determined and, in comparison to men, unworthy of celebration within the community. They are, in short, like Rousseau's festival-goers of the *Second Discourse*. Their lives are measured by comparison to others.

In a similar way, inequality and social oppression are motivating forces for Beauvoir's discussion of the festival in *The Ethics of Ambiguity*. The goal of "emancipation of oppressed natives" is juxtaposed with the festival; she shows that in the festival, "Existence must be asserted in the present if one does not want all life to be defined as an escape toward nothingness. That is the reason societies institute festivals whose role is to stop the movement of transcendence, to set up the end as an end" (Beauvoir 1948, 125). The festival is a discrete moment in time wherein "in songs, laughter, dances, eroticism, and drunkenness one seeks both an exaltation of the moment and a complicity with other men" (Beauvoir 1948, 126). Fighting for emancipation or seeking the socialist revolution to end inequality, in contrast, are long-term goals.[8]

For both Rousseau and Beauvoir, the festival brings to light social inequality. Festivals are a "gathering" and a "complicity with other men," but they also stand as a vehicle for comparisons that reveal social inequality (for Rousseau), or, through their contrast with more long-range movements, reveal the project to ameliorate oppressive social inequalities (for Beauvoir). Both thinkers situate at least some of their philosophical discussion of the festival in the context of a discussion of social inequality and liberation from it.

COLLECTIVE FREEDOM AND FREEDOM IN THE COLLECTIVE

Beauvoir launches her discussion of festivals in *The Ethics of Ambiguity* with a statement that could very well be a description of Rousseau's general will, which may be understood as the will of each member of the sovereign whole wherein each wills for the whole while maintaining independence and obedience only to self:[9] "the affirmation of the collectivity over against the individual is opposed, not on the plane of fact, but on the moral plane, *to the assertion of a collectivity of individuals each existing for himself*" (Beauvoir 1948, 124; emphasis added). Whether or not she has the general will in mind here or elsewhere (140), Rousseau and Beauvoir do seem to agree that the individual must partake in a collective; both see the project of the collective as ending oppression or injustice, but that the collective can never subsume the individual. As Rousseau so eloquently puts it, "each giving himself to all, gives himself to nobody" (1967, 18).

Festivals also celebrate the collective itself. Rousseau offers the festival as the ideal means of recovering natural virtue through social entertainment. The festival illustrates social entertainment in a republic free from pernicious social inequalities. His most developed articulation and defense of this notion of festival appears in *Letter to M. D'Alembert on the Theatre*, where he also forcefully argues against the creation of a theater in Geneva and proposes open-air festivals as the proper entertainment for well-governed and virtuous people.

> To what peoples is it more fitting to assemble often and form among themselves sweet bonds of pleasure and joy than to those who have so many reasons to like one another and remain forever united? We already

have many of these public festivals; let us have even more; I will be only the more charmed for it. But let us not adopt these exclusive entertainments which close up a small number of people in melancholy fashion in a gloomy cavern, which keep them fearful and immobile in silence and inaction, which give them only prisons, lances, soldiers, and afflicting images of servitude and inequality to see. No, happy peoples, these are not your festivals. It is in the open air, under the sky, that you ought to gather and give yourselves to the sweet sentiment of your happiness. (1960, 125)

These festivals arise in response to hard work and involve everyone in the play, thus avoiding the displays of inequality evident in the festival of the *Second Discourse*. Arising rather spontaneously, they also foster virtue by being both public and open air. There are no opportunities to stray from virtue when the watchful eyes of the entire community are present. Festivals, Rousseau argues, are an "important component of the training in law and order and good morals (manners)" (1960, 130). In a way, these are the progeny of that first festival of the essay *On the Origin of Language*. In the *Letter to M. D'Alembert*, Rousseau's positive appraisal of the festival is rooted in the potential he sees for fostering unity, much like the "cradle of a nation" alluded to earlier.

Rousseau clearly saw social entertainment as reflective of communal and political values. His moralizing over the festival and his condemnation of the theater for Geneva provide ample evidence to suggest that "good art" was a moral evaluation of a people rather than (or in addition to) an aesthetic judgment. Good art can only truly be appreciated by good individuals, that is, individuals who have somehow escaped or been liberated from the oppressive social mores that dictate behavior. In short, individuals must be free in all aspects of life—and that is the deeply libratory element to Rousseau's festivals.

In this account of festivals, rather than comparing oneself to others in a way that fosters inequality, the festival offers a place for mutual appreciation. Of course, this assessment is drawn in part from the contrast he makes between the festival and the theater. In the latter, one is either a spectator or part of the spectacle. The spectacle in theater, he argues, tends to celebrate vice rather than virtue, whereas in a festival there is no role distinction and at least a greater possibility that it will serve morality rather than flout it. Although some festivals might invite comparisons and competition among people, Rousseau describes the desirable festival as characterized by joyful, open air, spontaneous dancing, preferably situated in country or mountain villages rather than bustling cities.[10] Cities were too prone to pernicious inequality, sordid behavior, and the rule of public opinion. Rousseau championed the festival in part because it supported his philosophical commitment to scorn public opinion. Costumes might be worn but, in his view, these contributed to the amusement rather than served as a means by which one was judged.

Rousseau himself was no stranger to festivals. During his stay in Venice in 1743, he was an enthusiastic participant in carnival, even donning a mask. Leo Damrosch describes carnival, "which was celebrated in several stages that occupied fully half the year," as a means of liberation from constraint, a theme that surely resonated with Rousseau. One could don a mask and thereby shake off the proprieties of social roles. Indeed, Damrosch quotes a letter Rousseau wrote to the Comtesse de Montaigu on November 23, 1743: "I have altered my philosophy a bit to appear like the others, so that I go to the piazzas and theaters in mask and *bautta* [the typical mask in eighteenth-century Venice] as proudly as if I'd worn that outfit all my life" (quoted in Damrosch 2005, 174).[11]

The festival is an opportunity to shake off socially imposed roles and join together collectively. In mountain villages, like Clarens, the setting for Rousseau's epistolary novel *Julie*, hard work and healthy space left people simple and virtuous—closer to their true natural selves, as opposed to the socially constructed selves of the cities. Thus the festival enhances the unity of the community:

> Plant a stake crowned with flowers in the middle of a square; gather the people together there, and you will have a festival. Do better yet; let the spectators become an entertainment to themselves; make them actors themselves; do it so that each sees and loves himself in the others so that all will be better united. (1960, 126)

Paul Thomas discusses the revolutionary aspects of Rousseau's festival as providing "an opportunity for collective moral regrounding, serving to sustain the principles of a community by reaffirming *les sentiments de sociabilité*" (1997, 666). Communal or collective recognition is necessary, according to Thomas, for democratic politics. Others have suggested that Rousseau lays the groundwork for revolutionary solidarity with his discussion of the collective (Cladis 2003). The festival, in that context, may be seen as "collective self-expression" based in equality. In essence, that is the general will of *The Social Contract* (1997, 667–669). Freedom, however, and not the collective self-expression itself, is the goal of the festival.

Beauvoir is less explicit than Rousseau about the unifying potential of the festival though it is present in the communication among existents. Her most extensive discussion of festivals is found in the third section, part IV, "The Present and the Future," of *Ethics of Ambiguity*. In the festival, she sees the ethics of existence manifest. Citing Bataille and clearly drawing on the Hegelian notion of recognition, Beauvoir sees in the festival a rejection of being. Her discussion is worth quoting at length:

> Existence attempts in the festival to confirm itself positively as existence. That is why, as Bataille has shown, it is characterized by destruction; the ethics of being is the ethics of saving: by storing up, one aims at the stationary plenitude of the in-itself, existence, on the contrary, is consumption; it makes itself only by destroying; the festival carries out this negative movement in order to indicate clearly its independence in

relationship to the thing: one eats, drinks, lights fires, breaks things, and spends time and money; one spends them for nothing. The spending is also a matter of establishing a communication of the existents, for it is by the movement of recognition which goes from one to the other that existence is confirmed. (Beauvoir 1948, 126)

The communication of existents confirms existence for Beauvoir; the unity of peoples allows members to enjoy freedom for Rousseau. Both conceive freedom as encompassed in community with others. As Beauvoir says, the festival is notable because it actively negates being. It cannot maintain that stance but its affirmation of existence is at least momentarily a collective experience of freedom. The festival shows that the present existence must be surpassed, "that is what gives festivals their pathetic and deceptive character" (Beauvoir 1948, 127). The festival ends and it must end. The present cannot be held.

It is noteworthy that both Beauvoir and Rousseau conceive of the festival as demonstrative of relations between people.[12] Moreover, both see in the festival a positive articulation of ethics. In addition, before Hegel, Bataille, Kojève, or Sartre, Rousseau laid the groundwork for seeing the festival as socially and politically important and philosophically interesting. The communication among existents reverberates from the community of Rousseau.

In *The Second Sex* Beauvoir suggests that festivals celebrate the transcendence of the existent (Beauvoir 2009, 74). She ends her discussion of festivals in *The Ethics of Ambiguity* by instructing us to understand "that every living movement is a sliding toward death. But if they are willing to look it in the face they discover that every movement toward death is life. . . . the present must die so that it may live. . . . it must assert itself as an absolute in its very finiteness" (Beauvoir 1948, 127). The idea, in other words, is that our undertakings are transitory and finite but we must "will them absolutely." That is what gives meaning to existence and affirms freedom. Festivals, far from abstractions, are brief moments of existence in freedom. Beauvoir's discussion of freedom at the end of *The Ethics of Ambiguity* carries stirrings of a festival:

> in order for the idea of liberation to have a concrete meaning, the joy of existence must be asserted in each one, at every instant; the movement toward freedom assumes its real, flesh and blood figure in the world by thickening into pleasure, into happiness. . . . The saving of time and the conquest of leisure have no meaning if we are not moved by the laugh of a child at play. (Beauvoir 1948, 135)

Like Rousseau before her, Beauvoir argues that freedom is an individual experience, but one that is always mediated by a community. That community might curtail freedom through socially constructed class and gender roles or expectations, or it might, with all of the individuals equally, engage freedom in joy and festivity.[13]

Festivals play a special role in the philosophical work of Rousseau and Beauvoir. Whether they are seen as a break in history, the start of social construction and inequality, or an idealized form of social entertainment for enhancing communal togetherness, festivals highlight the best and the worst of human freedom.

WOMEN, WORK, AND THE LESSONS OF THE FESTIVAL

Both Rousseau and Beauvoir use festivals to address the practical issues of oppression of women and workers. In the context of festivals, their discussion of women and workers illustrates the prospects as well as the obstacles to human freedom discussed above. Rousseau and Beauvoir are rather famously in opposing camps on the issue of women. However, it is also clear that Beauvoir found in Rousseau some inspiration for her understanding of freedom. The problem is that he did not extend his account of freedom far enough. The festival, and in particular adornment for the festival, illustrates both the potential for liberation from socially constructed gender roles and Rousseau's failure to extend that liberation quite far enough. I explore these connections in the following subsection.

In a slightly different vein, the festival may also be used to illustrate the importance of work for both Rousseau and Beauvoir. Both see the possibility for oppression in work that is not freely undertaken, but both also argue that through work individuals realize their freedom. The festival is a sort of counter-point to work in both regards. That is, it might both be a means of throwing off oppression temporarily or permanently and a suitable climax for work done in freedom. The second subsection explores these relations for Rousseau and Beauvoir.

Festivals and Women

Rousseau's "woman of nature," Sophie, is a result of proper training in accordance with feminine virtue, but as Mary Wollstonecraft, Beauvoir, and numerous others have pointed out, the virtues that Rousseau identifies for Sophie are mere proprieties.[14] Her freedom is already neatly constrained according to what Rousseau calls her feminine virtue. Beauvoir's analysis of women's situation in both *The Second Sex* and *The Ethics of Ambiguity* reveals the extent of these constraints. But since the work critiquing Rousseau from a Beauvoirian perspective has been done, it might be worth looking at Rousseau and Beauvoir as allies rather than opponents, up to a certain point. Rousseau's *Emile* demonstrates the damaging effects of social construction and seeks to provide a style of education rooted in freedom.[15] Beauvoir demonstrates the effects of social construction on women's lives throughout *The Second Sex*. Both aim to uncover and transform oppressive systems; that is, both have freedom as their aim.

Given both the divergence and the alliance, the juxtaposition of their respective accounts of the adornment and courtship at festivals and dinner parties is informative. According to Rousseau, whatever form of amusement is pursued, it ought not to flaunt the natural differences between the sexes. On the contrary, each sex has natural virtues that ought to be preserved and maintained; men ought to act like men and women act like women (according to what Rousseau believes to be their natural virtues), each under the supervision of the entire community.[16] A festival accomplishes just the sort of verification of natural virtue that Rousseau desires.

At the end of the *Letter to M. D'Alembert*, Rousseau lists a number of purposes or benefits of the festival, which he also claims make them "an important component of the training in law and order and good morals" (130). Interestingly, all of the benefits he lists pertain to the relationship between the sexes and the establishment of a family. The first two cover courtship: the sexes would have a suitable meeting place at the festival and would be content at other times, when they are forced to be separated, knowing that the festival will provide a leisurely expanse of time during which they may mingle. The next three address intrafamily relations: everyone in the family would enjoy the entertainment of the festival, mothers would further enjoy adorning their daughters for the activity, and that adornment would also "provide diversion for many others" (131). Next, Rousseau suggests an interfamily benefit: the festivals, in addition to creating a space for the forming of unions, might also serve to reconcile feuding families—an activity clearly conducive to the peace of the community. Further, in accordance with equality, he claims "the inclinations of children would be somewhat freer; the first choice would depend somewhat more on their hearts; the agreements of age, temperament, taste, and character would be consulted somewhat more; and less attention would be paid to those of station and fortune which make bad matches when they are satisfied at the expense of the others" (131). Finally, for the state as a whole, he offers festivals as a means to create more unity and to "maintain the body of the people better in the spirit of its constitution" (131). In short, festivals, according to Rousseau, are the ideal form of entertainment for bringing the sexes together and maintaining a stable society.

Somewhat ironically, Rousseau cautions women against too much adornment in numerous places in his work (Rousseau 1960; 1992; 1993, Book V). However, as is clear from the above, at least some adornment is part of what makes the festival festive for mother, daughter, and potential admirers.

This is an apt spot to see Beauvoir breaking in. Both Beauvoir and Rousseau see the festival as potentially exhibiting social inequality. Rousseau, however, sees it only in terms of class, while Beauvoir sees it in terms of class and gender. In *The Second Sex*, Beauvoir talks about adornment, festivities, and interaction between the sexes. The chapter on "Social Life" offers a lengthy analysis of the rituals women undergo to dress appropriately for a dinner party. Just as Rousseau criticized the theater saying that it introduces luxury as women seek to adorn themselves according to their social station (Rousseau 1960, 63), so too, Beauvoir says that one of two significations of dressing up is that "it is meant to show the woman's social standing (her standard of living, her wealth, the social class she belongs to)" (Beauvoir 2009, 571); the other is that "it concretizes feminine narcissism." Adornment for public entertainment is an outward sign of one's social status or standing; it is also a sign of woman's own value: "As a woman is an object, it is obvious that how she is adorned and dressed affects her intrinsic value" (Beauvoir 2009, 577). Interestingly, Beauvoir also argues that "by adorning herself, woman is akin to nature, while attesting to nature's need for artifice" (572). This resembles how Sophie is instructed to dress by Rousseau; she ought to be attired in clothes that bring out her simple beauty but do not obscure it or overwhelm it. The adornment he recommends for daughters at the festival is surely of this sort. Rather than being grounded in luxury, it aims at enhancing woman's natural merit. Beauvoir, of course, faults both sorts of adornment for turning woman into an object for men and for the envy of other women. As she explains, "From one man to another, the festivity takes on the appearance of a potlatch; each of them gives the vision of this body that is his property to all the others as a gift. In her evening dress, the woman is disguised as woman for all the males' pleasure and the pride of her owner" (Beauvoir 2009, 575). While there is no direct reference to Rousseau, her criticism cuts directly to the patriarchal attitude that is evident in Rousseau's appeal to the adornment of women in the festival. Moreover, the effects adornment for festivities has on freedom is profound. Beauvoir speaks at great length about the clothes that impede woman's walk, the exposed flesh that makes her object, the delicate dress that restricts movement, and the "laws" that dictate the appropriate clothing "so as to attract suitors" (574–575). Whereas Rousseau begins by chastising the inequality evident in luxurious adornment for the theater and ends by proposing the "innocent and laudable" aim of the adornment for the festival, Beauvoir recognizes both the social inequality present in and the objectifying function of adornment as women become gifts for the vision (or to use Rousseau's term, *diversion*), if not also the embrace of others. Given that "potlatch" is a ceremony wherein hosts give gifts to their guests, thereby reinforcing their social status and potentially also cementing bonds within the community, Beauvoir's claim that woman is a gift of the potlatch highlights her oppressed condition in the community.

Festivals and Work

Rousseau notes the virtue of festivals in his novel *Julie*. There, and in contrast to the *Second Discourse*, festivals are a reward for hard work.[17] The workers at Clarens, Julie's home, transform the labor of a grape harvest into a festival (*Julie*, 603; discussed in Damrosch 2005, 321). Indeed, in a number of places in his writing, Rousseau extols the virtue of a hard day's work. A good society, furthermore, makes certain that each individual works in order to contribute to the whole and in order to avoid the social and personal vices that emerge through idleness (see especially Rousseau 1993, 177–178). The most important social vice is inequality and, as we have seen, the festival plays a significant role as a source of inequality according to the *Second Discourse*. But, as we have also seen, the festival might rather be a fitting form of social intercourse after a day well spent in hard work. In the education of

Emile, Rousseau introduces him to human companionship or social interaction first through work. Social interaction in work sees its fulfillment in the festival; both work and festival are shared equally by all members of the community. The point is that work—evenly distributed and sufficiently occupying—is the balance for the festival and ensures equality for society: "Do you then want to make a people active and laborious? Give them festivals, offer them amusements which make them like their stations and prevent them from craving for a sweeter one" (1960, 126; see also 70).

Work plays an important role for Beauvoir as well. As she says, "It is through work that woman has been able, to a large extent, to close the gap separating her from the male; work alone can guarantee her concrete freedom" (Beauvoir 2009, 721). Like Rousseau, Beauvoir understands idleness to result in vices and exacerbate inequality. In the case of gender inequality specifically, she writes: "The curse on the woman vassal is that she is not allowed to do anything; so she stubbornly pursues the impossible quest for being through narcissism, love, or religion; when she is productive and active, she regains her transcendence; she affirms herself concretely as subject in her projects; she senses her responsibility relative to the goals she pursues and to the money and rights she appropriates" (721). Work enables transcendence. A woman worker, or rather a nonoppressed woman worker, is better able to attain equality in transcendence. An important element for both Beauvoir and Rousseau is that freedom is nothing without equality (Rousseau 1967, 55), or to put it another way, "To will oneself free is to will others free" (Beauvoir 1948, 73).

In addition, Beauvoir also discusses the festival as a fitting site of entertainment to balance work, as well as a counterbalance to a project once completed. She acknowledges the potentially oppressive nature of work for some when she offers an effective criticism of the festivals that Salazar mandated at the expense of schooling. This criticism echoes Rousseau in a number of important ways:

> Here we see, in its extreme form, the absurdity of a choice which prefers the Thing to Man from whom alone the Thing can receive its value. We may be moved by dances, songs, and regional costumes because these inventions represent the only free accomplishment which was allowed the peasants amidst the hard conditions under which they formerly lived; by means of these creations they tore themselves away from their service work, transcended their situation, and asserted themselves as men before the beasts of burden. Wherever these festivals still exist spontaneously, where they have retained this character, they have their meaning and their value. (Beauvoir 1948, 94)

Notice that Beauvoir decries the service work wherein individuals are constrained to perform tasks determined for them and the work (or product) takes its place over and against them. The festival is a fitting counterpoint to such oppressive labor; in it, the workers express their transcendence. This reflects the theme discussed earlier: existence is affirmed in the festival. Moreover, work that relegates the worker to immanence, like the service work Beauvoir mentions, is countered by the assertion of transcendence in the festival. This festival of peasants in Portugal features villagers, not city dwellers, who engage in the amusement after a hard day's work. Beauvoir claims that they used the festival to "transcend their situation" (1948, 94). The contrast or display of such transcendence "before the beasts of burden" highlights the importance of the festival for freedom. Of course, we must be careful not to overstate the case. Even the workers who find their transcendence in the festival will sink back into the oppression of their work tomorrow. This signals the need to confront the future, to recognize that the fleeting festival, as discussed earlier, is also a contrast to the more lasting projects of liberation from oppressive labor structures.

CONCLUSION

Rousseau's proposals regarding the festival were not altogether welcomed (and certainly did not reflect the actually existing festivals of eighteenth-century Europe). Damrosch notes that "the popular festivals that Rousseau celebrated were perceived by the patricians as invitations to subversion. Throughout Europe, in fact, the ruling elites were committed to repressing such festivals" (Damrosch 2005, 300).[18] In a way, perhaps Rousseau's proposal is a bit tongue-in-cheek: he uses the very form of social entertainment that those in power consider most damaging to social life as *the* form of entertainment for a virtuous republic. Clearly, part of the revolutionary aspect of his festivals is to call into question the accepted values and social hierarchies of his time. Equality and liberty, rather than propriety and wealth, ought to inform social interactions of every sort: ethics, politics, arts, and romance.

With their ability to fold the spectator and spectacle into one, festivals remind us of ourselves. As Rousseau and Beauvoir agree, each person is a freedom. The festival invites us to cast off those aspects of society that constrain and obscure us from ourselves. In festivals, the individual or the existent may exhibit and inspire freedom for the collective. The collective itself might be born of the festival or reinvigorated by it. It might discover the completion of a collective project or the announcing of a new age.

Festivals offer an intense period of social relations that underscores our human achievements as well as our possibilities. They also reveal our collective flaws, throwing into stark relief those atrocities from which we celebrate our liberation. In this way, festivals illustrate our most vibrant human characteristics—those we embrace as well as those we scorn—while also simply providing a space for communal celebration. At least one of the most enduring lessons for Rousseau's and Beauvoir's philosophical exploration of the festival is that by breaking into history, festivals invite us to revel in liberation: our own and others.

NOTES

1. In *Simone de Beauvoir*, a film by Joseé Dayan and Malka Ribowska (1979), GMF Productions.
2. Beauvoir's concept of childhood was heavily influenced by her reading of Rousseau (Scholz 2010).
3. In "Virtuous Bacchanalia: Creolizing Rousseau's Festival," Chiji Akoma and I present Rousseau's seemingly disparate accounts of the festival. One account is found in the *Discourse on the Origin of Inequality Among Mankind*, and the other, a more detailed and more positive account, is found in the *Letter to D'Alembert on the Theatre*. Taken together, these two accounts of the festival reveal its role in fostering virtue and providing a suitable site for social intercourse.
4. The celebration at the liberation of Paris also appears early in her prize-winning novel *Les Mandarins*.
5. Cladis (2003) and Crocker (1967) suggest that we read the *Second Discourse* as the "fall."
6. The two accounts of festival from Rousseau discussed here mirror his central concepts: *amour-propre* (vanity) and *amour de soi* (self-love).
7. Although I would argue that Beauvoir is actually following the work of anthropologist Johann Jakob Bachofen, whom she cites, and whose work on mother right was used by Engels, whom she also cites; it is clear that there is also the intellectual trajectory from Rousseau's *Second Discourse* to Marx and Engels to Beauvoir. This trajectory is most evident in the third chapter of *The Second Sex*, "The Point of View of Historical Materialism."
8. Throughout *The Ethics of Ambiguity* Beauvoir argues for the liberation of the oppressed and challenges individuals to see their own project as contributing to that project. While her account of this solidarity does not require the sort of shared sentiment we see in Rousseau's idyllic festival or even the moral regrounding Thomas mentions, one can nevertheless see in Beauvoir the same critique of social oppression and appeal for transformative action that one sees in Rousseau: "whatever the virtues of a civilization may be, it immediately belies them if it buys them by means of injustice and tyranny" (Beauvoir 1948, 125).
9. The general will is notoriously difficult to define, summarize, or explain. I have merely tried to capture its spirit here. That is, that each of us, in committing ourselves to the community, thereby keep ourselves from dependence on any single person but must will for the whole in order to maintain that powerful communal bond that also ensures our individual freedom.
10. See also Cladis's *Public Vision, Private Lives* (2003, 173) and Paul Thomas's essay, "The Revolutionary Festival and Rousseau's Quest for Transparency" (1997, 667), for an elaboration on this point.

11. This stands as something of a contrast to his boyhood experience of "the spontaneous dancing in the Place Saint-Gervais" (Damrosch 2005, 187). He used this purified youthful memory of the festival in casting judgment on Parisian celebrations that seemed deliberately designed to "divert the people" and make them drink until they were ill (187; see also 289–290).
12. Kimberly Hutchings sees Beauvoir's discussion of festivals as an illustration of "relations between individual and collective, subject and object, self and other and their implications for ethics" (Hutchings 2003, 60, she cites p. 126, of *The Ethics of Ambiguity*). She contrasts Beauvoir's use of the festival as an "illustration of the temporality of existence" with Hegel's use in the *Phenomenology*. Both authors reveal, according to Hutchings, first, "The author's conception of the relation between individual and collective identities and ends"; second, "the author's conception of the relation of individual existents to external nature"; and third, "the author's conception of the relations between existents" (61). Hegel's revel continues through the "recollection of the whole movement," but Beauvoir's revel "cannot be sustained as each existent moves beyond the moment towards death." Hutchings concludes that Beauvoir's use of the festival (equating existence with destruction and consumption) follows Bataille, Kojèvian, and Sartrean versions of Hegel's emergence of self-consciousness from life in the *Phenomenology*.
13. Lori Jo Marso and Patricia Moynagh offer an apt description of Beauvoir's method in *Simone de Beauvoir's Political Thinking*: Looking at the lives of particular individuals is a means "for understanding and transforming our collective existence. Universal categories are thereby unsettled, yet opportunities to create bonds within common political projects emerge" (2006, 1).
14. See, for example, Wollstonecraft's *A Vindication of the Rights of Women*, chapter 5; Beauvoir's *The Second Sex*, p. 124; and Pateman's *The Sexual Contract*, chapter 4, for a start.
15. Beauvoir offers us two accounts of childhood—one is an apprenticeship to freedom and the other is an apprenticeship to the serious. Rousseau's Emile, a male child, serves as a model for the former. The childhood of most women, on the contrary, demonstrates the apprenticeship to the serious. The importance of this argument for freedom is in part that the limits to one's transcendence begin to be interiorized during childhood (Scholz 2010).
16. Notice how that dictum rules out the theater, which Rousseau claims invites men to adopt the virtues of women (especially regarding adornment). Rousseau's play, *Narcissus*, is an amusing portrayal of some of the moral problems that might transpire when men are adorned like women (1992). Beauvoir connects the theater and the festival in a way that the Rousseau of the *Letter* would not: "One of art's roles is to fix this passionate assertion of existence in a more durable way: the festival is at the origin of the theatre, music, the dance, and poetry. In telling a story, in depicting it, one makes it exist in its is particularity with its beginning and its end, its glory or its shame; and this

is the way it actually must be lived. In the festival, in art, men express their need to feel that they exist absolutely" (127). Rousseau would agree with the festival's ability to affirm and express existence, but his disdain for the finer arts seems clearly skeptical of the extension of this assertion into theater.

17. Recall that in the *Second Discourse* festivals arose because of leisure time.
18. Compare, also, to the bacchanalia described by Beauvoir in the "Myth" section of *The Second Sex*, p. 171.

WORKS CITED

Akoma, Chiji and Sally J. Scholz. Spring 2009. "Virtuous Bacchanalia: Creolizing Rousseau's Festival." *CLR James Journal* 15(1).

Arp, Kristana. 2001. *The Bonds of Freedom*. Chicago: Open Court Press.

Bauer, Nancy. 2001. *Simone de Beauvoir, Philosophy, and Feminism*. New York: Columbia University Press.

Beauvoir, Simone de. 1948. *The Ethics of Ambiguity*. Trans. Bernard Frechtman. Secaucus, NJ: Citadel Press.

———. 1962. Must We Burn Sade. In *The Marquis de Sade? An Essay by Simone de Beauvoir*. Ed. Paul Dinnage. London: John Calder.

———. 2009 [1949]. *The Second Sex*. Trans. Constance Borde and Sheila Malovany-Chevallier. New York: Alfred Knopf.

Cladis, Mark. 2003. *Public Vision, Private Lives: Rousseau, Religion, and Twenty-First Century Democracy*. Oxford, UK: Oxford University Press.

Damrosch, Leo. 2005. *Jean-Jacques Rousseau: Restless Genius*. Boston: Mariner Books, Houghton Mifflin.

Hutchings, Kimberly. 2003. *Hegel and Feminist Philosophy*. Cambridge: Polity Press.

Marso, Lori Jo and Patricia Moynagh. 2006. *Simone de Beauvoir's Political Thinking*. Urbana: University of Illinois Press.

Pateman, Carole. 1988. *The Sexual Contract*. Palo Alto, CA: Stanford University Press.

Rousseau, Jean-Jacques. 1960. *Letter to M. D'Alembert*. In *Politics and the Arts*. Trans. Allan Bloom. Ithaca, NY: Cornell University Press.

———. 1966. *On the Origin of Language*. Trans. John H. Moran and Alexander Gode. New York: Frederick Ungar Publishing.

———. 1967. *The Social Contract and Discourse on the Origin of Inequality*. Ed. and with an introduction by Lester G. Crocker. New York: Pocket Books.

———. 1992. Preface to Narcissus. Collected Writings. In *Discourse on the Sciences and Arts* (First Discourse) and *Polemics* (Collected Writings of Rousseau), vol. 2. Trans. Judith R. Bush, Roger D. Masters, and Christopher Kelly. Hanover, NH: University Press of New England.

———. 1993. *Émile*. Trans. Barbara Foxley. London: J. M. Dent.

———. 1997. *The Discourses and Other Early Political Writings*. Cambridge: University of Cambridge University Press.

Scholz, Sally. 2000. *On de Beauvoir*. Belmont, CA: Wadsworth.
———. 2001. *On Rousseau*. Belmont, CA: Wadsworth.
———. Spring 2010. That All Children Should Be Free: Beauvoir, Rousseau, and Childhood. *Hypatia* 25(2):394–411.
Thomas, Paul. Winter 1997. The Revolutionary Festival and Rousseau's Quest for Transparency. *History of Political Thought* 18.4: 652–676.
Vintges, Karen. 1996. *Philosophy as Passion*. Bloomington, IN: Indiana University Press.
Wollstonecraft, Mary. 1989. A Vindication of the Rights of Women. Buffalo, NY: Prometheus Books.

A Different Kind of Universality

Beauvoir and Kant on Universal Ethics

WILLIAM S. WILKERSON

> At the limit, the Beauvoirian ethics would take place under the sign of its own impossibility. This is not to suggest that it would simply not take place or that there is no Beauvoirian ethics, but rather that a Beauvoirian ethics must be affirmed as paradoxical.
> —Penelope Deutscher

Beauvoir's ethics reconciles individual freedom with the need for the Other. From her moral conversion during the war,[1] through the moral and philosophical essays of the 1940s, to *Le deuxième sexe* and *Les Mandarins*, one idea characterizes this reconciliation: all free individuals have a reciprocal need for the Other, which only mutual generosity satisfies. Another's freedom both completes and sustains my freedom. Generosity must ground these reciprocal relationships, because granting freedom to others means that I can *demand* nothing. I can only appeal to their generosity. Freely responding to others' freedom is thus a pure *gift*, because it expects nothing in exchange. Yet paradoxically, this gift is in all of our interests: Beauvoir thinks that any who seek justification and freedom must desire both their own and others' freedom as a part of their own fulfillment (Beauvoir 1976, 24, 72; Beauvoir 2008c 32, 91–92).[2]

Two important conclusions follow from this ethical perspective:

1. No pregiven or ready-made moral law determines my response to the Other's appeal in advance and independently of our situation. Beauvoir's ethics offers no equivalent to Kant's categorical imperative. Two or more individual freedoms cannot, *in principle*, decide in advance how to live together, how to resolve conflict, or even how to fulfill their own interests, since freedom must always adapt itself to situation and since our continual surpassing renders our futures unknown and totally open. We can be guided by our generosity and our desire for

freedom and justification, but this guidance leads me only to openness to another real individual, and to the uncertain possibilities we face: "To treat the other as a freedom so that his end may be freedom; in using this conducting wire one will have to incur the risk, in each case, of an *original solution*" (Beauvoir 1976, 142; Beauvoir 2008c 176–177).

2. *If* there is an imperative in Beauvoir's ethics—and it is not clear that there is—it is decidedly hypothetical and practical. Seeking justification leads me to generosity and to the Other, but fulfilling these needs comes by virtue of my own need and desire for justification and freedom. "Contrary to the formal rigor of Kantianism that considers the act as more virtuous as it is more abstract, generosity seems to us to be better grounded . . . the less distinction there is between the other and ourselves and the more we fulfill ourselves in taking the other as an end" (Beauvoir 1976, 144; Beauvoir 2008c 178). As a consequence, her counsels on ethical living often have the character of practical advice for living a creative, free kind of living. Similarly, much of the discussion of the independent woman in *The Second Sex* amounts to practical guidance for women to negotiate their oppression.[3] This practical advice, combined with a lack of a universal principal and Beauvoir's own desire to create a life in literature and autobiography, have led some, like Karen Vingtes, to claim that Beauvoir presents an ethic that avoids imperatives altogether. Rather, her ethics offers an "art of living" similar to Foucault's care of the self.[4]

Certainly, by offering no ready-made ethical principle and eschewing the ideal of ethical universality in favor of practical advice, Beauvoir rejects the Kantian ethic of an a priori universal principle that is absolute and completely binding. Yet her most sustained, complex, and explicitly ethical work, *The Ethics of Ambiguity*, speaks of an "ethics of autonomy" with a universal requirement of freedom (Beauvoir 1976, 24; Beauvoir 2008c, 32), a want for all people to be free (Beauvoir 1976, 86–87; Beauvoir 2008c, 108), and a "principle of action" (*principe d'action*) whose range is universal (Beauvoir 1976, 23; Beauvoir 2008c, 32). Indeed, the seemingly Kantian features of this book have been a constant source of difficulty and irritation for both Beauvoir and her interpreters. Beauvoir told biographer Deirdre Bair that she was using Kantian ideas and style when she was writing it (Bair 1990, 271), even though her own autobiography famously claimed that of all her books *The Ethics of Ambiguity* was the most irritating to her. She claimed that

> the fact remains that on the whole I went to a great deal of trouble to present inaccurately a problem to which I then offered a solution quite as hollow as the Kantian maxims. . . . I was in error when I thought I could define a morality independent of social context. (Beauvoir 1992, 67)[5]

Beauvoir thus disavows the work for both its Kantian language and its apparent abstract solution to human problems of action that require social context to be thought and understood correctly. In turn, her interpreters have ironically spent a great deal of ink trying to understand the universality of my need for the freedom of others. Most who read the book find her claim that my freedom requires the Other, and her apparent attempt to elevate this to a principle, puzzling, if not mistaken. These interpreters have either sought an argument for this universal principle of mutually required freedom, or avoided the problem altogether by claiming she presented antiformal ethics.[6]

I would like to propose, explain, and defend the following three theses about the issue of universality and the relationship to Kant: (1) Beauvoir never intended her ethics to be universal in anything like the Kantian sense, indeed from the Kantian perspective, her ethics is explicitly *anti-universal*; (2) What universality her ethics does possess must be seen as *temporal* and *practical-hypothetical* rather than *spatial* and *categorical*; and (3) these differences emerge because of their different ontologies of freedom. Following a discussion of these three theses, I conclude with some speculations as to why Beauvoir put her ethical ideas into Kantian language.

KANTIAN UNIVERSALITY

Although Kant's commitment to universality as the criteria for selecting which rules ("maxims") we should follow is famous, both the nature and the source of this universality has seemed unclear to many commentators.[7] Nonetheless, a fairly straightforward reconstruction of his ethical thinking follows the familiar "regressive" reasoning pattern so common to Kant's ethical and theoretical thinking: begin with an actual aspect of our experience, in this case moral judgment, and then regress back to the conditions of its possibility. If we look at the arguments of both the *Groundwork* and especially the second *Critique* schematically, they reveal this same regressive line of reasoning:

1. Morality is actual, insofar as people know themselves to be morally obligated even in the most extreme of circumstances (Kant 1956, AK30).[8] This runs parallel to the *Groundwork* where Kant begins with the concept of duty, a notion he claims "dwells already in the natural sound understanding" (Kant 1981, AK 397), in other words, a concept of morality that we all take to be actual. Moral obligation is characterized both by its strictness and its universally binding character.
2. Neither happiness, nor moral sense, nor self-interest can be the source of this universally binding morality. Kant argues this in several locations in the second *Critique* (Kant 1956, AK 25–27, 35–42) and similar arguments exist in the *Groundwork*, where he argues that neither prudential reasoning (Kant 1981, AK 402–403) nor hypothetical imperatives

(Kant 1981, AK 414–421) can produce genuine moral principles. One can also read the discussion of the end-in-itself as a derivation of the absolute value that belongs to a rational being, a value that cannot be derived simply from some particular (i.e., nonuniversal) good.

3. Since there is no other source of our moral obligation, it must be our existence as rational beings that makes this kind of universal moral obligation possible.

Now it appears that Kant assumes universality from the start, as a first and essential feature of anything worthy of the name morality. After all, the arguments in support of (2) all begin and end with the assumption that happiness and other sources of moral obligation fail to provide for a sufficiently binding and *universal* moral law. Kant himself could not state this problem more clearly in the *Critique*: "In this inquiry no objection can be raised that the *Critique* begins with pure practical laws and their reality" (Kant 1956, AK 46). He calls the apparently evident consciousness of universally binding moral laws the Fact of Reason. Recognizing that he assumes the reality of a pure practical law—of a universally binding and entirely formal moral law—Kant argues that this presupposition is no objection because these laws are then grounded in the freedom of a rational being. Thus, the argument of the second *Critique* "makes the concept of their existence in the intelligible world, i.e., it makes freedom, its foundation . . . these laws are possible only in relation to the freedom of the will; but if the will is presupposed as free, then they are necessary. Conversely, freedom is necessary because those laws are necessary, being practical postulates. *How this consciousness of the moral laws or—what amounts to the same thing—how this consciousness of freedom is possible cannot be further explained*; its permissibility, however, is established in the theoretical *Critique*" (Kant 1956, AK 46; emphasis mine).

Hence, the universally binding character of the moral law originates in the freedom of the subject, the possibility of which is established in Third Antinomy of the first *Critique*. How does the freedom of the subject ground this universality? We are negatively free insofar as the world of sense and its laws of causality do not bind us. This premise Kant establishes in the first *Critique*, but in his ethical thought he gives it a practical value, insofar as he thinks we discover our freedom from empirical determination ("negative freedom") when we discover that universal moral laws, which require freedom, bind us. Our consciousness of the moral law (the Fact of Reason) leads us to the consciousness of our freedom in the intelligible world. Since freedom in the intelligible world must be thoroughly unconditioned by anything in the sensible world, it cannot be motivated by any particular cause that would belong to that world. Yet, freedom cannot be pure spontaneity: it cannot act without any reason or motivation, for that would be a meaningless indeterminacy (Kant 1981, AK 446).[9] The negative sense of freedom takes us directly to a positive sense—autonomy—according to which we must give ourselves a law of action if our freedom is to have any meaning. By hypothesis, the requirement that this law be given in the intelligible world means that it can have no particular or sensuous object or motive, and so it must be pure universality itself that characterizes this law.

Universality thus derives from autonomy. Using language that is decidedly not Kant's: knowledge of moral principles, either in the form of pure practical laws or in the form of the ordinary concept of duty is *first in the order of knowing*; we know ourselves to be morally obligated. Although morality is first in the order of knowing, the freedom that makes morality possible, and the pure practical law that comprises morality are *equal in the order of being*. Or as Kant puts it, the moral law and our autonomy are reciprocally implicating.

While commentators typically agree that autonomy is the source of universality, Korsgaard does the best job of explaining how this universality works in practice (Korsgaard 1996, 64). Using Kant's own example: when a person wills a maxim of lying, he wills at once two things—that all other beings should follow a standard of truth telling and that he should exempt himself from this rule. Hence this will stands in contradiction to itself and the maxim of lying shows itself to be immoral because it cannot be willed universally.[10] The interesting feature of this example, however, is precisely that the moral obligation of truth telling does not originate from prudence or happiness, nor does it originate from *any other external principle*: the source of the moral obligation is the subject's own willing. In other words, in willing to lie, the subject wills that truth telling should be a moral obligation followed by all other rational beings, while also willing an exception for himself. Autonomy of the will or freedom in the positive sense—the will's capacity to give itself laws—creates the moral obligation. This is why Kant says that autonomy is the only source of genuine moral obligation, all others being heteronymous. Only if we as rational beings have a source of moral obligation internal to our own willing can it be genuinely binding on us; any other source of moral obligation would be external and therefore require some additional incentive beyond the structure of the subject's own will. Yet, because this obligation originates by virtue of being a rational being, it is binding upon all other rational beings: it is universal.[11]

Kant effectively squares the circle: moral obligation originates in the individual subject's will, and *for that very reason*, it stands as a universal obligation. The subject does not escape being rational and free, and so all willing is under the same moral obligation as a condition of being a rational and free will. The universality of Kantian ethics is thus *categorical*, exactly as Kant says, and it is further fully *a priori*, prior to any particularities of the subject. *Spatiality* suggests itself as another way of characterizing this kind of universal obligation precisely because a spatial dimension will be one in which all points are simultaneous, in contrast to a temporal dimension, in which points succeed each other.[12] Kantian universality spreads itself across each free individual equally and at the same time, even as saying this is quite literally wrong within the Kantian scheme. The time in which individuals are morally obligated is a time that is literally outside of time as an experienced succession. Our moral obligation originates in the intelligible world, and thus comes from a dimension of our being that cuts through each of us before we locate ourselves in the flow of time. Yet, as we experience ourselves in time, as beings experiencing the flow of successive time, we find ourselves always already obligated by virtue of this "simultaneous" fact of rational freedom that precedes both simultaneity and succession in time. Insofar as a universal moral law always already obligates us, obligation holds for all of us before we can even conceive of ourselves as empirical beings in the world, and there is no experienced time where moral obligation does not have its hold on us.

BEAUVOIR'S ANTI-UNIVERSAL STANCE

Beauvoir never intended, even in *The Ethics of Ambiguity*, to establish a universal ethical principle of this Kantian form. She makes this point in three different ways. First, from *Pyrrhus and Cineas* forward, Beauvoir denies both the possibility that our wills and desires could harmonize or that we could share a universal human good or happiness. This flows directly from the fact of *individual* freedoms: "precisely because they are free, they do not agree among themselves" (Beauvoir 2004a, 131; Beauvoir 2008c, 294). Individual freedoms by necessity differ, cannot be predicted, and seek their own unique way of disclosing and understanding the world, rendering an ultimate harmonizing impossible. Beauvoir uses this claim to dismiss a humanism that would offer a transcendent end to be achieved in *Pyrrhus and Cineas* (Beauvoir 2004a, 106–113; Beauvoir 2008c, 237–253) and to repudiate utilitarianism in *Ethics* (Beauvoir 1976, 112–113; Beauvoir 2008c, 139–140). In *Pyrrhus and Cineas*, she argues that any universal human good or purpose would be generated from the finite perspective of an individual or group of individuals, and for this reason could not legitimately claim to transcend those individuals. All the purposes and notions of the human good that have so far been proposed reveal themselves to be limited to a particular historical situation when they have been transcended by later historical periods and their own notions of the human good. (She even extends this same kind of argument against the notion of a religious purpose, arguing that any understanding of an ultimate reality like god could again only be the work of a finite human perspective.) In *Ethics*, she claims that any notion of utility or collective happiness cannot be made prior to a particular way of disclosing the world and the human place in it. This prior "decision" about how to disclose the world does not originate solely from a radical human freedom (as it does in *Being and Nothingness*) but rather from the interplay of socially given meanings and choices individuals make in response to this already given world. This large role for socialization (explained in *Ethics* in terms of childhood development) results in an even greater difficulty in establishing a transcendent human good or utility, since it means that we are always already working within a particular way of disclosing the world that colors and directs choices about the good.

Indeed, although the antinomy of action that she confronts in the final section of *Ethics* mostly concerns the legitimacy of violence, in fact the antinomy itself is none other than the general problem of individual freedoms in conflict: "Thus one finds oneself in the presence of the paradox that no action can be generated [*se faire*] for man [*pour l'homme*] without being generated against some men [*contre des hommes*]" (Beauvoir 1976, 112; Beauvoir 2008c, 124). Beauvoir could not be clearer: one cannot will for all without willing against some; in short, one cannot will for all. Beauvoir concludes that we cannot transcend or resolve this paradox, we can only work within it and make concrete decisions with the hope of realizing further freedoms. This point, made here in the abstract, becomes more concrete and situated in both *The Second Sex* and *The Mandarins*. The great literary success of *The Mandarins* stems in part from the fact that none of the characters find it possible to act for freedom without simultaneously creating conflict amongst themselves.

Second, Kant's moral universal willing is an "abstract" willing, for it is a willing independent of any particular content. This point, as we saw, is essential to Kantian ethics. The moral law functions as a higher-order law that provides only formal criteria for selecting maxims. No specific content can be given for this law, as it originates in the intelligible world and must stand universally for all rational beings: "the practical rule, which is thus here a law, absolutely and directly determines the will objectively, for pure reason, practical in itself, is here directly legislative. The will is thought of as independent of any empirical conditions and consequently as pure will" (Kant 1956, AK 31). It is precisely this abstract character of Kant's universality that leads to the apparent difficulty in generating convincing examples of its application.

In contrast, Beauvoir claims repeatedly that I cannot will in the abstract—I cannot will myself free *as such*. Rather, I must will freedom in the concrete and by means of engaging actual, individual projects. "Freedom requires realization of concrete ends, or particular projects" (Beauvoir 1976, 24; Beauvoir 2008c, 32) and freedom "must, by giving itself a particular content, aim by means of it an end which is nothing else but the precisely the free movement of existence" (Beauvoir 1976, 29; Beauvoir 2008c, 38–39). While those who want to lead meaningful and justified lives should be interested in their own freedom as the end of all their projects, the fact that they always exist *in situation* means that they cannot will this freedom as a project unto itself, but, rather, must find ways to realize that attitude of authentic freedom in the midst of making concrete choices about how to live in their situation. Moreover, individual projects are precisely that—individual—and thus inevitably come into contact and conflict with others' projects. In realizing my freedom, what she says of the adventurer holds for all of us: our projects conflict and we must take sides (Beauvoir 1976, 60; Beauvoir 2008c, 77).[13] Adopting neutrality in a conflict is always a false choice, because neutrality simply allows the stronger side of the conflict to win. As a consequence, one again cannot choose freedom for oneself without choosing against other freedoms.

Third, and most importantly, Beauvoir thinks that the impossibility of willing the universal derives from the ontology of our finite freedom itself. "Without failure, no ethics" Beauvoir writes, and this problem cannot be transcended (Beauvoir 1976, 10; Beauvoir 2008c, 15). Value originates in our lack of being—from the fact that we lack both a determinate nature and a completed way of being. Without a ready-made way of being, we must create our way of being. As we move toward the future, we propose to ourselves an "ought-to-be" (*devoir-être*)—a term I will discuss in detail below. Since the lack that defines us can be neither fulfilled, nor completed, nor transcended, we cannot fulfill such a "should." The very condition that requires ethics, our lack of being, thus makes its fulfillment impossible. We cannot become a being with a determinate nature without ceasing to be human; to put it in Sartrean language, we cannot solidify into being-in-itself. Bad faith will always get us, because the possibility of bad faith makes ethics necessary in the first place.

Hence, this third reason against universality underwrites the previous two: it is a direct consequence of our incomplete being that we will always be in conflict with one another and individuals will always fail to realize their proposed standards and their desire for freedom. Ethical perfection would render ethics itself unnecessary; even if we could all will freedom as our ultimate and universal goal, we could never achieve this freedom in anything but a partial and limited way.[14] I want and will my freedom in a world where that freedom can never be fully realized and where I will necessarily have to fight for freedom by embracing the antinomy and depriving others of their freedom. Just as Kant does not overcome the antinomies but explains how they arise, Beauvoir does not solve the problem of conflicting freedoms in a higher universality; she only shows how it arises and offers practical advice for living with it. The extremely close connection between ethics and politics, evident in all her writing, also has its basis in this nonuniversality of individual willing and the inevitable failure that humanity is. We will always be fighting for freedom in concrete action.

Moral principles do not predate our willing in the world, cannot be willed in the abstract, and cannot serve all finite freedoms at once. Nor can ethics even consider itself as a completed form of thought that could generate principles that could function simultaneously for all. For all these reasons, Beauvoir rejects a spatial and categorical universality of the Kantian form.[15]

ONTOLOGIES OF FREEDOM

Beauvoir and Kant both begin with human freedom. Why do they end in different places? How is it that Beauvoir reasons from freedom to an apparent denial of universality, while Kant reasons from freedom to a fully categorical and spatial universal? Beauvoir herself gives us the answer, in a remarkably perspicuous discussion of Kant in the *Ethics*. In accounting for evil, Beauvoir draws a distinction between two kinds of ethical approaches, what are today called externalist and internalist views on ethical obligation. In the externalist view, exemplified for Beauvoir in the thought of Plato, the good is a transcendent standard independent of human existence. With this view, one accounts for an evil will by arguing that ignorance of this standard produces moral evil. In contrast, if we are internalists and grant that the force of moral obligation originates from human willing itself; if—in Beauvoir's own language—we

> grant that the moral world is the world authentically willed [*voulu*] by man all possibility of error is eliminated. . . . in Kantian ethics, which is at the origin of all ethics of autonomy, it is very difficult to account for an evil will. As the choice of his character which the subject makes is achieved in the intelligible world by a purely rational will, one can not [*sic*] understand how the latter expressly rejects the law which it gives to itself. (Beauvoir 1976, 32–33; Beauvoir 2008c, 43)

The charge that Kant cannot account for evil is a common one,[16] and I will not debate its merits here, because it seems less important than Beauvoir's characterization of an "ethics of autonomy" as a standard that originates in willing itself and her clear allegiance to this kind of moral thinking. She places her own ethics in the school of autonomy, and then proceeds to explain its unique place in this school: while Kant defined the human will as essentially positive, she sees the will as a negativity that "can coincide with [itself] only by agreeing never to rejoin [itself]" (Beauvoir 1976, 33; Beauvoir 2008c, 43). At least as a rational will, the nature and being of the will in Kant's view are fully determined. Such a will has neither the need nor the ability to be something other than what it is. As we saw, the will in its intelligible form is pure spontaneity governed by rational law. From both the theoretical and practical writings, we know that Kant believed it to be at least possible that the will can be a cause unto itself, but even such a spontaneity must not be lawless, otherwise the problem of a completely indeterminate willing arises. Without law, the will does not act purposefully or even meaningfully, so it must give itself a law. As we also saw, this connection between the spontaneity of the will and the law it must give itself plays an important role in establishing the existence and legitimacy of the moral law in both the *Groundwork* and the second *Critique*. It is because the will acts in the intelligible world, not under lawlike causality, but rather under a rational form of causality, that it must give itself a rational law. By its nature, such a rational law is universally binding, since all other rational beings, willing freely but lawfully in the intelligible world would will the same law.

Yet this also means that the will cannot be otherwise than rational in its spontaneous willing (and hence, the difficulty with evil). In striving to link freedom to morality, Kant disregards the human capacity to "play with the negative" (Beauvoir 1976, 33; Beauvoir 2008c, 43). Beauvoir begins with human spontaneity as well, but shares with Sartre the conviction that such spontaneity cannot be governed in advance by any standard. Original choice, the choice of how one will relate to one's own freedom, "occurs without reason, before any reason" because it discloses the world and makes it meaningful to humankind (Beauvoir 1976, 40; Beauvoir 2008c, 54). The freedom of the Kantian subject must be bound by a rational law, because Kant cannot envision how a free subject could "bind itself" apart from a rational standard. For Beauvoir, as we have seen, the human being is always in process and always radically incomplete. Lacking a predetermined way of being, its negativity prohibits it ever *being* anything. If the subject is to follow a standard, it must both choose and bind itself to this standard.

And indeed, even though Beauvoir notes that a nearly absolute spontaneity lies at the base of our willing, and even though she disagrees that a pregiven form of law must make our freedom meaningful, she nonetheless agrees with Kant that our freedom must supply itself with a standard to judge itself against, what she calls a *devoir-être*. This hyphenated term has no easy translation; it has been rendered as "have-to-be," "ought-to-be" and even "duty-to-be."[17] I will leave it in French because of its unique difficulties of translation and also to capture the fact that it is a term with a "technical status" in Beauvoir's thought: it names that obligation we stand under as free beings to use our freedom. Both Kant and Beauvoir see the force of moral obligation, its binding nature, originating in our free will, and not in anything external to it. But if the intelligible nature of a rational and free will provides a ready-made and always already binding law for Kant, what is the source of this "necessity" to have a *devoir-être* for Beauvoir, who wishes to deny to the will any genuine nature or being? Why must completely spontaneous subjects bind themselves to a *devoir-être*?

The answer is that the *devoir-être* arises as a practical necessity born out of a metaphysical fact about human intentionality and consciousness. As a practical fact, humans lack a predetermined way of being, seek justification for our lives, and want our lives to have meaning. In order to give it meaning and especially justification, we require some kind of standard by which we can judge our progress and development. Yet, when compared with the practical metaphysics of Kant, Beauvoir's more existentialist answer seems lacking because we can always ask the further question: *Why* do we need or seek justification? Aside from Beauvoir's argument that the nihilism such a question implies always fails to sustain itself consistently,[18] can we explain the origin of the need for justification? Given that we do not have the strong Kantian commitment to a law as the necessary grounding for making freedom free, and given the fairly radical nature of spontaneity, which seems to undercut the ability to value freedom, there would seem to be nothing from which to derive the *devoir-être*, unless there were some feature of consciousness that leads us to seek it and the justification it provides.

This is just what we find: the need for justification originates in the very intentionality of our being. Beauvoir views consciousness as an expression of both freedom and desire. Consciousness is freedom in that I am free to ask any question of being; I do not experience the world as passive receptacle but shape how I approach it and how I choose to disclose it, through the kind of questions I ask of it. Yet consciousness is also desire in that, as negativity, as a lack of being it seeks fulfillment; consciousness is driven toward being and toward an unbroken relation to the world. Together, this free desire that is consciousness represents Beauvoir's view of intentionality: a synthesis of a centrifugal, Sartrean-Husserlian view in which consciousness bestows meaning,[19] and a view more like Merleau-Ponty's and Heidegger's, in which consciousness lies at the nexus of world and body interaction.[20]

Debra Bergoffen further complicates this picture by arguing for two "moments" of intentionality in Beauvoir's view of consciousness (Bergoffen 1997, 76–85). In the first moment, my consciousness seeks to disclose being, to reveal meaning on the basis of particular style of disclosure. In a fully embodied relation to the world, I locate myself within a nexus of meanings, social, natural, and even spiritual. I would be tempted to revel in this joyful attraction to being—in this disclosure and openness—because it fills my incomplete existence with meaning and possibility, except that I am anxious to have meaning remain and to fix it in being. Nothing overcomes lack and desire (as we have already seen), and in this second moment arises the possibility of a desire to go from the openness of possibility and my free disclosure of the world to a narrowing and valorization of the meaning I have revealed. In short, the possibility of bad faith arises within the very structure of intentionality as my desire for *meaning* becomes a desire to *be*.

Both moments reveal to me the possibility of a *devoir-être*—of a possibility for my being that sets forward an end to be achieved and a standard by which I can judge myself in relation to this end. Yet this desire for being does not lead inevitably to a freezing of being and to bad faith. Even though it would seem that willing a *devoir-être* is an expression of bad faith, since it seems to be a way to freeze being, it is not (and in this she clearly distances herself from Sartre). I seek meaning as a part of desire/intentionality, and this must be the revelation of more than a moment; it must give birth to an actual desire that moves it forward in the form of a style of disclosing the world and the project. The difficulty comes in the anxiety of the second moment, which wants to hold this *devoir-être* in a single, frozen time. This is why Beauvoir speaks of 'winning' (*gagner*) by choosing to disclose being—to stay with the first moment of intentionality, and the inevitable tension and ambiguity that such a choice produces (Beauvoir 1976, 23–24; Beauvoir 2008c, 32–33).

Such a willing is one that needs a standard, a direction, a *devoir-être* in order to realize its freedom. Yet this willing does not have—in advance—a single form of a rational law as in Kant. We have seen two reasons for this: both because the subject discloses being within a particular situation and because willing disclosure means willing a perpetual tension. Of these, willing tension (*vouloir tension*) becomes a central feature of her ethical outlook, because it amounts to the will contesting its own tendency to seek a finalized and full being or determined state of itself. Effectively, it means willing to stay with the first moment of intentionality, even as one must commit oneself to a *devoir-être* into an uncertain future. One must sustain one's willing without willing in bad faith, and this generates a tension in the individual.

To recapitulate this discussion: the source of obligation in Kant is our rational freedom—our ability to give ourselves our own law and thus express the fact of our involvement in a supersensible realm where abstract, practical reason reigns supreme and universal. Our will, at once free and rational, is the source of the binding force of any morality. The source of obligation in Beauvoir is equally our freedom, but the similarity ends with that word—freedom signaling such radically different conceptions of our existence that one is virtually unrecognizable from the point of view of the other. While Kant remains attached to the notion that self-given law is the only possible source of our freedom and obligation, Beauvoir argues instead that all our freedom points us toward the project, with its *devoir-être* and the need for an ethic that we can use to judge and justify our actions, but which we can never fulfill since our will never fulfills its lack. The human condition is to need a *devoir-être* just because we cannot fulfill one, and because we have no predetermined way of being and therefore no universal way of being that we all share. Hence, the will remains negativity and the existentialist freedom that emerges can never elevate itself to the status of a universal law because there was no universal subject to begin with. Whatever standard I give myself as my unique 'ought,' it originates instead from a particularity that cannot be transcended, but the *fact* that we all need to seek and reveal meaning implies that a *devoir-être* stands over us all. In fact, this is why nihilism fails: it makes of avoiding meaning into a *devoir-être* and so immediately falls into an unstable contradiction.

BEAUVOIR'S UNIQUE UNIVERSALITY

Nonetheless, there is still something "universal" about Beauvoir's ethical stance. I would claim that her rejection of a *spatial* and *categorical* Kantian universality does not mean that she rejects any form of universality. Rather, she proposes a *temporal* and *hypothetical* universality that fits with her general ethical outlook. I can explain this kind of universality by taking up the familiar distinction between levels of freedoms found in *Ethics of Ambiguity*: an original or ontological freedom akin to Sartre's radical freedom, and a moral freedom that humans establish through taking up a particular attitude toward this ontological freedom.[21] I will avoid a lengthy discussion of this distinction, and simply stress that she characterizes moral freedom by its relationship with *time*. To want freedom and to want disclosure of the world are one and the same, and to want disclosure requires that perpetual tension spoken of above. She repeats this point throughout *Ethics*: "to will is to engage myself to persevere in my willing" (Beauvoir 1976, 27; Beauvoir 2008c, 36).[22] Again, much later in the text: "This requires that each action be considered as a finished form whose different moments, instead of fleeing toward the future in order to find their justification, reflect and confirm one another so well that there is no longer a sharp separation between present and future, between means and ends" (Beauvoir 1976, 131; Beauvoir 2008c, 162). Moreover, although only I can found my project, the anguish of this permanent and unending choice leads me to flee into bad faith, and we saw that the struggle against this tendency is for her the primary moral struggle.

Underneath these claims lies her view that human existence is perpetual transcendence; that we are a lack of being thrown forward by this lack, and that we never escape this continual process of transcendence. Indeed, in *Pyrrhus and Cineas*, this transcendence becomes the very source of our anguish and our temptation to give into nihilism. Thus a *temporal universality* is a willing in which freedom does not deny itself by trapping itself in bad faith but perpetually (universally at each successive moment) tries to reestablish itself in an individual's existence. It wills the tension of fighting bad faith. This kind of *se vouloir libre* cannot be willed for all other individuals; for reasons we have seen I cannot will *for* Others and cannot will universally, but *my* freedom can be willed throughout *my* lifetime. Beauvoir takes care to point out that such a freedom does not pre-exist our activity of willing ourselves free, but is summoned up in the act of establishing itself; I make moral freedom in the act of willing and wanting moral freedom. This fact explains both why her ethic is an ethic of autonomy, and also why the universality of my willing is not spatial. Her ethic is one of autonomy because (once again) the binding force of a *devoir-être* originates from my willing, and yet it is not a spatial universality because moral freedom does not pre-exist the very act of willing it, and so it cannot be the pre-existent universality of a Kantian moral law. A *devoir-être* comes into being in the continual process of an individual's life coming into being. Beauvoir can thus consistently claim that willing oneself free can "require itself universally [*elle s'exige universellement*]" and "can not [sic] establish a denial of itself [*elle ne peut pas fonder un refus d'elle-même*]" (Beauvoir 1976, 24; Beauvoir 2008c, 32), because choosing freedom means refusing to congeal into bad faith, which requires a *perpetual* or temporally universal willing.

Still, one might object, isn't Beauvoir claiming that all humans—all free beings—must will moral freedom? Isn't her claim about the peculiar temporality of moral freedom one that applies to all who would read her text? Doesn't it spread itself *spatially* across individuals? There is no easy answer to this question, but I believe Beauvoir thinks that the universality of her own ethical exhortation is hypothetical rather than categorical, because it begins with my individual desire and radiates outward toward others. Categorical and spatial universality always already applies to all individuals without reference to the specific object or desire of willing. Kant's moral willing is disinterested (except insofar as reason itself can be said to have an interest). But Beauvoir believes that all ethics ultimately appeals to our interests. In this particular case, individuals will freedom because they want it and the justification that it brings, and they cannot, really, escape this interest. Beauvoir then simply points out that I can attain this genuine freedom and this genuine justification only in relation to the freedom of the Other because I have a need for the Other. The Other plays a constitutive role in defining my project and myself, sustains the human meaning of my project, and keeps me from slipping into bad faith. I want a genuine disclosure of the world; an authentic recognition of the conditions necessary for this disclosure lead me to want the freedom of the Other and to call for the gift of the Other's free recognition.

In the Kantian scheme, I always act *as if* all other beings are rational and deserving of moral treatment. As rational beings, the moral law obligates certain actions and motives prior to any specific willing. I should treat others according to the moral law because they are also subject to rationality. But in Beauvoir's scheme, this is completely impossible. A *devoir-être* is called into being by the very act of my willing and cannot predate it. Moreover, I do not and cannot act *as if* all others have attained moral freedom. In *this* world where (spatial) universal willing is impossible, and where our finitude undercuts all attempts at being, the inescapable paradox of my wanting to be free is that this will must necessarily take account of the antinomy of action and even act *against* the freedom of some in the name of a more complete freedom. Hence the curious paradox of a *universal hypothetical*: *if* you want to be free, *then* you must will perpetual disclosure and recognize your need for others. Yet we must always act under the recognition that this will take us into conflict, and not harmony. There is no need to reconstruct an argument that would take us to a spatial universal, spread across individuals, for the "principle" at work here already rules out that kind of universal.

In saying this, I am not denying that Beauvoir thought an individual had a profound need for the Other and that the relationship between the self and Other was not fundamental in all her thinking, beginning with *L'invitée*. Rather, I am saying that a *need* for the Other, which appears in all of her texts from *Pyrrhus and Cineas* forward, cannot be elevated to the status of a universal principle and that she did not in fact mean for it to be a universal principle in *Ethics*. The Kantian language of universality leads us to think that the need for the Other should be a principle and as a consequence *Ethics* points away from some of its best insights.

As further justification for this interpretation of *Ethics*, we should note that although Beauvoir undoubtedly feels the inescapability of this need for the Other, she seems uncertain *how* to justify or explain this need, especially if we begin with the self and its freedom. This can be seen from the fact that her justifications for this need change through the texts being considered. In *Pyrrhus and Cineas*, she claims that only the Other can overcome the nihilism brought on by our continual surpassing of each moment: "in order for the object that I founded to appear as a good, the other must make it into his own good, and then I would be justified for having created it. The other's freedom alone is capable of necessitating my being" (Beauvoir 2004a, 129; Beauvoir 2008c, 289). In *Ethics of Ambiguity*, the Other not only prevents this nihilism, but also keeps us from falling into the absurdity of bad faith (Beauvoir 1976, 71; Beauvoir 2008c, 90–91). Yet even in this text, she also presents the Hegelian idea that my consciousness of my finite self requires another freedom for its existence. This Hegelian ideal becomes completely dominant in *The Second Sex*, where she simply begins with the idea that one consciousness requires another—it is only a matter of overcoming the deformities of the master/slave form of this mutual need: "the conflict can be overcome by the free recognition of each individual in the other, each one positing itself and the other as object and as subject in a reciprocal movement. But friendship and generosity, which accomplish this recognition of freedoms concretely . . . are undoubtedly man's highest accomplishment; this is where he is in his truth" (Beauvoir, 2011, 159–160; Beauvoir, 2008a, 240).

Although brief, this summary shows that Beauvoir, no matter how committed to the relationship of self and Other, struggled to understand that relationship. The fact that *Ethics* stands as a transitional text between the fully Hegelian view of *Second Sex* and the more Sartrean sounding view of *Pyrrhus and Cineas* no doubt contributes to the difficulty people have with finding her "argument" for her claim that an individual freedom requires the freedom of others.

Even in *Ethics*, however, I believe that the Hegel-influenced line of thought is her strongest way to connect self and Other, given her starting point of individual freedom. Since authentic willing of disclosure requires a particular consciousness of my self as that which raises the *devoir-être* into being, the conditions of this particular kind of willing is self-recognition. Others are necessary to this self-recognition; without others there would be no sense of the unique character, values, and projects that make me myself, even if this means that others continually threaten the stability of my self. Or, as Beauvoir puts it in *Ethics*, after an explicit reference to the master-slave dialectic, "if I really were everything, there would be nothing else beside me; the world would be empty. There would be nothing to possess and I myself would be nothing" (Beauvoir 1976, 71; Beauvoir 2008c, 90–91). We can only recognize the concrete singularity of ourselves in contrast to others, and we can only develop our projects and our selves in genuine contact with others who challenge and question our being.

So while we need the Other, this need leads to no spatial and categorical universal. Rather it points out that, if I seek justification, I must recognize the need for the Other's freedom. This need can only by asked for in an appeal to the Other's generosity, since one cannot *compel* a free response, and the Other can only appeal to my own freedom in turn. This free generosity, as we have seen, cannot be guided by a categorical principle because it is not itself a categorical principle but a concrete, lived relation. Even more, I need others' freedom within a human situation that makes the realization of this need fraught with the conflict that individual freedoms necessarily create. I need other individuals in a world of conflicting individuals, and neither this need, nor the conflict, can be transcended. This bitter lesson, we might say, is the moral of ambiguity.

CONCLUSION: WHY USE KANTIAN LANGUAGE?

There can be little doubt why Beauvoir later found the *Ethics* irritating: the Kantian language of universality leads *away* from the point of the book and its overall ethical argument. Evidence of this is found in the continual attempt by scholars to find the argument for the claim that my freedom requires other freedoms *universally*. Such a quest simply misses the point of the book altogether. But while the content of the ethic is not Kantian, the language and style of presentation shares much in common with Kant. Why write non-Kantian ideas in a Kantian idiom? There are many possible reasons why she felt the need to express herself in this way, and here I admit to engaging in some speculation. One credible reason is found in her short essay "Moral Idealism and Political Realism," written between *Pyrrhus and Cineas* and *Ethics*. There, she claims that modern societies almost exclusively regulate themselves according to an "adulterated legacy of Kantian ethics" (Beauvoir 2004b, 177). To speak to such a society one must adapt the language of this Kantian ethics to a new purpose. The passage in *Ethics* examined earlier corroborates this idea, stating that Kantian ethics are at the origin of all ethics of autonomy—including Beauvoir's—but that her approach succeeds where Kant's fails because it first defines humanity as a lack and explains both the origin of value and our inevitable failure to attain our proposed values (Beauvoir 1976, 33; Beauvoir 2008c, 43). Beauvoir thought she could construct an anti-Kantian ethics using the language of Kantian ethics, and thus her most sustained and explicitly ethical text directs the reader away from its chief innovation.

Even if this is only speculation, I believe it points to an interesting problem that was definitely central to Beauvoir. Just as many discussions of the last century have pointed out that one cannot displace metaphysical thinking without creating one's own metaphysical scheme, it appears that one cannot speak the language of modern, philosophical ethics without falling into the trap of "doing" modern-style ethics. To speak in the philosophico-ethical register it seems almost like one must speak with a universalizing voice, and it is just this problem that irritated Beauvoir, and led her to view works like *The Mandarins* and *The Second Sex* as her best works; for they confront human problems in the complexity of their situation and in an explicitly nonuniversal way. At the heart of her ethical thought, then, we find the same thinking that drove her to connect philosophy and literature to attain a more genuine expression of human existence: the thought that one cannot speak for all and yet each action requires that others are taken into consideration in the concrete particularity and that no ready-made solution exists for how to consider the others.

NOTES

1. The conversion can be witnessed in the *Wartime Diary* (Beauvoir 2009, 319–320). Margaret Simons explains the importance of this moral conversion from solipsism to a Hegelian-influenced social view in her introduction to the same volume (Beauvoir 2009, 28–31).
2. Penelope Deutscher's discussion of Beauvoir's ethics (used as an epigram for this paper) points out that the requirement of a pure generosity under these circumstances makes her ethics virtually paradoxical: my own interest *requires* a reciprocal gift. I shall return to this problem later. See Deutscher 2008.
3. So much so that she even advises her woman readers that "choosing defiance is a risky tactic unless it is a positively effective action; more time and energy are spent than saved" (Beauvoir 2011, 724; Beauvoir 2008c, 591–592). I am

grateful to Margaret Simons for much helpful discussion of the idea of practical guidance in *The Second Sex*.
4. See the middle chapters of Vingtes 1996, 67–119.
5. The statement in its entirety reads: "Of all my books [the *Ethics of Ambiguity*] is the one that irritates me the most today. . . . the fact remains that on the whole I went to a great deal of trouble to present inaccurately a problem to which I then offered a solution quite as hollow as the Kantian maxims. My descriptions of the nihilist, the adventurer, the esthete, obviously influenced by those of Hegel, are even more arbitrary and abstract than his, since they are not even linked together by a historical development; the attitudes I examine are explained by objective conditions; I limited myself to isolating their moral significance to such an extent that my portraits are not situated on any level of reality. I was in error when I thought I could define a morality independent of social context."
6. Vingtes (1996, 68–69) summarizes the early debate (1979–1990) between Thomas Anderson, Robert Stone, and Sonia Kruks over this matter, before dismissing the universality as a matter of Kantian "style" and arguing that Beauvoir sought an ethics as an "art of life." Kristana Arp (2001, 68–74) also attempts to reconstruct the argument. Even Bergoffen's nuanced discussion of generosity and risk directs itself to the question of my obligation to the Other (Bergoffen, 1997, 85–110). More recently, Matthew Eshleman takes up the question again and argues that the universality of the ethical requirement in *Ethics of Ambiguity* is underdeveloped before he tries to provide his own justification for the universality requirement (Eshleman, 2009, 81–82).
7. For a sample of this literature see (Aune, 1979; Korsgaard, 1996; Rickless, 2004; Wood, 1999). Since my focus lies in contrasting Kantian-style universality with Beauvoir's ethics, I will not attempt to justify the interpretation of Kantian universality I present here, although it owes much to my reading of these sources.
8. All future Kant references will be to the Prussian Academy Edition page numbers ("AK").
9. See also the Third Antinomy of the first Critique (A442/B473-A456/B484 and A532/B500-A558/B586) and Wilkerson 2009.
10. Once again, there are many interpretations of Kant's universality and contradiction test. For a summary and critical discussion of this issue, see Korsgaard 1996, 77–105.
11. Wood is thus right (1999, 156), and in fact Beauvoir agrees, that autonomy is Kant's most original and important contribution to moral thought.
12. Yes, this is a Bergsonian way of conceiving it, and it's worth remarking that *Essai sur les données immédiates de la conscience* is, among other things, an attack on Kantian thought.
13. I have changed the translators' "he must declare himself" to match the French idiom: "*Il lui faut prendre parti.*"

14. Hence, the quote from Deutscher that serves as this paper's epigraph, "Beauvoirian ethics would take place under the sign of its own impossibility. . . . a Beauvoirian ethics must be affirmed as paradoxical," is in fact Beauvoir's *own* insight into ethical thought (Deutscher 2008, 52–53).
15. As a final example of her denial of Kantian universality, consider two aspects of *The Mandarins*. First, the character of Paula: in a rather delicious dig at her own work, Beauvoir places a full statement of her own ethical view into the mouth of this pathetic creature: "'I told you I've now learned to love you with complete generosity, with an absolute respect for your freedom. That means I require no explanation of you'" (Beauvoir 1999, 305). The irony here is that Paula is a perfect example of the "woman in love" Beauvoir describes in part 2 of *The Second Sex*. Her point seems to be that even her own ideals of generosity and freedom must be taken in situation and willed concretely in order to be realized. In the case of somebody like Paula, they actually become an ideal of bad faith. Second, the novel ends with all the principles, Henri, Anne, and Dubrueilh, deciding to take up political action again, even after their miserable failure with *L'Espoir*. The point seems to be that the struggle for freedom must be engaged continually but without hope of final success.
16. See Korsgaard, 1996, 170–71.
17. Frechtman's original translation of *Ethics* used the English "have-to-be." The newer (and superior) translation of the introduction to the *Ethics* in *Philosophical Writings* by Marybeth Timmerman and Mary Beth Mader uses "ought-to-be." Joseph Bien, in translating the term in Merleau-Ponty's *Adventures of the Dialectic* uses "duty-to-be."
18. This is an argument that is made across the entirety of *Pyrrhus and Cineas* and in Beauvoir's discussion of the nihilist in *Ethics*.
19. This claim is certainly not without controversy, but a good defense of it can be found in Føllesdal 1981.
20. A fine discussion of this point can be found in the first chapter of Deutscher 2008.
21. Several interpreters have read this distinction into this text. See Arp 2001, 55 for a prime example. Vingtes takes these two and adds a third, for *three* levels of freedom (Vingtes 1996, 70). Eshelman's (2009) discussion in "Beauvoir and Sartre on Freedom" also distinguishes two levels of freedom. I believe there is something correct about this, as long as we think that we never *experience* radical freedom, but, rather, always experience a situated freedom that is basically moral freedom.
22. The French reads, "*vouloir, c'est m'engager à persévérer dans ma volunté.*"

WORKS CITED

Arp, Kristana. 2001. *The Bonds of Freedom*. Chicago and La Salle, IL: Open Court.
Aune, Bruce. 1979. *Kant's Theory of Morals*. Princeton, NJ: Princeton University Press.

Bair, Deirdre. 1990. *Simone de Beauvoir: A Biography*. New York: Summit Books.
Beauvoir, Simone de. 1976. *The Ethics of Ambiguity*. Trans. Bernard Frechtman. New York: Citadel Press.
———. 1992. *The Autobiography of Simone de Beauvoir: Force of Circumstance*, vol. 1. Trans. Richard Howard. New York: Paragon House.
———. 1999. *The Mandarins*. Trans. Leonard Freidman. New York: W. W. Norton.
———. 2004a. Pyrrhus and Cineas. In *Philosophical Writings*, 77–150. Ed. Margaret A. Simons and Sylvie Le Bon de Beauvoir. Trans. Marybeth Timmermann and Mary Beth Mader. Urbana: University of Illinois Press.
———. 2004b. Moral Realism and Political Idealism. In *Philosophical Writings*, 175–193. Ed. Margaret A. Simons and Sylvie Le Bon de Beauvoir. Trans. Marybeth Timmermann and Mary Beth Mader. Urbana: University of Illinois Press.
———. 2008a. *Le deuxième sexe*, vol. 1. Paris: Gallimard.
———. 2008b. *Le deuxième sexe*, vol. 2. Paris: Gallimard.
———. 2008c. *Pour une Morale de l'aminguïté suivi Pyrrhus et Cinéas*. Paris: Editions Gallimard.
———. 2009. *Wartime Diary*. Ed. Margaret Simons and Sylvie Le Bon de Beauvoir. Trans. Anne Deing Cordero. Urbana, IL: University of Illinois Press.
———. 2011. *The Second Sex*. Trans. Constance Borde and Sheila Malovany-Chevallier. New York: Vintage Books.
Bergoffen, Debra B. 1997. *The Philosophy of Simone de Beauvoir: Gendered Phenomenologies, Erotic Generosities*. Albany, NY: State University of New York Press.
Deutscher, Penelope. 2008. *The Philosophy of Simone de Beauvoir: Conversion, Ambiguity, Resistance*. Cambridge, UK: Cambridge University Press.
Eshleman, Matthew. 2009. Beauvoir and Sartre on Freedom, Intersubjectivity, and Normative Justification. In *Beauvoir and Sartre: The Riddle of Influence*. Ed. Christine Daigle and Jacob Golomb, 65–89. Bloomington: Indiana University Press.
Føllesdal, Dagfinn. 1981. Sartre on Freedom. In *The Philosophy of Jean-Paul Sartre*. Ed. Paul Arthur Schlipp, 392–407. La Salle, IL: Open Court.
Immanuel Kant. 1956. *Critique of Practical Reason*. Trans. Lewis White Beck. Indianapolis: Bobbs-Merrill Company (Liberal Arts Press).
———. 1981. *Groundwork for the Metaphysics of Morals*. Trans. James Ellington. Indianapolis: Hackett Editions.
Korsgaard, Christine. 1996. *Creating the Kingdom of Ends*. Cambridge, UK: Cambridge University Press.
Rickless, Samuel. 2004. From the Good Will to the Formula of Universal Law. *Philosophy and Phenomenological Research* 68:554–577.
Vingtes, Karen. 1996. *Philosophy as Passion: The Thinking of Simone de Beauvoir*. Bloomington: Indiana University Press.
Wilkerson, William. 2009. In the World but Not Of the World: The Relationship of Freedom to Time in Kant and Sartre. *Epoché* 14:113–130.
Wood, Allen. 1999. *Kant's Ethical Thought*. Cambridge, UK: Cambridge University Press.

Simone de Beauvoir and the Marquis de Sade

Contesting the Logic of Sovereignty and the Politics of Terror and Rape

DEBRA BERGOFFEN

Sade the person was a torturer and a rapist. Sade the author created characters and spectacles that justified torture and rape. Yet Simone de Beauvoir refused to dismiss him as a mere pornographer or a common criminal. In accordance with the principles of *The Ethics of Ambiguity*, she credited him with having formulated an authentic ethics. She recognized him as articulating and epitomizing the existential ethical drama—the conflict between the demands of individuality and the necessities of intersubjectivity. In "Must We Burn Sade?" Beauvoir phrased this ethical dilemma in terms of a question: "[Is it] only by the sacrifice of our individual differences that we can integrate ourselves into the community?" (Beauvoir 1966, 4). In *The Ethics of Ambiguity* she framed it in terms of a refusal "to deny *a priori* that separate existents can at the same time be bound to each other, that their individual freedom can forge laws valid for all" (Beauvoir 1948, 18). In writing "Must We Burn Sade?," Beauvoir pitted her existential answer to the question of the relationship between the desire to express one's singularity and the demands of communal life against Sade's sexual terrorist solution. She interrogated Sade's life and literature to demonstrate the difference between the perverse subject who thinks of her- or himself as an absolute sovereign with unfettered freedom and the right to terrorize and victimize others, and the ethical subject who recognizes the difference between individuality and sovereignty, acknowledges their ambiguity, affirms her or his bond with others and accepts the limitations of freedom imposed by these bonds. Sade's ethic was authentic according to Beauvoir, because he assumed responsibility for his choices and actions. It was perverse because in assuming this responsibility he used his freedom to deprive others of theirs. The case of Sade is an important reminder that authenticity is a necessary but not sufficient condition of an existential ethic.

Had Beauvoir not already have written *The Second Sex*, her critique of Sade might have stayed focused on the ways that Sade forced us to confront the human consequences of resolving the ethical dilemma by rejecting the idea that a dilemma exists—that is, by insisting that since there are no ontological human bonds nothing can legitimately limit individual freedom. As the author of *The Second Sex*, however, Beauvoir complicates the ethical landscape. Now she frames the ethical question within the political context of oppression—specifically the oppression of women. Further, the ethical relationship is no longer confined to the ethics of mutual recognition necessary for the politics of the project; it is also envisioned in terms of the erotic body and its ethic of generosity (Bergoffen 1997). As complicated by *The Second Sex*, the ethical problem posed by Sade's affirmation of libertine freedom is unavoidably embodied. Now it concerns whether the truth of the erotic in revealing our mutual vulnerability to the passions of the flesh and each other will be experienced as a paradigmatic ethical moment or as an invitation to tyranny.

In bringing a gendered lens to Sade's life and work, Beauvoir reminds us that the ethical dilemma posed by Sade is not lived by asexual disembodied human beings. It is lived by particular men and women living gendered lives in sexist societies where men claim the privileges of freedom, and women are situated as the Other. As Beauvoir surveys the scenes of this sexist arrangement, she cites the harem as an extreme example of women's oppression. In citing this example she was thinking of Middle Eastern harems, not Sade's libertine ones. Though it is doubtful that the realities of harem life are mirrored in Sade's libertine harems, it is also doubtful that Sade was mistaken in his account of the secret of the harem world. For Sade, as for Beauvoir, the extremes of the harem are magnifications, but not distortions, of the forces at work in the sexist social order of the world at large. For both Beauvoir and Sade the harem provides an image of a world where the dream of unfettered sovereignty reigns—where the sovereign has the power and the freedom to subject others to his sexual desires and appetites. The harem is the place where the erotic ethic of response to and affirmation of the dignity of vulnerability is willfully violated. Beauvoir is acutely sensitive to the evil of this violation and this, I think, is why Sade's philosophy of the bedroom struck such a chord. In taking up the argument with Sade, Beauvoir believed that she won her case. Sade, of course, could not dispute her. He continued, however, to stalk her.

THE LOGIC OF SOVEREIGNTY

Years later, during the French Algerian war, Sade's ghost appeared in the guise of the French government. Though Beauvoir's France claimed to adhere to the principles of democracy it, like the revolutionaries of Sade's day, justified the violation of these principles and the practices of terror and torture in the name of higher political imperatives. Knowing that Sade refused to be a henchman for the Revolution, that he refused to grant the state the right to murder, terrorize, or judge, Beauvoir knew that she could not, strictly speaking, hold Sade responsible for the ways in which his imaginary scenes became blueprints for the very real politics of terror, rape, and torture. Understanding this, she also found that Sade could not be absolved of the charge of complicity; for it was not the what or how of state power (torture or murder) that Sade rejected, but the fact that a state, an illegitimate sovereign claimed the right to this power. In Sade's view, a sovereign may use power however it wishes. Cruelty, murder, and torture are legitimate expressions of individual freedom and passion because individuals may legitimately claim sovereignty. Once deployed to serve the calculated interests of a state, however, Sade finds these practices unsupportable. They violate the sovereignty of the individual by creating a "fantasmatic" sovereign—the state.

Though this logic is straightforward, it is belied by Sade's plots and life. Not all individuals in his stories or world are granted equal sovereign status. Sovereignty is neither inherent in the human condition nor a human right. A sovereign person is the one who has, by virtue of the privilege of birth or exercise of power, either convinced or terrorized others into recognizing and submitting to their sovereignty. Though Sade and his imaginary libertine sovereigns claim to be autonomous individuals, the context of Sade's claim and the settings of his libertine orgies are at odds with the claims themselves. Sade's actual exploits were enactments of the taken-for-granted privileges of his class. The arguments of his characters are delivered in communal orgy settings. Given that these contexts create the enabling conditions for Sade's and his characters' affirmation of sovereignty, I do not see how we can accept Sade's argument that only the individual qua individual can claim sovereignty.

According to Beauvoir, Sade never wished to renounce the privileges of his rank or his wife's fortune. He never rebelled against his aristocratic lineage. His position gave him the right to imagine that he could indulge his passions as he saw fit. His fortune made it possible to live his dreams. Would a working-class man imagine that he had a right to do whatever he wished to and with others? It was as a member of a privileged class that Sade claimed the privilege of his individuality. When his class, in the person of his mother-in-law, revoked his privileges, when he could no longer "revive symbolically, in the privacy of the bedroom, the status for which [he was] nostalgic: that of the lone and feudal despot" (Beauvoir 1966, 8), he re-created this illusion of power in his novels. Sade is clear about one of these illusions—the illusion of power—when he writes, "What does one want when one is engaged in the sexual act? . . . every man wants to be a tyrant when he fornicates" (Beauvoir 1966, 8). He does not detect the other—the illusion of the sovereign individual. He does not foreground the fact that his imaginary sovereigns depend on the recognition of others and on a strictly organized social order that legitimates the expression of their individuality. Both illusions, however, presume that the desire to be a tyrant is natural—that the pleasures of cruelty are universally desired—and that all attempts to suppress these desires and pleasures are unnatural. As long as we are working within the Sadean frame we cannot dissociate the demands of sovereignty from the idea of a tyrannical human nature.

There are two strains of thought in Sade's logic of sovereignty. Taken in one direction, sovereignty accrues to any individual who has the power to claim it. As a sovereign individual you cannot give the state or any other collective the right to restrict your passions. Taken in another direction, one's claim to sovereignty requires a social order that supports your claim either because you are a member of a privileged class or because you have been recognized by members of the privileged class as having earned the right to join them. Whatever direction you follow, however, in claiming the rights of sovereignty, you claim the right to oppress terrorize or destroy others according to your desire. Working with the first strain of thought, individuals control the direction of their passions. No collective authority may interfere. Working with the second strain of thought, the state or collective that supports the sovereignty claims of its members may legitimately claim the right to direct, but not repress, their expression of passion. Here the sovereignty of the individual is beholden to the sovereignty of the class, tribe, or state. Here there is nothing fantasmatic about the state's claim to the authority bestowed by sovereignty. As the guarantor of a social contract that designates one group of people as available to another, the sovereignty claimed by the collective cannot, however, be invoked to violate the original intent of the contract. It can neither criminalize acts of passion, whatever form they may take, nor stigmatize any of its expressions. If we follow this logic from the perspective of those who are recognized as sovereigns, we see that neither strain supports the repression of their desire. If we follow it from the perspective of those who are not recognized as sovereigns, however, we find that both strains support their repression and exploitation. At stake between these logics are the parameters and the direction of desire. Will the passion of the individual be manipulated to serve the revolutionary, nationalist, racist, and so on agenda of a collective—will passion be subjected to a Sadean version of sublimation—or will it be individualistic? Will the right to the libertarian pursuit of pleasure be secured by a sovereign, or will libertine life, unsecured by the authority of a collective sovereign, be pleasurable, passionate, and always at risk?

Beauvoir is aware of the tension between Sade's seemingly straightforward defense of individual freedom and the class privilege asserted in this defense. She describes Sade as "an aristocrat haunted by dreams of despotism" (Beauvoir 1966, 18) who was caught in a time when the power of his class was in decline. His aristocratic right to dominate others, at risk in the real world, could only be lived in the illusions of his imagination. Though Beauvoir notes the relationship between Sade's sense of aristocratic entitlement and his defense of his right to tyrannical domination, she does not link his inability to experience solidarity with others to his aristocratic sense of belonging to a superior class—a class that might assert class solidarity but would never acknowledge a common human bond that joined all classes. Seeing this, however, and noting that Sade's enactments of sovereign freedom are always set in communal scenes that mimic the strict class segregation of his dying aristocratic world (his libertine harems are populated by a class of servants, a class of victims, and a class of tyrants), we cannot sever his defense of individual freedom from his refusal to see all human beings as individuals. Individual freedom only belongs to those who are positioned as individuals in the social order. If you belong to a class where the possibility of being recognized as an individual is foreclosed, you only exist as an object for the sovereign's pleasure.

To see the way Sade's logic of sovereignty flourishes today, we merely need to substitute the phrase *human being* for the word *individual.* The logic that circumscribes the possibility of being an individual in Sade's world by making it a matter of class privilege or terrorist power operates today when certain peoples claim the right and use their power to expel others from the sphere of the human. Like Sade's sovereigns, who claim the right to determine how and whether their inferiors will live, our contemporary sovereigns claim genocidal rights. Any person or group not identified with the privileged ethnicity, religion, race, or nationality will be stripped of their humanity and eliminated.

Beauvoir challenges this logic of sovereignty with her logic of ambiguity. This logic recognizes the truth of the experience of sovereignty as part of a more complicated truth—the truth that the experience of individuality is a shared human experience; each of us feels the singularity of our existence. Further, she does not accept Sade's assumption that we can only express the singularity of our existence as the desire to be tyrants. Finally, she insists that the truth of individual sovereignty is only a partial truth. As sovereign subjects to and for ourselves, we are also and necessarily objects for others. In Beauvoir's words: "The privilege, which he alone possesses, of being a sovereign and unique subject amidst a universe of objects, is what he shares with all his fellow-men. In turn an object for others, he is nothing more than an individual in the collectivity on which he depends" (Beauvoir 1948, 7). Beauvoir rejects those ethical systems that deny the complex truth that constitutes "the tragic ambiguity of [our] condition" (Beauvoir 1948, 6) and argues for her alternative to these systems by asking us "to assume our fundamental ambiguity" (Beauvoir 1948, 9).

THE POLITICS OF SOVEREIGNTY

Beauvoir did not return to the question of Sade after writing the preface to *Djamila Boupacha* (Beauvoir 1962). Just as we can see how her concern with the oppression of women brought certain facets of Sade's ethical violations into focus, we can also discern how her encounter with the Boupacha case might have refocused her analysis of Sade's politics. It is not a question of imagining how Beauvoir might have rewritten the Sade essay but of seeing how the essay as written clarifies the particular challenges posed by the horrors of torture, genocidal rape, and racist nationalist politics.

Reading the Sade essay from the perspective of the questions raised by the Boupacha preface, we are still guided by the basic themes of Beauvoir's critique. What Beauvoir calls Sade's perversion is not a matter of his sexual tastes (e.g., sodomy) but of his misuse of freedom and misunderstanding of the ambiguous relationship between our existential experience of singularity and our existential condition of sociality. Read through the preface to *Boupacha*, the meaning of Sade's criminality is no longer confined to the impact of his perversion on the politics of gender oppression. Now it is a matter of the ways that the everyday perverse politics of gender become political terrorist tactics that threaten democratic principles. From this perspective, the crucial question raised by Sade concerns the politics of sovereignty. Read through the Boupacha case, Sade's challenge to our sense of decency has less to do with the ways that he unleashes the destructive powers of the erotic and more to do with the ways in which he affirms the practices of dehumanization that ground all colonialist politics and bear the more contemporary names Auschwitz, the gulag, the killing fields, ethnic cleansing, and genocide.

To get to the heart of the importance of hearing Beauvoir's Sade essay through the sounds of her *Boupacha* preface, we need to remember that the *Boupacha* case is not simply a case of torture. It is a case of a young virgin Muslim woman who was raped and tortured. The French authorities determined that raping her, destroying her sexual embodied and symbolic identity, was the surest way to destroy her. In her case they were wrong. In other cases they were not. Boupacha's case ended with the end of the Algerian War. Sade's case for a politics of rape and torture did not.

Having long found a home in secret torture rooms, Sade's logic of absolute sovereignty has migrated to very public war zones, where raping and mutilating women has now become a military tactic. Rape, long considered a spoil of war, is now used as war weapon in its own right. No longer closeted, as in the Algerian war, state-authorized rape is now staged as a public pornographic spectacle. In this it takes its cue from Sade's script. Sade understood rape and torture as a political act. As a politics, rape and torture had to be public, visible, and calculated. As an affirmation of the rights of the libertine sovereign the point of Sade's sexual terrorist spectacles was to affirm and justify what he saw as the natural laws of freedom and domination and validate the truth of pain. Though today's use of women's bodies as weapons of war follow Sade in understanding rape and torture as a political act whose effectiveness is enhanced by being publically staged, they diverge from Sade in their objectives. Those who direct contemporary spectacles of rape and torture claim that they are justified by the laws of race and ethnic purity and validated by the promise of history and the rights of national sovereignty. Sade's exhibitions were enacted for the pleasure of the libertines. Today's rape scenes are staged for the destruction of enemies.

The contest between Sade's rape politics and Beauvoir's existential politics is now being waged between the architects of military strategies who use rape as a weapon of war and international jurists who invoke human rights laws to criminalize these tactics. As Beauvoir, in taking up the Boupacha case, may be read as returning to her quarrel with Sade, I return to this quarrel by taking up the question of the ethical ground of legal, human rights based condemnations of wartime rape. My question concerns the adequacy of Beauvoir's response to Sade. It may be put as follows: Can Beauvoir's critique of Sade offer principles for addressing and redressing the pandemic use of women's bodies as war weapons?

SADE AS RORSCHACH TEST

In writing "Must We Burn Sade?" Beauvoir became part of a conversation regarding Sade that had become quite heated. Sade's last wish was that he disappear—that all traces of his tomb be erased—and that his memory vanish from the memory of man (Bataille 1985, 109). His wish was almost granted in the eighteenth and nineteenth centuries. His books were banned. When he wasn't being censored he was being ignored. During these centuries his name was absent from the lists of significant literary figures. The twentieth century changed that. The surrealists anointed him as the father of their revolutionary agenda. Georges Bataille was more cautious. Though he rejected the surrealist unconditional embrace of Sade, he accepted Sade as ally—someone who also understood the truth of the erotic as the truth of the irresistible and gratuitous desire to destroy everything that is born, lives, and strives to last (Bataille 1962, 185). Joining the surrealists and Bataille in saving him from his wished for oblivion, *Yale French Studies* devoted a special issue to his work in 1965. Reading these twentieth-century interpretations of Sade, it is difficult to avoid the idea that his writings function like a Rorschach test—they tell us more about the times in which Sade is being read and the people reading him than about Sade and his literary talent or philosophical acumen.

I do not think that is an accident. If Sade wanted to be effaced after his death, he also refused to be pinned down while he lived. He insisted that none of his characters spoke in his name. Appealing to his readers' freedom in ways that Beauvoir would appreciate, he makes his elusiveness a matter of principle. In *Aline et Valcour*, for example, rather than advocating a single philosophical position or justifying one or another of his character's claims, he offers his readers various possibilities and asks them to choose the system that best suits their temperament and inclinations (Roger 1995, 88).

Beauvoir's question, Must we burn Sade? and her ambiguous answer—no, but we save him from the flames not to endorse his principles but to confront the way that he crystallizes the problem of evil—allows us to understand Sade's Rorschach power as more than an effect of his literary style. If it is a matter of confronting the reality of the destructive drives that Sade says we harbor within ourselves, then our response to Sade will register our ability to digest the truth of the pleasure we take in cruelty and our willingness confront the particular historical and material ideologies that mask and justify this pleasure.

Anne Le Brun alerts us to Sade's Rorschach effect when instead of asking Beauvoir's question, Must we burn Sade? she asks why we still read him. Le Brun writes: "Considering, therefore, that we have seen so much, that we have memories so chocked with blood, what is so appalling about Sade? Aren't we being ridiculously squeamish, given that for the last fifty years the words 'final solution,' 'nuclear menace,' and 'extermination camp' have all carried meaning? . . . Condemned as we are to drag along this constantly renewable burden of horror, how can we still find it unbearable to read *The One Hundred and Twenty Days of Sodom*? What nerve is it that Sade touches to upset us in this manner?" (Le Brun 1990, 15–16). Responding to her own question, Le Brun accounts for Sade's continued relevance in two ways: first, in defrocking the ideologies that justify our criminality, he forces us to face our criminal desires; second, that he reveals the "unbearable infinity of freedom" (Le Brun 1990, 75). Neither Beauvoir nor Le Brun, however, are content to justify preserving Sade with reasons and arguments. Both turn to emotional and visceral justifications. In taking this turn, they suggest that the antidote to Sade's poisonous politics may be found within Sade's writings themselves.

Beauvoir concludes her Sade essay telling us that the value of Sade's testimony to our selfishness and injustice lies in its ability to disturb us (Beauvoir 1966, 63–64). Le Brun makes a more guttural claim. She finds that Sade, in forcing us to face the criminal abuse of our infinite freedom, evokes our disgust (Le Brun 1990, 67). If Sade teaches us that we cannot rationally contest the truth of passion—that reason is the servant of desire—he also teaches us to respect the truth of the body. The bodily truths of disturbance and disgust signal our rejection of Sade's politics. If we burn Sade, we risk losing the experience of revulsion that recoils at the sovereign abuse of freedom. We risk losing the truth of the body that speaks of our common humanity. There is also a warning in Beauvoir's and Le Brun's observations: The time when Sade fails to disturb and disgust us will signal the end of the sense of ourselves as bound to each other. It will be a time when the demand for justice that comes from the affirmation of this bond is silenced. When this time comes, the question Must we burn Sade? will be irrelevant. No one will be disturbed or disgusted enough to ask it. Neither will anyone object to Sade's logic of sovereignty, freedom, tyranny, and horror. No revulsion. No calls for justice. W. H. Gass, reviewing the 1968 publication of *Juliette* in the *New York Times Book Review* put it this way: "Isn't the Marquis warning us that if we will not recognize the humanity of man and respond to our human outcries, *Juliette* will be our future? It is a future close at hand" (Gass 1968, 4).

THE PROBLEM OF OUR AGE

At the end of the *Sade* essay, Beauvoir joins those who identify their era with a single driving question. For W. E. B. Du Bois it is the question of the color line (Du Bois 1999, 5); for Luce Irigaray it is the question of sexual difference (Irigaray 1993, 5); and for Beauvoir it is the problem of "the true relation between man and man" (Beauvoir 1966, 64). Sade, according to Beauvoir, understood this last problem (her problem) in all of its dimensions. He, like she, neither argued for an original human community nor for an inherent species sympathy. He, like she, begins with the fact of our basic separateness and confronts the realities of our selfishness and injustice. Unlike Beauvoir, who in complicating the idea of sovereignty refuses to allow the absence of an original ontological bond to negate the legitimacy of forged bonds that foster and respect our ambiguous freedom, Sade uses the absence of an original ontological bond to reduce the idea of "fraternity" to an illusion.

The fact that we desire each other despite the absence of an original ontological bond means that our relationship to the other remains a problem. If not "fraternity," what? Sade's answer is brief: cruelty. The illusions of the ideal of "fraternity" justify torture. As he sees it, since it is the case that we are not inherently connected to each other; and since it is the case that we desire an existential relationship with each other, then, in the absence of any a priori moral laws prohibiting violence, the fact that pain indubitably connects us to each other means that we can satisfy our desire to be bound to each other through the screams that register the cuts of the flesh.

If we look more closely, however, the problem of the relation between man and man, a problem to which Beauvoir and Sade offer radically different solutions, is the problem of our age, because our age, as prophesized by Nietzsche, is the age of the abyss created by the death of God. So long as God lived, the relation between man and man was mediated by His law. It was not a problem we were charged with solving. That is not to say that before God's death human relations were just and harmonious. Violations of God's law were plentiful. They could not, however, be justified with Sadean claims of absolute sovereignty. So long as God lived, only He could claim absolute sovereignty rights. Human beings who claimed sovereignty rights, for example, state rulers and popes, were limited by His law. After God's death, however, all restraints on human claims to sovereign power are lifted. Sade expresses the logic of atheist sovereignty with alarming clarity. Against Beauvoir's argument that the death of God leaves human beings more responsible for the ethical use of freedom than ever (Beauvoir 1948, 16), Sade sides with Dostoyevsky: If God is dead, everything is permitted.

According to Sade's logic of sovereignty, the sovereign is the one whose right to freedom is absolute. There is nothing abstract or transcendent about this freedom. It is human, immanent, and embodied. It is the right to use the bodies of others according to the sovereign's desire. Others may be designated as objects of pleasure, experimentation, or oppression. They are disposable.

Identified as the problem of sovereignty, the Sadean problem of our age lies at the nexus of embodiment, violence, and vulnerability. It incorporates Irigaray's problem of sexual difference insofar as it is lived as the problem of genocidal and wartime rape. It incorporates Du Bois's problem of the color line insofar as it is lived as the problem of ethnic cleansing and genocide. In our age, Sade's class politics of the sovereign individual has morphed into the global politics of sovereign people. In this politics a people declares itself sovereign. Where Sade's characters claimed that their sovereign freedom gave them the right to cut individuals into pieces, thereby destroying them, sovereign people claim the right to cut humanity into pieces and to wipe out one piece for the sake of the other. The idea of human rights is supplanted by the idea of sovereign rights. The particular Sadean sexual nature of this politics of sovereignty was gruesomely displayed in the Bosnian-Serb ethnic cleansing campaign in the wars in the former Yugoslavia and in the genocide in Rwanda. The enactments of these declarations of sovereignty were neither the product of a prisoner's imagination nor confined to the pages of a book.

In these war zones, more civilians than soldiers were military targets. Civilian rape moved from the sidelines to the frontlines of battle zones. It was transformed from its ancillary role in victory celebrations and soldiers' rest and relaxation into a lethal combat weapon. This may be seen as one of the consequences of entering the era of biopower; for despite their ideological differences, the framers of the genocides in the former Yugoslavia and Rwanda shared a common goal—to replace a diverse population with a homogeneous one, and thereby to destroy a world where sovereignty was contested to one where a single sovereign people could claim absolute sovereign rights. Further, these genocidal rape campaigns shared another feature—ethnic and/or racial claims to sovereignty were aligned with patriarchal masculine claims to sovereignty. Enemy men were murdered or imprisoned leaving enemy women available for the genocidal perpetrators to affirm their masculinity by exercising Sadean libertine freedom. The women are not "just" raped; they are transformed into bodies to be used, abused, ridiculed, and humiliated. They become objects of disgust to themselves and others. In Sade's world pain established the bond between the torturer and his victim. In our genocidal world the raped women's pain and shame signal the perpetrators' power to cut the bond of humanity.

In Rwanda the genocidal intent of the rapes was tied to a politics of gendered grievances. The destruction of the Tutsi had to be done in such a way as to destroy the idea that a Tutsi woman could be proud that she could decide whether or not to be sexually available. The similarity between this intent and the intent of the libertines to destroy the moral pride of Justine and her claim to be able to control her sexuality is eerily disconcerting. Like Justine and the women in the harem, the Tutsi women were gang-raped (Human Rights Watch 1996, 25). Like Justine and Sade's harem women, Tutsi women were raped in groups so that they became witnesses to each others' degradation (Human Rights Watch 1996, 29). While some men raped them, others watched and cheered (Human Rights Watch 1996, 31, 37). Like Justine, the Tutsi women became pornographic spectacles. We cannot, of course, push this analogy too far. Justine's rapes are part of a libertine project. The assaults on Tutsi women were part of a genocidal strategy. Neither, however, should we dismiss it. In both cases the women are taught the first rule of femininity: You cannot say no.

The degrading intent and effect of transforming "proud" Tutsi women into rapable bodies is graphically described by Marie. She was among a group of women kept as sex slaves by the Interahamwe. Marie and the other women in her group were forced to travel along the roads naked, covered in filth and blood, "like a group of cattle" (Human Rights Watch 1996, 35–36). For many of the rapists, displaying the women like cattle was not enough. The women had to be mutilated and their mutilated sexually available bodies had to be publically displayed. Elizabeth describes the militia storming her home. They killed her husband and two of her children and gang-raped two women before slashing them and leaving them to die with their legs spread apart (Human Rights Watch 1996, 30). Denise's story is even more chilling. She presents us with the following scene: "When he finished [raping me] he took me inside and put me on the bed. He held one of my legs open and another held the other leg. He called anyone who was outside and said, 'You come and see how Tutsikazi are on the inside.' Then he cut out the inside of my vagina. He took the flesh outside, took a small stick and put what he had on top. He stuck the stick in the ground outside the door and was shouting 'Everyone who comes here will see how Tutsikazi look'" (Human Rights Watch 1996, 43).

Like the Tutsi women in Rwanda, the Muslim women and girls in the former Yugoslavia were raped, sexually enslaved, humiliated, and degraded. Almost all of the rapes were gang rapes. Whether they occurred in the women's homes, on the road as they attempted to flee, or in detention centers, women were exhibited before their families, civilian strangers, or enemy men as sexual objects available for abuse (Human Rights Watch 2000, 11). Wherever they occurred, the rapes were organized as spectacles. They exemplified Joanna Bourke's observation that rape is a ritualized form of social performance (Bourke 2007, 6). Bourke writes: "It is never enough to merely inflict suffering: those causing injury insist that even victims give meaning to their anguish" (Bourke 2007, 6). The Muslim women who were willing to tell their stories make it clear that it is the rapists who instruct the women on the meaning of their abuse. One woman reported being dragged off a tractor by Serb paramilitary and being sexually assaulted in front of dozens of other refugees (Human Rights Watch 2000, 15–16). Another describes paramilitaries entering a room in a detention center with knives and masks. They would threaten to cut her. They beat and bit her. They raped and tortured her until she was unconscious. When she awoke her assailant was standing over her and laughing (Human Rights Watch 2000, 20). A third woman's description of her ordeal follows: She was placed in a room and forced to strip naked. Five men entered the room. The first four stood around looking at her body. As the fifth man raped her the others watched and shouted at her through a walkie-talkie under the bed (Human Rights Watch 2000, 22). Here the walkie-talkie simulated the effects of a recording studio. Beverly Allen and Catharine MacKinnon report that some massacres, rapes, and executions were videotaped (Allen 1996, 34; MacKinnon 1994, 75). In MacKinnon's words: "With this war, pornography emerges as a tool of genocide. . . . the world has never seen sex used this consciously, this cynically, this elaborately, this openly, this systematically, with this degree of technological and psychological sophistication as means of destroying a whole people" (MacKinnon 1994, 74–75). The stories multiply. Some women are held for months as a time; others for days or hours; but always, their tormentors make the point that the women are nothing more than hypervisible sexual objects to be used, abused, and ridiculed. The ways that the rapes are performed are intended to shame the women and through this shame to make them accomplices in their own and their people's degradation. As Susan Brownmiller writes: "Rape of an object doubly dehumanized *as woman, as enemy* carries its own terrible logic. In one act of aggression the collective spirit of woman and of the nation is broken, leaving a reminder long after the troops depart. And if she survives the assault, what does the victim of wartime rape become to her people? Evidence of the enemy's bestiality. Symbol of her nation's defeat. A pariah. Damaged property. A pawn in the subtle wars of international propaganda" (Brownmiller 1994, 181).

INVOKING THE SHOCKED CONSCIENCE OF HUMANITY TO CHALLENGE THE LOGIC OF SOVEREIGNTY

Living in an age of genocide, we are also living in an age where the affirmation of human rights has become a central feature of international law. Reading the United Nations Declaration we see that this affirmation is one of our century's responses to feelings of disturbance and disgust evoked by the Aryan race ideology of death camps and Final Solutions. This becomes clear if we compare the justification in the American Declaration of Independence for the idea of human rights with the justification in the United Nations Declaration of Human Rights. The Americans justified their rebellion against the misuse of sovereignty by the king of England by citing the fact that all men were endowed by their Creator with the inalienable rights of life, liberty, and pursuit of happiness. The post–World War II international community makes no such appeal. No transcendent power is called on to guarantee the truth of our shared human right to be treated as fully human. In language that Beauvoir would approve, the UN declaration holds human beings responsible for warranting the truth of our common humanity. It appeals to the shocked conscience of humanity to justify its claim that our shared humanity requires that all human beings be recognized as possessing inalienable rights.

In legitimating the immanent and emotional grounds of human rights claims, the United Nations also gave itself the power to establish criminal courts to prosecute human rights violations. It established the International Criminal Court for the former Yugoslavia and the International Criminal Court for Rwanda in response to the genocides that took place during those wars. Determining that an ad hoc approach to human rights violations was inadequate, the UN has now established a permanent International Criminal Court in The Hague. Though all of these courts invoke judicial standards of evidence and require that trials proceed in accordance with legal standards of logic and truth, their judgments also register the fact that the court, as a witness to these genocides, cannot contain its disgust. The courts, of course, cannot say this outright. They cannot speak as freely as Beauvoir, Le Brun, and Gass. They can, however, speak of humiliating and degrading treatment and use this language to express their horror.

Speaking in this way, the Rwanda court defines humiliating or degrading treatment as "Subjecting victims to treatment designed to subvert their self-regard" (Human Rights Watch 2004, 59). The offenders, in other words, know how the victim will subjectively experience their actions. How is this possible? Here the Yugoslavia court is more specific. It says that any reasonable person would know this (Human Rights Watch 2004, 154). The perpetrators, in other words, cannot claim not to know the degrading and humiliating effects of their actions. So with regard to outrages on personal dignity, we are in the presence of a cross-cultural universal idea that is not, à la Descartes, arrived at through meditation, but encountered through the emotion of humiliation and the experience of destroyed self-regard. Further, this experience of an outrage on personal dignity, as the examples of the Yugoslavia court show, are above all bodily. They are: "[I]nappropriate conditions of confinement, performing subservient acts, being forced to relieve bodily functions in their clothing, and endur[ing] the constant fear of being subjected to physical, mental, or sexual violence." (Human Rights Watch 2004, 156).

Ironically, in rejecting Sade's logic of absolute sovereignty by declaring that no human being has the right to humiliate or degrade another, but accepting Sade's argument that the infliction of pain ties us to each other when it asserts that the torturer cannot claim to be ignorant of the victim's humiliation, these courts alert us to the limits of the rationality on which the legal system depends. If the torturer could claim ignorance of the effects of his or her actions on the victim, he or she could evade responsibility for the victim's degradation. Though such a claim might be rational, the courts do not find it credible. If the courts only relied on reason, Sade's logic of sovereignty might prevail. By relying on the body to alert us to the common experience of humiliation, however, the courts allow the emotions that disturb and outrage us to carry legal weight.

The UN human rights court system is perhaps the most visible difference between our very real genocidal world, Beauvoir's Algerian War world, and Sade's imaginary libertine universe. Sade's victims suffered and died without leaving a trace. Only the libertine sovereigns had the power of speech. Whatever meaning the victims' lives had was given by the part they played in satisfying the libertine's desires. During the French-Algerian War Beauvoir had to prod, lobby. and shame the French courts into giving a victim of state-authorized torture, sexual abuse, and rape the right to hold her assailants accountable. The UN criminal court system, in conjunction with domestic courts, state legislatures, and NGO actions are changing this. Those who claim to be absolute sovereigns with the epistemic authority to speak the truth of their victims' experience are seeing their claims rejected. The objects of sovereign desire are asserting their rights as subjects to define the meaning of their lives. In the name of a shared humanity, they are insisting that their dignity be recognized and respected. Invoking the language of human rights, they are speaking Beauvoir's language of ambiguity; for if the torturers see their victims as mere objects, these victims are rendering the torturers objects of their accusations. Neither torturer nor victim can be reduced to a single dimension of existence. Each in their ambiguity is vulnerable to the power of the other. Both in their ambiguity are morally obliged to recognize each other as vulnerable rather than as sovereign subjects. Invoking the language of our shared humanity, human rights advocates insist that the dignity of each individual be recognized and protected. In seeing our individual dignity as the ground of the law of a shared humanity, those who invoke the language of human rights may be seen as addressing the problem Beauvoir identifies as the problem of our age: the problem of "the true relation between man and man." by "refus[ing] to deny *a priori* that separate existents can at the same time be bound to each other, that their individual freedom can forge laws valid for all" (Beauvoir 1948, 18).

This is not to say that Beauvoir has won her argument with Sade. Human rights laws are not established in the abstract. They respond to the facts on the ground. It is as though there is a contest between our material capacities for violence and our symbolic capacities for naming and criminalizing them. So far our material capacities seem to be winning. What is not named is not judged, but we only name after the fact, and even then we do not have a good record of protecting victims of already-named criminal aggressions. We also know, however, that naming a crime is a prerequisite for judging and convicting the criminal, and that if genocidal violence goes unnamed, its power will not be checked. There is power in the word, the question concerns our will to invoke it, and the institutional resources committed to supporting it.

The jury deciding the outcome of the contest between the power of the human rights word and the force of libertine desire is still out; but while the verdict remains unclear, so long as the Sadean justification of sovereign freedom disturbs and disgusts, us we can hope that the bonds forged by our desire for each other will be fixed by the gratification of joy rather than the torment of pain. This is not a utopian hope for the end of violence. Such a hope would ignore what Beauvoir called the tragic reality of the human condition, but rather the hope that libertine violence will be named, will continue to disturb, disgust, and outrage us and will, as far as is humanly possible, be checked.

WORKS CITED

Allen, B. 1996. *Rape Warfare: The Hidden Genocide in Bosnia Herzegovina and Croatia.* Minneapolis: University of Minnesota Press.

Bataille, G. 1962. *Eroticism: Death and Sensuality.* Trans. M. Dalwood. San Francisco: City Lights Books.

———. 1985. *Literature and Evil.* Trans. A. Hamilton. New York: Marion Boyars.

Beauvoir, S. de. 1948. *The Ethics of Ambiguity.* Trans. B. Frechtman. New York: Philosophical Library.

———. 1962. *Djamila Boupacha: The Story of the Torture of a Young Algerian Girl Which Shocked Liberal French Opinion.* Trans. P. Green. New York: Macmillan Books.

———. 1966. Must We Burn Sade? In Marquis de Sade, *The Marquis de Sade: The 120 Days of Sodom and Other Writings,* 3–64. Trans. Seaver, R. and Wainhouse, A. New York: Grove Press.

Bergoffen, D. 1997. *The Philosophy of Simone de Beauvoir: Gendered Phenomenologies, Erotic Generosities.* Albany: State University of New York Press.

Bourke, J. 2007. *Rape: A History from 1860 to the present.* London: Virago.

Brownmiller, S. 1994. Making Female Bodies the Battlefield. In *Mass Rape: The War Against Women in Bosnia-Herzegovina*, 180–182. Ed. A. Stiglmayer. Lincoln: University of Nebraska Press.
Du Bois, W. E. B. 1999. *The Souls of Black Folk*. New York: W. W. Norton.
Gass, W. H. 1968. Written with a Hose. *New York Times Sunday Book Review*, September 22.
Human Right Watch. 1996. *Shattered Lives: Sexual Violence During the Rwandan Genocide and Its Aftermath*. Washington, DC: Human Rights Watch.
———. 2000. *Kosovo: Rape as a Weapon of Ethnic Cleansing: Federal Republic of Yugoslavia*. New York: Human Rights Watch.
———. 2004. *Genocide, War Crimes, Crimes Against Humanity: Topical Digests of the Case Law of the International Criminal Tribunal for Rwanda and the International Criminal Tribunal of the Former Yugoslavia*. New York: Human Rights Watch.
Irigaray, L. 1993. *An Ethics of Sexual Difference*. Trans. C. Burke and F. Gillian. Ithaca, NY: Cornell University Press.
Le Brun, A. 1990. *Sade: A Sudden Abyss*. San Francisco: City Lights Books.
MacKinnon, C. 1994. Turning Rape into Pornography: Postmodern Genocide, 73–81. In *Mass Rape: The War Against Women in Bosnia-Herzegovina*. Ed. A. Stiglmayer. Lincoln: University of Nebraska.
Roger, P. 1995. A Political Minimalist. In *Sade and the Narrative of Transgression*, 76–99. Ed. D. B. Allison and A. S. Weiss. Cambridge, UK: Cambridge University Press.

Beauvoir and Marx

WILLIAM L. MCBRIDE

For someone like me whose early exposure to philosophy as a student occurred in the United States of the mid-twentieth century, when the heavy Cold War atmosphere so well described by Simone de Beauvoir in *The Mandarins*[1] was still quite prevalent (though somewhat modified by virtue of the real though tenuous "thaw" resulting from Nikita Khrushchev's acknowledgment of Stalinist atrocities), it is difficult to realize just how infrequently the names of Marx or even Hegel had ever been mentioned in the institutions of higher education that she attended during the late 1920s. We students of the next generation took it for granted that the existentialists, the label that had by then become irrevocably attached to Beauvoir and her associates, were part of a Continental European tradition going back to those nineteenth-century figures. True, some doubted Marx's credentials as a "real" philosopher, but, despite the obvious role that the invocation of his name played in the pronouncements of Communist parties worldwide, the study of his ideas (if only, all too often, under the rubric of "Know your enemy!"), was commonplace in American universities in the late 1950s. But that had clearly not been the case at the Sorbonne or the École Normale of Beauvoir's student days, as she herself asserted on many later occasions, and as is evidenced by near-total absence of Marx's name from the hundreds of pages of her diary from those years (a diary that contains a truly astonishing number of author names and book titles). She was, of course, already acquainted with the reality of the Communist Party and with some committed Communists, but she simply failed, at least as all evidence suggests, to connect this reality with the idea of Marx as a philosopher, or indeed as a relevant writer of whatever sort. And in reading her autobiographical writings produced over so many subsequent years, in numerous sections of which one finds philosophical discussions and analyses, one cannot help but be struck by the continued relative dearth of references to Marx, despite the enormous and well-documented importance of Communism and Communists during those same years.

However, there is a very paradoxical aspect to this, an aspect that is epitomized in one significant reference to Marxism (though, N.B., not to Marx himself) that Beauvoir makes in reviewing the varied reactions, so many of them negative and hostile, that greeted the publication of *The Second Sex*: "Our relations with the Communists couldn't have been worse; all the same, my thesis [in *The Second Sex*] owed so much to Marxism and showed it in such a favorable light that I did at least expect some impartiality from them!" (Beauvoir 1994, 190).² It should be noted immediately that, while in this sentence Beauvoir seems simply to be equating Communists with Marxists, as so many ordinary people did at the time, and as the Communists themselves preferred, she then goes on to speak of some "non-Stalinist Marxists"—whose reactions, however, were equally negative. In short, there has been little or no direct discussion of Marx's thought over many hundreds of pages of texts, and yet there is a taken-for-granted assumption that her own thought was deeply indebted to Marxism. Moreover, whenever Beauvoir does refer in passing to Marx or Marxism in her later years, particularly in interviews, I find her quick generalizations to be almost invariably on-target.

In Beauvoir's more strictly philosophically oriented writings there are, in fact, three brief but serious discussions of Marx and Marxism that I propose to consider in turn. They occur in *Pour une morale de l'ambiguïté* (I have first cited the French title because that of the English translation, *The Ethics of Ambiguity*, is so distortive of its spirit), *The Second Sex* itself, and the long essay titled "*La pensée de droite, aujourd'hui.*" Then, in conclusion, I shall discuss the historical paradox, larger and much more important than the textual one, whereby Beauvoir's thinking, even if we accept at face value (as I think we should) her assertion of a debt to Marxism, in fact contributed in a major way to rethinking fundamental Marxist premises.

ETHICS OF AMBIGUITY

It is noteworthy that Beauvoir later criticized this book for, among other things, its idealistic tendencies, but for the moment let us set this aside. In any event, she is clearly seeking, in this work, to move away from any such remaining tendencies, toward a philosophy focused on the given *situation*—an emphasis that, as she asserts, existentialism shares with Marxism, which she characterizes, interestingly enough, as one form of "radical humanism" (Beauvoir 1994, 18). She of course shares with Marxism a deep antipathy toward oppression, and she finds common cause with Marx (mentioned by name), in various passages, concerning at least two of her own book's most central ideas: that freedom from oppression must come to all human beings before it can be said that any individual is fully free; and that ethical action—despite Beauvoir's awareness that Marx hesitated to use the language of traditional morality—needs to be oriented toward a future that is projected as open and indefinite rather than as an end state. The negative side of her treatment of Marx and Marxism revolves around one point above all: Marxism's alleged denial of the reality of human freedom at the ontological level.

There is a sense in which, Beauvoir says, Marxism emphasizes subjectivity, in the tradition of Kant and Hegel. But at the same time, according to her, it puts so much stress on the determination of choices and actions by objective material conditions that Marxists are distrustful of bourgeois intellectuals who appear to be sympathetic to their ideas, because by definition they, as bourgeois, are incapable of grasping the standpoint of the proletariat from the inside. Marxists, she claims, simply deny the reality of free choice, so strongly asserted by existentialists. She goes so far as to attribute to dialectical materialism a "psychology of behavior" (Beauvoir 1994, 20). But, she goes on to say, it is counterintuitive (my word, not hers) to think that there is no element of freedom involved in the choice, for example, to become a member of the Communist Party. Moreover, Marxists, in practice, often do admit the reality of freedom that they deny in theory. Indeed, as she points out when she returns to some of these issues later in the book, Marxists have been quite aware, from early on, that it is sometimes a great struggle to develop within actual members of the proletariat the revolutionary consciousness that they theoretically should have by virtue of their class status.

Beauvoir also shows here that she has some familiarity with the ideas of Lenin, as well as, of course, much experience in interacting with her Communist contemporaries. Perhaps this goes some way toward explaining her point about Marxists' distrust of bourgeois intellectuals, because such distrust was fairly common in Communist circles at that time. Nevertheless, she would have done well to say something more here about the capital role of bourgeois intellectuals within the entire Marxist tradition, beginning with Marx himself. As Marx (and Engels) pointedly observe in a famous paragraph in *The Communist Manifesto*, in obvious self-reference:

> Finally, when the class struggle nears the decisive hour, the process of dissolution going on within the ruling class, in fact within the whole range of old society, assumes such a violent, glaring character, that a small section of the ruling class cuts itself adrift, and joins the revolutionary class. . . . a portion of the bourgeoisie goes over to the proletariat, and in particular, a portion of the bourgeois ideologists, who have raised themselves to the level of comprehending theoretically the historical movement as a whole. (Marx 1988, 64)

The wording of this text, especially of its conclusion, strongly implies that those Communists who, according to Beauvoir in *The Ethics of Ambiguity*, maintain that the bourgeois intellectual can only attain to a proletarian standpoint "from the outside, by abstract recognition" (Beauvoir 1957, 19) have not read their Marx carefully enough, have not fully understood him. (As we shall see, she was in fact well aware of this.)

But can the same be said with respect to these same Communists' denial of the reality of human freedom, even in the face of seemingly overwhelming evidence to the contrary? Ah, how many millions of words have been written and spoken on this question of determinism in Marxist theory, beginning with Marx himself! I do not intend to try to summarize them here. I shall merely note that, once again,

Beauvoir was surely on solid ground in imputing such a determinist view, of a fairly "hard" sort, to the contemporary "Marxists" with whom she was familiar; but she was on somewhat shakier ground when imputing it, if indeed she intended to do so, to Marx himself. (Throughout this text, she refers much more frequently to "Marxists" than to "Marx," and in a couple of those sentences in which she invokes Marx's name she actually contrasts him with "the Marxists," though not directly concerning the question of the reality of freedom.) I shall further note that her colleague Sartre, in the interview that he gave late in life for the Library of Living Philosophers, declared very unambiguously and in answer to several different questions that he no longer considered himself a Marxist, as he once had, and referred to "the freedom that seems to be missing in Marxist thought" (Sartre 1981, 21). Thus, his attempt to reconcile Marxism with existentialism, about which Beauvoir herself had never seemed quite so enthusiastic, eventually foundered in large measure on this reef of freedom that had been central to her critique of Marxism in *The Ethics of Ambiguity* so many years earlier.

THE SECOND SEX

The references to Marx in this book, which is of so much greater length than *The Ethics of Ambiguity*, are equally sparse, but they are strategically situated. Of course, there is the well-known short chapter near the beginning of this book titled "The Point of View of Historical Materialism," but it focuses almost exclusively on Engels's *The Origin of the Family, Private Property, and the State*—a work of considerable historical importance, no doubt, especially in the context of feminist theory, but one that is not usually regarded as very central to the Marxist canon. (Engels wrote it some years after Marx's death, though he claimed to have taken his inspiration for it from Marx's notes on Lewis Morgan's book, *Ancient Society*, which he had come across.) In that chapter, Beauvoir characterizes Engels's contribution as an advance, but nonetheless disappointing, and she subjects it to a close analysis that discloses illicit inferences and gaps in thinking, including in particular his failure to justify the close connection between the "historical defeat" of the female sex and the development of the institution of private property. She acknowledges that there are parallels between the oppression of women and class oppression, but insists that they are merely that—parallels—and that there is no exact similarity. (I shall return to this crucial point later.) She concludes this discussion by attributing to Engels (and by extension to historical materialism in general) an "economic monism" that, as a monism, falls as far short in explaining the condition of "the second sex" as does the sexual monism of Freud that had been the focus of her previous chapter (Beauvoir 1957, 60; Beauvoir 1976a, 105).

Later, in the historical section of *The Second Sex*, Beauvoir cites one long footnote from Marx's *Capital* in which, according to her, Marx recounts a conversation that he had with manufacturer, Mr. E., in which the latter "informed me that he employed females exclusively at his power looms . . . gives a decided preference to married females, especially those who have families at home dependent on them for support; they are attentive, docile, more so than unmarried females, and are compelled to use their utmost exertions to procure the necessaries of life." Then, writes Beauvoir, Marx adds: "Thus are the virtues, the peculiar virtues of the female character to be perverted to her injury—thus all that is most dutiful and tender in her nature is made a means of her bondage and suffering" (Marx 1961, 402).[3] I think it is of some importance both because it affirms that Marx was a strong sympathizer with the plight of women (and there are numerous other footnotes and texts in *Capital* with a similar theme) and because it treats his magnum opus as a serious reference work. Then, a little further on in *The Second Sex*, early in the chapter on myths, there is a long paragraph on the myth of woman as Other that ranges from the ancient Greeks to modern times; in the middle of it, Beauvoir rather casually refers to the egalitarianism of socialist ideology and says that "in the authentically democratic society proclaimed by Marx there is no place for the Other" (Beauvoir 1957, 142; Beauvoir 1976a, 241). In these few, very straightforward words, so typical of her style, Beauvoir at once identifies Marx as a principal spokesperson for the socialist ideal and, rightly in my opinion, identifies the Marxian socialist ideal as a democratic one.

But the single reference to Marx in *The Second Sex* that is probably best known is the quotation from his *1844 Manuscripts* with which, after making a concluding comment, she ends her book. In this very brief, somewhat cryptic text, Marx says that the relationship of man to woman, being the most natural of human relationships, is the best index of the extent to which what is natural has become human and human beings have become natural—human nature being regarded as an ideal. Beauvoir remarks that it could not have been said better, and she concludes that, in order for the triumph of the reign of freedom to occur, it will be necessary "that by and through their natural differentiation men and women unequivocally affirm their brotherhood" (Beauvoir 1957, 732; Beauvoir 1976b, 663). Let us not be diverted by the word *fraternité* here: the French language has no gender-neutral word for this (neither does the English language, for that matter), and of course this word in French immediately recalls the great slogan of the French Revolution. What interests me more, at any rate, is Beauvoir's allusion to the reign, or realm, of freedom, because that is an expression used by Marx in both his early and later works as the shorthand expression for what he conceived (here following Hegel, but with a strong awareness of the severe inadequacy of Hegel's understanding of it) as the highest aspiration of humanity. (In Marx's later work the standard formulation became "the ascent from the realm of necessity to the realm of freedom.") At the end of *The Second Sex*, then, it seems clear that Beauvoir, having just cited Marx concerning the relationship between men and women, is consciously appropriating this phrase of his for her own liberatory purposes; in other words, she makes evident just how much, as she affirmed in the passage in her autobiography that I cited earlier, her thesis in this work owed to Marxism.

LA PENSÉE DE DROITE, AUJOURD'HUI

This long, interesting study, originally published in *Les Temps Modernes* in 1954, focuses on some figures who at the time would have been, and in some cases still are, well known to Anglophone readers—for example, Spengler, Nietzsche, Toynbee, Jaspers—and others with, now as then, less "name recognition" outside France, such as Drieu La Rochelle, Monnerot, and Maulnier. What may surprise some readers is the extent to which Beauvoir attributes an influence on some of the latter group to the conservative, virulently anti-Communist American political scientist, still remembered by some for his works in defense of Machiavelli and on the Cold War and the "managerial revolution," James Burnham. The world of right-wing thought into which this essay plunges us bears some uncanny resemblances to the contemporary version of the same world, but in at least one way it seems remote: while Beauvoir very well depicts right-wing ambivalences about "intellectuals" and about thinking itself, it is primarily with intellectuals that she is dealing; whereas there are very few of those, at least of any comparable quality, in the ranks of today's Right. In this regard, Beauvoir asserts early in her essay that, "on the Right, the word 'intellectual' easily takes on a pejorative meaning" (Beauvoir 1955, 102).[4] It is true, she continues, that among the proletariat there is also a suspicion of intellectuals, but only because they are bourgeois; however, she points out, Marx himself affirmed the capacity of some bourgeois intellectuals to rise to the level of comprehending the historical movement as a whole, and she quotes the final line of the passage from the *Communist Manifesto* that I cited. She thus corrects the more negative characterization of Marxism's stance toward intellectuals with which she had left her readers in *The Ethics of Ambiguity*.

Most of Beauvoir's references to Marx and Marxism in "*La pensée de droite, aujourd'hui*" occur in the early pages of the essay. That is precisely because she takes Marxism as her principal point of departure, since it is also the current point of departure for most if not all of the writers whom she analyzes here. For them, she asserts, prior to the Second World War there was a sense of impending doom, of a mortal menace to Western civilization, but they were somewhat uncertain as to its exact nature; "now," however, "barbarism has a name: communism" (Beauvoir 1955, 98). It is the Marxist-Communist menace that preoccupies them and occasions such great fear and loathing on their parts. However, while a few right-wing writers claim to be experts in Marxist doctrine, that is not the case for the vast majority of them; it is, she cites Thierry Maulnier as admitting, "most certainly virtually unknown to those who are fighting against it or think they are doing so" (Beauvoir 1955, 113).[5] But this does not prevent them, of course, from offering psychological explanations of both Marx and Marxism, the most popular of these being that it is actually a (false) religion. To Monnerot, for example, Communism "is the Islam of the 20th Century" (Beauvoir 1955, 115).

One aspect of Marxist theory with which they *are* familiar is its claim that there is such a thing as class struggle, and that is a claim that, in one way or another, they all try to deny. What they all assert, on the other hand—at least all of those whom Beauvoir is analyzing—is *pluralism*, that is, the alleged fact that the world is so very complicated that there are different kinds of slaveries, different kinds of feudalisms, and different kinds of capitalisms, as Jules Monnerot, among others, maintains. This position serves their ideological interests very well, concludes Beauvoir: "For Marx's 'simplistic' schema which contrasts exploiters and exploited they substitute a pattern so complex that, with the oppressors differing as much among themselves as they differ from the oppressed, this latter distinction loses its importance" (Beauvoir 1955, 140–141).

While it would be a very interesting exercise to consider at length Beauvoir's in-depth portrait of right-wing thought as it appeared to her in 1954, the present chapter is obviously not the place in which to undertake this task. Here, I would like only to reflect on two points: first, very briefly, the relevance of this analysis to our time, nearly sixty years later; second, the additional light that it may cast on Beauvoir's relation to Marx and Marxism. Concerning the first point, ironies and similarities abound. Very much in keeping with Beauvoir's observation that the Right relies much too heavily on analogies, we can find quite a few contemporary right-wing politicians in both the United States and Europe who, with the retreat of Communism, play heavily on a theme that is the reverse of Monnerot's, to wit, that Islam is the Communism of the twenty-first century. Today, one finds similar warnings to the effect that Western civilization is under severe threat, similar denials that there is any such thing as class struggle, a similar effort on the part of many on the Right to conjoin religion with capitalism,[6] and a similar anti-intellectualism and distrust of thinking itself. The greatest single difference between the Right of the mid-century as depicted by Beauvoir and the Right of today is, as it seems to me and to repeat an earlier remark, the far greater prevalence today of this last-mentioned characteristic.

As for what "*La pensée de droite, aujourd'hui*" may tell us about the evolution of Beauvoir's relationship to Marx and Marxism, I think that it should be seen, at a minimum, as reinforcing what she was to say years later, in her autobiography, concerning her deep indebtedness to him and it, even in *The Second Sex*, the publication of which antedated this essay by five years. But in "*La pensée de droite . . .*" her reliance on Marx as a basic reference point is much more unreserved, much less ambiguous than it could possibly have been in a book that included a chapter highly critical of his closest collaborator and indeed, at least as it was presented, of "the point of view of historical materialism" as such. Near the beginning of this later essay, Beauvoir writes approvingly and without any apparent reservation concerning Marx's "denunciation" of idealism (Beauvoir 1955, 98), and she takes a text of his, in which he observes that every new class proposes its ideas as the only universally true and valid ones (Beauvoir 1955, 101), as a sort of guide to the unraveling of bourgeois ideological justification that she is about to undertake. In short, Beauvoir does not engage in the somewhat theatrical, if not downright sophistic, intellectual acrobatics wherewith Sartre attempted to demonstrate, in the opening pages of an essay first published three years later, that Marxism was the one and only dominant thought system of that era[7] (and, hence, she also did not feel obliged later, as Sartre did, to recant any such extravagant proclamations). Rather, Beauvoir here simply takes that worldview, with its commitment to ideological critique and so many of its other fundamental premises such as the reality of class struggle, as a given.

AND YET...

On the basis of what I have shown up to now, it would seem that Beauvoir would have to be regarded, at least by 1954, as closer to Marx than to any of the other philosophers considered in the present volume, even though she had less to say about him explicitly than about many of the others. Why, then—to paraphrase a key sentence of Sartre's that occurs shortly after his above-mentioned declaration of obeisance to Marxism in *Search for a Method*—is she not simply a Marxist?[8]

The principal, though far from the only, answer to this question is to be found, of course, in *The Second Sex*—not just in certain of its texts, important as they may be, but even more in its global effects on the history of thought—effects so profound that a good case could be made for her being the philosopher who exerted the greatest influence on the culture of the twentieth century—greater, perhaps, than Sartre, Heidegger, or Wittgenstein, to mention three of the most prominent alternative candidates.[9] What Beauvoir demonstrated throughout that long work, after the initial three chapters detailing the inadequacies of biological, Freudian, and Engelsian historical materialist accounts of gender difference, was precisely that such "monistic" theories must be modified and partially replaced by an existentialist-phenomenological approach, rooted in past and present lived experience, and leading to a freely chosen reorientation of future societies in the direction of equality. Despite her well-known protestations to the effect that she was not a "philosopher," meaning a system-builder in the tradition of Hegel or Sartre, what she gave the world in *The Second Sex* was a new comprehensive worldview, involving, as she put it in concluding her first chapter on biology, "an ontological, economic, social, and psychological context" (Beauvoir 1957, 36; Beauvoir 1976a, 77), and at the same time avoiding the sort of confused, ideologically driven "pluralism" that she attributed to right-wing thought in her essay on that topic. And, as I have noted, she very cleverly established a link between this quite revolutionary contribution to thought and the core element of Marx's philosophy, its liberatory message, by citing him at the very end of her book.

But of course what emerged from *The Second Sex* and the vast intellectual movement that it ultimately generated was in fact no longer the Marxism of Marx, for whom "The history of all hitherto existing society is the history of class struggles" (Marx 1988, 55).[10] Now, it is clear that Marx never intended to claim—and it would have been supremely fatuous to have done so—that in order to understand history one needs *only* to look at it through the lens of class struggle. His own historical writings show subtlety and sophistication even while retaining an orientation in which classes and subclasses play a leading role. But the net effect of Beauvoir's analyses is, to a degree that I suspect that she herself was not fully aware at the time (or perhaps ever), to reject that claim as being in some important sense false; she does this by showing that there is at least one other major key to understanding history—the very key that Marx, in the once-obscure passage in the *1844 Manuscripts*, which were not even published until decades after his death, identified as "the relation of man to woman." The many varieties of Marxist feminism, socialist feminism, or both that were spawned in the latter part of the twentieth century took their inspiration from Beauvoir's seminal work, as did other approaches to feminism for which Marx no longer held any importance.[11] Thus, the "destiny" of Beauvoir's "Marxist" contribution was, as one might put it in a paraphrase of Engels's single most famous line in *The Origin of the Family . . .* , in which he referred to "the great historical defeat of the female sex," the great historical defeat of the Marxian worldview, at least as the overwhelmingly dominant worldview that Sartre had considered it to be in *Search for a Method*.

"Destiny": that is the general title that Beauvoir assigned to the first three chapters of *The Second Sex*, in which she discusses, respectively, biology, Freudian psychoanalysis, and Engels's work. She explains her reason for choosing this word at the end of her introduction. After enumerating the several key questions concerning the limitations on women's freedom and the possibilities of surmounting them that will be the driving themes of her work, she says that these issues would be meaningless "*si nous supposions que pèse sur la femme un destin physiologique, psychologique ou économique*" (Beauvoir 1976a, 32).[12] The old Parshley English translation, "if we were to believe that women's destiny is inevitably determined by physiological, psychological, or economic forces" (Beauvoir 1957, xxix) retains the essential sense of what Beauvoir wrote but subtly alters it by implying that "women's destiny," although not inevitably shaped by these "forces," is nevertheless somehow a reality of sorts; whereas what Beauvoir's French implies is that the very notion of any such "destiny" is a myth, an illusion. If we take this idea literally and apply it to chapter 3, "The Point of View of Historical Materialism," then it is not only Engels's faulty account of women's history as understood through the lens of class struggle that Beauvoir is challenging, but indeed the whole underlying presupposition (to which Marx himself also appeared to subscribe all too often, even though it was not necessary for him to do so, and there are texts in which he explicitly denies it), that there is an underlying pattern, a *fatum*, which the human race is doomed to follow. This challenge certainly ran counter to the triumphalist Marxism of her contemporaries in the French Communist Party, which helps to explain their very negative reaction to *The Second Sex* when it was published. Their so-called orthodox version of Marxism had in fact descended, as it were, from the realm of freedom to that of necessity and dogma. Probably some of them even sensed, at a time at which the Party was still very strong, the future decline that was betokened by such a radically alternative reading of history and society as Beauvoir's was to theirs.

Did Beauvoir's "challenge," as I have put it, run counter to the spirit of Marx himself, to the point of being ultimately non-Marxist? Well, yes and no. For, as paradoxical as it may be to say this, it is true both that Beauvoir's thought is deeply Marxist in inspiration (or at least "*marxisant*," as the apt French expression would have it), and yet that it amounted to a revolutionary, world-historically original, break with the entire Marxian tradition.

NOTES

1. *Les Mandarins* was written between 1951 and 1954 and published in the latter year. For some reflections on this work that connect with the theme of the present essay, see McBride 2005.
2. Two studies of Beauvoir that are especially worthwhile for understanding the background of this statement are by Deutscher 2008 and Lundgren-Gothlin 1996. Eva Lundgren-Gothlin's is a voice that was silenced far too soon.
3. I am citing directly from the English version of *Capital*, whereas Beauvoir presumably cited from a French translation. However, the translation as she reports it is quite faithful to the English, the one somewhat noteworthy difference being that, instead of the words "the virtues, the peculiar virtues of the female character," the French reads "*les qualités propres de la femme.*"
4. This and all subsequent translations from this essay are my own.
5. Beauvoir does not annotate this citation.
6. In this context, Beauvoir offers us a marvelous citation from an eighteenth-century priest, Hyacinthe de Gasquet: "Jesus Christ himself is the guarantor of your debt [*est votre caution*]; it is still between his divine hands and on his adorable head that you invest [*placez*] capital" (Beauvoir 1955, 122).
7. See Sartre 1963.
8. "Why, then, are we not simply Marxists?" (Sartre 1963, 35). In fact, the French text reads "*Qu'est-ce donc qui fait que nous ne soyons pas tout simplement marxiste?*" (Sartre 1985, 40). Note that he writes "*marxiste*" in the singular, which implies that he is using the word as an adjective rather than, as the English translation would have it, as a noun. This may seem to be a pedantic point, but I am not sure that it is. While Sartre, during this period, often came closer than Beauvoir ever did to identifying himself as *a* Marxist "*tout simplement*," Beauvoir's perspective in "La pensée de droite, aujourd'hui" could very well, as I think I have shown, be characterized as a "Marxist" perspective—especially if one were to read this essay in isolation from the rest of her work.
9. I make similar comments concerning Beauvoir's preeminent importance in McBride 2006.
10. In later editions, published after Marx's death, Engels already qualified this claim, in a footnote, by restricting the assertion to all *written* history, in light of the more recent findings of anthropologists and especially of Morgan. In

this same footnote, he also called attention, significantly enough, to his *The Origin of the Family.*
11. As Alison M. Jaggar, herself not a close student of Beauvoir's at the time, wrote in her long, definitive (at least for American feminist philosophy of the period) work: "Indeed, *The Second Sex*, published in 1949 by the existentialist Simone de Beauvoir, must be considered a forerunner of the contemporary women's liberation movement" (*Feminist Politics and Human Nature* [Totowa, NJ: Rowman & Allenheld, 1983], p. 10). Or, as another prominent feminist philosopher, Sandra Bartky, writes in recalling her intellectual evolution out of classical phenomenology: "I turned instead to an examination of the embodied consciousness of a feminine subject, indeed, of a subject with a specific social and historical location. Simone de Beauvoir had pointed me down this path" (*Femininity and Domination: Studies in the Phenomenology of Oppression* [New York and London: Routledge], 1990). Such testimonials in the relevant philosophical literature are legion.
12. Literally, "if we were to suppose that a physiological, psychological, or economic destiny weighs on woman."

WORKS CITED

Beauvoir, Simone de. 1955. La pensée de droite, aujourd'hui, 99–200. In *Privilèges*. Paris: Gallimard.
———. 1957. *The Second Sex*. Tran. H. M. Parshley. New York: Alfred A. Knopf.
———. 1964. *Force of Circumstance*. Trans. R. Howard. New York: G. P. Putnam's Sons.
———. 1976a. *Le deuxième sexe* I. Paris: Gallimard.
———. 1976b. *Le deuxième sexe* II. Paris: Gallimard.
———. 1994. *The Ethics of Ambiguity*. Trans. B. Frechtman. New York: Citadel Press.
Deutscher, Penelope. 2008. *The Philosophy of Simone de Beauvoir: Ambiguity, Conversion, Resistance*. Cambridge, UK: Cambridge University Press.
Lundgren-Gothlin, Eva. 1996. *Sex and Existence: Simone de Beauvoir's 'The Second Sex.'* Trans. L. Schenck. London: Athlone Press.
Marx, Karl. 1961. *Capital*, vol. I. Moscow: Foreign Languages Publishing House.
———. 1988. *The Communist Manifesto*. Ed. F. L. Bender. New York: W. W. Norton & Co.
McBride, William. 2005. The Conflict of Ideologies in *The Mandarins*: Communism and Democracy, Then and Now. In *The Contradictions of Freedom: Philosophical Essays on Simone de Beauvoir's* The Mandarins, 33-45. Edited by S. Scholz and S. Mussett. Albany: State University of New York Press.
———. 2006. Sartre e Beauvoir all'asse del ventesimo secolo. Trans. P. Invitto from the original French ("Sartre et Beauvoir à l'axe du vingtième siècle"). In

La fenomenologia e l'oltre-fenomenologia: Prendendo spunto dal pensiero francese, 91–101. Ed. G. Invitto. Milan: Mimesis Edizioni.

Sartre, Jean-Paul. 1963. *Search for a Method*. Trans. Hazel Barnes. New York: Alfred A. Knopf.

———. 1981. Interview with Jean-Paul Sartre. In *The Philosophy of Jean-Paul Sartre*, 5–51. Ed. P. Schilpp. La Salle: Open Court.

Sartre, Jean-Paul. 1985. Sartre, *Critique de la raison dialectique, précédé de Questions de méthode*, Tome I. Paris: Gallimard.

Saving Time

Temporality, Recurrence, and Transcendence in Beauvoir's Nietzschean Cycles

ELAINE P. MILLER

> This inequality will be particularly noticeable because the time they spend together—and that fallaciously seems to be the same time—does not have the same value for both partners. . . . For a man . . . time is a positive asset. For the . . . woman time is a burden she aspires to get rid of . . .
>
> —Simone de Beauvoir, *The Second Sex*

In *The Second Sex* Simone de Beauvoir primarily uses Friedrich Nietzsche as a source of quotations that convey, like stinging arrows, exactly what is wrong with the feminine condition. Although she writes in her autobiography that she read Nietzsche with enthusiasm as a student, and she quotes very different, and more positive passages from his work in her journals, nevertheless in her critique of the historical role accorded to the second sex, she mostly relegates him to the role of spokesperson for—or at least indicator of—the very views of women that she seeks to expose and problematize. Nevertheless, I will argue in this essay that Nietzsche's understanding of the will, and in particular of the temporal transformation that can take place through the willing of the eternal return, holds an important place in Beauvoir's conception of how the relegation of woman to pure immanence (a fixed natural and cultural position reducible to pure "facticity") might be overcome and transformed.

In *The Ethics of Ambiguity*, Beauvoir criticizes Nietzsche's thought more for being solipsistic than for being sexist, but her earlier writings also manifest a positive appropriation of Nietzschean ideas, in particular that of self-actualization through a transformation of one's relation to time. By looking at Beauvoir's philosophical writings predating *The Second Sex*, we can gain a clearer understanding of the Nietzschean nature of temporality and will in her understanding of the self-affirmation that must accompany authentic existence, which can then be specifically applied to women's historical situation. I will illustrate how Beauvoir's analysis of domestic labor elaborates on and extends a Hegelian-Marxist critique of estrangement, calling for a transformation in economic, political, and social conditions for women. At the same time, complementing these changes, Beauvoir borrows from Nietzsche the idea of a reattunement of the will as the means by which the mode of circular repetitive temporality—a tiresome existential temporality relegated primarily to women, according to Beauvoir's critique—might be overcome.

In what follows I will first outline what I take to be Beauvoir's critique of housework along Hegelian and Marxist lines, further characterizing this activity in temporal terms. I will then consider the remarks Beauvoir makes on time and temporality in her early writings, in order to situate the discussion in terms of concrete examples of the temporal dimensions of existence. I will specifically focus on Beauvoir's articulation of authentic temporality, a conception of which I will argue she inherits from Nietzsche, by looking at *Pyrrhus and Cineas* (Beauvoir 2005) and *The Ethics of Ambiguity* (Beauvoir 1948). I will conclude by revisiting the critique of housework from the perspective of the temporality outlined in these works and explain how authentic temporality transforms the circular temporality of work that merely repeats the cycle of life-labor (domestic labor) into a temporality of eternally renewed willing in a manner that recalls Nietzsche's description of the transformation of "it was" into "thus I willed it" in *Thus Spoke Zarathustra* (Nietzsche 1978).

However, I will emphasize that for Beauvoir, Nietzsche's critique needed to be supplemented by a specific account of women's time, in order to shift the focus from resentment to oppression. I will use Kristeva's account of "women's time" to articulate the distinction between the circularity of biological or thinglike repetition (what Beauvoir calls "immanence") and the temporality of free transcendence (also Beauvoir's term), the cyclical nature of which I argue is a Nietzschean-influenced theme in Beauvoir's work.[1] Although Beauvoir's discussion of "willing oneself free" is not initially a specifically feminist theme (*The Ethics of Ambiguity* presents it as a human imperative), it has special implications for Beauvoir's critique of domestic labor in its repetition, renewal, and transformation of the cyclicality of what has historically been deemed women's work.

DOMESTIC ESTRANGED LABOR

As has already been argued,[2] Beauvoir's reading of Hegel was influenced by Alexandre Kojève's *Introduction to the Reading of Hegel*, which freely mixed concepts taken from Marx and from Existentialism into its interpretation of Hegel. From Hegel's *Phenomenology of Spirit*, the most salient figure that Beauvoir discusses and utilizes is the master-slave dialectic, which Hegel leads into with a discussion of what might be described as human life in the state of nature, a state that will be transformed through the struggle between master and slave. Hegel refers to the processes that constitute (mere) biological life as "the pure movement of axial rotation" (*die reine achsendrehende Bewegung*), a "universal flux," and a "whole *round* of activity"

(*Kreislauf*; my emphasis; Hegel 1977, 104–110). Life in the form of humans as an animal species "points to something other than itself," namely to consciousness, which in its individual form metamorphoses into self-consciousness through the process of facing and reacting to another consciousness that also presents itself as independent. Both sides are characterized by a desire that orients itself toward something outside itself, and both self-constitute through their mutual attempts to overcome the Other. Self-consciousness thus arises through a conflict, otherwise known as a fight for recognition. However, as one self-consciousness bends to the other in order to save itself (it must stake its life in order to prove its nonattachment to mere life), it is forced to work for the master consciousness, and it is this work that eventually brings about an unexpected conversion; the slave consciousness emerges as the truth of self-consciousness, for through its work it rids itself of its attachment to natural existence by transforming nature into something humanly wrought (Hegel 1977, 117), a process that the master consciousness fails to accomplish.

Kojève singles out the importance of work in this process, emphasizing a Marxist interpretation of labor as the primary essential activity by which humans transform their natural environment into an intersubjective world. Furthermore, Kojève interprets labor as temporalization, as the transformation of the change of the natural world into the development or progress of history. In "A Note on Time, Eternity, and the Concept," Kojève identifies the Hegelian Concept with time, and time with human existence: "if Work temporalizes Space the existence of Work in the World is the existence in this world of Time. Now, if Man is the Concept, and if the Concept is Work, Man and the Concept are also Time" (Kojève 1980, 145). The identification of human existence with time or temporalizing plays an important, if implicit, role in Beauvoir's existential analysis, which I will turn to in the next section.[3]

Kojève brings together Hegel's brief, yet important, discussion of work in the master-slave dialectic, with Marx's more extensive and influential discussion of estranged labor. Marx's word "estrangement" (*Entfremdung*) is used as a privative modification of *externalization* (*Entäusserung*), Hegel's (and Marx's) word for the human being's necessary positing of itself in otherness. Normally, this otherness is eventually superseded in an enrichment of self or self-actualization that overcomes the dichotomy between subjectivity and objectivity. Estrangement, by contrast, occurs when human existence becomes reified in something outside of itself in which it cannot recognize itself, cementing the subject-object divide and preventing a return to self. I will argue that Beauvoir sees both housework and the menial labor that some of the working class is relegated to as forms of estranged labor.[4]

Marx defines estranged labor as labor into which the worker puts his life but that nonetheless does not belong to him: "Whatever the product of his labor is, he is not. The greater this product is, the less he himself is" (Marx 1988, 72). Estranged labor is external to the worker, that is, it does not belong to the worker's essential being. This labor does not affirm, but rather denies the worker's self, and makes her unhappy or apathetic rather than content or energized; it "does not develop [the worker's] mind and body freely but mortifies and ruins them" (Marx 1988, 73). The laborer therefore feels her*self* only outside of her work and in her work feels outside of herself. She is "at home" only when she is not working, and when she is working she is not "at home." Her labor is therefore "forced" (Marx 1988, 73). "As soon as no outside compulsion exists to engage in it, it is shunned like the plague. It is not her own, but someone else's; in it she belongs to another; it is thus a loss of self" (Marx 1988, 73; all gendered pronouns altered).

Another type of estranged labor that we might add, though Marx does not discuss it, is labor that has *no* product and *no* end. Hegel and Marx both insist that the human being has a need to both posit and recognize itself in an other. Externalization is a necessary constituent of both individual actualization and actualization at the level of the species. Other animal species, as Marx notes explicitly and Hegel implicitly, "produce" only for their immediate, bodily needs (see Marx 1988, 77; Hegel 1977, 108). Humans, by contrast, produce even when free of physical need, and moreover "freely confront their product" (Marx 1988, 77). For Marx, estrangement occurs when the product worked on belongs to someone else, to the owner of the given means of production, so that the worker cannot reflect himself in it and make it a part of his broader individual and species being. However, a job like housework, of which Beauvoir provides a brilliant phenomenological analysis, does not exactly fit this schema, for it has no product and no end. Like the worker on the assembly line, the woman who cleans a house engages in a repetitive cycle of tasks that provide no self-fulfillment, no self-othering followed by a return to self in the form of recognition. But her estranged labor, unlike his, has more in common with the mere "axial rotation" of life than with an interrupted spiritual process.

BEAUVOIR'S ANALYSIS OF HOUSEWORK

Beauvoir famously likens housework to "the torture of Sisyphus" in its endless repetition of the same, and to a Manichean labor that seeks to "abolish" a perceived "evil," in this case dirt and decay, "not by positive action," but through a negation of the endless piles of dust, dirt, and, lint that accumulate day after day and threaten to overwhelm without constant vigilance. Work may define human existence,

> But the wife is not called upon to build a better world: the house, the bedroom, the dirty laundry, the wooden floors, are fixed things: she can do no more than rout out indefinitely the foul causes that creep in; she attacks the dust, stains, mud and filth; she fights sin, she fights with Satan. But it is a sad destiny to have to repel an enemy without respite instead of being turned toward positive aims. (Beauvoir 2009, 476)

Here Beauvoir clearly refers to the Kojèvian idea of work as the world-building essential activity of the human species.[5] Woman, traditionally, has not been called on to contribute to that world-building; furthermore, her labor is "fixed" rather than subject to temporalization. This is why (or because—the logic is circular)[6] she still remains aligned with Nature, with a natural realm unmarked by recognition, untransformed by work, and not measured by time:

> With the invention of the tool, maintenance of life became activity and project for man, while motherhood left woman riveted to her body like the animal. It is because humanity puts itself into question in its being—that is, values reasons for living over life—that man has set himself as master over woman; man's project is not to repeat himself in time: it is to reign over the instant and to forge the future. Male activity, creating values, has constituted existence itself as a value; it has prevailed over the indistinct forces of life; and it has subjugated Nature and Woman. (Beauvoir 2009, 75)

Beauvoir points out that through her identification with maternity woman becomes, at least in the traditional male definition of her, bound to her body and thus to a natural, repetitive, animal life. Housework reflects this role: "Eat, sleep, clean . . . the years no longer reach toward the sky, they spread out identical and gray as a horizontal tablecloth; every day looks like the previous one; the present is eternal, useless and hopeless" (Beauvoir 2009, 475). Natural "time" is horizontal rather than vertical, immanent rather than transcendent, eternal in the sense of lacking any true temporality. Woman's work within the home "does not grant her autonomy. . . . it does not open onto the future, it does not produce anything" (Beauvoir 2009, 484). Most heavily, "the very meaning of her existence is not in her hands" (Beauvoir 2009, 484). This echoes Marx's analysis of the assembly-line worker, whose life "is not his own, but someone else's . . . it does not belong to him . . . in it he belongs . . . to another . . . it is a loss of his self (Marx 1988, 73).

Like Marx, Beauvoir links consciousness to the production of a human-created world out of the natural. Marx writes that animals' existence is immediately identical with their life-activity, and this immediacy has both an ontological and a temporal significance, consisting of the endless chain of unconscious actions undertaken in order to preserve life. Humans make their life-activity an object for their will and consciousness, creating out of their consciousness a durable world parallel to and constructed out of nature (Marx 1988, 76). Beauvoir notes the paradoxical behavior of the housewife who bakes a perfect cake and sighs, "It's a shame to eat it!" or who waxes the hardwood floors and then does not want her husband and children to tramp over them with their muddy feet, calling this phenomenon the "temptation" of woman "to consider her work as an end in itself," as something lasting that reflects her subjectivity, even as she recognizes this impossibility.

> But time cannot be stopped; supplies attract rats, worms start their work; Covers, curtains, and clothes are eaten by moths: the world is not a dream

carved in stone; it is made of a suspicious-looking substance threatened by decomposition. (Beauvoir 2009, 483)

The housewife who attaches herself to such fleeting things is bound to be disappointed, for "it is impossible to obtain permanence and security through them" (Beauvoir 2009, 483). The products of domestic work are designed and destined for consumption, and while, as Hegel points out, human desire, with consumption as its natural outcome, is the first step toward self-consciousness, it is only through work as "desire held in check," fleetingness or immediacy "staved off" that the truth of self-consciousness emerges (Hegel 1977, 118).

It is primarily through marriage that woman enters into the role of caretaker of the house, a transformation that is as radical as it is unforeseen in romantic dreams of domestic harmony prior to marriage. In *The Second Sex* Beauvoir cites Nietzsche's critique of marriage from the perspective of the young girl entering into it:

> And then to be hurled as if by a gruesome lightning bolt into reality and knowledge, with marriage—and precisely by the man they love and esteem the most: to catch love and shame in a contradiction and to have to experience all at once delight, surrender, duty, pity, terror at the unexpected proximity of god and beast, and who knows what else! There one has tied a psychic knot that may have no equal. (Nietzsche 2001, section 71)

Here, "the unexpected proximity of god and beast" refers to the sexual act and the inexperienced woman's relation to her husband, as, from her perspective, what was entered into as a spiritual undertaking reveals itself to be nothing more than an animal act. In citing this critique of marriage, we see that Beauvoir recognized (and assumed that readers would do likewise) the complexity of Nietzsche's views on women, even if other quotations, taken out of context, might mark him as a misogynist. Beauvoir's early journals from her days as a philosophy student show that she appreciated the multilayered signification of Nietzsche's philosophy, including his views on women, and she never simply sets Nietzsche up as a foil for feminist theory. In the next section I will attempt to show, moreover, that Beauvoir found in Nietzsche a resource for articulating what might be called a feminist existentialist temporality that specifically engages with and attempts to transform the concept of woman as a merely natural being. First, however, I will briefly remind the reader of Nietzsche's doctrine of willing the eternal recurrence, in particular of what he sees to be at stake in this idea.

TEMPORALITY AND ETERNAL RECURRENCE

The philosophical and narrative climax of Nietzsche's *Thus Spoke Zarathustra* is the section "On the Vision and the Riddle," which narrates a dreamlike encounter Zarathustra has with a dwarflike creature he calls the "spirit of gravity," who sits on his back and mutters discouraging words in his ear as he climbs a steep rocky mountain path, thus weighing him down both mentally and physically. As Zarathustra finally stops to confront the dwarf, he notices a gateway at which two paths meet and stretch off eternally in opposite directions; these are past and future, and the gateway is the moment or instant (*Augenblick*), a term that, as we saw in the quote above—"Man's design is not to repeat himself in time: it is to take control of the instant and mould the future"—also holds a significance for Beauvoir's articulation of transcendence.

Zarathustra asks the dwarf whether he believes that these two paths contradict one another eternally, and the dwarf replies contemptuously that "all truth is crooked," and "time itself is a circle" (Nietzsche 1978, 158). To this Zarathustra responds in anger, admonishing the dwarf not to make things too easy for himself. Yet Nietzsche, himself, through Zarathustra, goes on to articulate a vision of time that is also circular. So in what way is the dwarf's version of time "too easy," and how will Zarathustra's version complicate it? I think that the contrast between the inauthentic, overly "easy" circular temporality of the dwarf and the willed cycle of eternal recurrence mirrors the contrast in temporality that Beauvoir implicitly articulates in criticizing the unfulfilling nature of the eternally renewed cyclical drudgery of housework and the general task of "maintaining and caring for life in its pure and identical generality" (Beauvoir 2009, 443), while nonetheless advocating the repetition of an eternally willed circular temporality as a requisite of an authentically lived existence.

Beauvoir describes the temporality of women's lives as confined to the domestic sphere, as we have already seen, as "endless repetition," as years spreading out ahead "gray and identical," but also as the "denial of life," as nothing more than the negative aspect of time, that is, the halt of decay, as opposed to time's usual dual function of creation and destruction (Beauvoir 2009, 475). The home is a "kind of counter-universe" (Bachelard, cited in Beauvoir 2009, 471), where reality is concentrated within the domestic space and the external world becomes unreal. As Hegel describes it, the realm of merely life-perpetuating activity is "the simple essence of Time which, in this equality with itself, has the stable shape of Space," a "simple universal medium" or "universal flux" in which the different moments cannot be superseded "if they do not have an enduring existence" (Hegel 1977, 106). Julia Kristeva writes in "Women's Time" that "the evocation of women's name and fate privileges the *space* that *generates* the human species more than it does *time*, destiny, or history" (Kristeva 1995, 204). Kristeva adds that female temporality has traditionally been associated with an eternal repetition that "preserves a solid temporality that is faultless and impenetrable, one that has so little to do with linear time that the very term 'temporality' seems inappropriate" (Kristeva 1995, 205).[7] Beauvoir describes the wife as the one who "ensures the even rhythm of the days and the permanence of the home she guards with locked doors"; such an existence "is given no direct grasp on the future" (Beauvoir 2009, 443). If feminine temporality is interpreted in this way (as following the biological cycle of reproduction and the perpetuation of the identity and permanence of immanence), we can see a parallel to the "too easy" circular time of Zarathustra's nemesis, the spirit of gravity, to a "time" that is not even temporal in the usual sense of the word.

Zarathustra speaks explicitly of a temporal vision of redemption that I will argue is also manifest in Beauvoir's articulation of the authentic existential project. In "On Redemption," Zarathustra describes the one who will create a salubrious and cohesive future out of the "fragments, riddles and dreadful accidents" of the past as one who can "redeem those who lived in the past and . . . recreate all 'it was' into a 'thus I willed it'" (Nietzsche 1978, 139). To live predominantly in the past is, according to Nietzsche, to remain determined by and resentful of the accidents that gave rise to your existence: for example, being born at a certain time or place, or having what one deems to be particular congenital disadvantages of a multiplicity of varieties. The "cripples" and "beggars" (*Krüppel und Bettler*) whom Zarathustra meets on a "great bridge" in this section are crippled or impoverished spiritually, however, rather than literally. They cannot overcome whatever it is that they deem to be holding them back from success or happiness in existence, and so they demand either to be reimbursed for their suffering or cured of their ills. Both of these remedies are exclusively past-oriented, according to Nietzsche. Instead of transforming the "handicap" into a strength, persons who are excessively oriented toward their past want to go back and reverse it; they want "revenge" on their past, something that is in any case impossible. Whatever they do to seek to remedy a past wrong itself becomes part of the past, so that what results is another specious cycling of time, this time in the form of the pathological repetition compulsion.[8] What is more, however, "When one takes away the hump from the hunchback one takes away his spirit" (Nietzsche 1978, 137).

This means that it is only in having the strength to transform every "it was" (past) into a "thus I willed it" (future) that humans are capable of overcoming existential resentment and the futile effort to will backward in order to change the past. This is what is known as the eternal recurrence, or sometimes the eternal recurrence of the same. The *willing* of the recurrence of what is, that is, the transformation of what has passively occurred *to* one into something that one actively takes responsibility for, transforms what appears to be a mere circular repetition into a revolution or return that transforms, in an intellectual and spiritual sense.[9]

EXISTENTIAL TEMPORAL PROJECTION IN *PYRRHUS AND CINEAS* AND *THE ETHICS OF AMBIGUITY*

In her earliest philosophical work, *Pyrrhus and Cineas*, Beauvoir frames an account of human existence through the story reported in Plutarch's *Lives* of an interchange between Pyrrhus, the Greek general of the fourth century B.C.E., and Cineas, one of his ambassadors and advisers. The discussion concerns Pyrrhus's unwillingness to stop after several successful battles in which he has vanquished various states, and his desire to go on to conquer more and more territory indefinitely. As Pyrrhus announces each plan to vanquish Africa, India, and Asia Minor, in turn, Cineas asks, "And after that?" At one seemingly arbitrary point Pyrrhus states that after that he will rest and enjoy life, whereupon Cineas asks, then, "why not rest right away?" The point Beauvoir makes of this story is that, while Cineas appears reasonable and Pyrrhus rash, nonetheless each of us lives in a day-to-day manner just as Pyrrhus did, although of course our chosen projects are rarely as grandiose or as violent. Life is a series of finite plans that, once accomplished, are immediately replaced by a new set of projections, as one limit is placed and then surpassed (*dépassé*): "In spite of everything, my heart beats, my hand reaches out, new projects are born and push me forward" (Beauvoir 2005, 91). This succession of projects, one end immediately turning into a new departure, may seem meaningless, a Sisyphean repetition: "Isn't Pyrrhus absurd to leave in order to return home? Isn't the tennis player absurd to hit a ball in order for someone to send it back to him and the skier absurd to climb a slope in order to immediately come back down?" (Beauvoir 2005, 99). But each of us is condemned to repeat this fundamental, futile choice: "Time continues to flow by, the instants push me forward. So I am wise, and what will I do now? I live, even if I judge that life is absurd, like Achilles always catching up with the tortoise despite Zeno" (Beauvoir 2005, 100). The cyclical temporality of this substitution of one mundane plan for another resembles that of housework, even if each segment of it is not as identical in nature to the others. They share a circularity that is Sisyphean, in that, as tasks, they never seem to come to a point where one can simply rest.

What is revealed in the anxiety that arises as a result of this recognition of the concomitant futility and necessity of free choice is neither death nor paralysis in this earlier account, but rather what Beauvoir refers to as Kierkegaardian or Nietzschean irony (Beauvoir 2005, 114). By Nietzschean irony she clearly refers to the cycle of events of this life that must be affirmed rather than denied, that can be transformed only through an affirmative willing ("thus I willed it"), not a resentful denial in the hope of achieving revenge or a better life elsewhere ("it was"). Beauvoir writes that "in this game of relationships there is no other absolute than the totality of these very relationships, emerging in the void, without support" (Beauvoir 2005, 114–115). It is in the acceptance and indeed embrace of the "heaviest thought" that the existential choices of life are never finished once and for all, but recur indefinitely, that one is able to face rather than flee from existence. In *The Ethics of Ambiguity*, Beauvoir gives the example of the Dutch painter Vincent van Gogh, who, when he recognized the extent of his own illness, faced a future in which he would no longer be able to paint. His was, she writes, no "sterile resignation":

> The past will be integrated and freedom will be confirmed in a renunciation of this kind. It will be lived in both heartbreak and joy. In heartbreak, because the project is then robbed of its particularity—it sacrifices its flesh and blood. But in joy, since at the moment one releases his hold, he again finds his hands free and ready to stretch out toward a new future. But this

act of passing beyond is conceivable only if what the content has in view is not to bar up the future, but, on the contrary, to plan new possibilities. (Beauvoir 1948, 29–30)

Beauvoir's reference to Kierkegaardian irony ties this discussion to the Danish philosopher's concept of repetition, a theme that she affirmed goes to the heart of what she tried to accomplish in her novel *The Mandarins*. In discussing writing this novel in her autobiography, *Force of Circumstance*, Beauvoir explains that repetition in this sense presupposes the loss and rediscovery of a goal, an intentional act of returning to a point of departure or decision that one had earlier abandoned, this time with the decisive assumption of the difficulties and failures that one knows will inevitably go along with it, since they are the same difficulties that directly led to its being left behind in the first place (Beauvoir 1965, 282). This active avowal of both the suffering and the value behind every act accords exactly with Nietzsche's conception of willing the eternal recurrence. Transcendence, for Beauvoir, involves surpassing one's given facticity, including the handicaps, in and with which one finds oneself, by integrating them within a free project that does not simply leave behind or deny the past.

In "The Age of Discretion," Beauvoir constructs a narrative around an aging female academic who, within a short period of time, begins to lose confidence in her writing, her passion for her husband, her aging body, and her success in raising her son to be the kind of man she wanted him to be. The character recounts that "I was frightened by the wasteland through which I was going to have to drag myself until death came for me" (Beauvoir 1969, 70). The story is an extended meditation on what happens when even the best and most fulfilling of women's lives (she has had a successful career, love, a family, intellectual satisfaction) comes face to face with the inexorable repetition of time. The character's redemption comes, at the end, not in some event that changes the pattern of her life from a cycle of repetition to a linear pathway of achievement and overcoming of anxiety, but rather in a reorientation within the character of her relationship to temporality and repetition, a reorientation that takes place in the story momentarily, through a reevaluation of her relationship to her son and husband, and through the intervention of language, in this case a literary reference to the medieval French chante-fable *Aucassin et Nicolette*, a story of love and resourcefulness in times of spiritual trial:

> *Little star that I see, Drawn by the moon.* The old words, just as they were first written, were there on my lips. They were a link joining me to the past centuries, when the stars shone exactly as they do today. And this rebirth and this permanence gave me a feeling of eternity. The world seemed to me as fresh and new as it had been in the first ages, and this moment sufficed to itself. I was there, and I was looking at the tiled roofs at our feet, bathed in the moonlight, looking at them for no reason, looking at them for the pleasure of seeing them. There was a piercing charm in this lack

of involvement. "That's the great thing about writing," I said. "Pictures lose their shape; their colors fade. But words you carry away with you." (Beauvoir 1969, 82)

The temporality that the story recounts is that of a cycle of rebirth, and it reorients the narrator away from her preoccupation with life as a pathway along which she would definitively achieve a series of goals (publication of her work, accolades from critics, her son choosing the right partner and espousing the political views of herself and her husband). Yet this interpretation may seem to conflict with Beauvoir's contention in *The Second Sex* that "by transcending Life through Existence, man guarantees the repetition of Life: by this surpassing, he creates values that deny any value to pure repetition" (Beauvoir 2009, 74), a passage that seems to advocate leaving repetition behind. In *Pyrrhus and Cineas* Beauvoir writes that "Man seeks to grasp his being again but he can always transcend anew the object in which his transcendence is engaged" (Beauvoir 2005, 115). The initial disagreement between Pyrrhus and Cineas that begins the essay concerns exactly the question of whether one can ever lay repetition aside and simply rest, a question that is eventually answered in the negative. This conclusion implies that there is more than one kind of repetition; the second kind of repetition, the repetition of the "and after that?" of existential projects, is indeed a form of repetition, but one that is essentially different than the "pure" or mere repetition of natural life, domestic work, and procreation. This authentically existential repetition is a form of overcoming that must be eternally renewed through affirmatively willing, in the way Nietzsche speaks of eternally putting one's will into what has already happened and will eternally recur.

Beauvoir seems to contrast this affirmative self-generated willing of what recurs to a lifetime of dependence on others for affirmation and for meaning. In *Pyrrhus and Cineas* she considers lives devoted to care for another, such as that of a slave, of someone who nurses an invalid, or of a mother caring for a child. Such existences are especially risky, Beauvoir suggests, because they falsely infer a seamless unity of existential time. The mother may be disappointed even when her son follows her wishes and makes of his life what she wanted, for she did not want what was good for the young man so much as "what was good for the little boy insofar as he would still exist in the young man." Time, Beauvoir writes here, "is not progress but division. . . . There is no instant in a life where all instants are reconciled" (Beauvoir 2005, 120).

Still further, just as one can never act "for one entire man," since his life does not remain the same throughout his life, "one cannot act for humanity as whole."[11] One therefore devotes oneself "amid risk and doubt" (Beauvoir 1948, 120). Indeed, Beauvoir sees one of the biggest pitfalls of old age, particularly for women, as coming to the realization that one has lived one's whole life devoted to another who now (especially in the case of a child one has raised) no longer needs one, thus depriving the person of what formerly gave her life significance. In addition, the "whole of humanity" may be understood in a sense parallel to that of the "entirety of time." If time is not progress but division, then perhaps humanity is never a whole but only, as Beauvoir puts it in the later work, "detotalized totalities," separate but interrelated (Beauvoir 1948, 122). The concomitant conception of time and in particular of human history would be one that denies the false either/or of adhering either to a continuous, rational view of history or to an historical unintelligibility. Beauvoir describes society and history as making "a multiplicity of coherent ensembles stand out against the unique background of the world" (Beauvoir 1948, 122).

OVERCOMING SUBHUMANITY

Beauvoir clearly distances herself from her interpretation of one aspect of Nietzsche's philosophy, namely, what she takes to be his solipsistic version of existentialism that privileges bare will to power (Beauvoir 1948, 72). Nevertheless, in *The Ethics of Ambiguity* she draws heavily on Nietzsche's analysis of the sub-man and the serious man from *Thus Spoke Zarathustra*, both of whom, in different ways, could be understood to be "crippled" in Zarathustra's sense of the word. The sub-men, Beauvoir writes, "have eyes and ears, but from their childhood on they make themselves blind and deaf, without love and without desire" (Beauvoir 1948, 42). This recalls Zarathustra's depiction of the last men (*letzte Menschen*) who ask, "What is love? What is creation? What is longing? What is a star?" and blink in the response to these profound questions that requires the least possible effort (Nietzsche 1978, 17). The sub-man exists as a brute fact, whose acts are never positive choices, whom one can accuse of "not willing himself" (Beauvoir 1948, 43). Beauvoir echoes Nietzsche in describing the danger of such people, who believe that "whoever feels differently" should "go voluntarily into a madhouse" (Nietzsche 1978, 18); she writes that "in lynching, in pogroms, in all the great bloody movements organized by the fanaticism of seriousness and passion . . . those who do the actual dirty work are recruited from among the sub-men" (Beauvoir 1948, 44).

Beauvoir calls an existential ethics a "triumph of freedom over facticity," a formulation that recalls the transformation of "it was" (the "brute facts" that characterize ones existence) into "thus I willed it," a free choice (Beauvoir 1948, 44). Indeed, Beauvoir distinguishes explicitly between freedom as a given quality of human being, and freedom as willed. She acknowledges the bewilderment that might greet the phrase "will oneself free" in the minds of those who assume we are always already free, yet insists that it is only through "making itself be" through willing that a genuine freedom can be established and actualized (Beauvoir 1948, 25). This kind of active willing can only be developed over time and indeed assumes a unity of time, an eclipse of the fiction of the pure instant (Beauvoir 1948, 26).

This freedom is frightening for the sub-man, for he has but an indistinct awareness of the world's dangers (war, sickness, racism, sexism, political problems), and he wants to efface his own part in any responsibility for these perils by thinking of his own existence as a mere flash or instant in contrast to the totality of historical time. Thus "the attitude of the sub-man passes logically over into that of the serious man" (Beauvoir 1948, 45) who chooses to submerge his freedom into a ready-made content given to him by an external authority such as society, organized religion, or a political cause. For Nietzsche the serious man epitomizes resentment, or raging impotently backward against time, negating life by affirming only its refutation. For Beauvoir, he is the one who negates his own freedom by handing it over to an authority who will tell him how to believe and act. Furthermore, "as soon as the Idol is no longer concerned, the serious man slips into the attitude of the sub-man" (Beauvoir 1948, 50). Finally, Beauvoir notes the same link between seriousness and nihilism argued by Nietzsche (Beauvoir 1948, 56, 100).[12]

So the authentic "existential" attitude must avoid the extremes of indifference, on the one hand, and fanaticism in service of an external cause, on the other. Humans are free, Beauvoir writes, but it is not enough that they formally recognize this freedom. They must, as we have seen, "will themselves free," a process that takes time and renewed effort: "It is in time that the goal is pursued and that freedom confirms itself. And this assumes that it is realized as a unity in the unfolding of time" (Beauvoir 1948, 26), a conscious assumption of responsibility for one's past, present, and future actions in the unity of one's existential project. This unity is only achieved through an eternally recurring willing of one's action:

> I must ceaselessly return to it and justify it in the unity of the project in which I am engaged. Setting up the movement of my transcendence requires that I never let it uselessly fall back upon itself, that I prolong it indefinitely. Thus I can not [sic] genuinely desire an end today without desiring it through my whole existence, insofar as it is the future of this present moment and insofar as it is the surpassed past of days to come. To will is to engage myself to persevere in my will. This does not mean that I ought not aim at any limited end. I may desire absolutely and forever a revelation of a moment. This means that the value of this provisional end will be confirmed indefinitely. But this living confirmation can not be merely contemplative and verbal. It is carried out in an act. The goal toward which I surpass myself must appear to me as a point of departure toward a new act of surpassing. Thus, a creative freedom develops happily without ever congealing into unjustified facticity." (Beauvoir 1948, 27–28)

Echoing Pyrrhus's resolution, she writes that "the goal toward which I surpass myself must appear to me as a point of departure toward a new act of surpassing." This new act of surpassing is a "creative freedom" that resists "congealing" into "unjustified facticity" (Beauvoir 1948, 27–28). The world is only disclosed to humans through the very resistance it opposes to humans' efforts, and the will is only defined by raising obstacles (Beauvoir 1948, 28). As Nietzsche writes in *Twilight of the Idols*, "what does not kill me makes me stronger" (Nietzsche 2003). And if the project results in failure, we must use our freedom to pursue its own movement "in the face of failure," so that it can "by giving itself a particular content, aim by means of it at an end which is nothing else but precisely the free movement of existence" (Beauvoir 1948, 29).

TRANSCENDENCE AS SELF-OVERCOMING: IMPLICATIONS FOR *THE SECOND SEX*

While Beauvoir uses the language of "man" and "mankind" in her early philosophical writings, it is clear from the context that she intends to refer to the entirety of humankind. However, and equally clearly, her research into the specificities of women's existence in *The Second Sex* led her to a consideration of the activity of domestic labor that sounds very similar to her castigation of the life of the sub-man in *The Ethics of Ambiguity*. The difference lies, of course, in the fact that sub-men choose their form of existence, whereas women have it relegated to them. Beauvoir writes, "It is easy to see why she is ruled by routine; time has no dimension of novelty for her, it is not a creative spring; because she is doomed to repetition, she does not see in the future anything but a duplication of the past" (Beauvoir 2009, 640).

In *The Ethics of Ambiguity*, Beauvoir calls the oppressed of all kinds "those who are condemned to mark time hopelessly," those whose lives are nothing more than "a pure repetition of mechanical gestures" (Beauvoir 1948, 83). In her comprehensive study of Beauvoir on repetition, Penelope Deutscher concludes that "Beauvoir's many strengths did not include a determination to locate difference within repetition" (Deutscher 2008, 108). Noting the complexity of her discourse on repetition, Deutscher nonetheless contrasts Beauvoir's notion of repetition and its concomitant sameness with the transformation or dislocation in repetition found in the work of Butler, Derrida, and Deleuze. I would agree that Beauvoir's existentially authentic notion of repetition does not anticipate the philosophy of these later thinkers, but to the extent that she is, like they, influenced by Nietzsche's understanding of the eternal recurrence, one can find at least a nascent conception of difference in repetition in her work.[12] It is a theme that is perhaps more explicitly articulated in the work of Beauvoir's contemporary, Albert Camus, who also was more vocally a follower of Nietzsche, but this adds to the notion that difference in repetition is not solely a late-twentieth-century theme.[13] I would argue that Beauvoir's notion of conversion, which Deutscher also carefully follows throughout her works, can be understood to be part of the same intellectual trajectory.

The Second Sex primarily provides a historical and phenomenological catalog of woman's many-faceted historical relegation to the realm of immanence, to a bodily thinglike identity within the realm of mere life, including procreation and labor in the domestic sphere. Not until the very end of the book does the question of the repetition of transcendence get addressed. I would like very briefly to address this theme in Beauvoir, and then to return to the issue of domestic labor. The question remains whether an activity like housework—which is both repetitive in the sense of the "axial rotation" of mere life, and traditionally accorded largely to women—can ever be redeemed in the Nietzschean sense of transforming an "it was" into a "thus I willed it."

Beauvoir writes in *The Second Sex* that the patriarchal tradition that calls for women to stay and work at home defines her solely as sentiment, interiority, and immanence; however, "in fact, every existent is simultaneously immanence and transcendence; when [s]he is offered no goal, or is prevented from reaching any goal, or denied the victory of it, [her] transcendence falls uselessly into the past" (Beauvoir 2009, 267). When this happens, woman becomes interiority and immanence, but "this is in no way a vocation, any more than slavery is the slave's vocation" (Beauvoir 2009, 267). The word *vocation*, derives from the Latin *vocatio*, or calling, and further from *vocare* or voice. Nietzsche uses the German *Beruf* to indicate the same idea of a spiritual calling to which one devotes one's life, and Hegel and Kojève would likely accord to work this same significance. Woman has *no* vocation when she is forced to engage ceaselessly in the nonproductive and never-ending cycle of domestic work.

Art, literature, and philosophy, activities that are on the opposite end of the work continuum, by contrast, are "attempts to found the world *anew* on a human freedom" (Beauvoir 2009, 748; my emphasis). Every individual concerned with "justifying" her existence—a process that involves taking one's givenness or one's facticity, and willing it in such a way that one "makes it right" or "deals justly with it"—will "experience [her] existence as an indefinite need to transcend *herself*" (Beauvoir 2009, 16–17). This is a refounding of the world, a founding anew, a nonidentical repetition.

What does it meant to transcend, not the world, not one's projects, but oneself? We can perhaps gain a clearer sense of this project by again looking back to Nietzsche, this time to the trope of self-overcoming that is so prominent in *Thus Spoke Zarathustra*. Here, Life, personified as a feminine character, speaks to Zarathustra with the words "I am that which must always overcome itself" (Nietzsche 1978, 115). Indeed, Nietzsche equates self-overcoming with the temporal version of redemption discussed above. Beauvoir also sees (mere) life, or immanence, as that which must overcome itself, and argues that, just as for Nietzsche, this process is never achieved once and for all, but must "always" surpass itself "anew." This is the meaning Beauvoir indicates when she writes that "every subject . . . accomplishes its freedom only by *perpetual* surpassing toward other freedoms" (Beauvoir 2009, 16). The truth of the highest human achievement "demands that man surpass *himself* at each instant" (Beauvoir 2009, 160). This is a repetition with difference, the self-overcoming that is manifest in the renewed willing of one's vocation, of one's life as a project, as a work, as a transcendence that never allows itself to fall back into a fulfilled opacity or thinglike being, but always renews its willing in an endless cycle of self-transformation. Contrary to the surpassing of a temporal, present state in favor of a static, metaphysical ideal, self-overcoming, or transcendence, in Beauvoir's terminology, is a self-surpassing that takes place firmly within this existence, and one that will always give rise to further self-overcomings.

Beauvoir's answer to the question of whether housework can ever be a part of this renewed self-willing both rejects the complete relegation of *any* subject's existence to the sphere of immanence and recognizes the necessity of tasks that maintain the realm of life that we all participate in. Such tasks can in themselves not be "redeemed" in the Nietzschean sense, if the person who performs them is wholly doomed to the realm of mere life. However, "If the individual who executes them is himself a producer or creator, they are integrated into his existence as naturally as bodily functions; this is why everyday chores seem less dismal when performed by men; they represent for them only a negative and contingent moment they hurry to escape" (Beauvoir 2009, 481). Such work "becomes meaningful and dignified only if it is integrated into existences that go beyond themselves, toward the society in production or action" (Beauvoir 2009, 484).

It will benefit both men and women, Beauvoir argues, if marriage as a "career" is prohibited (Beauvoir 2009, 523). For woman, this prohibition will allow her to take the meaning of her existence into her own hands, through her work that goes beyond the mere care for life. Man, in turn, will be freed from the dependence of women that weighs so heavily on him: "He will free himself by freeing her, that is, by giving her something to *do* in this world" (Beauvoir 2009, 523). Until women's freedom becomes concrete and fulfilled, "it cannot authentically assume itself except in revolt" (Beauvoir 2009, 664). Only when women are freed from the constraint of marriage, motherhood, and domestic labor as an exclusive and forced "vocation" can they have a chance "to build anything" (Beauvoir 2009, 664). This means that both women and men must take on their share of the necessary labor of maintaining and caring for life and immanence, incorporating it into their existence alongside their meaning-giving work, without thereby being overtaken by it, just as they do with their own inescapable natural bodily functions (Beauvoir 2009, 481).

CONCLUSION

I would argue that throughout *The Ethics of Ambiguity*, conversion understood temporally, as a transformation of temporality and history and human undertaking in general, operates explicitly and repeatedly with a Hegelian assumption of the necessity of meaningful self-externalization through work, but in opposition to a Hegelian conception of ethics and of history.[14] The recuperation and transformation of repetition into the willing of eternal recurrence plays an essential role in resisting the appropriation of contingency and overcoming of all absurdity carried out by a Hegelian rational schema that eventually prevails over all apparent contradiction and ends in a unified and absolute oneness. Beauvoir's chosen word to characterize ethics, "ambiguity," from "ambi-" or "both," evokes an irreducible and paradoxical twoness that is closer to Nietzsche.

In her discussion of the festival near the end of *The Ethics of Ambiguity*, the idea of resisting the Hegelian "ethics of saving," as Beauvoir calls it, comes to the fore most explicitly. In the section "Between Past and Future," Beauvoir discusses the temporality of authentic human existence in terms of Bataille's account of the festival (which in turn is based on Nietzsche's description of the Dionysian celebration), as a celebration of pure expenditure without expectation or even desire for reimbursement or profit (Beauvoir 1948, 126). Beauvoir suggests that the Hegelian approach—which she characterizes in terms of the economic metaphorics of investment and return—when applied to human existence miscarries in its blindness to the inevitable ambiguity and even tragic failure inherent in every true human endeavor, even when viewed from the perspective of the whole trajectory of history:

> What we maintain is that one must not expect that this goal be justified as a point of departure of a new future; insofar as we no longer have a hold on the time which will flow beyond its coming, we must not expect anything of that time for which we have worked; other men will have to live its joys and sorrows. As for us, the goal must be considered as an end; we have to justify it on the basis of our freedom which has projected it, by the ensemble of the movement which ends in its fulfillment. The tasks we have set up for ourselves and which, through exceeding the limits of our lives, are ours, must find their meaning in themselves and not in a mythical Historical end. (Beauvoir 1948, 128)

Beauvoir's Nietzschean cycles of repeatedly and eternally willing oneself free thus work against both the passivity of the spectator and the optimism of the belief in inevitable progress. Beauvoir immediately notes the limitations of pure expenditure. The "pure affirmation of the subjective present" that the festival represents is overly abstract, according to Beauvoir, and eventually and inevitably results in fatigue and emptiness. It is art's role to "fix this passionate assertion of existence in a more durable way," to turn the festival into theater, dance, and poetry (Beauvoir 1948, 127), a theme that pervades Nietzsche's *The Birth of Tragedy*. As in that work, the recognition of death and the finitude of human existence in all its aspects is an essential part of this fixing: "Existence must not deny this death which it carries in its heart; it must assert itself as an absolute in its very finiteness; man fulfills himself within the transitory or not at all. He must regard his undertakings as finite and will them absolutely" (Beauvoir 1948, 127).

To "will absolutely" does not mean to "will for all humanity," or "for all men," as Sartre puts it.[15] Beauvoir does of course insist on the fact that every human action necessarily and essentially touches the existence of others; "the individual is defined only by his relationship to the world and to other individuals. . . . his freedom can be achieved only through the freedom of others" (Beauvoir 1948, 156). However, the absoluteness of willing comes from the intensification of the repeated and temporally unified willing of one's own existential life project rather than from an abstract principle of ethical universalization. This willing, which must constantly be renewed, is a matter of "taking the given, which, at the start, is there without any reason, *as something willed by man* (Beauvoir 1948, 156; my emphasis). Taking what is given, and making it into something willed humanly, absolutely, and eternally, is the very meaning of transforming "it was" (facticity) into "thus I willed it" (transcendence).

NOTES

1. To illustrate the distinction between transcendence and immanence, Beauvoir writes, "Every subject posits itself as a transcendence concretely, through projects; it accomplishes its freedom only by perpetual surpassing toward other freedoms; there is no other justification for present existence than its expansion toward an indefinitely open future. Every time transcendence lapses into immanence, there is degradation of existence into 'in-itself,' of freedom into facticity; this fall is a moral fault if the subject consents to it; if this fall is inflicted on the subject, it takes the form of frustration and oppression; in both cases it is an absolute evil" (Beauvoir 2009, 16).
2. See, for example, Lundgren-Gothlin 1998.
3. For the purposes of this paper, it is not important that Kojève misreads Hegel's Concept (*Begriff*) as equivalent to the human being here.
4. Penelope Deutscher discusses the parallels between Marx and Beauvoir's humanistic analyses of the estrangement of women and workers in terms of the physical and affective condition brought about by factory work and housework, but she also argues that Beauvoir does not think that women can be estranged in the Marxist sense from domestic labor (Deutscher 2008, 116f).
5. The nonproductive nature of "women's work," in addition to the fact that she does not risk her life, also explains why, despite Beauvoir's analogy of the relationship between men and women to that of the master and slave in Hegel, woman nonetheless does not historically emerge as the truth of that conflict, that is, as fully actualized self-consciousness (Beauvoir 2009, 74). For more on this topic, see also Miller 2000.
6. In other words, woman is aligned with nature because her labor, that of bearing and caring for children and tending the household, is fixed, like the determinate cycles of nature; however, it is precisely because of this perceived alignment with nature that she is given this fixed labor in the first place.
7. Kristeva's analysis is only partly relevant here in that she complicates the discussion of traditionally "feminine" temporality in that she is also and even predominantly considering the experience of maternity. Of course, the temporality of the reproductive cycle and maternity also has some elements in common with that of housework, such as, obviously, its repetitiveness and cyclical nature, but maternity cannot be considered estranged labor in the same way as housework because it does have an end and "product," one in which, however potentially problematically, the woman can reflect herself and actualize herself.

8. For the full discussion of this phenomenon, see Freud 1961, 43–51.
9. I am using *recurrence* (Nietzsche's *Wiederkehr*) analogously to the way in which Kristeva articulates *revolt*, which, given the etymology of both, seems entirely appropriate (both the German *kehren* and the Latin *volvere* mean "to turn": See, for example, Kristeva 1996: "the Latin verb *revolvere* engenders intellectual meanings: 'to consult or reread' (Horace) and 'to tell' (Virgil)" (3). *Recurrence* can also be used to signify "coming up again for consideration." The "working through" or verbal reliving of an experience, in an analytic situation, can be a form of nonidentical repetition, in which a repressed memory—perhaps of a traumatic event—which has been repeating itself through neurotic symptoms, is remembered and repeated in a way that is fundamentally modified by interpretation, ideally resulting in a capacity to be freed from the cause of the debilitating repetition. We can see here the proximity and yet absolute distinction between the two types of cyclical movement that is analogous to the relationship between the two types of cyclical temporality for Beauvoir and Nietzsche. As Kristeva puts it with reference to the shifting temporality of feminist inquiry, the focus of a new generation of feminists "will combine the sexual with the symbolic in order to discover first the specificity of the feminine, and then the specificity of each woman" (Kristeva 1995, 210). For a convincing argument as to why Beauvoir should be included within this new generation of feminists, see Zakin 2000.
10. In the introduction to *The Second Sex*, Beauvoir reiterates this claim: "Every subject posits itself as a transcendence concretely, through projects; it accomplishes its freedom only by perpetual surpassing toward other freedoms; there is no other justification for present existence than its expansion toward an indefinitely open future" (Beauvoir 2009, 16).
11. This claim changes somewhat in *The Second Sex*. Here Beauvoir writes that "individuals who appear exceptional to us, the ones we honor with the name of genius, are those who tried to work out the fate of all humanity in their particular lives. No woman has thought herself authorized to do that" (Beauvoir 2009, 749–750).
12. See, for example, Nietzsche 1978, "On Those Who Are Sublime," and "On the Spirit of Gravity." Nietzsche's claim is that seriousness is linked to negation of the value of this life, while for Beauvoir it is linked to a dishonest or self-deceptive negation of anything that is not the object of the particular serious endeavor.
12. See, for example, Deleuze 1983: "Why is mechanism such a bad interpretation of the eternal return? Because it . . . entails the false consequence of a final state . . . [which] is held to be identical with the initial state, so that one concludes that the mechanical process would once again run through the same set of differences. The cyclical hypothesis is incapable of accounting for either the diversity of coexisting cycles or the existence of diversity within the cycle. We

can only understand the eternal return as the expression of a principle that serves to explain diversity and the reproduction of diversity, or difference and its repetition (49, translation revised).
13. See in particular Camus's *The Plague* (Camus 1991), in which multiple forms of mundane repetition—the rounds of a doctor fighting against the seeming inevitable destructiveness of the epidemic, a writer who spends his life attempting to construct and constantly revising a single perfect sentence that is to open his novel, a man emerging into the sunlight and spitting on homeless cats—are the symbols of resistance to the plague, which is both physical and spiritual in significance. Camus's theoretical work *L'Homme Révolté* articulates art as a nongrandiose repetition of conscious creativity to counter the absurd. The title's implicit referral to repetition can be gleaned from the etymological linkage of "revolt" to "return" discussed above in note 15.
14. Most explicitly Beauvoir writes, "In Hegelian terms it might be said that we have here a negation of the negation by which the positive is re-established. Man makes himself a lack, but he can deny the lack as lack and affirm himself as a positive existence. He then assumes the failure. And the condemned action, insofar as it is an effort to be, finds its validity insofar as it is a manifestation of existence. However, rather than being a Hegelian act of surpassing, it is a matter of a conversion. For in Hegel the surpassed terms are preserved only as abstract moments, whereas we consider that existence still remains a negativity in the positive affirmation of itself. And it does not appear, in its turn, as the term of a further synthesis. The failure is not surpassed, but assumed. . . . To attain his truth, man must not attempt to dispel the ambiguity of his being but, on the contrary, accept the task of realizing it" (Beauvoir 1948, 13).
15. See Sartre 2000, especially pp. 17–18.

WORKS CITED

Beauvoir, Simone de. 1948. *The Ethics of Ambiguity*. Trans. Bernard Frechtman. New York: Philosophical Library.

———. 1965. *Force of Circumstance*. Trans. Richard Howard. New York: Putnam.

———. 1969. The Age of Discretion. In *The Woman Destroyed*, 11–85. Trans. Patrick O'Brian. New York: Pantheon Books.

———. 2005. Pyrrhus and Cineas. In *Simone de Beauvoir: Philosophical Writings*. Ed. Margaret Simons. Urbana: University of Illinois Press

———. 2009. *The Second Sex*. Trans. Constance Borde and Sheila Malovany-Chevallier. New York: Alfred A. Knopf.

Camus, Albert. 1991. *The Plague*. Trans. Stuart Gilbert. New York: Random House.

———. 1992. *The Rebel* [*L'Homme Révolté*]. Trans. Anthony Bower. New York: Vintage International.

Deleuze, Gilles. 1983. *Nietzsche and Philosophy*. Trans. Hugh Tomlinson. New York: Columbia University Press.

Deutscher, Penelope. 2008. *The Philosophy of Simone de Beauvoir: Ambiguity, Conversion, Resistance*. Cambridge, UK: Cambridge University Press.

Hegel, G. W. F. 1977. *Phenomenology of Spirit*. Trans. A. V. Miller. Oxford: Oxford University Press.

Freud, Sigmund. 1961. *Beyond the Pleasure Principle*. Trans. and Ed. James Strachey. New York: W. W. Norton.

Kojève, Alexandre. 1980. *Introduction to the Philosophy of Hegel: Lectures on the Phenomenology of Spirit*. Trans. Allan Bloom. Ithaca, NY: Cornell University Press.

Kristeva, Julia. 1995. Women's Time. In *New Maladies of the Soul*, 201–224. Translated by Ross Guberman. New York: Columbia University Press.

———. 1996. *The Sense and Non-sense of Revolt*. Trans. Jeanine Herman. New York: Columbia University Press

Lundgren-Gothlin, Eva. 1998. The Master-Slave Dialectic in *The Second Sex*. In *Simone de Beauvoir: A Critical Reader*. Ed. Elizabeth Fallaize. New York: Routledge.

Marx, Karl. 1988. Estranged Labor. In *1844 Economic and Philosophic Manuscripts*. Trans, Martin Milligan. New York: Prometheus Books.

Miller, Elaine. 2000. The Paradoxical Displacement: Beauvoir and Irigaray on Hegel's Antigone. *Journal of Speculative Philosophy* 14(2):121–137.

Nietzsche, Friedrich. 1978. *Thus Spoke Zarathustra*. Trans. Walter Kaufmann. New York: Penguin Books.

———. 2001. *The Gay Science*. Trans. Josefine Nauckhoff. Cambridge, UK: Cambridge University Press.

———. 2003. *Twilight of the Idols*. Trans. R. J. Hollingdale. London: Penguin Books.

Sartre, Jean Paul. 2000. Existentialism. In *Existentialism and Human Emotions*, 9–51. Trans. Bernard Frechtman. New York: Citadel Press.

Zakin, Emily. 2000. Differences in Equality: Beauvoir's Unsettling of the Universal. *Journal of Speculative Philosophy* 14:2, 104–120.

Beauvoir and Husserl

An Unorthodox Approach to The Second Sex

SARA HEINÄMAA

In the introduction to *The Second Sex*, Simone de Beauvoir illuminates the philosophical starting points of her inquiry as follows:

> As for the present study, I categorically reject the notion of psycho-physiological parallelism, for it is a doctrine whose foundations have long since been thoroughly undermined. . . . I reject also any comparative system that assumes the existence of a *natural* hierarchy or scale of values—for example, an evolutionary hierarchy. . . . All these dissertations which mingle a vague naturalism with a still more vague ethics or aesthetics are pure verbiage. (Beauvoir 1993, 73; Beauvoir 1987, 66)

With these very explicit words Beauvoir breaks away from two frameworks that have structured and overshadowed our theorization of the mind-body relationship since early modernity. On the one hand, she rejects all versions of psycho-physical *parallelism*, the earlier ontological versions as well as more recent methodological versions;[1] on the other hand, she also abandons all varieties of *ethical naturalism* and its conceptions of good life and human excellence.

Having surveyed huge numbers of scientific, cosmological, and religious sources (Beauvoir 1997, 244–445; Beauvoir 1981b, 195), Beauvoir came to see that our ethical and political ideas of men and women rest on a premature and prejudged understanding of the human body—an understanding that is limited by dualistic and naturalistic assumptions about the constitution of the world. Either mind and body are taken as two separate systems that run their courses independently of one another, or else the mental is theorized as an epiphenomenon or emergent property of physical reality. In both cases, the human body is conceived as one particular type of physiological and biomechanical system, comparable to animal bodies and inanimate objects. As a consequence, ethical and political disputes concerning women, their functions, roles, and positions in human communities, are confined by theories of animality and material nature (see, e.g., Beauvoir 1993, 262–264; Beauvoir 1987, 188–189; cf. Heinämaa 2010).

Beauvoir completely rejects this approach. For her, woman is not a female animal. Woman's very being, like the being of man, unites signification and sensibility, consciousness and materiality in a unique way that transcends the present and the past and opens onto a future. She is not defined by the animal prehistory or by the actual conditions of human life, but by her possibilities (Beauvoir 1993, 31, 73; Beauvoir 1987, 28–29, 66). Moreover woman manifests the openness of her being in all her activities and passivities. Even in the most "animal" functions of sexuality and reproduction, she displays the singularity and openness of her existence. Beauvoir concludes:

> To tell the truth, man, like woman, is flesh, and therefore a passivity. . . . And she, like him, in the midst of her carnal fever, is a consenting, a voluntary gift, an activity; they live in their different ways the strange ambiguity of existence made body. (Beauvoir 1991, 658; Beauvoir 1987, 737)

I will argue in this chapter that with respect to embodiment one of Beauvoir's most important philosophical starting points is Husserlian phenomenology, which she knew through the works of her contemporary phenomenologists. I will not discuss the historical relations of influence here in detail, since I have discussed them elsewhere (Heinämaa 2003b). It is enough to point out that Beauvoir knew classical phenomenological sources well not only because she worked through the early critical commentaries of Levinas (1963, 1994), Sartre (1998), and Merleau-Ponty (1993), published in the 1930s and 1940s, but also because she studied some central Husserlian sources independently (Heinämaa 2003a, 71–73). Instead of an exegetic account of historical relations of influence, however, I will offer a systematic explication of Beauvoir's existential-phenomenological discourse of feminine embodiment and develop my own interpretation of the significance of her feminist insight.

ONE'S OWN BODY: "OUR GRASP UPON THE WORLD"

While rejecting traditional notions of the mind-body relation, Beauvoir clarifies her approach to embodiment by writing: "However, it is said, in the perspective which I adopt—that of Heidegger, Sartre, and Merleau-Ponty—that if the body is not a *thing*, it is a situation: it is our grasp upon the world and an outline of our projects" (Beauvoir, 1993, 73; Beauvoir 1987, 66; translation modified).

In this summary sentence, Beauvoir condenses four fundamental claims. First, she argues that we do not experience our bodies as *mere things*; second, she asserts that our bodies are given to us as complex *situations* with operative fields and whole histories of embodiment; third, she claims that as such our bodies provide us with the *access* to the world as a whole; and, finally, she states that our bodies outline or rough out our *projects*. All these ideas stem from Husserl's analyses of human embodiment, and the phenomenologists that Beauvoir mentions—Heidegger, Sartre, and Merleau-Ponty—all used Husserl's analyses as starting points for their own interpretations of human existence.[2]

From Beauvoir's point of view, Husserl's most important result is the thesis that the human body cannot be identified with a material thing given in the perceptual field. In the second volume of his *Ideas*, Husserl states: "The same body which serves me as means for all my perceptions obstructs me in the perception of itself and is a remarkably imperfectly constituted thing" (Husserl 1952, 159; Husserl 1993, 167; cf. Sartre 369/433–434; Merleau-Ponty 1993, 108, 465; Merleau-Ponty 1995, 92, 406–407). Husserl argues that our own bodies are not just material things but also provide the necessary link or joint, the anchor, that connects us to all material things (cf. Merleau-Ponty 1993, 136, 157–160; Merleau-Ponty 1995, 121, 144–146). My own living body is my privileged point of orientation in space and my way of moving among things, and it includes all the organs that I need in order to grasp and manipulate objects. I can extend my bodily grasp of things with the help of tools, but in order to integrate any tool with my moving and perceiving body, I need to use organs that already belong to me (Husserl 1962b, 108–110; Husserl 1988, 106–108).[3]

Husserl grants that the human body can be conceived as a mechanism, but only within the naturalistic attitude in which all meaning and all sense is abstracted from the objects that are studied (Husserl 1952, 174–175, 183–184; Husserl 1993, 184, 193; cf. Sartre 1998, 349–353; Sartre 1993, 409–415, Merleau-Ponty 1993, 1993 87–105; Merleau-Ponty 1995, 73–89). This is a particular intellectual attitude that is motivated by certain theoretical interests; it is one of our cognitive possibilities, but not necessary for our practical lives. In this attitude, all properties, all relations, and all processes that depend on experiencing persons are put aside, since the aim is to capture realities as they are in themselves, independently of our experiences of them. Thus all value-properties and all goals must be set aside, along with secondary sensory qualities—color, taste, smell, and sound—since they all vary in our experiences and clearly depend on our capacities, dispositions, and habits (Husserl 1952, 85–86; Husserl 1993, 90–91). This naturalistic attitude studies things, animals and human bodies as physical substances in a universal network of causal interaction. The only prevailing qualities are the causally relevant primary qualities of extension, motion, number, shape, and solidity. All other properties are conceptualized as epiphenomena or emergent features with no causal efficiency in their own right (Husserl 1952, 175, 184–185; Husserl 1993, 184–185, 193–194).

As pointed out, this way of apprehending human bodies belongs among our intellectual possibilities, but it is neither the only way of grasping human bodies, nor the predominant one. In our everyday life, we conceive our own bodies and the bodies of other human beings as significative and communicating units that affect and motivate us directly and not through some hidden mechanisms. In the naturalistic attitude, such interpersonal influence by distance comes out as "mere appearance" (see Husserl 1962b, 112–113, 127–128; Husserl 1988, 110–111, 125). The communicative chain is theorized as a complicated series of causes and effects that is governed by the very same laws of force and information transmission that apply to other material things. The speaking face of the person and the attending ear of the hearer are studied as information processors, and the naturalistic philosopher concludes that ultimately the face is nothing but such a processor.[4]

Husserl opposes a simple experiential truth to this metaphysical position. He points out that even if we may conclude or "judge" that human bodies are machines (cf. Descartes ATVIII 32; cf. Merleau-Ponty 2003, 51–58; Merleau-Ponty 1964a, 175–178), we cannot *perceive* them as such mechanisms, but grasp them as significative systems composed of meaningful gestures and postures: "The facial expressions are seen facial expressions, and they are immediately bearers of sense for the other's consciousness, e.g. his will, which, in empathy, is characterized as the actual will of the person and as a will which addresses me in communication. . . . There is no question here of a causal relation . . . and equally no question of any other psycho-physical relation" (Husserl 1952, 235; Husserl 1993, 246; translation modified; cf. Merleau-Ponty 1993, 231–232; Merleau-Ponty 1995, 197–199).

Moreover, Husserl argues that all scientists and all philosophers of nature remain dependent in their activities of investigation and argumentation on instrumental and personal realities. The scientist and the philosopher have to operate in the lifeworld peopled by persons in order to develop, secure, and justify their theoretical results, and this operation is possible only if they take certain validities of the life-world for granted: the usability of their scientific instruments and their communicative media and the expressivity of their own bodies and the bodies of others (Husserl 1988, 125–127). Scientists may neglect this dependency for particular explanatory purposes—and they have to, in order to develop their materialistic theory—but if they proceed to *absolutize* this worldview, then they overstep limits of validity (Husserl 1952, 183–184; Husserl 1993, 193; Heinämaa 2003, 2011).

AN ANDROCENTRIC PERSPECTIVE: "DIRECT AND NORMAL CONNECTION"

Beauvoir accepts the classical phenomenological analysis of the sense of the body, but she takes distance from the universalistic aspirations of her contemporary phenomenologists, and argues that human bodies come in different variations with several criteria of normality. One of her main arguments is that the male body is falsely taken as the single standard and norm of human existence: "He conceives his body as a direct and normal connection with the world, which he believes he apprehends in its objectivity, whereas he regards the body of woman as weighted down by everything which specifies it: as an obstacle, a prison" (Beauvoir 1993, 15; Beauvoir 1987, 15–16). For Beauvoir this androcentric conception is part of the problem to be studied, and should not be used to explain the hierarchical relations that obtain between the sexes. It strains and distorts psychological and bio-scientific accounts of human bodies, but it also compromises philosophical discourses on embodiment.

Beauvoir points out that women's bodies are usually compared to men's bodies on the basis of physical strength and reproductive functions, and that in such comparisons these bodies come out as a limited means of grasping the world (Beauvoir 1993, 73–74; Beauvoir 1987, 67). Women's arms are shorter, it is argued, and thus their reach must be lesser; their muscles are weaker and thus their effects are minor; she is burdened with the child that she carries inside her womb or in her arms, and cannot take part in the explorative and militant practices that differentiate humans from other primates (Beauvoir 1991, 112–114; Beauvoir, 1987, 95–96; Heinämaa 2003, 105–109).

For Beauvoir such comparisons cannot account for the prevalence of the hierarchical relations between the sexes or for the actual subordination of women to men; on the contrary, any identification of contemporary women with their animal or prehuman ancestors begs the question and contributes to the reestablishment of the hierarchy. The task of the philosopher is not to repeat such accounts but to problematize the naturalness and necessity of the scales of values on which they rest. Beauvoir writes: "It is not merely as a body, but rather as a body subject to taboos, to laws, that the subject is conscious of himself and realizes itself—it is with reference to certain values that he evaluates himself. And once again, it is not upon physiology that values are based; rather facts of biology take on the values that the existent bestows upon them" (Beauvoir 1993, 76, 94–95; Beauvoir 1987, 68–69, 83).

Thus Beauvoir contrives a powerful analysis of the sexual hierarchy by connecting the phenomenological discourse of the body to her existential theory of values. She explicates her value theory in her essays of the 1940s, *Pyrrhus and Cineas* and *The Ethics of Ambiguity*. According to this theory, no values are natural or independent of the activities of human individuals and communities; rather, all values are constituted by the choices, practices, and actions of human beings: "It is desire which creates the desirable, and the project which posits the goal. It is human existence which makes values spring up in the world on the basis of which it will be able to judge the enterprises in which it will be engaged" (Beauvoir 1947, 22; Beauvoir 1994, 14–15, translation modified).

This implies that the sexual hierarchy cannot be derived from any natural law or from any cosmological or divine order. Its formation must be tracked down to the activities and actions of human beings, ourselves and our predecessors. *The Second Sex* takes on this task: the first part of the book inquires into the real and mythical history and prehistory of the sexual hierarchy, and the second studies its repetition and effects in our lived experiences (see Heinämaa 2003, 103–105).

It is important to notice that Beauvoir's axiological approach is more radical than the social constructionist approach of her successors. Beauvoir does not just reject the idea of a natural or divine grounding of values but also urges us to question the idea of a social agreement. She argues that women are measured by standards of superiority and excellence that have been established in mutual recognition and valorization that only includes men (Beauvoir 1993, 14–15; Beauvoir 1987, 15; Beauvoir 1991, 237–243; Beauvoir 1987, 171–175; Heinämaa 2003, 101–102). Women have not questioned the norms created within male communality, but neither have they actively taken part in their institution and reinstitution (Beauvoir 1993, 114; Beauvoir 1987, 15–16, 29, 96).

So when Iris Marion Young wonders why Beauvoir does not explain women's "inhibited intentionality" or their "discontinuous movements" by cultural-social conditioning but instead chooses to study the parameters of woman's bodily existence (Young 1989, 145), she imposes a false dichotomy of cultural/natural on Beauvoir's reflections on embodiment and existence. The human body is not a natural reality for Beauvoir, but is always involved in cultural practices. By implication, all bodily functions and all bodily capacities of human beings imply nexuses of values. There is no objective physiological level on which men and women could be compared independently of value positings: "[T]he 'weakness' is revealed as such only in the light of the *ends* man proposes, the *instruments* he has available, and the *laws* he establishes" (Beauvoir 1993, 74; Beauvoir 1987, 67; emphasis mine). Each comparison implies a valuation, and each objective measurement is laden with interests (Beauvoir 1993, 30; Beauvoir 1987, 28).

So if Beauvoir does not introduce social-cultural conditioning as an explanation of the fact that women's bodily movements are "discontinuous" and their motor intentionality is "inhibited" (Young 1989, 149), this is not because she would offer a physiological explanation instead. She does not aim at explaining such facts, neither by culture nor by biology, because she does not accept any such "facts" as simply given. In her understanding, woman's movements can indeed be characterized as "restricted," "discontinuous," and "inhibited," but only on the basis of some presupposed standard of normality, and each such standard implies a set of interests. The task of a feminist philosopher is not to put forward such accounts without questioning their axiological foundations. The real challenge is to study the origin and constitution of the values involved in the activities at issue.

THE LIFE WORLD AS A PRACTICAL AND AFFECTIVE FIELD

Husserl argues that the Lifeworld which surrounds us in our everyday activities is not a collection of physical objects but is composed of different sorts of practical things: tools, instruments, machines, buildings, utensils, pictures, signs, symbols, and material elements that are used in the construction of such objects. He uses the experience of warmth and the practice of heating to exemplify and illuminate the practical character of our common surroundings: "I see coal, for instance, as heating material; I recognize it and recognize it as useful and as used for heating, as appropriate for and as destined to produce warmth" (Husserl 1952, 187; Husserl 1993, 197).

The Lifeworld is also given as a field of affective relations. All things in it have motivating powers and we respond to their movements and properties by turning toward them or away from them, and by actively positing value or by passively yielding to stimuli (Husserl 1952, 189–190; Husserl 1993, 199; Husserl 1962b, 110; Husserl 1988, 108).

Husserl's analyses of the givenness of value-objects and practical objects include two ideas. First, Husserl argues that all value characteristics and all practical characteristics of real things are constituted on the basis of straightforward sense-perception. Thus the most fundamental level of reality is that of sensible materiality, and all practical or axiological determinations are constituted on the basis of simple perceptual presence: "To begin with, the world is, in its *core*, a world appearing to the senses and characterized as 'on hand' or 'present at hand' [*vorhanden*]. . . . The ego finds itself then related to this empirical world in new acts, e.g., in acts of valuing or in acts of pleasure and displeasure. In these acts, the object is brought to consciousness as valuable, pleasant, beautiful, etc. . . . In that case, there is built, upon the substratum of mere intuitive presenting, an evaluating . . . in which the value character is given in original intuition" (Husserl 1952, 186; Husserl 1993, 196; cf. Husserl 1962a, 298–306). This does not mean that we would first relate to mere things and only subsequently to practical and valuable objects. Value-neutral presence is not a separate part of our factual experience but a constitutive factor disclosed by abstractive analysis.[5]

Second, Husserl also argues that through the processes of association, habituation, and sedimentation things appear to us as useful and valuable as such. Goals and values are not experienced to us as subjective inventions but as shared realities: "I 'can use it for that,' it is useful to me for that. Others also apprehend it in the same way, and it acquires an intersubjective use-value and in a social context is appreciated and is valuable as serving such and such a purpose, as useful to man, etc." (Husserl 1952, 188; Husserl 1993, 197).

On the basis of Husserl's analyses of value-objects and practical objects, Heidegger and the existentialists developed their own critical discourses on the lifeworld and our being-in-the-world. Heidegger attacked the notion of perceptual presence and argued that the most fundamental type of givenness is not presence-at hand or being-there but practical readiness-to hand (*zu-handen*). If we abandon the habit of privileging our cognitive interests, he reasoned, and study the way in which things are given to us in our daily lives, we can conceive the givenness of the world in a new way. Such a study shows that originally we do not just observe things or record their presence but are practically involved with them (Heidegger 1992, 95; Heidegger 1993, 67). Accordingly, things appear to us in the modes of serviceability, conductiveness, usability, and manipulability. These are not any secondary determinations but belong to things as such.

Studying Husserl's and Heidegger's interchange on thinghood and presence, Sartre and Merleau-Ponty developed an argument to the effect that the fundamental objects of our experience are not theoretical objects, and not even practical instruments, but affective percepts that move, attract and repulse our bodies (e.g., Sartre 1998, 649–651; Sartre 1993, 769–771; Merleau-Ponty 1993, 235–242, 371–373; Merleau-Ponty 1995, 203–209, 321–323). For example, we see a table neither primarily as a structure of wood fibers, cells, or molecules, nor as a seat that supports and bears objects in use. As a perceptual thing, the table is neither a theoretical object of natural sciences nor a practical object of everyday affairs. Primarily, we *see* the table as an attractive thing that invites our bodies to move in certain ways: we slide our hand on its smooth, cool surface, as if it "demanded those movements of convergence that will endow it with its 'true' aspect" (Merleau-Ponty 1993 367; Merleau-Ponty 1995, 318).

So according to Sartre and Merleau-Ponty, perceptual things do not just stand there in front of us or opposite to us, as if in mute presence, but invite us to movement and direct our moving bodies with their motivating powers of attraction and repulsion.

THE FEMININE WORLD: "INDOMITABLE"

Beauvoir's *The Second Sex* includes many descriptions of the practical relations that obtain between sexually different bodies and their environments. However, like her French contemporaries, she also argues that the practical-instrumental analysis does not capture all the intentional relations that we have to our environments and to the surrounding world. She states:

> The world does not appear to woman "an assemblage of utensils," intermediate between her will and her goals, as Heidegger defines it: it is, on the contrary, obstinately resistant, indomitable. (Beauvoir 1991, 485; Beauvoir 1987, 609)

This argument has two aspects. First, the idea is that the environing world does not always or predominantly give itself to women as a practical field in which they manipulate things and work to advance their personal projects and the projects of their communities. In certain lived situations, the practical-instrumental relations of everyday life move aside and give way to affective relations that connect the person to her environment independently of her decisions and plans. Second, her own body is not given to the woman in these situations as the instrument of her will but appears in another mode: it reveals and includes an *alien vitality* that does not contribute to her personal projects or to the projects of her community but instead serves a future new life.[6] This phenomenon is highlighted by the experiences of pregnancy and nursing.[7] Beauvoir describes the former as follows:

> The mystery of a collar of blood that inside the mother's belly changes into a human being is one no mathematics can put in equation, no

machine can hasten or delay; she feels the resistance of duration that the most ingenious instruments fail to divide or multiply; she feels it in her flesh, submitted to the lunar rhythms, and first ripened, then corrupted, by the years. (Beauvoir 1991, 485; Beauvoir 1987, 609)

Beauvoir's argument here must be taken in a fundamental way. She is not suggesting that the environing objects would appear to women as obstacles or their own feminine bodies as burdens, as many readers have concluded (Heinämaa 2003).[8] Rather than using the concepts of obstacle, hindrance, and burden, Beauvoir suggests that the whole conceptual framework of instruments is inadequate in the description and analysis of certain feminine experiences. In these experiences, things are not given as useful or suitable, but neither do they appear as useless or unsuitable; bodies are not given as effective instruments but neither do their appear as broken tools or as burdensome loads.[9] The oppositions of usefulness/uselessness, suitability/unsuitability, and manipulability/nonmanipulability fail to capture the specifications under which the environing world appears to women. The "feminine world" is not just, or even predominantly, a practical environment ready to hand; it is a world "dominated by fatality and traversed by mysterious caprices" (Beauvoir 1991, 485; Beauvoir 1987, 609).

We should not let Beauvoir's provocative formulation and the scattered character of her discourse lead us disregard the critical thrust of her approach. In the rest of the chapter I will argue that her discourse on feminine experience implies fundamental claims about human existence and that by developing this discourse further we can question certain dominant ideas of twentieth-century phenomenology of embodiment.

The first thing to notice is that by "fatalities," "mysteries," and "uncertainties," Beauvoir does not merely refer to some contingent incidents but to the uncontrollable process of *life itself*, as it is appears in certain feminine experiences. This is not a psychological and cultural-historical claim to the effect that women tend to mystify natural phenomena for the lack systematic knowledge and political power.[10] Nor is the point merely in the experiential fact that the Lifeworld includes ungovernable or uncontrollable events. More importantly, and more fundamentally, Beauvoir suggests that pregnancy and childbirth reveal life themselves as processes that escape our grasp and control and confuse the boundaries of own and alien, self and other.

Second, the critical edge of Beauvoir's argument does not concern merely women but also our philosophical (and supposedly unprejudiced) discourses on human life and existence. By thematizing and explicating women's experiences and the world as it appears to women (Beauvoir 1993, 32; Beauvoir 1987, 29; Beauvoir 1991, 9; Beauvoir 1987, 33), Beauvoir discloses an androcentric bias and a universalizing tendency in her contemporary phenomenology and philosophy: what is called "human existence" and what is called the "human world" turn out to be generalizations based on men's experiences. The traditional position that women have in such a world is that of a mirror image (Beauvoir 1993, 242; Beauvoir 1987, 175).

Thus, and this is the third point, the intentional structures that are disclosed in women's experiences and the "feminine world" are not exclusive to women. Rather, Beauvoir suggests that by studying the neglected and marginalized aspects of women's lives as they are given to women themselves, we can *all* gain a more valid and more profound understanding of *human existence*. The philosophical question that drives her inquiries into women's lives concerns the sense of being human. What is at issue concerns us all: "the relation between the facticity of the individual and the freedom which assumes this facticity is the most difficult enigma involved in the human condition, and this enigma presents itself in the most uncanny manner in woman" (Beauvoir 1993, 400; Beauvoir 1987, 286).

In order to see what is at issue here, it is useful to compare Beauvoir's discourse on feminine experience to Merleau-Ponty's discourse on the experience of illness (Merleau-Ponty 1995, 120–127).[11] The point of the comparison is not to suggest that the feminine body would be an invalid body, but to highlight and articulate the different aspects of vitality as it is given in our varying experiences.

PREGNANT EXPERIENCE AND PRENATAL LIFE

In his *Phenomenology of Perception*, Merleau-Ponty argues that phenomenologists need to inquire into the experiences of people who suffer mental and physical illnesses because their abnormal experiences reveal certain operations of perceptual consciousness that remain latent or marginal in the experience of the healthy. The most important of these latent operations is the functioning of our perceptual organs, their sensitivity and motility. Merleau-Ponty calls these functions the "anonymous" aspects of our perception and he characterizes them as follows: "By sensation I grasp, on the fringe of my own personal life and my own acts, a life of a given consciousness from which these latter emerge, the life of my eyes, my hands, my ears, which are so many natural selves" (Merleau-Ponty 1993, 250; Merleau-Ponty 1995, 215–216).

The anonymous operations of our sense-organs are not under the control of our will and are not directed by our explicit emotions, plans, or projects. When I explore things, my eyes constantly react to the salient features of the perceptual field; similarly when I palpate something the movements of my hands respond to the surfaces and elements that they encounter. These movements are part of our sensory-motor consciousness and they constitute our responsiveness to the environment: "While I am overcome by some grief and wholly given over to my distress, my eyes already stray in front of me, and are drawn, despite everything, to some shining object" (Merleau-Ponty 1993, 113–114; Merleau-Ponty 1995, 97). The movements of the sense-organs are not intentional in the sense of being intended by the perceiving ego, but they prepare for such movements and allow the perceiver to focus her attention to significant things of the environment.

Normally the functions of our sense-organs proceed without our notice, and as such they contribute to our perceptions. In other words, they form a hidden ground on which our attentive perception rests. In sickness they come to the fore through pain and discomfort. The movements of my eyes which yesterday went unnoticed now announce themselves in tenderness and soreness (see Sartre 1998 371–379; Sartre 1993, 436–437). I do not recognize or live through these movements as external processes, but as operations that belong to my own body, and have belonged to it all along. The functions of our sense-organs are anonymous in the sense that they do not issue from our personal decisions (Merleau-Ponty 1993 xiii, 191–194; Merleau-Ponty 1995, xviii, 164–166; Merleau-Ponty 1964b, 17, 187–188; Merleau-Ponty 1968, 3, 142–143), but they are not external to our lived bodies. As such they are always connected to and integrated with the most personal and egoic aspects of our worldly relations. This means that the anonymous is not a separate or separable part of the human being, but is the hidden substratum on which our personal activities rest (Merleau-Ponty 1993, 513–514; Merleau-Ponty 1995, 450–451).

Beauvoir points out that, like the perceiving body, the feminine body entails functions that proceed independently of personal preferences, volitions, and decisions. These are the reproductive functions of pregnancy and nursing in which the woman's body houses and sustains an alien life, an other sensing body.[12] Beauvoir combines physiological and poetic descriptions of such conditions, and interprets them with her existential concepts:

> Mystery for man, woman is considered to be mystery in itself. To be true, her [bodily] situation makes woman very liable to such a view. Her physiological destiny is very complex: she herself submits to it as to some foreign rigmarole; her body is not for her a clear expression of herself; within it she feels alienated. (Beauvoir 1993, 400; Beauvoir, 1987, 286)

Moreover, Beauvoir's discourse includes descriptions of the processes in which woman's body prepares for pregnancy, and she gives an existential formulation also of such bodily experiences:

> [her body] is, indeed, beset by a persistent and foreign life that each month makes and unmakes a birthplace within it; each month preparations are made for a child to be born and then aborted in the dissolution of the crimson fabrics. Woman, like man, *is* her body; but her body is something other than she. (Beauvoir 1993, 67; Beauvoir 1987, 61)

Beauvoir's account is provocative in drawing a parallel between birth of life and abortion as two recurring phases of one continuous process. In the 1940s and 1950s, her existential formulations were considered scandalous;[13] they were equated with her political arguments for women's abortion rights and rejected together with them. Contemporary reactions, as well as subsequent interpretations, focused on the ethical-political aspects of her discourse and neglected its ontological implications or else subjected them to the political debate.

In order to get to the philosophical core of Beauvoir's insight, it is important to study closely the context of her claims. The statement above is put forward as a direct comment on Merleau-Ponty's influential thesis on human embodiment, formulated in *Phenomenology of Perception* as follows: "I am my body, at least wholly to the extent that I posses experience, and yet at the same time my body is as it were a 'natural' subject, a provisional sketch of my total being" (Beauvoir 1987, 61; cf. Merleau-Ponty 1995, 198).

One of Merleau-Ponty's main ideas in *Phenomenology* argues that the anonymous life of the human body provides a sketch for our worldly relations and that our egoic acts forge personal ways of intending out of this intentional "material." Thus our conscious lives can be characterized as "variations" of a human way or style of relating to the world (Merleau-Ponty 1993, 145–147; Merleau-Ponty 1995, 124–126).

Beauvoir's description of feminine embodiment complicates this line of thought. Her main idea is that the human body, as it is given to women, is not just a general sketch for multiple personal modifications but is also a concrete point of contact between two separate selves.[14] In addition to the anonymous operations of the sense-organs which serve our personal acts of experiencing, a woman's lived body entails functions that contribute to the emergence and sustenance of another sensing being and potentially another person. This means that the operations of the human body do not just incorporate general world-relations with personal intendings, or past activities with futural spontaneity, as Merleau-Ponty argues (1993, 277; Merleau-Ponty 1995, 240, 441–442), but that some of them also serve to establish a division between two sensory-motor subjects. The following is my own explication of the remarks and discussions that we find in *The Second Sex*.

First, the functions of pregnant and nursing bodies resemble the anonymous operations of our perceptual organs in providing a foundation for certain kinds of experiences. Whereas the anonymous functions of our sense-organs contribute to the personal relations of attentive perception, the vital functions of the maternal body contribute to the establishment of interpersonal relations of affection and proto-communication between two subjects, the fetus and the mother, one of whom is nested in the other. Such experiences become possible when the fetus reaches the level of articulated sensation and autonomous movement.

When a developed fetus moves in the womb, the mother is able to experience its movements both from inside and from outside.[15] On the one hand, she can feel these movement in the inner tissues of her belly.[16] Women describe the early movements of their fetuses by comparing them to muscular cramps and pangs of their own organs, and to nonliving entities that move inside their bodies, for example, food entering and passing though the throat or bubbles imagined bumping against the sensitive inner surfaces of the belly. When the fetus grows and develops, its sensory-motor capacities develop and its movements become directed and responsive to the given environment. Its comportment can then be experienced by the mother as proto-intentional activity of an independent sensing being.[17] Some felt movements are identified as taps, kicks, pokes, and strokes; others are experienced as more complicated forms of behavior and compared to stepping, jumping, diving, and fluttering. The phenomenologist Loiuse Levesque-Lopman gives a personal account of such experiences:

> By about the fourth month I was able to distinguish, with great excitement, the movement of my baby in my body. That gentle movement, which was to become more forceful later, as well as the continuing physical changes, provided immediate and continuous reminders of my pregnancy. The reality of the movements of the fetus gave me the promise of a baby in the near future, but it was not yet the recipient of maternal love. (Levesque-Lopman 1983 260–261)

Another source gives the following description:

> I cannot describe what I feel when I look at my belly which moves according to you, and not me. I cannot influence these movements, you are an independent being; and I feel that my space will soon become too small for you. (Reim 1984 25)

The woman can also feel the effects of the infant's movements on the outer surface of her belly in later states of pregnancy: she can touch the belly with her hands and through the medium of her own flesh reach the moving child. Moreover, others also can feel these movements by touching her belly and they can see effects of the inner movements on the outer surface of the belly.[18]

The experience of one's own body changes accordingly. In early phases of pregnancy, the belly appears as a solid undivided body-part, but in late phases, it is given as including a hidden inner space, a birth place and dwelling place of an alien living being. Thus it can be compared to cradles and nests (Martin 1987; Young 1990,162; Gahlings 2006, 486).[19]

The possibility of identifying movements and positions of a sensuous moving being allows a relation of gestural communication to develop between the two. Actual concrete experience confirms this: The mother can both pacify and stimulate the movements of the child with the movements of her own body and her hands. Many women report that they experience no movements of the child when they move heavily, but when they settle down the child starts moving (Reim 1984, 115, 180).[20] Moreover, recent experimental studies confirm what pregnant women have argued on the basis of their own experience: a developed fetus responds to external sounds and is also able to identify voices, melodies, and rhythms (DeCasper and Fifter 1980; DeCasper, Lecanuet, Busnel, Deferre-Garnier, and Maugeais 1986; DeCasper and Spence 1994; Moon, Cooper, and Fufer 1993).

The prenatal practices of sensory-motor proto-communication can be continued after the birth of the infant and they can be developed further.[21] This means that the sense of sight (or smell) does not establish the first link between the two sensory-motor subjects but rather enriches and refines the connections of affection and communication already established on the basis of the senses of touch and movement (kinesthesia).[22] The privilege of the sense of sight may be justified in the larger communal setting in which third parties relate to the newborn primarily through vision,[23] but this overlooks the primordial sensory link between the infant and the mother.[24]

As this description clearly shows, the vital functions of the feminine body cannot by themselves provide ground for intersubjective experiences without the operations of the sense organs. In other words, the vital functions of the feminine body depend on the sensory operations of both the mother and the infant in their potential to ground specific types of intersubjective experiences. The pregnant woman is able to experience the fetus as a living being only because she is able to feel its spontaneous and receptive movements and she is able to touch her own body and sense its movements (cf. Husserl 1952, 147–150; Husserl 1993, 155–158).[25]

The coordination of different kinds of operations and functions in pregnancy complicates the phenomenon, and for this reason it is necessary to explicate the essential differences between them. The next section is dedicated to this task. After the explication, I return to the topic of the mother-fetus pair and end my chapter by discussing Beauvoir's understanding of this very specific type of human relating.

COMPLICATIONS: "AN EQUIVOCAL COUPLE"

The vital functions of the feminine body differ in important respects from the anonymous operations of perception. Phenomenologically considered, the main difference is that the latter but not the former are "presentational" and thus allow for two different types of apprehensions, one external and the other internal *to the living body*. The presentational sensation of warmth, for example, can be grasped either as a quality external to the body or as a state of the sensing organ itself. When I press my back on the cliff, I can perceive the warmness of the surface of the cliff but I can also disregard the external thing and capture the state of warmness in my own back. Similarly the sensation of light can be grasped as an outer effect on the eye or as a state of the eye itself.

In contrast, the phenomena that make up the reproductive functions of the feminine body remain on either side of the dividing line of own/alien and cannot be apprehended as belonging to the other side. In other words, an occurrence is grasped either as a state of one's own living body or else as an event external to it. For example, the swelling of the breasts and the belly during pregnancy are experienced as changes in one's own body. Similarly menstrual cramps are experienced as unpleasant violent movements of the inner organs of one's lived body; they are not grasped as effects of alien entities operating on the body from inside.[26] On the other hand, no such change of focus can establish lactated milk or menstrual blood as a part of the sensing moving body;[27] the flow is insensitive and thus grasped as an excretion or secretion expelled from the lived body.[28] The sensitive orifices and vessels through which these fluids travel are, however, experienced as belonging to the lived body.

As such the functions of the feminine body can be compared to the vital functions of the lungs and the digestive system.[29] The main difference here is that whereas respiration and nutrition involve reception of an external element (the element of air, or some liquid or solid element), the feminine functions operate, as if, on their own, without any external material (cf. Leder 1990 47, 50–51). Another difference is in their temporal character: feminine functions are not constant or diurinal but periodic.[30]

There is one aspect in which the feminine functions differ *both* from the operations of our sense-organs *and* from the functions of the our viscera: All these three types of prepersonal functions come to the fore in discomfort and pain, but whereas pain indicates damage or illness in the case of the sense-organs and the viscera, it lacks this meaning in the case of feminine functions. Menstruation, swelling of breasts, expansion of the belly, and lactation are not grasped as signals of an abnormal or anomalous condition that diverts from the optimal state of the feminine body.[31] On the contrary, they contribute to the establishment of another norm.[32] To be sure, such occurrences and developments divert from the daily processes of women's bodies, but at the same time they constitute a norm that covers these bodies from sexual maturity to menopause.

The most remarkable difference, however, between the vital functions of the feminine body, on the one hand, and the functions of our sense-organs and our viscera, on the other hand, is in their teleology. The functions of the feminine body point to and make possible a rearticulation of one's own body: pregnancy involves an experience of bodily self-estrangement and the reproductive functions prepare for this condition. In pregnancy the bodily inside is not simply one's own but appears also as a habitat of another living being.

This teleology is not just a medical fact or a theological dogma, but is part of the bodily experience of women themselves. The main point is captured well by Julia Kristeva who in "Stabat mater" states that a woman with a child is "a division of the very flesh" (1983 240–241; Kristeva 1995, 177–179; cf. Kristeva 1977 and 1979). Beauvoir describes the same phenomenon by her existential concepts of immanence and transcendence:

> What is specific to the pregnant woman is that the body is experienced as immanent at the moment when it transcends itself. . . . The transcendence of the artisan, of the man of action is inhabited by *one subjectivity*, but in the becoming mother the opposition between subject and object is

abolished. She forms with this child from which she is swollen *an equivocal couple* overwhelmed by life. (Beauvoir 1991, 349–350; Beauvoir 1987, 512; my emphasis)

The functions of the feminine body, as it is lived by women, are specific in that they prepare for an opening of an inner space, a space that houses another living sensing-moving being. The two—the inner space and its fetal inhabitant—are constituted together for the pregnant woman, and the constitution involves several different types of sensations and a complex nexus of them.

Beauvoir characterizes the phenomenon by calling it an "equivocal couple." This suggests two ideas: on the one hand, the pregnant woman and the fetus form an intersubjective relation, but on the other hand, their relation is "equivocal" in the sense that it differs in crucial respects from other forms of human intersubjectivity.[33] In order to complete my interpretation of Beauvoir's argument on feminine experience, I will close my paper with a short discussion of the main aspects of the concept of *couple* as it is used in *The Second Sex*.

Beauvoir's thinking about couples is influenced by the works of several philosophers, some of whom are explicitly mentioned while others remain in the background.[34] Her discourse has multiple facets and serves several different purposes of argumentation. For this reason it is necessary to study carefully Beauvoir's formulations, to insert her claims in the framework of the whole study, and to compare her remarks of different types of couples. The central idea is explicated in the case of the man-woman couple.

In the introduction to *The Second Sex*, Beauvoir argues that man and woman do not simply stand, and have never simply stood, in opposition to one another, but form in their very *being* a couple. In this context she also claims, in passing, that the couple is the fundamental unit of all human communality or *Mitsein* (Beauvoir 1993, 19–20; Beauvoir 1987, 19–20). This means that human beings could not belong to larger communities and societies without also belonging to pairs and couples.

The point is not to affirm the traditional assumption that the heterosexual couple is the fundamental unit of human societies, but to argue that human beings need to form couples—some kinds of couples—in order to establish larger intersubjective wholes. In other words, communicative and affective couples are necessary elements of all human sociality and communality. Without them no larger wholes would be possible. Thus, the couple is not just a relation or a duality for Beauvoir, but is the basic building block of all human sociality.

Against this background, Beauvoir's characterization of the mother-fetus relation as an "equivocal couple" is rather radical. Her concept of a couple implies a crucial claim about dependency: in so far as the mother and the fetus form a couple, they are not just dependent parts of human communities, but on the contrary constitute a unit on which such larger wholes depend. Moreover, this particular type of couple is "equivocal" and not as fully articulate as the couples that we form in our adult lives. This means that human communality and sociality can be established on ambiguous grounds and are not necessarily composed of fully developed individuals.

CONCLUSIONS

We can draw several different kinds of conclusions from the interpretations and explications of this chapter. The main conclusion concerns Beauvoir's argument about androcentricism: The explication of the experience of pregnancy developed here helps to make sense of Beauvoir's claim that her contemporary philosophy suffers from an androcentric approach to human embodiment. Moreover, my explication also shows how the experience of pregnancy relates to the existential-phenomenological discourse on embodiment and intersubjectivity. The main result, in this respect, is that the mother and the fetus form a pair of two lived bodies. I have argued that in order to see the critical potential of this statement, it is necessary to realize its Husserlian parameters.

My second conclusion concerns the conceptual basis of Beauvoir's thinking. Our inquiry demonstrates that Beauvoir's discussion on pregnancy, and feminine embodiment more generally, depends on the phenomenological concepts of the lived body and the lifeworld, and on phenomenological analyses of subjectivity and its constitution in sensation and motility. Her main insight is that the lifeworld is not just a practical field of utensils and tools but also a field of affective relations. Correspondingly, our lived bodies are not just "instruments of instrument," as Sartre contends, but also receptive and communicative gestures.

Third, we have also reached interesting results concerning the experience of pregnancy as such. First, we can conclude that pregnancy is not a state of blurred or lessened subjectivity, as often assumed, but involves a particular kind of experience of intersubjective relating. Second, human coexistence can be established between two sensory-motor subjects, one of which is nested in the body of the other. All this complicates our received notions of lived space and the traditional equation between the inner and the own. Finally we can conclude that intersubjectivity is not a structure established in birth or after birth, but has roots in prenatal existence. This has interesting implications for the traditional hierarchization of the visible over the tangible. I have suggested that Beauvoir follows Husserl's constitutional analyses, which show that touch, and not vision, is necessary for the constitution of all living bodies.

NOTES

Please note that this essay uses the British Edition of Parshley's translation of The Second Sex and special editions of the French, *Le deuxième sexe*, resulting in different paginations from editions available in the United States.

1. Beauvoir does not discuss occasionalism or interactionism because these positions were not seriously defended by any contemporary philosophers.
2. For the differences between Heidegger's, Sartre's, and Merleau-Ponty's discussions of embodiment, see Langer 1998; Heinämaa 2003, 61–64; Hoffman 2006; Heinämaa 2007; and Heinämaa 2010.
3. Compare Sartre 1998, 364–365; Sartre 1993, 428; Merleau-Ponty 1993, 166–172; Merleau-Ponty 1995, 142–147; Merleau-Ponty 2003, 58; Merleau-Ponty 1964a, 178; Slatman 2009, and Slatman and Widdershoven 2009.
4. For an example of such an account, see Mandik 2007.
5. Husserl argued that the idea of value-neutral being results from abstractions and is not part of factual experience. In his so-called Intersubjectivity manuscripts he writes: "Everything that is touches our feelings; every existent is apperceived in a value-apperception and thereby awakens desirous attitudes" (Husserl 1973, 404–405), and in another manuscript: "Mere sensation-data, and at a higher level, sensory objects, as things that are there for the subject, but there as value-free, are abstractions. There is nothing that does not affect the emotions" (Ms. A VI 26, 42a, cited in Drummond 2006).
6. Compare Beauvoir's anti-Heideggerian insight to that of Ricouer: "at a certain level of my existence I no longer appear to myself as a *task*, as a project. I am a *problem resolved* as though by a greater wisdom than myself. This wisdom is a nourishing one: when I have eaten, it is not up to me to make the food into myself and grow on it. It is a wisdom of movement: the circulation of my blood and the beating of my heart do not depend on me" (Ricoeur 1966, 418).
7. This feminist argument has later been developed by several feminist philosophers, influenced by Beauvoir's existential-phenomenological account. Following Beauvoir, both deconstructive thinkers, such as Kristeva (1983) and Irigaray (1984), and philosophers coming from the pragmatistic tradition, such as Young (1990), question the instrumental-practical account of the human body and instead develop aesthetic and ethical conceptualizations.
8. In this respect Beauvoir's account differs from that of Sartre (e.g., Sartre 1998, 498–500; Sartre 1993, 584–587).
9. The pregnant body can appear as unable, incapable, and invalided to an external observer who studies its movements in a third-person perspective. It can also appear in this way to the woman herself. The point, however, is not about an experiential possibility but about a necessity: this is not the only way nor the primary way in which the pregnant woman experiences her own body.
10. For the history of such claims, see, Easlea 1980, 38–40, Merchant [1980] 1989, 151–163.
11. Another important point of comparison is to be found in Beauvoir's own discourse on aging (Beauvoir 1970, 1988).
12. Merleau-Ponty's works include extensive discussions on pregnancy, birth, generativity, and natality, but he uses these concepts to reform the phenomenological

account of the emergence and formation of meaning and our intentional relations to the world, not to discuss childbirth (see Merleau-Ponty 1993, 29–30, 178–179, 271–272, 335–344; Merleau-Ponty 1995, 21–22, 152–153, 235, 290–297; Merleau-Ponty 1964b, 193, 259–267, 286–287; Merleau-Ponty 1968, 147, 206–213, 233–234). Thus, one should not equate his statements about of pregnancy or birth with claims concerning human infants (e.g., Leder 1990). However, one can well argue that Merleau-Ponty's thinking here is analogical and that uses the model of human birth and pregnancy to make sense of another kind of becoming and formation. This is one of Luce Irigaray's arguments in *An Ethics of Sexual Difference* (1984), and her critical conclusion is that this conceptual debt is never paid back by any inquiry into the phenomenon of sexual difference (1984, 152–157).

13. For Beauvoir's own account see her *Force of Circumstance* (Beauvoir 1997, 257–259; Beauvoir 1981b, 196–198).
14. Beauvoir's critical remarks against Merleau-Ponty and phenomenology of embodiment must be distinguished and kept separate from the more common suspicion according to which Merleau-Ponty and the phenomenologists privilege the "higher" operations of sense-perception at the expense of the "lower" presentational sensations of pain, contraction, fatigue, and so on (e.g., Leder 1990, 36–37). Beauvoir is not worried about the privilege of the perceptional but about the privilege of male experience. Moreover, her work demonstrates that the higher activities of consciousness, such as intending, willing, and judging, are traditionally associated with maleness and masculinity, and the "lower" functions, such as sensitivity, affectivity, and receptivity, with femaleness and femininity. She does not accept such equations but argues that both sexes manifest activity and passivity, reason and sensitivity.
15. The phenomenon is traditionally called *quickening*, a term derived from *quick*, in the sense of *alive* (*vivus, bios, zoe*). The term has been used in this sense in medical and legal discourse since ancient times. For example, William Blackstone explains the history of English law in the eighteenth century as follows: "if a woman is quick with child, and by a potion, or otherwise, killeth it in her womb; or if any one beat her, whereby the child dieth in her body, and she is delivered of a dead child; this, though not murder, was by the ancient law homicide or manslaughter" (Blackstone 1979, IX.I.1.).

    In early modernity, the quickening was usually taken as the first certain sign of new life and, thus, pregnancy. The mere missing of menstruation was not taken as a reliable sign of new life. Accordingly, women declared pregnancy only on the basis of experiences of child movements (Labouvie 1998, 19).
16. Physiologically put, the woman's uterine muscles, rather than her abdominal muscles, are the first to sense the fetal movement. For this reason, the body weight of the woman does not have a substantial effect on when she experiences these movements (i.e., which week of her pregnancy). The uterine muscles of women who have given birth are more relaxed than those of primiparas and

thus more sensitive, and some of these women can feel fetal motion as early as in the fourteenth week. Usually these experiences occur at about the middle of a pregnancy. A woman pregnant for the first time typically feels fetal movements at about the eighteenth to twentieth week, whereas a woman who has already given birth at least two times will typically feel movements around the fifteenth to seventeenth week.

17. Iris Marion Young argues that the experience of pregnancy helps to problematize and question the distinction between *own* and *Other* (1990, 161–163). Her argument is based on equivocation of the term *mine*, and it turns out invalid when the different senses of "mineness" are distinguished. Young claims that the pregnant mother experiences the movements of the fetus as "wholly hers." She bases this idea on the experiential fact that these movements happen within the mother's body and thus only the mother "has access to them" (Young 1990, 163). This neglects the sense of mineness or ipseity, in which these movements belong to the infant, and not to anybody else, including the mother: while the fetus moves, only it, and nobody else, undergoes the kinesthetic and touch sensations that originally constitute the movements. If we deny the fetus such sensations, then we compromise the sense in which we call it "living." Young's account is based on this sense of living: the movements of the fetus can be distinguished from those of inanimate entities, such as "bubbles" and "gurgles," only in that they are lived through and sensed by the fetus (and not just the mother) (cf. Young 1990, 162–163).

    A different line of critique is presented by Caroline Lundquist who in her article "Being Torn: Toward a Phenomenology of Unwanted Pregnancy" (2008) argues that even if Young emphasizes the uncontrollable aspects of pregnancy by introducing Kristeva's idea of a "split subject," her account privileges planned pregnancies and neglects two types of unwanted gravidities: forced and "rejected" pregnancies (by rape) and "denied" pregnancies (in psychotic and in nonpsychotic conditions).

18. In certain respects, the flesh of the mother's belly functions in a similar way as clothing that usually mediates the touching of two separate subjects: we can touch other persons through clothing and identify their postures and movements. The difference, of course, is that in the case of fetal touching, the medium is the sensing flesh of the mother and not any inanimate entity. I believe that this phenomenon has interesting implications for our interpretation of Merleau-Ponty's discourse of *flesh* as the element of all our worldly relations (Merleau-Ponty 1964b, 1968) and its background in Aristotle's remarks on *flesh* as a mediating element, comparable to air and water (Aristotle 1984).

19. As pointed out in the note above, women who have experienced several pregnancies are usually able to identify the movements of their fetuses earlier or to describe them more distinctly than primiparas.

20. Pregnant women may also attach verbal responses to their gestural and postural adjustments; they "may respond to fetal movements by talking, offering

reassurance, affection or reprimands for moving too quickly or forcefully" (Denmark and Paludi 1993, 447).

21. Empirical studies show that emotionally women react to the new life that develops within their bodies in several different ways. Many women welcome the new life that they are able to perceive, but many women are also emotionally indifferent. When the pregnancy is unwanted or forced, women may apprehend the fetus as a parasite or as a hostile intruder, or even as a monstrous alien (Lundquist 2008, 140–143). All these emotional reactions depend on the experience of a *living*, sensing, and moving being.

22. This insight counters the traditional idea of birth as a temporal *null point* of human existence—an idea that still dominates our philosophical discussions of existence and coexistence (e.g., Ricouer 1966, 433; Leder 1990, 59–60; Schüss 1997; 2000; cf. Merleau-Ponty 1993, 399; and Merleau-Ponty 1995, 347). For a discussion of the relevance of Husserl's ethics to motherhood and parenting, see Donohoe 2010.

23. Cf. Schüss 1997 and 2000; Oksala 2003.

24. It is remarkable that even theorists who focus their studies on the vital functions and operations of our lived bodies fail to study the phenomena of inner spatiality and sensory-motor intersubjectivity that characterize the experience of pregnancy. The discourse of birth and generation is still dominated by imaginary accounts of one's own birth and entry into the visual world (e.g., Ricoeur 1966, 433; and Leder 1990, 67, 89–90).

25. I will not discuss here Husserl's descriptions of embryos as proto-children [*Urkinder*]. His discussion is complicated and intimately tied with his theory of temporalization (e.g., Husserl 1973, 171–184).

26. The cultural interpretations of menstruation involve such conceptualizations, but the bodily experience of a menstrual cramp differs from the bodily experience of being struck by an external force and shares features with experiences of tic or tremor.

27. All cultural meanings, negative and positive, attached to menstrual blood build on this primary bodily meaning (cf. Beauvoir 1993, 249–253; Beauvoir 1987, 180–182).

28. The German philosopher Ute Gahlings studies menstrual bleeding in comparison to the bleeding of wounds and describes the difference as follows: "Whereas bleeding can be caused at any time in different parts of the skin, for example, by cutting, woman's bleeding, as it appears in menstruation and in the breaking of the hymen, cannot be caused by such strokes on the surface of the body or even on the genitals. It necessarily originates from the inner parts of the body. The blood appears on the genitals, but the *why*, the *where* and the *when* [of its origin] cannot be determined [by perception] and it does enter the realm of the visual, it remains hidden, even if different body parts can suffer sensations from mild ones to very strong ones. Blood streams, oozes, exudes, and drips from the genitals and makes them moist. Its streaming or dripping

does not proceed constantly or evenly, and also its constitution differs. The bleeding takes varying time spans and the blood does not form any scabs on the surface of the body; the streaming decreases and ends according to its own order. Menstrual blood can be flowing up to viscous, some times [*sic*] clumpy, but it never thickens or hardens at the point of exit from the body" (Gahlings 2006, 212).27 For a phenomenological descriptions of introception and somastosensory givenness, see Leder 1990, cf. Adam 1998, and Cameron 2002. Organ transplant operations (interior organs, e.g., heart and liver, limbs, hand, and face) have helped to thematize unnoticed aspects of lived embodiment. See, Varela 2001; Slatman 2009; and Slatman and Widdershoven 2009.

29. Leder argues that *introception* differs from *extroception* (and *proprioception*) in constituting spatially and temporally fragmented wholes, or wholes with "gaps" and "breaks." In consequence, he characterizes the givenness of the processes of digestion, respiration, pulsation, and circulation by the metaphors of silence and reticence: "By large the greatest part of my vegetative processes lies submerged in impenetrable silence" (Leder 1990, 42). The problem with this description is that it presupposes, but does not explicate, the sense in which the "missing elements" are given to the person whose lived body is at question: Are they originally experienced by this person, are they given to him by the analogy of other lived bodies (human or animal), or are they constituted in imagination (and/or recollection) (cf. the phenomenon of the phantom limb)? In any case, these sensations are of such kind that they do not constitute an inner organ of reception and movement (vs. the tongue).
30. Since the feminine functions proceed in the same, or similar, periodic and cyclic rhythms as the movements of the celestial bodies, they are traditionally associated with astronomic, extratelluric or extramundane, regularities (cf. Beauvoir 1993, 253; Beauvoir 1987, 181).
31. Renaissance physicians as well as laymen still believed that lactated milk is fundamentally the same substance as menstrual blood, only transformed into a colorless or whitened state by the thermoregulation of the human body. This belief was suggested by traditional wisdom and by clinical practice, but empirical observation seemed to confirm it also, since the emanation of menstrual blood and breast milk correlate negatively in time and positively in quantity. More generally, all physiological and mental states of men and women were explained on the basis of the idea of interconvertible or fungible fluids: blood, milk, sperm, vaginal mucus (e.g., "whites" or "menstrua alba"), sweat, water (tears), and so forth (Laquer 1990, 35–43, 103–108). This was the normal-scientific theory since Hippocratic times, and it prevailed over contrary observations and evidences (Laquer 1990, 104). The idea of interconvertable fluids also implied the possibility that men produce breast milk, and such conditions were reported as facts by Renaissance physicians (Laquer 1990, 106).
32. Leder (1990, 89–92) points out that feminine functions are not experienced as signs of pathological developments, but he fails to think the possibility that

our lived bodies are governed by several *different* norms. It seems to me that this neglect is due to a conceptual solution: Leder's discourse is dominated by the Heideggerian paradigm of broken tools that suggests a picture of unitary norms (1990, from 84 onward).

33. For possible objections against the intersubjective interpretation of the phenomenon of pregnancy and replies to these objections, see Heinämaa 2012.
34. Beauvoir's sources include the conflictual analyses of Hegel and Sartre as well as Heidegger's distinction between *Dasein* (*réalité humaine*) and *das Man*, but she is also strongly influenced by Husserl's (and Merleau-Ponty's) egological approach as well as Kierkegaard's and Levinas's Cartesian reflections, which emphasize the role of dual relationships, couples and pairs, in human existence (cf. Heinämaa 2003b, 1–20). She also develops her insight of the dynamics of couples versus larger communities in her major novels *She Came to Stay* and *The Mandarins* (Merleau-Ponty 1964b, 113–114, n. 1; Merleau-Ponty 1986, 81–82, n. 14).

WORKS CITED

Aristotle. 1984. *On the Soul.* Trans. W. S. Hett. Cambridge: Harvard University Press.

Beauvoir, Simone de. 1947. *Pour une morale de l'ambiguïté.* Paris: Gallimard.

———. 1970. *La vieillesse*, 2 vols. Paris: Gallimard.

———. 1981a. *La cérémonie des adieux, suivi de Entretiens avec Jean-Paul Sartre août-septembre 1974.* Paris: Gallimard.

———. 1981b. *Force of Circumstance.* Trans. Richard Howard. Harmondsworth, UK: Penguin.

———. 1984. *Adieux: A Farewell to Sartre.* Trans. Patrick O'Brian. New York: Pantheon Books.

———. 1987. *The Second Sex.* Trans. and ed. H. M. Parshley. Harmondsworth, UK: Penguin.

———. 1988. *Old Age.* Trans. Patrick O'Brian. London: Penguin Books.

———. 1993. *Le deuxième sexe I: les faits et les mythes.* Paris: Gallimard, 1993. *The Second Sex.* Trans. and ed. H. M. Parshley. Harmondsworth, UK: Penguin, 1987.

———. 1991. *Le deuxième sexe II: l'expérience vécue.* Paris: Gallimard. *The Second Sex.* Trans. and ed. H. M. Parshley. Harmondsworth, UK: Penguin, 1987.

———. 1997. *La force des choses I.* Paris: Gallimard.

———. 1994. *The Ethics of Ambiguity.* Trans. Bernard Frechtman. New York: Carol Publishing Group Editions.

Blackstone, William. 1979. *Commentaries on the Laws of England.* Chicago: University of Chicago Press.

DeCasper, Anthony and William Fifter. 1980. Of Human Bonding: Newborns Prefer Their Mother's Voices. *Science* 208(4448):1174–1176.

DeCasper, Anthony, J.-P. Lecanuet, M.-C. Busnel, C. Deferre-Garnier, and R. Maugeais. 1986. Prenatal Maternal Speech Influences Newborn's Perception of Speech Sounds. *Infant Behavior and Development* 9:133–150.

DeCasper, Anthony and M.-J. Spence. 1994. Fetal Reactions to Recurrent Maternal Speech. *Infant Behavior and Development* 17:159–164.

Denmark, Florence L. and Michele A. Paludi, M. 1993. *Psychology of Women*. Westport, CT: Greenwood Press.

Donohoe, Janet. 2010: The Vocation of Motherhood: Husserl and Feminist Ethics. *Continental Philosophy Review, Special Issue: Feminist Phenomenology.* Ed. Sara Heinämaa and Lanei Rodemeyer, 43:127–140.

Drummond, John. 2006. The Respect as a Moral Emotion. *Husserl Studies* 22(1):1–27.

Engel, Pascal. 2008. Psychology and Metaphysics from Maine de Biran to Bergson. In *Psychology and Philosophy: Inquiries into the Soul from Late Scholasticism to Contemporary Thought,* 235–246. Ed. Sara Heinämaa and Martina Reuter. Dordrecht, The Netherlands: Springer.

Easlea, Brian. 1980. *Witch Hunting, Magic and the New Philosophy: An Introduction to Debates of the Scientific Revolution, 1450–1750.* New York: Harvester Wheatsheaf.

Gahlings, Ute. 2006. *Phänomenologie der weiblichen Leiberfahrung*. München: Verlag Karl Alber.

Heinämaa, Sara. 1996. *Ele, tyyli ja sukupuoli: Beauvoirin ja Merleau-Pontyn ruumiinfenomenologia ja sen merkitys sukupuolikysymykselle.* Helsinki: Gaudeamus.

———. 2003a. The Phenomenological Starting Points of Beauvoir's *Le deuxième sexe*: The Body as an Instrument and the Body as an Expression. In *Cambridge Companion to Beauvoir,* 66–86. Ed. Claudia Card. Cambridge, UK: Cambridge University Press.

———. 2003b. *Toward a Phenomenology of Sexual Difference: Husserl, Merleau-Ponty, Beauvoir.* Lanham, Boulder, New York, Oxford: Rowman & Littlefield.

———. 2007. Selfhood, Consciousness, and Embodiment: A Husserlian Approach. In *Consciousness: From Perception to Reflection in the History of Philosophy,* 311–328. Ed. Sara Heinämaa, Pauliina Remes, and Vili Lähteenmäki. Dordrecht, The Netherlands: Springer.

———. 2010. Phenomenologies of Mortality and Generativity. In *Birth, Death and Femininity: Philosophies of Embodiment.* Ed. Robin M. Schott, Bloomington: Indiana University Press.

———. 2012. The Body." In *Companion to Phenomenology.* Ed. Sebastian Luft and Sören Øvergaard. London: Routledge.

———. 2012. Gender and Sexual Difference. *Handbook in Contemporary Phenomenology.* Ed. Dan Zahavi. Oxford University Press.

Heidegger, Martin. 1992. *Being and Time.* Trans. John Macquarrie and Edward Robinson. Oxford: Blackwell.

———. 1993. *Sein und Zeit.* Tübingen: Max Niemeyer.

Hoffman, Piotr. 2006. The Body. In *A Companion to Phenomenology and Existentialism*, 253–262. Ed. Hubert Dreyfus and Mark Wrathall. Malden, Oxford, Victoria: Blackwell.

Husserl, Edmund. 1950. *Ideen zu einer reinen Phänomenologie und phänomenologischen Philosophie, Erstes Buch: Allgemeine Einführung in die reine Phänomenologie, Husserliana, Band III*. Ed. Walter Biemel. Haag, The Netherlands: Martinus Nijhoff.

———. 1952. *Ideen zu einer reinen Phänomenologie und phänomenologischen Philosophie, Zweites Buch: Phänomenologische Untersuchungen zun Konstitution, Husserliana, Band IV*. Ed. Marly Bimel. Haag, The Netherlands: Martinus Nijhoff.

———. 1962a. *Ideas: General Introduction to Pure Phenomenology*. Trans. W. R. Boyce Gibson. New York, London: Collier.

———. 1962b. *Die Krisis der europäischen Wissenschaften und die transzendentale Phänomenologie: Eine Einleitung in die phänomenologische Philosophie, Husserliana, Band VI*. Ed. Walter Biemel. Haag, The Netherlands: Martinus Nijhoff.

———. 1973. *Zur Phänomenologie der Intersubjektivität: Texte aus dem Nachlass, Dritter Teil: 1929–1935, Husserliana, Band XV*. Ed. Iso Kern. Haag, The Netherlands: Martinus Nijhoff.

———. 1988. *The Crisis of European Sciences and Transcendental Phenomenology: An Introduction to Phenomenological Philosophy*. Ed. W. Biemel. Trans. D. Carr. Evanston, IL: Northwestern University.

———. 1993. *Ideas Pertaining to a Pure Phenomenology and to a Phenomenological Philosophy, Second Book: Studies in the Phenomenological Constitution*. Ed. M. Biemel. Trans. R. Rojcewicz and A. Schuwer. Dordrecht, The Netherlands: Kluwer Academic Publishers.

Irigaray, Luce. 1984. L'invisible de la chair: Lecture de Merleau-Ponty: *Le visible et l'invisible*, 'L'entrelacs—le chiasme.' In Éthique la différence sexuelle. Paris: Minuit.

James, Susan 2003: Complicity and Slavery in *The Second Sex, Cambridge Companion to Simone de Beauvoir*, 149–167. Cambridge, UK: Cambridge University Press.

Kristeva, Julia. 1977. Motherhood according to Giovanni Bellini. In *Desire in Language: A Semiotic Approach to Literature and Art*. Ed. Leon S. Roudiez; trans. Thomas Gora, Alice Jardine, and Leon S. Roudiez. New York: Columbia University Press.

———. 1979: Le temps des femmes, *34/44: Cahiers de recherche en sciences des textes et documents*, 5:5–19. [1981. In Woman's Time. Trans. Alice Jardine and Harry Blake. *Signs* 7(1):13–35.]

———. 1983. Stabat Mater. In *Histoires d'amour*, 223–247. Paris: Denöel.

———. 1995. Stabat Mater. In *The Kristeva Reader*, 160–186. Ed. Toril Moi; trans. Leon S. Roudiez.

Labouvie, Eva. 1998. *Andere Umstände: Eine Kulturgeschichte der Geburt.* Köln, Weimar, Germany; Wien, Vienna: Böhlau Verlag.

Lacquer, Thomas. 1990. *Making Sex: Body and Gender from the Greeks to Freud.* Cambridge: Harvard University Press.

Langer, Monika 1998: Sartre and Merleau-Ponty: A Reappraisal. In *The Debate between Sartre and Merleau-Ponty.* Ed. Jon Stewart, Evanston. IL: Northwestern University Press.

Levesque-Lopman, Louise. 1983. Decision and Experience: A Phenomenological Analysis of Pregnancy and Childbirth. *Human Studies* 6:247–277.

Lévinas, Emmanuel. 1963: *Théorie de l'intuition dans la phénoménologie de Husserl.* Paris: Vrin.

———. 1987. *Time and Other.* Trans. R. A. Cohen. Pittsburgh: Duquesne University Press.

———. 1995. *The Theory of Intuition in Husserl's Phenomenology.* Trans. André Orianne. Evanston, IL: Northwestern University Press.

———. 1994: *Le temps et l'autre.* Paris: Quadrige/PUF.

Lundquist, Caroline. 2008. Being Torn: Toward a Phenomenology of Unwanted Pregnancy. *Hypatia* 23:136–155.

Mandik, Peter. 2007. The Neurophilosophy of Consciousness. In *The Blackwell Companion to Consciousness,* 418–432. Ed. Max Velman and Susan Schneider. Oxford: Basil Blackwell.

Martin, Emily. 1987. *The Woman in the Body: A Cultural Analysis of Reproduction.* Milton Keynes, UK: Open University Press.

Merchant, Carolyn. 1989. *The Death of Nature: Women, Ecology and the Scientific Revolution.* New York: Harper.

Merleau-Ponty, Maurice. 1964a. Eye and Mind. In *The Primacy of Perception and Other Essays on Phenomenological Psychology, the Philosophy of Art, History and Politics,* 159–190. Ed. James M. Edie. Evanston, IL: Northwestern University Press.

———. 1964b. *Le visible et l'invisible.* Paris: Gallimard.

———. 1968. *The Visible and the Invisible.* Trans. Alphonso Lingis. Evanston, IL: Northwestern University Press.

———. 1993. *Phénoménologie de la perception.* Paris: Gallimard.

———. 1995. *Phenomenology of Perception.* Trans. Collin Smith. New York: Routledge & Kegan Paul.

———. 1997. *L'union de l'*âme *et du corps* (lectures at École Normale Supérieure in 1947–1948) Collected and ed. Jean Deprun. Paris: Vrin.

———. 2001. *The Incarnate Subject: Malebranche, Brian, and Bergson on the Union Body and Mind.* Trans. Paul B. Milan; ed. Andrew G. Bjelland Jr. and Patrick Burke. New York: Humanity Books.

———. 2003. *L'Œil et l'espri.* Paris: Gallimard.

Moon, C., R. P. Cooper, and W. P. Fufer. 1993. Two-Day-Olds Prefer Their Native Language. *Infant Behavior and Development* 16:495–500.

Oksala, Johanna. 2003. The Birth of Man. In *Metaphysics, Facticity, Interpretation: Phenomenology in the Nordic Countries*. Dordrecht, Netherlands; Boston; and London: Kluwer.
Ricoeur, Paul. 1966: *Freedom and Nature: The Voluntary and Involuntary*. Trans. Erazim Kohák. Evanston, IL: Northwestern University Press.
Sartre, Jean-Paul. 1993. *Being and Nothingness: A Phenomenological Essay on Ontology*. Trans. Hazel E. Barnes, New York: Washington Square Press.
———. 1998. *L'être et le néant: essai d'ontologie phénoménologique*. Paris: Gallimard.
Slatman, Jenny. 2009. A Strange Hand and Recognition of Another. *Phenomenology and Cognitive Sciences* 8:321–342.
Slatman, Jenny and Widdershoven, Guy. 2009. Being Whole After Amputation. *The American Journal of Bioethics* 9:48–49.
Schüss, Christina. 1997. The Birth of Difference. *Human Studies* 20:243–253.
———. 2000. Empirical and Transcendental Subjectivity: An Enigmatic Relation. In *The Empirical and the Transcendental: A Fusion of Horizons*. Ed. B. Cupta. New York: Rowman & Littlefield.
Stern, Daniel. 1985. *The Interpersonal World of the Infant: A View from Psychoanalysis and Developmental Psychology*. New York: Basic Books.
Varela, Francisco. 2001. Intimate Distances: Fragments for a Phenomenology of Organ Transplantation. *Journal of Consciousness Studies* 8:259–271.
Young, Iris Marion. 1990. *Throwing Like a Girl and Other Essays in Feminist Philosophy and Social Theory*. Bloomington: Indiana University Press.
Zahavi, Dan. 2004. The Embodied Self-Awareness of the Infant: A Challenge to the Theory-Theory of Mind? In *The Structure and Development of Self-Awareness: Interdisciplinary Perspectives*. Ed. Dan Zahavi, Thor Grünbaum, and Josef Parnas. Amsterdam and Philadelphia: John Benhamins.

Beauvoir and Bergson

A Question of Influence

MARGARET A. SIMONS

Simone de Beauvoir's early enthusiasm for the philosophy of Henri Bergson (1859–1941)—denied in her 1958 autobiography, *Memoirs of a Dutiful Daughter*—is a surprising discovery in her 1927 handwritten student diary, as I reported in 1999 and explored at more length in 2003 (Simons 1999; Simons 2003). Discovered by Sylvie Le Bon de Beauvoir after Beauvoir's death in 1986, and now housed in the Bibliothèque nationale, Beauvoir's student diary first appeared in print in the 2006 volume, *Diary of a Philosophy Student: 1926–27*, followed in 2008 by the French publication, *Cahiers de jeunesse: 1926–1930*. Since my 1999 analysis of the 1927 diary, the publication of the 1926 diary and other posthumously discovered texts has deepened and complicated the evidence of Bergson's influence.[1] In this chapter, I propose to take up and expand on my earlier analyses in the light of this new evidence, arguing that Beauvoir's methodological turn to the description of immediate experience, especially her method of writing philosophy in literature and her lifelong interest in describing the subjective experience of time, drew on Bergson's philosophy before her first encounter with Husserl's phenomenology, which may have come as early as 1927; that her concept of bad faith and interest in exposing distortions in perception and thinking, as in the chapters in *The Second Sex* on myths about women, drew on Bergson's philosophy long before she had read Marx; and that her earliest formulation of the problem of the Other drew on Bergson's distinction between the "social self and the deep self," two years before she met Jean-Paul Sartre and two decades before she first read Hegel's *Phenomenology*.

BERGSON IN BEAUVOIR'S STUDENT WRITINGS

Beauvoir's denial in *Memoirs* of her interest in Bergson, as part of a general denial of her interest in philosophy in 1926—the year she began studying not literature, but philosophy at the Sorbonne—is well known: "I toyed with the idea of writing; I preferred literature to philosophy, and I wouldn't have been at all pleased if someone had prophesized that I would become a kind of female Bergson; I didn't want to speak with that abstract voice which, whenever I heard it, failed to move me." "Literature took the place in my life that had once been occupied by religion," she writes. "The books I liked became a Bible . . . I copied out long passages from them" (Beauvoir 1958, 288, 259; Beauvoir 1974, 208,187).[2] Contradicting this autobiographical claim of the primacy of literature is the diary itself, which begins with an entry dated August 6, 1926, and whose first lengthy quotations, on the verso pages facing the entries for August 12 and 13, 1926, are not from literature but philosophy: Bergson's 1889 essay, *Time and Free Will: An Essay on the Immediate Data of Consciousness* (Beauvoir 2006, 58–61).

Of Beauvoir's eleven quotations from *Time and Free Will*, three (I, V, and VI) are discussed in both the student diary and *Memoirs*. Quotation I begins with Bergson's account of the threat posed by language and social convention to individual consciousness: "The word with well-defined outlines, the brutal word, which stores up the stable, common, and consequently impersonal element in the impressions of humanity, suppresses, or at least masks the delicate and fugitive impressions of our individual consciousness." This quotation also includes Bergson's celebration of "a bold novelist" who "tearing aside the cleverly woven web of our conventional self, shows us under this appearance of logic a fundamental absurdity, under this juxtaposition of simple states an infinite permeation of a thousand different impressions that have already ceased to be the instant they are named" (Beauvoir 2006, 58–59).

In quotation V, the second of the quotations discussed in both the diary and *Memoirs*, Bergson argues that the formation of the "conventional self" by language limits the freedom of our "living and concrete self": "Within the fundamental self is formed a parasitic self that continually encroaches upon the other. Many live like this, and die without having known true freedom. . . . [O]ur living and concrete self thus gets covered over with an outer crust of clean-cut psychological states, which are clearly delineated, separated from one another and consequently fixed." Finally, in quotation VI, Bergson relates his concepts of freedom and the two aspects of the self to his broader metaphysical view of reality as a temporal process accessible to intuition, rather than a spatial entity accessible to the intellect:

> [T]here are two different "selves," one of which is, as it were, the external projection of the other, its spatial and, so to speak, social representation. We reach the former by deep reflection, which leads us to grasp our inner states as living beings, constantly in the process of forming. . . .But the moments at which we again thus grasp ourselves are rare, and that is why we are rarely free. Most of the time we live outside ourselves, hardly perceiving anything of ourselves but our own colorless ghost, a shadow that pure duration projects into homogeneous space. Hence our existence unfolds in space rather than in time; we live for the external world rather than for ourselves; we speak rather than think; we 'are acted' rather than

act. To act freely is to recover possession of self, and to get back into pure duration. (Beauvoir 2006, 60)

Beauvoir's first discussion of Bergson's philosophy is in the diary entry dated August 16, 1926, where her enthusiasm for *Time and Free Will* is obvious. She describes it as a "great intellectual rapture" and lauds his methodological "appeal to intuition" in solving philosophical problems: "Whereas in reading other philosophers I have the impression of witnessing more or less logical constructions, here finally it is palpable reality that I touch, and I find life anew. . . . Simply an appeal to intuition, some dissociations of ideas by going more deeply into them, in short the method that I spontaneously applied when I wanted to know myself and the thorniest problems fade. So many things in the 180 pages of *Données immédiates de la conscience* by Bergson." Beauvoir writes of her "pleasure" in discovering themes of Bergson's philosophy in modern novelists: "There is a joyous astonishment in noting that these mysteries of the soul suggested by the artist have more than a subjective existence, and reciprocally that the abstract formulas of philosophy begin to live when they are clarified by quotes that resituate them in the current of individual consciousness" (Beauvoir 2006, 66).

But, anticipating her own decision to go further and write philosophy in literary form, Beauvoir expresses "a little bit of disappointment all the same" to see the "purely individual" discoveries of the novelists "lose their adventurous character" when "explained" in Bergson's "intellectual" essay. She critically contrasts Bergson's passage about the "brutal word" quoted above with a passage from Barrès ("Why words, this brutal precision that mistreats our complexity?"): "[Bergson] is first too general, scientific and not 'written for me'; and then it explains the observed fact whereas Barrès makes an observation in an elegant formula. It causes the intelligence to intervene in a region of the self that likes to remain obscure and unconscious. In summary, it is philosophy, Barrès is life." But Beauvoir concludes her discussion of *Time and Free Will* in her diary with enthusiastic admiration for his philosophy: "What really thrilled me was the analysis of the two aspects of the self; it is truly tremendous. This duality so often observed between the being that I am within myself and the being seen from outside, not deformed, seen exactly by me, having become an observer, between the true being considered from the exterior or the interior. . . . It would be fascinating to study the psychology of the great novelists in the light of Bergson. Nobody has better than he . . . defined the art of the modern novelist" (Beauvoir 2006, 66–67).

In her account of this same period in *Memoirs*, Beauvoir quotes Barrès on "the tyranny of language" and writes of "taking refuge in 'my deep self'" in the struggle against social convention—all without any mention of Bergson (Beauvoir 1974, 192–196; Beauvoir 1958, 266–268). Some pages later in *Memoirs*, Beauvoir does refer to her enthusiastic reading of Bergson's analysis of the two aspects of the self: "In Bergson's theories about 'the social self and the deep self' I enthusiastically recognized my own experience. But the impersonal voices of the philosophers didn't bring me the same consolation as those of my favorite authors" (Beauvoir 1974, 207; Beauvoir 1958, 287). Two paragraphs later comes the famous declaration, quoted above, that the "abstract voice" of Bergson's philosophy, "whenever I heard it, failed to move me." Gone are Beauvoir's description of *Time and Free Will* as a "great intellectual rapture" and her "joyous astonishment" at discovering the connection of Bergson's philosophy to modern literature and noting that the "mysteries of the soul suggested by the artist have more than a subjective existence."

Beauvoir's autobiographical erasure of her early enthusiasm for Bergson's philosophy is part of a wider autobiographical erasure of her work in philosophy, an erasure I have discussed in detail elsewhere (Simons 2010). Given this context, Beauvoir's brief account in *Memoirs* of her enthusiasm for Bergson's analysis of the two aspects of the self ("in Bergson's theories about 'the social self and the deep self' I enthusiastically recognized my own experience") takes on importance. It points to Bergson's possible influence on the "problem of the Other," the central theme of *She Came to Stay*, Beauvoir's metaphysical novel (written from 1937–41) about the collapse of solipsism in the subjective experience of oneself as an object of another consciousness.

Traditionally read as Beauvoir's illustration of Sartre's philosophy of "the Look" in his 1943 essay, *Being and Nothingness*, Beauvoir claimed in her autobiographical writings and interviews that her work on this problem came out of her own experience and not from Sartre. In her 1966 Japan lecture, "My Experience as a Writer," for example, Beauvoir recounts the novel's origination in her own "concrete psychological experience." When "a friend I was very fond of . . . was somewhat hostile to me . . . I discovered something that everyone knows," she writes, "the other's consciousness exists; . . . in his world I am an object with which he can more or less do as he likes" (2011b). The difficulty, of course, is that Beauvoir also denied being a philosopher and doing philosophy, which raises the question of how she could have originated the work on the problem of the Other. Jessica Benjamin posed exactly that question to Beauvoir in our 1979 interview, asking Beauvoir if she got the idea of the confrontation with another consciousness from Sartre, which Beauvoir heatedly denied: "It was I who thought about that! It was absolutely not Sartre! . . . This problem of the consciousness of the Other, this was my problem" (Simons and Benjamin 1999, 10).

Returning to the passage in *Memoirs* ("in Bergson's theories about 'the social self and the deep self' I enthusiastically recognized my own experience"), we see Beauvoir's claim about the problem of the Other arising from her own experience, a claim confirmed by the student diary, whose first entry, dated August 6, 1926, already shows Beauvoir grappling with the problem of the opposition of self and other. As the diary opens, Beauvoir is recounting a pilgrimage to Lourdes with an aunt. She recalls feeling "ashamed" when faced with the physical suffering of the invalids: "[O]nly a life that was a complete gift of oneself, a total self-abnegation, seemed possible to me." But then, anticipating her critique of self-abnegation in

The Second Sex, Beauvoir rejects it, describing the "absolute gift" as "moral suicide." She vows instead to achieve an "equilibrium" between the duty to self and the duty to others. In the August 12, 1926 diary entry, Beauvoir frames the problem in metaphysical terms, referring to one part of herself "made to be given away," and another "made to be kept and cultivated." These diary passages point to a difference in Beauvoir's and Bergson's concepts of relations with others. For Bergson, who sees social relations as a solely utilitarian concern, our sole responsibility is to the self and its freedom, while for Beauvoir our deepest emotions draw us to the other, which poses a different, more complicated ethical problem.

Beauvoir's first comments on Bergson's *Time and Free Will* appear in the diary several days later, in the entry dated August 16, 1926, with her enthusiasm for Bergson's "analysis of the two aspects of the self" reflecting a preexisting interest in a problem within her own experience. It's interesting to note her subjectivist reading of this passage from Bergson given her later account, in *She Came to Stay*, of the collapse of solipsism in the experience of oneself as an object of the other's gaze. As we've seen above, the passages from *Time and Free Will* quoted in her diary do not explain how the "crust" of "social self" is formed: "our living and concrete self thus gets covered over with an outer crust." But Bergson does provide an explanation in *Time and Free Will* in a passage that appears on the page following the passage selected by Beauvoir for quotation. His explanation refers to the roles of other consciousnesses in the formation of the "social self": "When our most trustworthy friends" advise us to take some important step, he writes, "the sentiments which they utter with so much insistence . . . "form a thick crust which will cover up our own sentiments" (Bergson 1928, 129; Bergson 1913b, 168–169).[3] Note as well Beauvoir's solipsistic reading of the passage she quotes in her diary. She describes a duality "between the being that I am within myself and the being seen from outside," seemingly referring to the experience of being seen by another consciousness. But Beauvoir denies this reading. She writes that the "being seen from outside" is "seen exactly by me, having become an observer." The other has no role in this solipsistic reading; one's own consciousness is the sole source of knowledge of the self.

Evidence of Beauvoir's interest in Bergson's philosophy is found throughout her diary from 1926–27, as I will discuss below, including an interest in Bergson's philosophical methodology that would be lifelong. But indirect evidence of Beauvoir's interest in his philosophy is evident in an even earlier manuscript—her 1924 student essay analyzing "*Introduction to the Study of Experimental Medicine*" (1865) by the nineteenth-century French physiologist and philosopher of science Claude Bernard, whose account of the experimental method influenced Bergson's account of a two-part philosophical method—beginning with the negative step of exposing distortions in thought and perception followed by the positive step of describing immediate experience, an interest shared by Beauvoir.[4] Her student essay admires Bernard's call for the rejection of every "philosophical and theological yoke" and his valuing of "the great experimental principle" of "philosophical doubt," which, according to Bernard, "leaves to the mind its freedom and initiative." Bernard, anticipating Bergson's methodological turn to immediate experience, argues that discoveries are engendered not by reason but by a "feeling for the complexity of natural phenomena" and calls for experimenters to "go down into the objective reality of things" (Beauvoir 2004b).[5]

Bergson's description of reality as a temporal process, a "perpetual becoming," can be seen as taking up Bernard's challenge (in Bergson's words) to develop a philosophy "capable of following concrete reality in all its sinuosities."[6] Bergson describes matter as characterized by "inertia," and mind by spontaneity, unforeseeability, and freedom. Once again drawing on Bernard, Bergson argues that distortions in perception arise when our utilitarian consciousness singles out features of interest from the mass of changing sense impressions: "Our needs are so many search lights which, directed upon the continuity of sensible qualities, single out in it distinct bodies" (Bergson 1911).[7] Consciousness is "tormented by an insatiable desire to make distinctions" and to perceive reality through symbols and words that distort our perceptions as it "arrests [their] mobility" (Bergson 1913b, 128–129, Bergson, 1928, 98). The effect is "to obscure some of its aspects, to diminish it by the greater part of itself" (Bergson 1911, 28). According to Bergson, the distortions of utilitarian consciousness cause problems for philosophers who mistakenly assume that words and symbols represent ontological distinctions rather than simply practical conveniences. "[I]t may be asked whether . . . by merely getting rid of the clumsy symbols round which [philosophers] are fighting, we might not bring the fight to an end" (Bergson 1913b, xx).

Beauvoir's 1927 diary points to the influence of Bernard and Bergson on her early formulation of the concept of "bad faith." Beauvoir admired Bernard's valuing of philosophical doubt and his criticism of "every philosophical and theological yoke" for "enslaving the mind." Bergson expands on this theme in *Time and Free Will* in his account of freedom as inhibited by self-deception: we tend to thrust "back into the darkest depths of our being" "feelings and ideas which are not unperceived, but rather which we do not want to consider" (Bergson 1913b, 169; Bergson 1928, 130). Beauvoir's valuing of doubt and lucidity in her diary entry dated April 30, 1927, points to the influence of Bernard and Bergson on her developing concept of "bad faith":

> Indeed, it is ridiculous to let myself be troubled again by the certainty of others. I cannot keep myself from envying them because it seems that in faith . . . there is something more complete than in doubt. . . . However I do indeed *know* that their God is not. . . . No, really; what I like more than anything is not ardent faith . . . but . . . intelligence and criticism . . . the beings who cannot let themselves be duped and who struggle to live in spite of their lucidity. (Beauvoir 2006, 241–242)

Beauvoir's student diary also reflects her early interest in the methodological turn to a description of immediate experience called for by both Bernard and

Bergson. Bernard's call for the scientist to "go down into the objective reality of things" is echoed in Bergson's *Matter and Memory*, where Bergson explains that exposing distortions is only the beginning: "To give up certain habits of thinking, and even of perceiving, is . . . but the negative part of the work to be done." The next step is "to seek experience at its source, or rather above that turn where, taking a bias in the direction of our utility, it becomes properly human experience" (Bergson 1911, 241). "This method . . . attributes a privileged value to immediate knowledge" (Bergson 1911, 245), which entails attending not to the intellect but to the feelings and impressions of our embodied engagement in the world, a method also meant to resolve or dissolve philosophical problems such as idealism and realism or freedom and determinism.

Beauvoir's interest in the description of immediate experience is evident in a diary entry dated May 6, 1927:

> This morning I experienced a strange minute whose memory has not yet died for me. I had just seen Barbier [a fellow philosophy student] again, who had so spontaneously come towards me. . . . And then . . . for an instant, I held a completely new life in my hands. . . . A new passion was blossoming in me. Splendid! I loved him. How can I put it? It was not speculation or reasoning, or dream or imagination. For an instant, it was. Still a bit even now, my life is no longer a traced path where, from the point that I have already reached, I can discover everything and have nothing more to do than to place one foot after another. It is an unmarked trail that my walking alone will create. . . . For an instant I was free, and I experienced [*vécu*] it. . . . This is how I see life: thousands of possibilities [*possibles*] in childhood fall by the wayside bit by bit, and so much so that on the last day there is no longer anything but *one reality*; you have lived *one life*. (Beauvoir 2006, 246–247)

An explicit reference to Bergson then follows: "But it is Bergson's *élan vital* that I am rediscovering here" (ibid.). This passage is interesting because of Beauvoir's use of Bergson's distinctive terminology in the references to the moment, memory, and the future pregnant with possibilities, as in quotation VIII from the August 1926 diary entry: "What makes hope such an intense pleasure is the fact that the future, which we dispose of to our liking, appears to us at the same time under a multitude of equally possible attractive forms. Even if the most desired of these is realized, it will be necessary to sacrifice the others, and we shall have lost a great deal. The idea of the future, pregnant with the infinite possibilities, is thus more fruitful than the future itself and this is why we find more charm in hope than in possession, in dreams than in reality" (Beauvoir 2006, 60–61).

But it is also interesting because of a very un-Bergsonian theme—the discovery of freedom through the experience of falling in love. While Bergson criticizes the influence of society and even friends as inhibiting individual freedom, Beauvoir saw her existence "for others," her social relationships as potentially supportive of the self—as in her 1944 essay *Pyrrhus and Cineas*, where responding to the appeal of the other opens a path out of solipsism. In the April 18, 1927, diary entry, Beauvoir describes herself as finding comfort and encouragement in the other's gaze: "I am lonely to the point of anxiety today. . . . To console myself, I must glance at this self with the multiple faces which my friends' eyes reflect." On May 20, 1927, Beauvoir writes: "even simple companionship is a very precious good! In it alone I can tear myself away from my own manner of thinking" (Beauvoir 2006, 228, 261). Thus the look of the other can be a solace, and not always a threat to the self.

Beauvoir's interest in Bergson's philosophy is also evident in the plans for her future work, as in the May 13, 1927 diary entry, in which she declares her intention to write philosophy in literary form: "Write 'essays on life' that would not be novelistic, but rather philosophical, by linking them vaguely with fiction. But let thought be the essential and let me seek to find the truth" (Beauvoir 2006, 258). An entry dated July 29, 1927 shows Beauvoir's clear determination to become a philosopher: "Oh! I see my life well now . . . a passionate, boundless research. No love will eclipse this. If I marry, my philosophy will have to be taken with me. . . . Marvelous intoxication of thought, solitude of the mind. I will dominate the world. Literature, works, undertakings—what are all these next to my austere resolution" (Beauvoir 2006, 296). "[T]he most profound part of my life is my thoughts," Beauvoir writes later in the same diary entry. "I was unaware that one could dream of death out of metaphysical despair, sacrifice everything for the desire to know, and live only to save oneself. I didn't know that every system is something ardent and tormented, effort of life, of being, drama in the full sense of the word, and does not engage only abstract intelligence. But I know it at present, and that I can no longer do anything else" (Beauvoir 2006, 297). These early references to doing philosophy are strikingly Bergsonian in the way in which they reject the conception of philosophy as engaging only the abstract intelligence.

BERGSON IN BEAUVOIR'S EARLY LITERATURE

Beauvoir's early novel, *When Things of the Spirit Come First*, written from 1935 to 1937 but not published until 1979, satirizes the intellectual passions of her youth, including Bergson's philosophy, as I discuss below, but the novel also provides evidence of her continuing interest in Bergson's philosophy, despite the erasure of this evidence in the account of *Spirit* in *Prime of Life*, the second volume of her autobiography. Beauvoir frames the discussion of *Spirit* in *Prime* with the lengthy passage, referred to above, disavowing any interest in philosophy. "Why was I not tempted to try my hand at philosophy?" she asks. "I did not consider myself a philosopher," she replies, explaining that she lacked "inventiveness." Besides, she writes, "the feminine condition" does not engender the "obstinacy" required for the "concerted delirium" of a philosophical system claiming for one's insights the "value of universal keys." This section of *Prime* immediately preceding the discussion of *Spirit* concludes: "I wanted to communicate that which was original in my experience. In order to succeed in that task, I knew that I had to orient myself towards literature" (Beauvoir 1960, 253–255; Beauvoir 1962, 265–266).[8] Despite Beauvoir's autobiographical disavowal of philosophy, a careful study of *Spirit* reveals its philosophical content.

In *Spirit* Beauvoir employs a Bergsonian methodology to address the philosophical problem of *bad faith*, apparently the earliest use of this important term in her work: "despite . . . my bad faith," remarks the character, Marguerite, in the concluding story of *Spirit*, "I had long . . . suspected the truth" (Beauvoir 1979, 246; Beauvoir 1982, 210).[9] In her preface to the 1979 French edition of *Spirit*, Beauvoir describes the novel as a work of "apprenticeship," where "many of the themes" of her later work first "took shape," thus "clarifying the genesis" of her work. Beauvoir also describes *Spirit* as a "satire," albeit a "timid" one, of her early intellectual passions. The fact that Bergson's philosophy is satirized along with Paul Claudel's morality of feminine self-sacrifice and André Breton's surrealism indirectly confirms Bergson's early importance for her (Beauvoir 1979, vii–viii). Beauvoir's preface reveals a Bergsonian account of her project in *Spirit*, as following Bergson's method of demonstrating the shortcomings of a philosophical position, in this case spiritual idealism, by exposing the distorted thoughts and bad faith of its proponents: "I was in revolt against the spiritual idealism [*spiritualisme*] that had oppressed me for so long and I wanted to express this disgust through the story of young women whom I knew and who had been its more or less consenting victims. I played a great deal on the bad faith that appeared to me—and still appears to me—as inseparable from it. Thus I was led to the difficult attempt to make the voices—and the silences—of lying heard" (Beauvoir 1979, vii).

Beauvoir uses the literary device of a private diary to expose the bad faith of her female protagonist in *Spirit*, Chantal, who tried "to give those who came into contact with her a brilliant image of her life and of herself" (Beauvoir 1982, 6). Echoing Bergson's critique of language as masking truth, Beauvoir, in her preface to the 1979 edition of *Spirit*, explains her method for portraying bad faith: "I used language to conceal the truth, as I did much later in *La femme rompue* (*The Woman Destroyed*). From that point of view Chantal's diary seems to me rather successful" (Beauvoir 1979, vii). Her interest in the problem of bad faith, Beauvoir explains in *Prime*, arose from her own experience: "If the bad habits I attributed to Chantal irked me so much, that was . . . because I had slipped into them myself . . . embellishing my life history with false items of information. . . . The novel that Françoise writes in *She Came to Stay* turns on a similar theme: it was a favorite preoccupation of mine" (Beauvoir 1962, 268; Beauvoir 1960, 257).

Beauvoir's critical distance from Bergson is apparent in *Spirit* in her satirical portrayal of Chantal as a Bergsonian, as in the following passage from Chantal's diary, echoing passages from Beauvoir's 1926 diary: "Today . . . I understood the truth of certain pages of Bergson that have long been close to my heart: dissecting our fleeting impressions, shutting them up in words, and turning them into thoughts very often means brutally destroying the impalpable shimmer that gives them all their value. Yes: what we must do is attune our consciousness to the changing flow of life" (Beauvoir 1979, 55; Beauvoir 1982, 55).[10] One aspect of Beauvoir's criticism of Bergson in *Spirit* is in her depiction of Chantal as unable to escape the self-deception and distortions in her thought through a turn to immediate experience alone, since that very experience is distorted by a tendency to romanticize it. A confrontation with other consciousnesses is necessary to break through Chantal's self-deception.

While Beauvoir's demonstration of the role of others in exposing distortions in thought is an implicit criticism of Bergson's epistemological subjectivism, the concluding story, described by Beauvoir as "a satire on my youth" mirroring her own religious education and "adolescent crisis," reveals Beauvoir's continued valuing of Bergson's method in the search for self. The story's young female protagonist, Marguerite, is forced to acknowledge her own bad faith when a young man, Denis, a surrealist whom she had made the romantic center of her life, opts instead for a marriage of convenience. Her response, as Beauvoir explains in the preface to the American edition, is a turn to immediate experience. "In the end her eyes are opened; she tosses mysteries, mirages and myths overboard and looks the world in the face" (Beauvoir 1982, 6). The world of immediate experience, freed from the categories imposed on it by Denis, appears to Marguerite in Bergsonian terms as "a vast and shapeless mass." "Suddenly, instead of symbolic scenery, I saw around me a host of objects that seemed to exist for themselves . . . I had no need of Denis to hear what they had to say to me." "They had burst their allegorical wrappings and now they showed themselves naked, living, and inexhaustible . . . and . . . there in the center of things, in the place Denis left empty, I had found myself." The story ends with a Bergsonian condemnation of "ready-made values": "all I have wished to do was to show how I was brought to try to look things straight in the face, without accepting oracles or ready-made values" (Beauvoir 1979, 247–249; Beauvoir 1982, 211–212). *Spirit* thus reflects Beauvoir's continued reliance on a Bergsonian turn to the description of lived experience for the recovery of a self lost in a relationship, while recognizing that such a turn may be unable to overcome tendencies of self-deception, as in the case of Chantal, whose distorted thought is exposed only through a relationship with others.

Beauvoir's implicit critique of Bergson's epistemological subjectivism in *Spirit* is carried further in her metaphysical novel, *She Came to Stay*, written in 1937–41, where she uses Bergson's subjectivist methodology to demonstrate the existence of other consciousnesses able to see the self as the self cannot—thus demonstrating the limits of subjectivism itself. Beauvoir's work on the philosophical problem of solipsism in *She Came to Stay* is erased in *Prime*, where she frames her account of writing SCTS with references to "literature" (Beauvoir 1962, 360): "I wanted to write a novel, that's all" (Beauvoir 1962, 393). But Beauvoir's novel is self-consciously philosophical, with a character describing the problem of the existence of other consciousnesses as "a problem that philosophers break their heads over" (Beauvoir 1954, 301).[11] The novel's innovative depiction of the collapse of metaphysical and epistemological solipsism in the objectifying experience of the other's gaze defines a key element in Beauvoir's prewar philosophy, as does the ethical solipsism of the novel's conclusion.

In *She Came to Stay*, Beauvoir—taking up a Bergsonian theme—traces the philosophical odyssey of a woman writer, Françoise, away from the distortions of utilitarian consciousness. In the opening pages of *She Came to Stay*, which is set in pre–World War II France, Françoise is hard at work in a theater office late at night revising a play. Her utilitarian consciousness is evident in Françoise's exaggerated awareness of her orientation in space and her tendency to define herself by her work and the objects surrounding her: "I wonder what he thinks of me . . . this office, the theater, my room, books, papers, work" (Beauvoir 1943, 15; Beauvoir 1954, 17). Habitually denying her feelings and forcing herself to work, Françoise denies her physical exhaustion and her sexual desire for the young man, Gerbert, working beside her.

Françoise's view of her inner life has been defined and solidified in response to social relations and language much as Bergson describes. To protect her image of herself as happy and free in her relationship with her partner, Pierre, the play's director, Françoise, refuses to acknowledge any feelings that threaten it, including her sadness at the denial of the desired intimacy with Gerbert: "In her heart rose a sadness as bitter and glowing as the dawn. And yet she had no regrets; she had not even a right to that melancholy which was beginning to numb her drowsy body" (Beauvoir 1943, 18; Beauvoir 1954, 21). Her bad faith is evident in Françoise first noticing and then denying a disturbing reality. Françoise's valuing of social relations is also apparent in her willingness to accept Pierre's characterizations of her own experience: "nothing that happened was completely real until she had told Pierre about it. . . . [S]he no longer knew solitude, but she had rid herself of that swarming confusion. Every moment of her life that she entrusted to [Pierre] was given back to her clear, polished, completed, and they became moments of their shared life." Françoise denies her separate consciousness and sees herself as merged with Pierre: "We are simply one" (Beauvoir 1943, 26; Beauvoir 1954, 30), and feels anguish at their separation: "separation was agony" (Beauvoir 1954, 108).

Beauvoir describes Françoise's reluctance to exercise her will and her freedom in Bergsonian terms: "If she were to take full responsibility for herself, she would first have to want to; but she didn't want to. . . . An act that was self-initiated and had no connection with [Pierre], was beyond her imagination. This, however, did not worry her; she would never find it necessary to call upon her own resources against Pierre" (Beauvoir 1954, 113). Françoise can experience the world of fleeting impressions at odds with her utilitarian consciousness: "There was nothing but this passing sound, the sky, the hesitant foliage of the trees . . . ; there was no Françoise any longer." But this only highlights her utilitarian consciousness: "She jumped to her feet. It was strange to become someone again, . . . a woman who must hurry because pressing work awaited her, and the moment was only one like so many others in her life" (Beauvoir 1954, 12–13). With the return of a substantive self,

Françoise denies the unique characteristics of this moment, dismissing it as interchangeable with other instants, thus reflecting, in Bergsonian terms, a utilitarian consciousness of time as interchangeable units in "a duration whose moments resemble one another" (Bergson 1913b, 221).

Françoise retreats to subjective idealism in order to suppress the regret that accompanies her dutifulness: "'It used to break my heart to think that I'd never know anything but one poor little corner of the world. . . . But now it doesn't bother me . . . because I feel that things which do not exist for me, simply do not exist at all. . . . [They have] no reality. [They are] nothing but hearsay'" (Beauvoir 1954, 14–16; Beauvoir 1943, 15–17). In a later scene at a night club, where she alone is not dancing, Françoise denies her embodiment, imagining herself to be a disembodied, sovereign subject: "I am there, impersonal and free. I contemplate at once all of these lives, all of these faces. If I were to turn away from them, they would disintegrate at once into a deserted landscape" (Beauvoir 1954, 29).

Françoise cannot help but notice the existence of the external world, since she experiences reality as overflowing her perception of it. But she denies it, wanting to regard reality as wholly encompassed by her perception. Walking through the empty theater, in the novel's opening scene, Françoise senses her power to "revive things from their inanimateness." But she also notes the limitations of her point of view: "She would have to be elsewhere as well; . . . she would have to be everywhere at the same time" (Beauvoir 1954, 12). In *Matter and Memory* Bergson argues that "[O]ur actual perception [is] always only a content in relation to a vaster, even an unlimited, experience which contains it" (Bergson 1911, 186). "In our perception we grasp a *state* of our consciousness and a *reality* independent of ourselves—this mixed character of our immediate perception . . . is the principal theoretical reason we have for believing in an external world which does not coincide absolutely with our perception" (Bergson 1911, 270).

Beauvoir portrays Françoise as denying her experience of the existence of other consciousnesses separate from her own in bad faith. Interestingly, these encounters with the other occur within relations of intimacy and dependency. In the novel's first scene, for example, Françoise discovers herself as an object in the eyes of Gerbert, who comments on her "rather well regulated" life. Françoise takes refuge in solipsism, denying the metaphysical possibility of a separate consciousness: "'One cannot realize that other people are consciousnesses that sense themselves from within as one senses oneself,' said Françoise. 'When one glimpses that, I find it terrifying. One has the impression of being nothing more than an image in someone else's head. But that almost never happens, and never completely.'" She refuses to acknowledge the reality of the other's judgment: "For me their thoughts are exactly like their words and their faces: objects in my own world" (Beauvoir 1954, 15–17; Beauvoir 1943, 17–18). So Françoise denies, in bad faith, realities of one's self revealed by the other's look.

The most serious challenge to Françoise's solipsism comes in her relationship with Xavière, a sensualist whose life seems to personify elements of both a Bergsonian ideal and the *femme-enfant* muse of Surrealism: "[Xavière] leaned her head back, half closed her eyes and lifted the glass [of aquavit] to her mouth. 'It burned all the way down my throat,' she said, running her fingers along her lovely slender neck. Then her hand slipped slowly down the length of her body. 'And it burns here. And here. It's odd. I feel as if I were being lighted up inside'" (Beauvoir 1954, 55). Xavière is like the dreamer whose quality of perception Bergson contrasts with that of the "man of action" in *Creative Evolution*: "in the almost instantaneous perception of a sensible quality, there may be trillions of oscillations which repeat themselves." The "man of action" is able to "embrace trillions of these oscillations in . . . [his] simple perception," and thus dominate them, while the dreamer is able, like some lower beings, to "vibrate almost in unison with the oscillation of the ether" (Bergson 1944, 327–328). In Beauvoir's novel, Xavière's body trembles in response to a dancer: "'I wish I could dance like that,' said Xavière. A light tremor passed over her shoulders and ran through her body" (Beauvoir 1954, 19; Beauvoir 1943, 21).

Xavière also mirrors Bergson's interest in the body, and especially "the surface of our body—the common limit of the external and the internal," "the only position of space which is both perceived and felt" (Bergson 1911, 58). In a scene in a bar, "Xavière was engaged in gently blowing the fine down on her arm which she was holding up to her mouth" (Beauvoir 1954, 60–61). Bergson's distinction between utilitarian memory (characterized by Françoise, the intellectual, who only remembers ideas relevant to her projects) and pure memory, "where our mind retains in all its details the picture of our past life" (Bergson 1911, 323) is also evident in Beauvoir's depiction of Xavière: "'I never forget anything,' [Xavière tells Pierre scornfully] 'I don't give a damn about understanding with my mind alone,' Xavière cried with unexpected violence. And with a kind of sneer, she added, 'I'm not an intellectual'" (Beauvoir 1954, 62).

Where Françoise is dutiful, Xavière is spontaneous, refusing to be bound by social obligations. "'You make appointments and then don't keep them,' said Françoise. 'You might also ruin some real friendships by going through life that way.' . . . 'Well, that's just too bad,' said Xavière. She pouted disdainfully. 'I've always ended up by quarreling with everyone'" (Beauvoir 1954, 57). Xavière, who criticizes Françoise for giving people rights over her, refuses all social demands: "'I'd rather live alone in the world and keep my freedom'" (Beauvoir 1954, 103). Reflecting Bergson's description of language as forcing conformity to social convention, Xavière refuses the demands of language, often choosing to remain silent: "There was a kind of intimacy that one could never achieve with Xavière . . . Xavière said nothing" (Beauvoir 1954, 47). For Xavière, as for Bergson, language and words overwhelm and thus distort fleeting impressions and feelings: "'The trouble is,' Xavière drawled, 'that big words immediately make everything so oppressive. . . . It's like a strait-jacket around me'" (Beauvoir 1954, 202–204; Beauvoir 1943, 253–255).

Françoise's involvement with Xavière challenges Françoise's solipsism, since in Xavière she confronts a consciousness that stubbornly refuses to be joined. Through her various attempts to relate to Xavière, we see Françoise increasingly turn to immediate experience, attending to her feelings and memories and losing her faith in language, just as Bergson would require. In the process, Françoise witnesses the collapse of her initial sense of self as a sovereign consciousness, and discovers her freedom. At first Françoise views Xavière as her possession ("now Xavière belonged to her") and savors the sense of being a sovereign consciousness: "Xavière's gestures, her face, her very life depended on Françoise for their existence" (Beauvoir 1954, 20; Beauvoir 1943, 23). When confronted by a contemptuous glance from Xavière early in the novel that signals her existence as a separate consciousness, Françoise's body registered her anxiety: "her throat was dry; her heart beat a little faster than usual." But Françoise uses her intellect to analyze away these troubling sensations: "This malaise brought her no pathetic revelation; it was only one accident among others, a brief and quasi foreseeable modulation which would be resolved in peace. She no longer ever took such instants violently; she knew well that none of them had any decisive value" (Beauvoir 1954, 32; Beauvoir 1943, 37). Beauvoir's use of Bergsonian terminology highlights Françoise's utilitarian consciousness in this scene, dismissing her feeling as "quasi-foreseeable," a quasi-mechanistic reaction, rather than a unique and spontaneous creation, just as she dismisses this poignant moment as interchangeable with any other.

Difficulties arise when Pierre becomes infatuated with Xavière. Françoise experiences a sense of exclusion and exile that challenges her sense of being the sole knowing subject. When Pierre says, "'We are one,'" Françoise no longer believes him, describing his words in Bergsonian terms, as a crust over reality: "'Your feelings . . . [are] like the white sepulchers of the Holy Bible. . . . They're firm, they're faithful, they can even be whitewashed periodically with beautiful words.' . . . 'Only, they must never be opened, because you'll find only dust and ashes inside.'" When Pierre appeals to her reason, Françoise rebels: "Presently he would find a whole slue of lovely arguments, and it would be so easy to give in to them. Françoise did not want to lie to herself. . . . She loathed the thought of that moment when she would cease crying and return to the world of merciful deception" (Beauvoir 1954, 162; Beauvoir 1943, 199–200). Language and intellect have become a means of deception and distortion for Françoise, who now trusts her feelings more than Pierre's words.

Françoise declares her love to Xavière, in a bad faith effort to create a trio. Xavière remains elusive, but in her longing and regret, Françoise discovers satisfaction in the emotional richness of the moment: "wholly drawn toward this infinitesimal golden head which she was unable to seize; . . . [h]er happiness was shattered, but it was falling around her in a shower of impassioned moments" (Beauvoir 1954, 250; Beauvoir 1943, 314). Focused on her desire, Françoise has entered the world of immediate experience, but it is a world in which Xavière undeniably exists as a separate consciousness, a reality Françoise experiences first as a visceral reaction to Xavière deliberately burning her hand with a cigarette: "The girl was pressing the lighted end against her skin, a bitter smile curling her lips. . . . Françoise flinched. It was not only her flesh that rose in revolt. . . . Behind that maniacal grin, was a danger more definitive than any [Françoise] had ever imagined" (Beauvoir 1954,

283–284; Beauvoir 1943, 354). In Xavière's jealous gaze later in the evening Françoise is confronted once again with the evidence of Xavière's existence as a separate consciousness: "Facing Françoise . . . an alien consciousness was rising. It was like death, a total negation, an eternal absence, and yet, by a staggering contradiction, this abyss of nothingness could make itself . . . exist for itself with plenitude. . . . Françoise . . . was herself dissolved in this void, the infinity of which no word, no image could encompass" (Beauvoir 1954, 291; Beauvoir 1943, 363–364).

Françoise later explains her experience to Pierre: "'I discovered she has a consciousness like mine. Has it ever happened to you to feel another's consciousness as something within?' Again she was trembling. . . . 'It's intolerable, you know'" (Beauvoir 1954, 295; Beauvoir 1943, 369). Here we see Beauvoir using Bergson's subjective methodology of describing one's own embodied, felt experience to demonstrate the existence of other consciousnesses, and thus the limits of subjectivism. "'What surprises me is that you are touched in so concrete a manner by a metaphysical situation,'" Pierre says. "'But it is something concrete,' said Françoise. . . . '[F]or me, an idea is not theoretical. . . . It is experienced [*s'éprouve*], or, if it remains theoretical, it doesn't count'" (Beauvoir 1954, 301; Beauvoir 1943, 375–376).

In the novel's melodramatic conclusion, Françoise murders Xavière to escape the image of herself as a jealous woman in the younger woman's eyes: "With horror Françoise saw the woman Xavière was confronting with blazing eyes, this woman who was herself. . . . I was jealous of her.'" As long as Xavière exists, Françoise's betrayal exists: "'My guilty face exists in the flesh.' . . . 'Either she or I. It shall be I.'" Beauvoir depicts the murder in which Françoise "had finally chosen herself" (Beauvoir 1954, 399–404; Beauvoir 1943, 497–503), in terms consistent with Bergson's description of the free act in *Time and Free Will*: "[I]n the depths of the self, below the most reasonable ponderings over most reasonable pieces of advice, something else was going on—a gradual heating and a sudden boiling over of feelings and ideas. . . . [A]nd this absence of any tangible reason is the more striking the deeper our freedom goes" (Bergson 1913b, 169–170). The murder would seem to be an act of genuine freedom, in Bergsonian terms—instinctual, irrational, and asocial. Beauvoir's conclusion thus remains consistent with Bergson's moral individualism, while the novel has demonstrated the limits of both metaphysical and epistemological solipsism.

CONCLUSION

Under the pressure of the Nazi Occupation, Beauvoir abandons the moral solipsism of SCTS and affirms in a January 1941 entry in her *Wartime Diary* a "metaphysical solidarity" that recognizes individual freedom as requiring a society in which freedom is valued universally. Her break with Bergson's philosophy is most evident in her postwar valuing of language and communication in overcoming isolation and furthering connections with others—a theme of the next three decades of her work.[12] But Beauvoir continued to draw on other elements of Bergson's philosophy throughout her life—writing metaphysical novels and relying on a turn to immediate experience as a means of disclosing reality and discovering the self. In her 1946 essay, "Literature and Metaphysics," for instance, Beauvoir gives a Bergsonian critique of intellectual understanding: "Since reality is not defined as graspable by the intelligence alone, no intellectual description could give an adequate expression of it. One must attempt to present it in its integrity, as it is disclosed in the living relation that is action and feeling before making itself thought" (Beauvoir 2004c, 275). And her description of reality, in "What Can Literature Do?" echoes Bergson: "reality is not a fixed being; it is a becoming. It is, I repeat, a swirling of singular experiences that envelop each other while remaining separate" (Beauvoir 2011c).

Finally, Beauvoir's essays in critical social philosophy, arguably her most influential works, employ Bergson's two-part method beginning with a critical exposé of distortions in perception and thought followed by a turn to a description of immediate experience. In *America Day by Day*, for example, Beauvoir exposes the mystification in white racist views of blacks in contrast with Richard Wright's description of blacks' lived experiences of racial segregation.[13] *The Second Sex* begins in volume one with an examination of myths of woman as the Other in the eyes of men, followed in volume two by an account of women's "lived experience," a method Beauvoir also follows in *La vieillesse*, her 1970 study of old age, where she exposes the sordid treatment of old people hidden behind "myths of expansion and affluence" (Beauvoir 1970, 2). Thus, Beauvoir's interest in the philosophy of Henri Bergson, first evident in her 1926 student diary, extended throughout her life, and provides a unifying methodological interest in the description of immediate experience that underlies the division of her work into the solipsism of the prewar writings and her postwar political engagement.

NOTES

1. For evidence of this claim see Simons 2010; Simons 2006; Beauvoir 2004a; Beauvoir 2009; and Beauvoir 2011a.
2. Revised translations from *Mémoires d'une jeune fille rangée* are my own.
3. Revised translations from *Essai sur les données immédiates de la conscience* and *Time and Free Will, An Essay on the Immediate Data of Consciousness* are my own.
4. Bergson wrote that he "never ceased to read and admire" Bernard's work (Bergson 1959, 1434).
5. For further discussion of Beauvoir's "Analysis," see Simons and Peters 2004.
6. The wording "a perpetual becoming" is from Bergson 1944, 296; "sinuosities" is from Bergson 1959, 1439.
7. Revised translations from *Matière et mémoire: Essai sur la relation du corps à l'esprit*, are my own.
8. Revised translations of *La force de l'âge* are my own.
9. Revised translations of *Quand prime le spirituel* are my own.

10. Same page in both editions; revised translations are my own.
11. Revised translations of *L'Invitée* are my own.
12. Central to her existentialist ethics in her 1944 essay, "Pyrrhus and Cineas," communication is a justification for the metaphysical novel in "Literature and Metaphysics": "The novel is justified only if it is a mode of communication irreducible to any other" (Beauvoir 2004c , 270, 272), and in her contribution to a 1965 debate on the topic, "What Can Literature Do?" where she writes: "Language reintegrates us into the human community; a hardship that finds words to express itself is no longer a radical exclusion and becomes less intolerable" (Beauvoir 2011c).
13. See my essay, "Beauvoir and the problem of racism," for more on Beauvoir and race (Simons 2002).

WORKS CITED

Beauvoir, Simone de. 1943. *L'Invitée*. Paris: Gallimard, 1943.

———. 1954. *She Came to Stay*. Trans. Yvonne Moyse and Roger Senhouse. New York: Norton; my revised translation.

———. 1958. *Mémoires d'une jeune fille rangée*. Folio. Paris: Gallimard.

———. 1960. *La force de l'âge*. Paris: Gallimard.

———. 1962. *The Prime of Life*. Trans. Peter Green. New York: Lancer.

———. 1963. Littérature et métaphysique. In *L'Existentialisme et la sagesse des nations*. Paris: Editions Nagel.

———. 1970. *La vieillesse*. Paris: Gallimard.

———. 1974. *Memoirs of a Dutiful Daughter*. Trans. James Kirkup. New York: Harper & Row.

———. 1979. *Quand prime le spirituel*. Paris: Gallimard.

———. 1982. *When Things of the Spirit Come First*. Trans. Patrick O'Brian. New York: Pantheon.

———. 2004a. *Philosophical Writings*. Ed. Margaret A. Simons, Marybeth Timmermann, and Mary Beth Mader. Urbana, IL: University of Illinois Press.

———. 2004b. Analysis of Claude Bernard's *Introduction to the Study of Experimental Medicine*. In Beauvoir 2004a, 23–30.

———. 2004c. Literature and Metaphysics. In Beauvoir 2004a, 269–277.

———. 2006. *Diary of a Philosophy Student: Vol. 1, 1926–27*. Ed. B. Klaw, S. Le Bon de Beauvoir, M. Simons, and M. Timmermann. Trans. Barbara Klaw Urbana, IL: University of Illinois Press.

———. 2009. *Wartime Diary*. Trans. Anne Deing Cordero; ed. Margaret A. Simons and Sylvie Le Bon de Beauvoir. Urbana, IL: University of Illinois Press.

———. 2011a. Simone de Beauvoir, *"The Useless Mouths" and Other Literary Writings*. Ed. Margaret A. Simons and Marybeth Timmerman. Urbana, IL: University of Illinois Press.

———. 2011b. My Experience as a Writer. In 2011a.

———. 2011c. What Can Literature Do? In 2011a.
Bergson, Henri. 1911. *Matter and Memory*. Trans. Nancy Margaret Paul and W. Scott Palmer. London: George Allen & Unwin.
———. 1913a. *Matière et mémoire: Essai sur la relation du corps à l'esprit*, 10th ed. Paris: Alcan.
———. 1913b. *Time and Free Will: An Essay on the Immediate Data of Consciousness*. Trans. F. L. Pogson. New York: Macmillan.
———. 1928. *Essai sur les données immédiates de la conscience*, 6th ed. Paris: Félix Alcan [1889].
———. 1944. *Creative Evolution*. Trans. Arthur Mitchell. New York: Modern Library.
———. 1959. La philosophie de Claude Bernard (1913). In *Oeuvres*. Paris: Presses Universitaires de France.
Simons, Margaret A. 1999. *Beauvoir and* The Second Sex*: Feminism, Race, and the Origins of Existentialism*. Lanham, MD: Rowman and Littlefield.
———. 2002. Beauvoir and the Problem of Racism. In *Philosophers on Race: Critical Essays*. Ed. Julie K. Ward and Tommy L. Lott. Oxford, UK: Blackwell, 260–284.
———. 2003. Bergson's Influence on Beauvoir's Philosophical Methodology. In The Cambridge Companion to Simone de Beauvoir. Ed. Claudia Card. Cambridge, UK: Cambridge University Press.
———. 2006. Beauvoir's Early Philosophy. In Simone de Beauvoir, *Diary of a Philosophy Student: Vol. 1, 1926–27*. Ed. B. Klaw, S. Le Bon de Beauvoir, M. Simons, and M. Timmermann. Trans. Barbara Klaw. Urbana, IL: University of Illinois Press.
———. 2010. Confronting an Impasse: Reflections on the Past and Future of Beauvoir Scholarship. *Hypatia* 25(Fall):4, 909–26.
Simons, Margaret A. and Jessica Benjamin. 1999. "Beauvoir Interview (1979)" in Simons 1999.
Simons, Margaret A. and Hélène N. Peters. 2004. Introduction. In Beauvoir 2004a, 15–22.

Beauvoir and Merleau-Ponty

Philosophers of Ambiguity

GAIL WEISS

INTRODUCTION: CONTEMPORANEOUS INFLUENCES

Most often, when we attempt to chart the influence of one scholar on another, what we are seeking to describe is a one-way relationship; we are usually trying to determine how one person's work set the stage for those who followed him or her. Famous examples of these types of relationships in the continental philosophical tradition include those in which the later thinker's work builds on themes addressed by her or his predecessor, taking them in a new direction (e.g., Schopenhauer and Nietzsche, Freud and Lacan, etc.), as well as cases where the subsequent work commences with a strong critique of a predecessor's position on one or more issues (e.g., Berkeley and Locke, Hegel and Kierkegaard, etc.). If we examine the connections between Simone de Beauvoir and Maurice Merleau-Ponty's work, however, something altogether different seems to be going on. For one thing, they were contemporaries, born the same year (1908), living only a short distance from one another in Paris for most of their careers, writing (and becoming famous) during the same time period. Moreover, their relationship predated their identity as authors; they first became close friends during their college years when they met as fellow philosophy students at the Sorbonne. They took the same final exams as twenty-year-olds in March 1928 (Simone Weil came in first, Beauvoir second, and Merleau-Ponty third), and were assigned to the same lycée the following January (along with Claude Lévi-Strauss) for their practice teaching.[1] Merleau-Ponty seriously dated and had hoped to marry Beauvoir's best friend, Zaza, before her early tragic death, and the three of them spent hours and hours together, with Beauvoir and Merleau-Ponty frequently arguing about philosophical themes with mutual respect and admiration, even though they often disagreed. Neither remained for very long at a lycée; unlike Beauvoir, who never taught again, Merleau-Ponty continued his academic career, occupying the Chair of Child Psychology formerly held by Jean Piaget at his alma mater, the Sorbonne, at the time of his sudden death in 1961.[2]

Despite their early philosophical differences, Beauvoir's and Merleau-Ponty's respective work often emphasizes common themes, three of which will be the focus of this essay: (1) the essential ambiguity that defines human existence implies that every situation we encounter has no fixed meaning, entails that new perspectives on one's current situation are always possible, and provides new ways to define oneself and one's situation; (2) an understanding of subjectivity as always already grounded in, and therefore arising out of, intersubjective experiences (or, to use Sartrean language, the view that being-for-others is a constitutive feature of being-for-itself); and (3) the powerful influence exercised by one's cultural, political, and historical situation in shaping the meanings and values an individual ascribes to her or his existence.

Although all three of these themes are worthy of extensive discussion in their own right, I focus the most on Beauvoir's and Merleau-Ponty's respective descriptions of the ambiguity of human existence. The very notion of ambiguity, I argue, plays foundational roles in both of their ideas; indeed, it is woven through, and central to, their respective discussions of intersubjectivity and the situation, those formative, yet ever-changing aspects of human existence that together help to shape the meanings we ascribe to our experiences from one moment to the next. Despite their agreement that human existence lacks a fixed meaning and is, therefore, essentially ambiguous, and further that this is a positive rather than a negative phenomenon (or, more accurately, as we shall see, series of phenomena), it is important to note that Beauvoir and Merleau-Ponty emphasize and explore very different existential dimensions of ambiguity. In particular, Merleau-Ponty develops an account of perceptual ambiguity as a lived, embodied experience, while Beauvoir explicates the ethical implications of the ambiguities of human desire. Yet both insist that ambiguity is an animating force in all human relationships and in the situation as such. Rather than seeing these different accounts of ambiguity as mutually exclusive, there is good evidence that Beauvoir and Merleau-Ponty saw their respective accounts as complementary to one another. Together, I suggest, their accounts present ambiguity as a dynamic phenomenon that is revealed in strikingly different ways throughout human existence.

Until fairly recently, Beauvoir's personal and philosophical relationship with Jean-Paul Sartre has received the lion's share of attention from scholars and non-scholars alike, leading to a very reductive understanding of Beauvoir's work in particular. Yet the influence of Beauvoir's thought and work on Merleau-Ponty and his on hers, predates the Sartre-Beauvoir relationship and also continued throughout their lives. In the characteristic French intellectual style of the time, this mutual influence is frequently quite subtle and therefore not always easy to detect, since these thinkers rarely use direct quotes from each other, and do not always name the authors whose ideas they are discussing. Indeed, only readers who are already familiar with these philosophers and the broader philosophical context in which they are writing are readily able to recognize the numerous indirect references they make to other scholars' work. Fortunately, however, we do have access to Beauvoir's favorable review of Merleau-Ponty's major work (*Phenomenology of Perception* [*Phenomenologie de la perception*]) and his laudatory review of her first published novel (*She Came to Stay* [*L'invitée*]). Interestingly, both reviews appeared in the same year, 1945, in two different contemporary French journals, *Cahiers du Sud* (Merleau-Ponty's review of Beauvoir) and *Les temps modernes* (Beauvoir's review of Merleau-Ponty). They offer, therefore, a perfect place to begin a discussion of common themes and mutual influences in their work.

MERLEAU-PONTY ON BEAUVOIR AND BEAUVOIR ON MERLEAU-PONTY: THE 1945 REVIEWS

In the following quotes from these two well-known reviews, each philosopher admires the other for providing an original, insightful treatment of a major theme that continues to resound in their respective bodies of work for years to come. In his review, "Metaphysics and the Novel," Merleau-Ponty (1964) claims that Beauvoir's 1943 novel powerfully demonstrates that:

> All life is undeniably ambiguous, and there is never any way to know the true meaning of what we do. Indeed, perhaps our actions have no *single* true meaning. (Merleau-Ponty 1964, 34)

While Merleau-Ponty celebrates Beauvoir's fictional depiction of the ambiguity of human experience for illustrating that there is "no *single* true meaning" for our actions, Beauvoir's "Review of the *Phenomenology of Perception*" approvingly affirms, with Merleau-Ponty, the interdependent relationship that exists at all times between an individual and the world such that an individual can only come to understand herself through the world in which she finds herself and vice-versa. In her words,

> Merleau-Ponty shows us that the phenomenological attitude allows man to access the world, and to find himself there: it is in giving myself to the world that I realize myself, and it is in assuming myself that I have a hold on the world. (Beauvoir 2004, 160)

It is notable that in both of these passages, Merleau-Ponty and Beauvoir do not merely praise one another's work but make their own declarative statements in support of the metaphysical claims they find depicted there. For instance, rather than simply stating that Beauvoir's novel makes a compelling case for the essential ambiguity, and therefore, the multiple meanings of human actions, Merleau-Ponty claims that our lives *are* ambiguous and that we therefore cannot fully know the meaning of what we do. In so doing, he not only accepts Beauvoir's view of ambiguity (as discussed below) but uses it to challenge the standard conception of the relationship between meaning and truth that emphasizes the singularity of each (i.e., the view that a single meaning gives rise to a single truth). To the extent that there is a true meaning to our experiences, he suggests, it is open-ended and multiple rather than fixed and singular. As open-ended, it is subject to continual change and revision over time. As multiple, it is never constituted by any one perspective alone, but, as we shall see, for both Beauvoir and Merleau-Ponty, the meaning of my action is always actively informed by other perspectives I have adopted in the past and will adopt in the future, by the changing, multiple perspectives of others, and by the situation in which I am immersed.

The quote from Beauvoir's review starts by affirming the power of the phenomenological attitude, as depicted by Merleau-Ponty, in giving us access to the world and our own place within it. However, rather than keeping the focus on the phenomenological attitude—what it consists in and what it reveals—the passage quickly goes on to make a more general statement about how the movement of self-understanding always already presupposes an outward movement toward and grasping of the world. This, Beauvoir suggests, in turn implies that any assertion of oneself as a distinct individual is mediated by and reflected within one's "hold" on (or what Edward S. Casey might call one's *implacement* within) the world.[3] Moving from a specific insight about Merleau-Ponty's depiction of the phenomenological attitude to a larger claim about how human beings' ongoing relationship to the world affects their self-understanding as well as their understanding of the world in which they dwell, Beauvoir displays their shared ontological commitment to an anti-Cartesian framework, stressing the impossibility of human beings' separating themselves from the world (as Descartes seeks to do at the outset of *The Meditations*), whether in thought or in reality.

As mentioned earlier, although Beauvoir and Merleau-Ponty (1) agree that human existence is essentially ambiguous; (2) affirm that one's understanding of oneself, others, and our shared world is always already mediated by my encounters with others; and (3) emphasize the ongoing influence of one's social, political, and historical situation on an individual's way of being in the world, they offer quite different perspectives on each of these phenomena. Turning now to their respective descriptions of ambiguity, I first explore Merleau-Ponty's emphasis on perceptual ambiguity in the *Phenomenology of Perception*, which is presented as a value-neutral description of how ambiguity structures human experience.[4] In contrast to Merleau-Ponty's dispassionate account of perceptual ambiguity, as I demonstrate in the subsequent section, Beauvoir's discussion of ambiguity in *The Ethics of Ambiguity*, published only two years later, explicitly acknowledges and critically analyzes the ethical and existential implications of human beings' encounters with, and responses to, the ambiguities that permeate their lives.

PERCEPTUAL AMBIGUITY: MERLEAU-PONTY

In the *Phenomenology of Perception* Merleau-Ponty appeals to the work of several Gestalt psychologists to explain how perceptual experience emerges out of ambiguity. On the surface, our ordinary perceptions seem to have little in common with famous Gestalt images such as the "duck/rabbit" or "old woman/young woman" where the same perceptual information is organized by the viewer in two different ways, producing two disparate perceptual experiences. However, Merleau-Ponty points out that perceptual experience is never static but always dynamic; this means that not only Gestalt images but the ordinary perceptions produced through our ongoing, embodied interactions with our environment can always be organized in more than one way. Gestalt images, from Merleau-Ponty's perspective, make the ambiguity that is a constitutive feature of the perceptual process explicit; they are not fundamentally different from all other perceptual experiences, even if the latter tend to exhibit more constancy than the rapidly changing perceptions provoked by the former. Thus, he observes, "It is precisely Gestalt psychology which has brought home to us the tensions which run like lines of force across the visual field and the system: own body-world, and which breathe into it a secret and magic life by exerting here and there forces of distortion, contraction, and expansion" (Merleau-Ponty 1986, 48–49).

The "secret and magic life" Merleau-Ponty refers to can, I think, best be understood as the inchoate or indeterminate aspect of all perceptual experience that arises out of the open-ended nature of our encounters with the objects, people, places, as well as social, political, and historical institutions that collectively comprise the world of our concern. Rather than viewing perception as emerging out of a self-conscious, reflective process, he argues that "the perception of our own body and the perception of external things provide an example of *non-positing* consciousness, that is, of consciousness not in possession of fully determinate objects, that of a *logic lived through* which cannot account for itself, and that of an *immanent* meaning which is not clear to itself and becomes fully aware of itself only through experiencing certain natural signs" (Merleau-Ponty 1986, 49). In this passage, Merleau-Ponty suggests, with the Gestalt psychologists, that there must be an indeterminate background against which determinate "figures" appear, a ground that has its own "immanent meaning" but that is not explicitly focused on in its own right (indeed, if we turn our focus to the latter, then it becomes the figure and what had hitherto been the figure recedes into the ground).

In the (explicitly) ambiguous Gestalt images, it is possible to reconstruct the process according to which a person perceives one figure or the other (e.g., duck or rabbit, old woman or young woman) by attending to the specific details in the image that are dominant in one perception but function as part of the ground in the other. However, such a retrospective analysis is a very artificial, analytic process that does not provide an accurate picture of the ordinary, spontaneous perceptual experience that is capable of generating, without any prior reflection, two successively different images out of the same perceptual data.

Ambiguity, for Merleau-Ponty, can thus be understood as a function of the figure/ground structure of perception; more precisely, our perceptual experience is ambiguous insofar as we possess the capacity to reverse the relationship between figure and ground on an ongoing basis.[5] New perceptual experiences can arise at any time even as we remain in the same situation, for as soon as we turn our attention from a given figure it becomes part of the ground and a new figure/ground relationship emerges. This reversible relationship between figure and ground then, is precisely what produces new perspectives, new contexts, and therefore new meanings. The figure/ground relationship, moreover, is not restricted to acts of perception but describes our intentional orientation to the world more generally for Merleau-Ponty. Indeed, we can readily see how it operates in conceptual acts when a particular idea we are contemplating functions as the figure and other ideas, memories, anticipations, and so on function as the ground. Accordingly, in "The Cogito" chapter of the *Phenomenology of Perception*, Merleau-Ponty claims that the clarity of an acquired thought "rests upon the fundamentally obscure operation" of "another thought which is struggling to establish itself, and succeeds only by bending the resources of constituted language to some fresh usage" (Merleau-Ponty 1986, 389).

For both Merleau-Ponty and Beauvoir, as we turn our attention from one phenomenon to another (whether this be the result of a voluntary intentional act or whether the world itself demands such a shift in our attention through its urgent solicitations), the meaning of any given experience alters accordingly. If being trapped within any one perspective would eliminate ambiguity, rendering our perceptions abnormal and dysfunctional, too much shifting of perspectives would become overwhelming, multiplying meaning to the point of meaninglessness. On perceptual grounds for Merleau-Ponty, and, as we shall see, on ethical grounds for Beauvoir, it is important to preserve a balance between fluidity and constancy in our everyday experiences such that we can move back and forth between perspectives (and the different possibilities they reveal) without being trapped in any one of them.

Ultimately, the implications of Merleau-Ponty's understanding of ambiguity far exceed the perceptual and even conceptual domains. This is readily evident in the final "Freedom" chapter of the *Phenomenology of Perception*, where he discusses the tension between social classes that can lead to a revolution, a new world order. No matter how fixed and repressive an existing political regime might be, he argues that "Neither the appointed order, nor the free act which destroys it, is represented: they are lived through in ambiguity" (Merleau-Ponty 1986, 445). Displacing the primacy that "clear and distinct" reflection (understood as a form of representation) is accorded within the rationalist philosophical tradition as final arbiter of meaning and truth, Merleau-Ponty locates meaning and truth within lived experience itself, and sees them as made possible, rather than nullified by, its ambiguity.

While both Merleau-Ponty and Beauvoir readily acknowledge that meaning sediments in specific traditions (whether we are talking about social classes, political movements, aesthetic trends, linguistic conventions, conceptual paradigms, cultural practices, religious rituals, or even perceptual traditions), both also maintain that ambiguity is never eliminated but always present, allowing for fresh encounters, fresh perspectives, and fresh meanings to emerge. Merleau-Ponty is arguably nowhere more eloquent concerning the open-ended meanings that emerge out of the fundamental ambiguity of human experience than when he discusses the ways in which painters take up the perceptual challenge of producing new perspectives through their aesthetic creations in the famous final sentences of his posthumously published essay "Eye and Mind." Emphasizing that no artistic endeavor occurs in a vacuum, but rather, that each new work is produced out of and in turn takes its place within a larger aesthetic tradition, he reveals that this very tradition is the source of, rather than the obstacle to, the new perspectives that transform it:

> If no painting completes painting, if no work is itself ever absolutely completed, still, each creation changes, alters, clarifies, deepens, confirms, exalts, re-creates, or creates by anticipation all the others. If creations are not permanent acquisitions, it is not just that, like all things, they pass away: it is also that they have almost their entire lives before them. (Merleau-Ponty 1993, 149)

As new artists and artworks find their own unique places within the aesthetic traditions out of which they emerge, they in turn serve as the springboard for the creative endeavors that follow them. Merleau-Ponty stresses in these powerful closing lines that rather than associating originality with the creation of something absolutely new or radically different than everything that precedes it, it is always possible to revisit a given work (as well as a given tradition) and see something novel in it, that is, to take up an original perspective toward it that fundamentally transforms its established meanings. Understood as essentially ambiguous then, each artwork (and each tradition) offers in the repeated interactions we have with it the possibility of being encountered differently; it is precisely as these possibilities are actualized, that new meanings are created and new futures are revealed.

THE AMBIGUITY OF DESIRE: BEAUVOIR

As earlier mentioned, a significant difference exists between Merleau-Ponty's and Beauvoir's respective discussions of ambiguity. The former describes the ambiguity of the perceptual process as a universal phenomenon functioning similarly for all human beings and persisting, albeit in somewhat altered form, even through serious perceptual impairments, while the latter focuses on the specific ethical implications that arise out of both individuals' and societies' *diverse* responses to the ambiguous, ontological dimensions of existence that confront them on a daily basis. Thus, in contrast to Merleau-Ponty, Beauvoir offers an explicitly normative account of existential ambiguity, even though the ethical hierarchy she introduces in *The Ethics of Ambiguity* of different types of individuals is presented, like Merleau-Ponty's account of perceptual ambiguity, in the form of a series of dispassionate phenomenological descriptions.[6]

Given Beauvoir's very positive review of Merleau-Ponty's *Phenomenology of Perception* in *Les temps modernes*, it is unlikely that she would have seen *The Ethics of Ambiguity* as in any way criticizing or undermining the account of ambiguity he provides there. Indeed, she suggests that his discussion of lived perceptual experience is the major contribution of this work, asserting that "what seems to me to be the most important [of the very rich suggestions] in his book, both by the method used and the results gained, is the phenomenological elucidation of a lived experience, the experience of perception" (Beauvoir 2004, 163). Though Beauvoir affirms at the outset of *The Ethics of Ambiguity* that ambiguity is part and parcel of the human condition—implying that it is a shared experience—this important text is best known for the critical commentary it provides on the many different ways in which ambiguity is lived. Indeed, she is much less interested in the common structure ambiguity gives to all of our perceptual experiences than in the range of responses human beings display in the face of this ambiguity as they seek to make sense of themselves and (their place in) the world. Taken together, I would argue, Merleau-Ponty's and Beauvoir's quite different descriptions of the essential ambiguity of human existence complement rather than oppose one another. By claiming that all perceptual experience is ambiguous, and that perception is the primary mode of human engagement with/in the world, Merleau-Ponty offers a strong ontological foundation for Beauvoir's subsequent discussion of the strikingly varied ways in which individuals actually contend (or even fail to contend) with this omnipresent ambiguity in their daily lives.

Even though she approvingly proclaims in her review of the *Phenomenology of Perception* that: "One of the great merits of [Merleau-Ponty's] phenomenology is to have given back to man the right to an authentic existence, by eliminating the opposition of the subject and the object," Beauvoir nonetheless identifies this opposition as a fundamental source of human ambiguity in an early passage from *The Ethics of Ambiguity* that credits Kierkegaard and Sartre, rather than Merleau-Ponty, with providing the existential basis for a "philosophy of ambiguity" (Beauvoir 2004, 160). She notes that:

> From the very beginning existentialism defined itself as a philosophy of ambiguity. It was by affirming the irreducible character of ambiguity that Kierkegaard opposed himself to Hegel, and it is by ambiguity that, in our own generation, Sartre, in *Being and Nothingness*, fundamentally defined man, that being whose being is not to be, that subjectivity that realizes itself only as a presence in the world, that engaged freedom, that surging of the for-oneself which is immediately given for others. (Beauvoir 1997, 9–10)

In contrast to a being-in-itself that "is what it is," and that lacks the freedom to recognize itself, much less define itself otherwise, Beauvoir approvingly invokes Sartre's definition of a human being, or being-for-itself, as "that being whose being is not to be," or, we might say, that being who alone possesses freedom of choice, the choice to be other than who she or he already is. Ultimately, as both Sartre and Beauvoir repeatedly remind us, a human being is not simply a being-for-itself but rather an uneasy synthesis of being-for-itself (subject) and being-in-itself (object) and, to complicate matters further, also a being-for-others.

Even though Beauvoir's discussion of ambiguity as a lived experience in these first few pages of *The Ethics of Ambiguity* uses Sartrean language to express why human existence is ambiguous, instead of sticking with the formal technical terminology of being-for-itself and being-in-itself that Sartre utilizes, she goes on to speak of human existence as marked by conflicting *desires*, namely, the desire to be, and the desire to disclose being.[7] While Beauvoir suggests that all human beings experience both desires, she portrays the latter desire alone, the desire to disclose being, as the ontological source of a genuine ethical existence. Before turning to see why the desire to disclose being has this privileged status, it is important to examine the other, equally human desire that she claims we are unable to satisfy, namely the desire to be.

Beauvoir describes the desire to be through Sartre's description of human being as a "failed project" to be God. From a Sartrean perspective, this desire takes the form of wanting to continue to exercise the freedom and subjectivity of a being-for-itself while at the same time possessing a clear, well-defined essence such that one's being is never in question, never contingent, but absolutely necessary and therefore absolutely justified. It should be noted that for both Beauvoir and Sartre, human beings do, in fact, live the duality of being-for-itself (due primarily to our distinctive consciousness that is always already a form of self-consciousness) and being-in-itself (due primarily to the facticity of our bodies, our pasts, and our situations). However, in contrast to God, these two dimensions of our existence are not reconciled in a perfect divine harmony. Rather, they remain in an uneasy tension from one moment to the next in our daily life, a tension compounded by the all too human tendency to embrace one and deny (or at the very least minimize) the other.[8]

A related strategy that is doomed to failure, which Beauvoir focuses on at length in *The Second Sex*, is to project on the Other the immanent qualities of a being-in-itself and to see oneself (or one's sex) alone as embodying the freedom and transcendence of a being-for-itself. An especially insidious version of this tendency plays out in the asymmetrical relations between men and women in a patriarchal society. Socialized to view themselves as sources of transcendence and to consign women (the Other) to the sphere of immanence associated with domestic life, she argues, men tend to blame women for their own "fallen" state. Within patriarchal society, she tells us,

> man's revolt against his carnal condition is more general; he considers himself a fallen god: his curse is to have fallen from a luminous and orderly heaven into the chaotic obscurity of the mother's womb. He desires to see himself in this fire, this active and pure breath, and it is woman who imprisons him in the mud of the earth. He would like himself to be as necessary as pure Idea, as One, All, absolute Spirit; and he finds himself enclosed in a limited body, in a place and time he did not choose, to

which he was not called, useless, awkward, absurd. His very being is carnal contingence to which he is subjected in his isolation, in his unjustifiable gratuitousness. It also dooms him to death. (Beauvoir 2010, 164–165)

Seeking to endow his existence with necessity and woman's with utter contingency by projecting the human qualities he finds undesirable in himself onto her, such a man is doomed not only to death but also to bad faith. Here the desire to be takes the form of a desire to be a pure being-for-itself, a noncorporeal thinking substance whose elevated status, it seems, can only be accomplished through the corresponding abasement of the other sex.

The desire to be, as Beauvoir describes it in *The Ethics of Ambiguity*, seeks to escape the unsettling contingency of one's existence as a finite being-for-itself not by projecting this quality onto an Other but by endowing oneself with a fixed essence, like that associated with a pure being-in-itself. A rock, for instance, is not uncertain of the meaning of its existence. It does not contemplate suicide. It is indifferent to its destruction. It just is what it is. The desire to be then, can also take the form of a desire to abandon the always uncertain fate of a being-for-itself who lacks a definitive essence, and this desire is consigned to failure precisely because it is a desire to be what one is not, namely, a being whose being is not in question. Interestingly, Beauvoir claims that the inevitable failure to achieve this "perfect" synthesis of being-for-itself and being-in-itself that we nonetheless continue to desire is an *ambiguous* failure because, as the desire of a human being, it is a passion that "is not inflicted upon him from without. He chooses it" (Beauvoir 1997, 11). In what sense, we might ask, does one *choose* this desire, and how does the choice of this unfulfillable desire render its failure ambiguous?

Beauvoir's response to these questions concerning the "choice" of the desire to be and the ambiguity of its failure is quite complex and requires careful unpacking. She asserts that, "the passion to which man has acquiesced finds no external justification. No outside appeal, no objective necessity permits of its being called useful. It *has no* reason to will itself. But this does not mean that it cannot justify itself, that it cannot *give itself* reasons for being that it does not *have*" (Beauvoir 1997, 12). Though we have no reason to persist in a "useless" passion that seeks to provide an absolute, external justification for our existence, she suggests that we can nonetheless justify our desire to be insofar as we recognize that it is a project that is chosen, not one that is imposed on us by outside forces. In a sense, Beauvoir seems to be saying, though one's daily existence as a being-for-itself forces one to recognize that the desire to be is a "useless" passion, to the extent that we persist in this desire, we are actively choosing to do so, choosing to let this desire govern other choices we make, including, most notably, our choice of the moral values according to which we assess the meaning and worth of our own and other people's lives. And, it is precisely when we recognize our *choice* to succumb to and/or act upon the desire to be that the failure to fulfill it becomes ambiguous. It is not an unmitigated or total failure, since it has the power to reveal our agency as free beings who can choose to persist in the unrealizable desire to be what we are not.

Beauvoir's account becomes more subtle, more nuanced, and more distinct from Sartre's at this point, because she maintains that the "nullity" of being or the lack at the heart of being-for-itself that generates and intensifies the desire to be but also guarantees its failure, reveals an even deeper desire, the desire to disclose the world (of being). In wanting to be what we are not, she implies, the very world in which we ourselves dwell (but to which we are not reducible) is disclosed and, she maintains, it is this very power to disclose the world that serves as a precondition for the desire to coincide with that which is disclosed. Thus, she proclaims, "Thanks to him, being is disclosed and he desires this disclosure. There is an original type of attachment to being which is not the relationship "wanting to be" but rather "wanting to disclose being" (Beauvoir 1997, 12).

By calling the desire to disclose being "an original type of attachment to being" Beauvoir seems to give it ontological priority over the desire to be, and to suggest that the desire to be is, in a crucial sense, a particular manifestation of, or at least a response to, a more fundamental desire to reveal the world and one's shifting place within it. Moreover, Beauvoir argues that it is precisely when one actively embraces the desire to disclose the world, or, in her words, "wills" to have this desire that (ultimately) one always already has, and when one repudiates the impossible project of coinciding with being-in-itself, that one "wins," ethically speaking. Affirming one's existence as a being-for-itself, as that unique being to whom a world is disclosed in and through the very movement of intentionality, "[t]his end, which man proposes to himself by making himself lack of being, is, in effect, realized by him. By uprooting himself from the world, man makes himself present to the world and makes the world present to him" (Beauvoir 1997, 12).

To desire to disclose the world, in short, is to confirm one's special, ambiguous relationship to the world as a human being-in-the-world; what is disclosed is not only the transcendent experience of bearing witness to the world's splendors and catastrophes but the simultaneous awareness that we too, as Merleau-Ponty so frequently reminds us, are *of* the world, immanent participants who cannot help but be affected by it. And it is precisely due to this latter recognition that the desire to be can never be renounced once and for all, but rather, persists at the very heart of the desire to disclose being as we seek to define ourselves, our possibilities, and our limitations through the people, places, and things that are disclosed to us. Both Beauvoir and Merleau-Ponty, in different registers, draw our attention to the fact that disclosing (or, for Merleau-Ponty, perceiving) the world is both an active and passive process: to desire to disclose the world is, at the same time, a desire to be disclosed by it. Beauvoir articulates this ambiguous relationship between the desire to disclose the world and the desire to be best, I think, in the sentences that immediately follow her preliminary description of the human capacity to disclose the world. Having just evoked, in very Merleau-Pontian language, both the activity and the passivity of this intentional movement whereby the world is disclosed to us and, at the same time, we disclose ourselves to the world, she exclaims:

> I should like to be the landscape which I am contemplating, I should like this sky, this quiet water to think themselves within me, that it might be I whom they express in flesh and bone, and I remain at a distance. But it is also by this distance that the sky and the water exist before me. My contemplation is an excruciation only because it is also a joy. **I cannot appropriate the snow field where I slide. It remains foreign, forbidden, but I take delight in this very effort toward an impossible possession. I experience it as a triumph, not as a defeat.** This means that man, in his vain attempt to *be* God, makes himself exist *as* man, and if he is satisfied with this existence, he coincides exactly with himself. **It is not granted him to exist without tending toward this being which he will never be. But it is possible for him to want this tension even with the failure which it involves.** His being is lack of being, but this lack has a way of being which is precisely existence. (Beauvoir 1997; 12–13; my emphasis in bold, italics original)

Here we see quite clearly the impossibility of renouncing once and for all the desire to be because, although it cannot be fulfilled without renouncing our existence as human beings who are both a part of and distinct from the world, the desire to be is also a quintessentially *human* desire that emerges only from this dual act of disclosing the world and being disclosed through this disclosure. Thus, it is not in renouncing the desire to be and embracing the desire to disclose the world, but in recognizing that the former is a necessary accompaniment of the latter, its underside if you will, that we can "win" both existentially and ethically.

Though she begins with the Sartrean observation that what makes our lives ambiguous is the way each human being is not only a being-for-itself but also a being-in-itself, Beauvoir, as we have seen, renders problematic any facile attempt to view the desire to be as simply an act of bad faith. And yet, to the extent that the desire to be is an admittedly failed project, how are we to authentically live this particular ambiguity in which we seem to see-saw back and forth perpetually from one type of desire to another? Beauvoir famously goes on to claim that it is only by *willing* to be a discloser of the world (a disclosure that a human being is, paradoxically, already enacting from one moment to the next insofar as one exists as a conscious being-for-itself) that we can achieve a genuinely ethical existence. Yet, as I have argued, the desire to be can never be renounced altogether for it, too, is a quintessentially human desire.

One way of reconciling these conflicting desires, a desire to remain open to the world and a desire to define oneself once and for all as occupying a particular place within it, a way that appears between the lines of Beauvoir's analysis but is never clearly or explicitly developed, is to claim that to will to be a disclosure of the world discloses not only the persistence of the world but also the persistence of one's desire to be. Such an interpretation preserves the ambiguity of both desires for each takes us to the heart of the other: in desiring to be, I desire to be part of the world I am always already disclosing, and in desiring to be a disclosure of the world, I desire to *embody* this very disclosure that I am, though I will necessarily fail in the process. Ultimately, I am claiming that for Beauvoir it is precisely in failing, acknowledging the failure, and in affirming the competing desires that produce the failure, that I succeed existentially and ethically in assuming the ambiguity of my existence.

AMBIGUITY, INTERSUBJECTIVITY, AND THE SITUATION: BEAUVOIR AND MERLEAU-PONTY

The sophisticated ontologies that issue from Beauvoir's and Merleau-Ponty's specific discussions of the ambiguity of experience, the primacy of intersubjectivity, and the ways in which one's self-understanding and understanding of others is always mediated by one's situation, are not only fascinating in their own right, but, I would argue, offer incredibly rich resources that provide ample ammunition against the oft-repeated criticisms of the phenomenological-existentialist tradition as solipsistic, universalistic, and apolitical. Both Beauvoir and Merleau-Ponty, as we have seen, offer very provocative and quite different accounts of how and why human experience is ambiguous. Merleau-Ponty concentrates on how unique perceptual experiences and context-specific perspectives develop on the basis of inherently ambiguous perceptual information. Beauvoir focuses on the ethical ambiguities that unfold as we cycle endlessly between our desire to reveal the world and our competing desire to possess the world that is revealed. However, both understand ambiguity as an essential feature of human existence that renders its meaning fluid, not fixed, insofar as it is perpetually open to new meanings and new interpretations from a never-ceasing flow of perspectives. While it is undeniable that individuals' experiences and perspectives tend to sediment over time, leading to habitual, stylized modes of behavior and thought that seemingly belie the ambiguity out of which they emerge, Beauvoir and Merleau-Ponty both emphasize that creative expressions and fresh perspectives can always be developed out of even the most settled or conventional ways of responding to others and the world of one's concern. A major impetus for altering one's habitual orientations is undoubtedly the central role other people play in offering us new perspectives on ourselves and on our shared situation.

In Merleau-Ponty's 1945 review of *She Came to Stay*, he credits Beauvoir for revealing, through the breakdown of the self-deceptive, solipsistic viewpoint of one of her main characters, Françoise, that the meanings other people ascribe to our actions directly affect and inform how we understand ourselves, others, and the world in which we dwell. Indeed, Françoise's illusory view of herself as a sovereign subjectivity crumbles in the face of her recognition of the incredible power a young girl (unwittingly) possesses not only to disrupt her long-established relationship with Pierre but also her very sense of herself and her place in the world.

For Merleau-Ponty, Beauvoir succeeds in expressing not merely one woman's tragic underestimation of her own autonomy in defining her relationships with others and determining the impact they will have upon her life, but rather, a general truth about human existence: "It is simply that all of our actions have several meanings, *especially as seen from the outside by others, and all these meanings are assumed in our actions because others are the permanent coordinates of our lives*" (Merleau-Ponty 1991, 37; my emphasis).

As "the permanent coordinates of our lives," Merleau-Ponty suggests, we are always already responsive to and reckoning with the perspectives of others. An implication of this account is that the meanings we give to our experiences are never purely individual, subjective accomplishments but rather more like what I would call collaborative "works in progress," emerging out of our interactions with different people who continually provide us with a series of disparate perspectives that, whether acknowledged or not, accepted or repudiated, continually inform our own. Whereas Sartre claims in *Being and Nothingness* that "being-for-others is not an ontological structure of the For-itself, we cannot think of deriving being-for-others from a being-for-itself. . . . nor conversely can we think of deriving being-for-itself from being-for-others" (Sartre 1984, 376), he affirms a Cartesian binary between being-for-itself and being-for-others that seems to posit an ineradicable gulf between one's own subjectivity and the subjectivity of the other. By contrast, Beauvoir, like Merleau-Ponty, repeatedly suggests that being-for-itself and being-for-others are co-constitutive.[9] In *The Ethics of Ambiguity*, Beauvoir develops the ethical implications of this latter insight, famously asserting that "to will oneself free is also to will others free." For both Beauvoir and Merleau-Ponty my own freedom is never a solipsistic affair: even when it seems most isolated from and opposed to the projects of others, it is nonetheless always bound up with, responsive to, and responsible for the freedom of others (Beauvoir 1997, 73).

Merleau-Ponty distances his own position forcefully from Sartre's view of being-for-itself as ontologically distinct from our being-for-others when he observes, "I can no longer pretend to be a nihilation [*néant*], and to choose myself continually out of nothing at all." Instead, he goes on to declare, in one of the best-known passages from the *Phenomenology of Perception*:

> True reflection presents me to myself not as idle and inaccessible subjectivity, but as identical with my presence in the world and to others, as I am now realizing it: I am all that I see, I am an intersubjective field, not despite my body and historical situation, but, on the contrary, by being this body and this situation, and through them, all the rest. (Merleau-Ponty 1986, 452)

Merleau-Ponty offers us a picture of an engaged, embodied subjectivity that is not detachable from, but rather is co-extensive with and co-constituted by, its network of social relationships, and its historical situation. Rather than viewing either others or the situation as having "the last word" in defining subjectivity, Merleau-Ponty presents us with a shifting constellation of multiple, dynamic forces whereby "we are involved in the world and with others in an inextricable tangle" (Merleau-Ponty 1986, 454). This suggests that the meaning of one's experiences or even of one's own existence as a unique being in the world, cannot be determined once and for all, nor can it be attributed to a single factor, but is continually renegotiated through ongoing interactions with others in the context of a specific historical situation that is itself never fixed but always evolving.

At the end of "The Lesbian" chapter in *The Second Sex,* Beauvoir offers us a similarly complex portrayal of how we should understand an individual's life choices. The adoption of a lesbian lifestyle, she maintains, is not the function of a purely subjective choice to pursue one type of existence or even one type of desire rather than another but:

> an attitude that is *chosen in situation*; it is both motivated and freely adopted. None of the factors the subject accepts in this choice—physiological facts, psychological history, or social circumstances—is determining, although all contribute to explaining it. It is one way among others for women to solve the problems posed by her condition in general and by her erotic situation in particular. (Beauvoir 2010, 436)

It is important to note that despite calling our attention to the multiple factors actively at work in constituting the meaning of an individual's experiences and her very sense of herself, Beauvoir nonetheless retains a strong notion of individual agency. A provocative implication of her account is that sexual desire, to the extent that it is taken up by the subject and becomes a meaningful part of her life, must itself be understood as more than a mere desire. As a meaningful lived experience it is an existential attitude that develops in response to challenges posed by specific as well as general features of one's situation; it is never reducible, as she observes, to any one factor alone.

Merleau-Ponty grounds the agency of each individual body-subject, not surprisingly, in the bodily motility that underlies our ongoing perceptual encounters with others and with the world of our concern. For Merleau-Ponty, the shifting meanings we ascribe to our experiences are formed not through an isolated subjectivity but in and through our embodied, engaged, and committed responses to the ambiguous call of the world and of the multiple beings (both animate and inanimate) who dwell within it. Just as the painter he describes in "Eye and Mind," "lends" his body to the world, so too do we incorporate the world within our bodies; this open-ended, interactive, and creative process Merleau-Ponty suggests, is never completed, and is not unique to the painter alone, but continues as long as each human being is alive (Merleau-Ponty 1993, 123).

CONCLUSION

Though both Merleau-Ponty and Beauvoir offer many positive descriptions of the plethora of possibilities available to us to transform the givens of our world, both also recognize that this is much easier said than done. The reality of oppression and its multiple sources (e.g., material, psychical, economic, social, political, etc.) was readily evident during their lifetimes and is certainly equally if not more evident today. Even as they emphasize that the ambiguity of human existence is the inexhaustible source of new meaning, new life, and new situations, both are also well aware that to embrace this ambiguity is also to embrace indeterminacy, vulnerability, and risk. To seek Cartesian certainty, for both Beauvoir and Merleau-Ponty, is to seek the end, not the beginning, of genuine philosophical inquiry, since it would destroy the ambiguity, and thereby the richness, of our experience as human beings in the world. By rejecting the established hierarchies of Cartesian ontological dualism, they call our attention, albeit in diverse ways, to those experiences and bodies that have, for the most part, gone unnoticed, or worse, as Beauvoir so frequently reminds us, have attracted such negative notice. As the explosion of new scholarship on both philosophers amply reveals, by challenging the taken-for-granted presumptions that often yield fixed perceptions (and conceptions) of ourselves, others, and the world we share, Beauvoir's and Merleau-Ponty's work continues to transform habitual ways of doing philosophy. Indeed, a major testimony to the far-reaching influence of their respective understandings of ambiguity, as well as to their own interdisciplinary approaches to the phenomena they explore, is the new insights they are generating in fields that didn't even exist as such during their lifetimes, including feminist theory, critical race studies, and disability studies. But that is another story!

NOTES

1. Deirdre Bair's *Simone de Beauvoir: A Biography* offers a detailed account of these early interactions between Beauvoir and Merleau-Ponty (Blair 1990). Beauvoir's published diary from that time period, *Simone de Beauvoir: Diary of a Philosophy Student*, Volume 1, 1926–27 is another important resource (Beauvoir 2006), as is her autobiographical narrative (Beauvoir 1974) *Memoirs of a Dutiful Daughter* (*Mémoires d'une jeune fille rangée*), where Merleau-Ponty appears as "Pradelle," one of the few pseudonyms in the book.
2. It should be noted that the lack of opportunities for women to teach at the college level may have had more to do with Beauvoir's decision than a definite choice not to try to become a university professor. In her autobiographies, continuing to teach at a lycée or trying to survive by her pen alone are the two options she considers; not surprisingly, and fortunately for posterity, she successfully pursued the latter, economically riskier path rather than the former.

3. See Casey 1993, *Getting Back into Place: Toward a Renewed Understanding of the Place-World*, for an extraordinarily rich discussion of the phenomenon of "implacement," inspired by Husserl, Heidegger, and Merleau-Ponty, as well as many others. Casey focuses in depth on the ongoing significance of the experience of finding oneself at all times actively "in" and "of" or, to use Heidegger's language, dwelling within the world.
4. I say "seemingly" value-neutral description for though this certainly is what Merleau-Ponty intended to provide, in keeping with a traditional Husserlian understanding of the goal of phenomenology, which was to offer a pure description of a given phenomenon free from all biases, Beauvoir herself, as well as Iris Young and other feminist philosophers have argued that one's gender socialization affects one's perceptions of oneself, others, and one's world and suggest that this process is always already value-laden.
5. Those who lack the capacity to reverse the relationship between figure and ground, that is, those whose perceptions are rigid and fixed, would presumably not experience the ambiguity Merleau-Ponty is describing; however, the stability of their resultant experience would, despite the perceptual constancy it would yield, be an affliction rather than a benefit since it would severely restrict the possible range and depth of meaningful human experience. In short, the more ambiguity one's experiences possess, the more possible perspectives (and contexts) they offer, and the richer the meanings they can provide for Merleau-Ponty.
6. Given the vast secondary literature that offers many insightful critical perspectives on Beauvoir's ethics of ambiguity, I will not be focusing in this section on her actual ethics but rather on a more meta-ethical concern that has received much less attention, namely the ambiguity that I am arguing defines the complex interdependent relationship she describes between the human desire to be and the equally human desire to disclose the world.
7. For two other discussions of this distinction see Weiss 2004 and Bergoffen 1997, 75–112.
8. And, Beauvoir and Sartre believe, it is precisely by succumbing to this latter tendency that human beings find themselves in bad faith. The catalog of different types of people Beauvoir presents in subsequent sections of *The Ethics of Ambiguity* and the women and elderly people she discusses at length in *The Second Sex* and in *The Coming of Age*, all bear testimony to the varied ways in which a lack of balance between being-in-itself and being-for-itself can play out in an individual's life, whether this lack of balance is more ascribable to how one regards oneself or to how one is judged by others. The serious man who utilizes his agency to declare his undying allegiance to ready-made values, the adventurer who refuses to commit himself once and for all to any particular cause, the individual woman living in an oppressive patriarchal society that consigns her to immanence and that offers her social rewards for accepting her

second-class status, and elderly men and women who are devalued and treated as an "inferior species," all illustrate the consequences of too readily embracing or being associated by others with one mode of being at the expense of the other (Beauvoir 1996, 286). Whether one affirms and/or whether others affirm one's being-for-itself over one's being-in-itself or vice versa, Beauvoir compellingly demonstrates, both efforts are equally doomed to failure because they seek to deny the ambiguity that arises out of these two inextricably (yet always paradoxically) conjoined features of human existence.

9. Beauvoir is, it must be noted, frequently ambivalent on this point. At times, she seems to affirm Sartre's strict separation between being-for-itself and being-for-others, as when she depicts the for-itself's freedom early on in *The Ethics of Ambiguity* in extremely individualist terms; yet she also argues that "no existence can be validly fulfilled if it is limited to itself. It appeals to the existence of others. The idea of such a dependence is frightening, and the separation and multiplicity of existents raises highly disturbing problems" (Beauvoir 1997, 67).

WORKS CITED

Bair, Deirdre. 1990 *Simone de Beauvoir: A Biography*. New York: Summit Books.

Beauvoir, Simone de. 1974. *Memoirs of a Dutiful Daughter*. Trans. James Kirkup. New York: Harper and Row.

———. 1990. *She Came to Stay*. New York: W. W. Norton and Company.

———. 2004. A Review of the *Phenomenology of Perception* by Maurice Merleau-Ponty (1945). In *Simone de Beauvoir: Philosophical Writings*, 159–164. Ed. Margaret A. Simons, with Marybeth Timmermann and Mary Beth Mader. Urbana: University of Illinois Press.

———. 1992. *The Prime of Life: The Autobiography of Simone de Beauvoir* (1929–1944). Trans. Peter Green. New York: Paragon House.

———. 1996. *The Coming of Age*. Trans. Patrick O'Brian. New York: W. W. Norton & Company.

———. 1997. *The Ethics of Ambiguity*. Trans. Bernard Frechtman. Secaucus, NJ: Citadel Press.

———. 2006. *Diary of a Philosophy Student*, Volume 1, 1926–27. Ed. Barbara Klaw, Sylvie Le Bon de Beauvoir, and Margaret A. Simons, with Marybeth Timmermann. Urbana: University of Illinois Press.

———. 2010. *The Second Sex*. Trans. Constance Borde and Sheila Malovany-Chevallier. New York: Alfred A. Knopf.

Bergoffen, Debra B. 1997. *The Philosophy of Simone de Beauvoir: Gendered Phenomenologies, Erotic Generosities*. Albany: New York.

Casey, Edward. 1993. *Getting Back into Place: Toward a Renewed Understanding of the Place-World*. Bloomington: Indiana University Press.

Heinämaa, Sara. 2003. *Toward a Phenomenology of Sexual Difference: Husserl, Merleau-Ponty, Beauvoir.* Lanham, MD: Rowman & Littlefield Publishers.

Merleau-Ponty, Maurice. 1964. "Metaphysics and the Novel." In *Sense and Non-Sense*, 26–40. Trans. Hubert L. Dreyfus and Patricia Allen Dreyfus. Evanston, IL: Northwestern University Press.

———. 1986. *Phenomenology of Perception.* Trans. Colin Smith. London: Routledge & Kegan Paul.

———. 1993. Eye and Mind. In *The Merleau-Ponty Aesthetics Reader*, 121–160. Ed. Galen A. Johnson; trans. Michael Smith. Evanston, IL: Northwestern University Press.

Sartre, Jean-Paul. 1984. *Being and Nothingness.* Trans. Hazel E. Barnes. New York: Pocket Books.

Weiss, Gail. 2004. Introduction to "Introduction to *The Ethics of Ambiguity.*" In Simone de Beauvoir, *Philosophical Writings*, 281–288. Ed. Margaret A. Simons and Sylvie Le Bon de Beauvoir. Urbana: University of Illinois Press.

Young, Iris. 2005. Throwing Like a Girl: A Phenomenology of Body Comportment, Mobility, and Spatiality, 27–45. In *On Female Body Experience: "Throwing Like a Girl" and Other Essays.* Oxford: Oxford University Press.

From Beauvoir to Irigaray

Making Meaning out of Maternity

ERIN MCCARTHY

INTRODUCTION

While Simone de Beauvoir and Luce Irigaray may differ on questions of sameness and difference, I believe that they share a common feminist project. Both Beauvoir and Irigaray work to articulate what is required for women to become subjects; both argue that woman is a project, a becoming. In this essay, I explain what I take to be their underlying shared phenomenological-existentialist approach to the question of meaning through their views on maternity. Clearly this is a complex project, for as soon as we begin to celebrate maternity, we find ourselves in a double bind—if we include maternity as part of woman's subjectivity, historically this has enslaved women. If, on the other hand we deny maternity as part of woman's subjectivity, this devalues maternity—paradoxically positing it as something other than woman; indeed, it becomes something dehumanizing, which is odd, to say the least, and false to many women's experiences.

As Beauvoir rightly fears, in celebrating maternity we risk essentializing women, linking the female body to maternity in severely limiting ways—roles that relegate them to the domains of "kinder, kirche, and küche." Confined to a mere reproductive role, Irigaray contends along with Beauvoir that women cannot find their own creativity; their own power and very subjectivity is denied them. As Beauvoir points out, woman is often seen as *only* her reproductive capacities: "'*Tota mulier inutero*: she is a womb,' some say," (Beauvoir 2010, 3), and "Woman has ovaries and a uterus; such are the particular conditions that lock her in her subjectivity; some even say that she thinks with her hormones" (Beauvoir 2010, 5). Beauvoir's and Irigaray's views of woman as a dynamic becoming suggest a way out of this essentialist way of defining her—a way to both acknowledge our relationship to our biology and a notion of maternity, without trapping us in either of them. The core of both Beauvoir's and Irigaray's views of woman's subjectivity as becoming inspires us to find meaning in maternity such that it could be something liberatory, rather than a prison or trap—liberatory not just for women, but ultimately for men and children too—providing an alternative, free from the oppressive patriarchal concept of maternity that is still pervasive today. I argue that while Beauvoir's analysis of maternity in *The Second Sex* is largely negative (and even though she herself does not see a way out of the double bind), in fact, her concept of woman as becoming implies that maternity does not have to be something feared or escaped. I go on to show how Irigaray pushes the concept of woman as becoming beyond Beauvoir's position, by including maternity as part of woman's possible subjectivity. Irigaray argues for a subjectivity that is embodied but does not trap us in that body, a subjectivity that embraces our relation to our biology but does not limit our understanding of it as centered around childbearing. Finally, I briefly explore how woman might make or find meaning in maternity whether or not she bears children. I elucidate how accepting maternity as integral to women's subjectivity does not necessarily mean that we have to condemn a woman's body to a maternal vessel and suggest that this reimagining might allow women to transcend the definitions of woman thus far imposed on them.

BEAUVOIR: BECOMING FREE IN THE CONTEXT OF MATERNITY

Well before her famous claim that "One is not born, but rather becomes, woman" (Beauvoir 2010, 283), Beauvoir points out that all humanity is in constant becoming (Beauvoir 2010, 73). She indicates that even though woman has been denied the discovery or creation of her own subjectivity, she can (or at least has the potential to) discover herself as a subjectivity that is not fixed, and certainly not static in the way she has traditionally been made to be. As Sara Heinämaa puts it, the "uniting idea of her treatise is the attempt to think about femininity in dynamic terms: to be a woman—to take part in the common feminine existence—is not to be subsumed under an exact concept or a general rule, and it is not to instantiate an eternal idea or a Platonic essence" (Heinämaa 2003, 83–84). Beauvoir's analysis in *The Second Sex* shows us how patriarchy has prevented woman from fully living her dynamic subjectivity as concrete individuality. More specifically, she shows us that one of the most significant and damaging ways in which woman has been trapped in immanence is through patriarchy's identification of woman as Mother. In fact, according to Alison Fell, "Beauvoir considers motherhood to be the most significant source of women's oppression in 1940's France" (Fell 2003, 82). One might think in light of this that she simply rejects the role of the mother and sees woman's biology as a trap, leaving us no way out of the double bind noted above. As we will see, despite its negative tone, Beauvoir's analysis of maternity and motherhood serves to challenge the reification of woman's biology and the very idea that woman's "natural purpose" is to become a mother. Beauvoir's aim regarding maternity and motherhood is to force us to first closely examine and then abandon our preconceptions and prejudices about maternity. This project, coupled with the idea of woman as becoming, I believe, is what allows us to go beyond her own analysis and to (re) imagine maternity outside of the masculine order of things.

As we saw from the first chapter of *The Second Sex* above, woman is more often than not defined as her body—she is a womb, a thing, a vessel. For Beauvoir, however—in line with Heidegger, Sartre and Merleau-Ponty—"the body is not a *thing*, it is a situation: it is our grasp on the world and the outline for our projects" (Beauvoir 2010, 46). This understanding of body as lived body, as that through and in which we experience life, means that ultimately, man's search in biology for justification of the feelings of "disquieting hostility woman triggers in him" (Beauvoir 2010, 21) is fruitless. Biology, as Beauvoir so astutely lays bare in the "Biological Data" chapter of *The Second Sex*, will only give answers that take the body as a thing, rather than as situation, and thus severely limits our understanding of woman if taken as the place from which to define her. As Linda Zerilli points out, Beauvoir demonstrates the absurdity of taking body as thing and in turn the absurdity of defining woman based on her biology alone. Taking on the language of biologists and physiologists, according to Zerilli, Beauvoir

> consciously employs the nomenclature of reproductive biology all the better to subvert its scientific authority. Speaking deviously, Beauvoir amplifies the male utterance to the point of absolute absurdity: "The egg is imagined to be a little female, the woman a giant egg." Now if our "theorizers" wish to deduce the passivity of the woman from the passivity of the egg, comments Beauvoir wryly, "in all honesty it must be admitted that in any case it is a long way from the egg to the woman." (Zerilli 1992, 118)

Indeed! Of course, Beauvoir does not entirely dismiss biology. What she refuses to buy into is that woman's biology is her destiny. Woman, she tell us, is her body (as situation) as much as man is his, but due to her specific biology—due to her reproductive capacities—"her body is something other than her" (Beauvoir 2010, 41). She does not have control over her body's biological processes such as menstruation and pregnancy. However, it is not that the female body is the cause in itself of woman's oppression, "but rather its interpretation and signification as 'a passive sexual object' at a particular historical moment, which is then accepted as destiny by the majority of both men and women" (Fell 2003, 86). This is a theme to which she returns time and again throughout *The Second Sex*. As Fredrika Scarth explains, "In *The Second Sex*, Beauvoir's focus on women led her to see that embodiment was not the same experience for women as it was for men. She began to see that the experience of embodiment was enmeshed in a web of social and material conditions. Indeed, she developed a very pointed thesis: that in patriarchal culture, men are very easily able to identify their bodies with freedom and transcendence and that women are led, almost inevitably, to identify their own bodies with immanence"

(Scarth 2004, 8). It is true that Beauvoir's discussions of woman's reproductive biology often seem negative. Indeed her claim that woman feels "that her body is an alienated opaque thing; it is the prey of a stubborn and foreign life that makes and unmakes a crib in her every month; every month a child is prepared to be born and is aborted in the flow of the crimson tide" (Beauvoir 2010, 41), can hardly be construed as positive. Nevertheless, the point she is making is that woman's biology does not necessarily bind her to a life of servitude to her body. However much the crises "of puberty and of the menopause, monthly 'curse,' long and often troubled pregnancy, illnesses, and accidents" alienate her and make her destiny appear "even more fraught the more she rebels against it by affirming herself as an individual" (Beauvoir 2010, 44), she is not bound by her reproductive capabilities to be anything other than Mother. Rather:

> Woman is not a fixed reality but a becoming; she has to be compared with man in her becoming; that is, her *possibilities* have to be defined: what skews the issues so much is that she is being reduced to what she was, to what she is today, while the question concerns her capacities; the fact is that her capacities manifest themselves clearly only when they have been realized: but the fact is also that when one considers a being who is transcendence and surpassing, it is never possible to close the books. (Beauvoir 2010, 45–46)

However, as Other, more particularly for our purposes here, as Mother, woman has no subjectivity of her own that can be concretized—she has been unable to concretize her being as "transcendence and surpassing"—no possibilities have been afforded her since she has not been free to define her own possibilities, and thus, she must find her meaning in the abstract, or, in the patriarchal structures outside herself, which lead to a deformed and limited subjectivity, particularly in the case of motherhood. Woman's freedom, her being as transcending and surpassing, is limited by the conditions imposed on it by man, for humanity "is male, and man defines woman ... [and] ... she is not considered an autonomous being" (Beauvoir 2010, 5). While she may not be *considered* an autonomous being by man—or indeed, even by herself, Beauvoir clearly believes there is a way out of these conditions, for woman is not a fixed, but rather, at her core, a free, autonomous being, whose being holds the possibility of transcendence, even as concrete expressions of it are systematically denied her. As we see expressed in Beauvoir's existentialist ethics in *The Ethics of Ambiguity*, the freedom which women, in order to become full subjects and not merely the Other, need to assume, requires an unending process, even when aimed at a particular goal. As she puts it: "The goal toward which I surpass myself must appear to me as a point of departure toward a new act of surpassing. Thus, a creative freedom develops happily without ever congealing into unjustified facticity" or immanence (Beauvoir 1948, 27–28). In other words, woman needs to continually create projects for herself, the same way that man does—but this possibility has been foreclosed to women, according to Beauvoir, almost from the beginning of human history.

In chapter 1 of the "History" section of *The Second Sex* (called "Nomads" in the Parshley translation), Beauvoir demonstrates that for most women, "pregnancy, giving birth and menstruation diminished their work capacity and condemned them to long periods of impotence" when they needed the protection of men (Beauvoir 2010, 72). Without birth control, woman became too fertile, her "absurd fertility" kept her from playing a role in the growth of the resources needed for the increasing population, and man controlled the balance between production and reproduction (ibid.). Hence, trapped by her own fecundity, Beauvoir tells us, "woman did not even have the privilege of maintaining life that the creator male had" (ibid.). What is more, she did not even take pride in "her" creation, for, as she points out in more depth later in the chapter on "The Mother," children are not really even her creation—she was "the passive plaything of obscure forces" (Beauvoir 2010, 73), and unlike man, who "has not only worked to preserve the given world: he has burst its borders; he has laid the ground for a new future" (ibid.), woman has been forced to stay home. She has had no projects, she has been given no opportunity to develop a creative freedom, she has not been able to create values, and she has been trapped in immanence, whereas men have been able to activate their transcendence. As Andrea Veltman explains, "transcendence encompasses activities that enable self-expression, create an enduring artifact, or in some other fashion contribute positively to the constructive endeavours of the human race. Labors of immanence required for the sheer perpetuation of existence, on the other hand, are characteristically futile—unable to provide a foundational justification for existence" (Veltman 2006, 115). This confinement to the home, the futility of being stuck in labors of immanence while man went to war is "the worst curse on woman," Beauvoir argues, for woman's ability to give life means nothing compared to man's risking of his life and taking of the lives of others: "throughout humanity, superiority has been granted not to the sex that gives birth but to the one that kills" (Beauvoir 2010, 74). And even though woman "aspires to and recognizes the values concretely attained by males" (ibid.), even though they reach toward the same moments of transcendence, man has denied this to woman. It is man, not woman, Beauvoir takes pains to argue, who has created a division between male and female values; man has created the "feminine domain—a rule of life, of immanence—only to lock woman in it" (ibid., 74) and a result, this prevents women from being existents with the same freedom and power that men enjoy.[1] With very few exceptions, men are, in fact, afraid of woman's freedom: "He would be liberated with their liberation. But this is exactly what he fears. And he persists in the mystifications meant to maintain woman in her chains" (Beauvoir 2010, 756).

Little wonder then, that in her detailed analysis of motherhood and the pregnant body in particular we find precious little to recommend it. In the patriarchal societal structure that Beauvoir's analysis lays bare, women are, as Toril Moi puts it, "slaves of the species. Every biological process in the female body is a 'crisis' or a 'trial,' and the result is always alienation" (Moi 1994, 165). Nowhere is this more emphasized, however, than in pregnancy:

> She experiences it both as an enrichment and a mutilation; the fetus is part of her body, and it is a parasite exploiting her; she possesses it, and she is possessed by it; it encapsulates the whole future, and in carrying it, she feels as vast as the world; but this very richness annihilates her, she has the impression of not being anything else. A new existence is going to manifest itself and justify her own existence, she is proud of it; but she also feels like the plaything of obscure forces, she is tossed about, assaulted. (Beauvoir 2010, 538)

Pregnancy overcomes woman, an alien parasite invades her body, roots her in immanence, yet at the same time justifies her existence in that it perpetuates the myth of woman's "'natural' vocation" (Beauvoir 2010, 524). The maternal body "is a body whose biological meaning is culturally produced by being inscribed in discourses of motherhood—discourses that uphold the mother as subject by denying mothers and women as subjects" (Zerilli 1992, 120). In other words, in the way in which it has been perpetuated by patriarchy, woman as mother seen through "the patriarchal myths that posit woman as one with nature, fulfilled and completed through maternity" (Scarth, 2004, 138) is a universal without any particulars to instantiate it. That is to say, through this mythology, all women are viewed not as individual women, as particular mothers with all their diversity and idiosyncrasies, rather, the discourses of motherhood are applied to all women without differentiation, without taking each woman's subjectivity into account.[2] So, unlike the work of an artisan or the existentialist man of action whose transcendence is driven by a unique subjectivity, what little subjectivity a pregnant woman has disappears, for, as we see above—pregnancy annihilates her: "the opposition between subject and object disappears; she and this child who swells in her form an ambivalent couple that life submerges; snared by nature, she is plant and animal" (Beauvoir 2010, 538), and her consciousness and freedom also disappear as she becomes a "passive instrument of life" (Beauvoir 2010, 538–539). On Beauvoir's analysis there is, in fact, nothing life-*giving* about the pregnant woman, her role is passive—the maternal body is a vessel only, a carrier for a life that will go on to determine itself, leaving that vessel behind.

It is impossible, in fact, Beauvoir argues, to see the pregnant woman as creative in herself. Impossible, as Beauvoir says, "to consider woman as a solely productive force: for man she is a sexual partner, a reproducer, an erotic object, an Other through whom he seeks himself" (Beauvoir 2010, 67). It is impossible to see woman as creative, productive in herself because on "a biological level, a species maintains itself only by re-creating itself . . . a repetition of the same Life in different forms. By transcending Life through Existence, man guarantees the repetition of Life: by this surpassing, he creates values that deny any value to pure repetition" (Beauvoir

2010, 74). Woman is relegated to the role of *re*-production of Life rather than being able to transcend it—she gets stuck in the labor of immanence, in the "pure repetition" of Life which, man determines, has no value in itself. Man goes on then to posit "*himself* as sovereign," and here "he encounters the complicity of woman herself: because she herself is also an existent, because transcendence also inhabits her and her project is not repetition, but surpassing herself toward another future; she finds the confirmation of the masculine claims in the core of her being" (ibid.; my emphasis). Woman finds this confirmation in *his* claims because, Beauvoir discloses, they are in fact, not masculine, but *human* claims. She implies that women originally did this unwittingly, seeing them as human rather than "man's" claims. Man, however, claimed them as his own and, to make matters worse, woman's "misfortune is to have been biologically destined to repeat Life, while in her own eyes Life in itself does not provide her reasons for being, and these reasons are more important than life itself" (ibid. 74). As Veltman explains, reasons "for living must be established through some activity that reaches beyond the maintenance of life itself toward the future; otherwise one labors to maintain life in the absence of an initial reason for laboring to maintain life" (Veltman 2006, 121).

While woman may have the illusion of being engaged in a project, of reaching toward the future in the creation of the child, it becomes clear that this is not the case. Beauvoir explains that "she does not really make the child: it is made in her; her flesh only engenders flesh: she is incapable of founding an existence that will have to found itself. . . . she engenders him in the generality of his body, not in the specificity of his existence" (Beauvoir 2010, 539).[3] Woman cannot activate her transcendence even in the creating of life because man has not given it value, for man needs her to merely repeat Life, yet not transcend it, so that he can surpass his own being, ignoring the fact that in this fundamental respect, men and women are equal, for woman is also a being "inhabited by transcendence."

IRIGARAY: WOMAN, BECOMING, MOTHER

For Irigaray, as for Beauvoir, woman is a becoming.[4] Like Beauvoir, Irigaray challenges Western philosophy to imagine a concept of self that is not bound by patriarchal frameworks, and she links this becoming to an ethical project. However, for Irigaray, Beauvoir does not go far enough. As Gail Schwab maintains, Irigaray does not deny the importance of Beauvoir's existentialist project, but finds the emphasis on transcendence "too limited and individualistic, and thus inadequate to create a way through or out of the predetermined Symbolic Order and the tangled web of networks it weaves" (Schwab 2011, 332). Transcendence is not enough for woman to found her subjectivity. For Irigaray, woman's subjectivity is one that is open and nondualistic in nature. Irigaray maintains that the dualism of mind and body that has so permeated Western philosophy renders impossible an adequate view of both female subjectivity and ethics. The primary point of contention with dualism for Irigaray, is that it tends to lead to the subjugation of one of the two terms: mind over body; subject over object; man over woman; self over other. The second term is subsumed into the first term; the first term becomes the norm and the second becomes the "other"; the first term is taken as "neutral" and either denies the second term its own subjectivity or makes its purpose the flourishing of the first term. If woman is always the Other—on the devalued side of the binary opposition and subsumed by the male subject, who is presented in the guise of something gender-neutral or even neuter—then she is defined only as that which is not male, and she has no subjectivity of her own. The world which claims to be neuter—in the sense of being stripped of its identification with any gender—has in fact, she maintains, been man's alone (Irigaray 1993b, 122). She argues that we need to construct or reconstruct ethics if a genuine female subjectivity is to be established. Her vision of woman's subjectivity is one that is not built on opposition to man, but rather on openness to the other and to continual becoming and challenging of the meaning of woman, all the while retaining difference: "In order to become, it is essential to have a gender or an essence . . . as *horizon*. Otherwise, becoming remains partial and subject to the subject. When we become parts or multiples without a future of our own this means simply that we are leaving it up to the other . . . to put us together" (Irigaray 1993b, 61), which is what Beauvoir so deftly demonstrates has happened—man has set up the conditions that have fixed the female subject as Other in place, and up until now, with the rare exception, woman has not been able to see the horizon toward which her becoming can strive.

On Irigaray's view, women have been denied their voice, in part, because their bodies have been denied their voice, relegated to mere object status and viewed as tools that reproduce, but which are not productive themselves (Grosz 1994, 8–10). This hierarchy has led to both body and women being subordinated in philosophy. Irigaray finds the key to woman's becoming and subjectivity in sexual difference rather than the Beauvoirean emphasis on equality. She maintains that to "demand equality as women is . . . a mistaken expression of a real objective. The demand to be equal presupposes a point of comparison. To whom or to what do women want to be equalized? To men? To a salary? To a public office? To what standard? Why not to themselves?" (Irigaray 1993a, 12). For Irigaray, woman's subjectivity is found in its difference from that of man. She argues throughout her work that before we can even move to a discussion of equality, we first need to establish woman's own subjectivity, for up to this point, woman has only been a lack, the Other. "Women's exploitation," she continues, "is based upon sexual difference; its solution will come only through sexual difference" (Irigaray 1993a, 12). And: "It is quite simply a matter of social justice," she writes, "to balance out this power of the one sex over the other by giving, or giving back, cultural values to female sexuality" (Irigaray 1993a, 13). Irigaray goes further than Beauvoir when she urges us to be comfortable with ambiguities that will result from understanding woman as becoming on her own terms in the construction of a new subjectivity:

It would no longer constitute itself in opposition to a self-definition that forms a part of male effectiveness. The female gender, according to the order of its ethical duty, struggles with itself, between light and shadow, in order to become what it is individually and collectively. This growth, which is partly polemical, between conscious and unconscious, immediacy and mediations, mother and women, has to remain open and infinite for and in the female gender. This growth is essential if the two genders are to meet. (Irigaray 1993b, 120)

On Irigaray's view, as for Beauvoir, woman is a becoming. Woman's subjectivity for Irigaray is a project on which "the books are never closed." Since woman's subjectivity has up to this point never been positively defined, it has struggled to grasp onto whatever meaning, however limited, it could find in the values posited by patriarchy. However, once woman's subjectivity is no longer part of the definition of male subjectivity, Irigaray contends above, it can find a creative outlet through which to express and generate her becoming. Irigaray's philosophy, from a perspective that aims to value the difference between the sexes, also aims to reveal a woman's subjectivity, wherein woman would be brought into the philosophical (and political) dialogue. "To become," Irigaray writes, echoing perhaps, Beauvoir's existentialist ethics, "means fulfilling the wholeness of what we are capable of being. Obviously, this road never ends" (Irigaray 1993b, 61). However, where Beauvoir seeks to escape the myth of maternity through first exposing and then rejecting it, Irigaray embraces the maternal as a metaphor, as we see when she states that the "becoming of women is never over and done with, is always in gestation" (Irigaray 1993b, 61). The commonality between Beauvoir and Irigaray here, is in their shared "sense of a fundamental openness of meaning" (Moi 1994, 150), which is key to both of their understandings of (re)imagining what it is to be a woman, and which in turn allows for the (re)imagining of maternity. Their difference, however, is that Beauvoir would never conceive of becoming along such a—to her mind—problematic and overdetermined function as gestation.

In "Body Against Body: In Relation to the Mother," from *Sexes and Genealogies*, we can see Irigaray's radical (re)imagining of all women as creative, of maternity as something productive in itself and not necessarily linked to the act or possibility of childbirth:

> Our urgent task is to refuse to submit to a desubjectivized social role, the role of the mother, which is dictated by an order subject to the division of labor—he produces, she reproduces—that wall us up in the ghetto of a single function. When did society ever ask fathers to choose between being men or citizens? We don't have to give up being women to be mothers. (Irigaray 1993b, 18)

Yet being mothers here is clearly not to be taken (only) literally. And Irigaray refuses to define woman's subjectivity in a way that keeps her in the double bind of having to choose between being mother or being woman. This is precisely the idea she is trying to escape and why, for example, she even urges us to be suspicious of artificial reproductive technologies when they are lauded for liberating women—for allowing woman to procreate without man. For, she says, and this is forty-one years after the publication of *The Second Sex*, "the framework for women's existence is exclusively maternal. And there's a real risk that some women, who think themselves freed from their nature such as it was defined by patriarchy, will once again subject themselves body and 'soul' to this variant on their fate called artificial procreation" (Irigaray 1993a, 134). For Irigaray, artificial procreation is a "precarious liberty," for what has not yet changed is the myth of maternity and the notion that maternity is a "natural" function and end for women. In fact, Irigaray makes an argument similar to Beauvoir's—that man perpetuates the myth of motherhood to avoid facing his own subjectivity. Irigaray explains that "the mother represents only a mute soil, a mystery beyond metaphor" to man, and says, echoing Beauvoir's descriptions of the horrors of pregnancy and childbirth, that as such, "Obviously you will find opaqueness and resistance in the mother, even the repulsiveness of matter, the horror of blood, the ambivalence of milk, the threatening traces of the father's phallus, and even that hole that you left behind when you came into the world" (Irigaray 1985, 228). Here, as Beauvoir herself pointed out, and as Irigaray so graphically describes it, we see that men are largely afraid of woman's freedom and becoming. Rather than honor the place where both genders originated, where man is given life, the pregnant body is turned away from in horror as it reveals a power that man has no control over. Woman has not had the conditions under which to make maternity a free choice—as Beauvoir so powerfully demonstrates—patriarchy has constructed it as something that is meant to define women for once and for all; be the source of *all* her happiness and fulfillment, which, for an autonomous subject, is impossible. This description, this experience of maternity is a limit placed on woman by patriarchy. Woman as becoming lacks such fixity, but man cannot face this, as it brings him face to face with the fragility of his own subjectivity. So woman is mythologized, fixed in place, as Mother, in order for man to not see her as a becoming, as having a subjectivity of her own.

Irigaray's project is to rethink maternity through woman's subjectivity rather than through man's or through the ways in which woman's confinement to motherhood has been perpetuated by patriarchy. Immediately following the above citation about refusing the "desubjectivized social role" of the mother—the same myth we saw trapping woman in immanence for Beauvoir—we find one of Irigaray's most provocative and inspiring statements about maternity that indicates how radically we might change the meaning of what it means to be a mother:

> We also need to discover and declare that we are always mothers just by being women. We bring many things into the world apart from children, we give birth to many other things apart from children: love, desire,

language, art, social things, political things, religious things, but this kind of creativity has been forbidden to us for centuries. We must take back this maternal creative dimension that is our birthright as women. (Irigaray 1993b, 18)

So maternity, in this (re)imagining includes creation of things well beyond children. A view of the female body and maternity as creative and powerful or productive in itself and not merely reproductive has been systematically denied women, as *The Second Sex* and much feminist literature that has followed has shown. As Rachel Jones points out, "Irigaray's texts work to reveal and reclaim the *mater*-iality of matter, revaluing the maternal by rethinking the material, and acknowledging both as actively generative" (Jones 2011, 79).

In *Between East and West,* Irigaray turns to the body and Asian thought through her own embodied practice of yoga (more so than any rigorous examination of Asian philosophy), to find sources for the maternal creative or generative dimension, stating that: "These traditions are feminine, which does not mean maternal. The accent put solely on the maternity of women is rather a masculine perspective in the evolution of the tradition" (Irigaray 2002, 60).[5] The patriarchal appropriation of these traditions has, not surprisingly, created an identity between the feminine and the maternal, yet as Irigaray points out, there remains there a concept of the feminine that is *not* defined solely as maternal but does not deny the maternal either. The valuable contribution of her turn to Asian philosophy, I maintain, is that it brings to light the fact that characteristics that we might identify in the West as maternal or feminine are not necessarily or essentially "feminine" characteristics in sharp contradistinction to "masculine" characteristics. These so-called feminine characteristics, such as compassion, a connection between body and mind, a nondualistic way of conceptualizing self, a focus on the relational, for example, have nothing *essentially female* about them and can be held up as simply human characteristics in Japanese philosophy, for example (McCarthy 2010, 3–6). And thus, an analysis or desire to find new meaning in or (re)imagine maternity does not necessarily fall prey to the fears of feminists like Beauvoir who, rightly, resist the "woman as Mother" kind of feminism for its potential to limit women, that has so often come out of the attempt to celebrate maternity in some way. Rather, finding traditions wherein the "feminine" and "masculine" are differently conceived allows us to burst the borders of the idea of female subjectivity and imagine it anew.

As we saw above, all women, those who have actually given birth and those who have not, are, on Irigaray's view, mothers. Her philosophy recognizes that the fullness of female subjectivity comes out of a tradition that has long kept body and mind or spirit separate and challenges that separation: "development of spirit," she says, "was presented to me in the form of philosophical or religious texts, of abstract imperatives of (an) absent God(s), at best of politeness and of love. But why could love not come about in the respect and cultivation of my/our bodies?" (Irigaray 2002, 60). For Irigaray, respect for and cultivation of a woman's body includes woman's reproductive capacities, but does not limit cultivation of women's bodies to the reproductive. Her philosophical reflections on, and analyses of yoga, and the Indian tradition in *Between East and West*, for example, remind us that through our bodies and our breath we can give birth to and create energy and love even if we do not or cannot create a child. Such cultivation of embodied creativity as maternal, such cultivation of love and, I believe, its concomitant cultivation of intersubjectivity has the potential to link us ever closer to others. One powerful example Irigaray gives of an intersubjectivity that is nondualistic but does not erase difference, is that of what she calls the "placental relation" between mother and fetus which, she argues, "the patriarchal imagination often presents (for example, in psychoanalysis) as in a state of fusion, [but which is] in fact strangely organized and respectful of the life of both" (Irigaray 1993a, 38). In this model of the "placental economy," as she calls it, "the mother's self and the other that is the embryo" manage to negotiate the space of the same (the maternal body) and the other (the embryo), the "difference between the 'self' [maternal body] and other [embryo] is . . . continually negotiated. It's as if the mother always knew that the embryo (and thus the placenta) was other, and that she lets the placenta know this, which then produce the factors enabling the maternal organism to accept it as other" (Irigaray 1993a, 41). As Laurel Bollinger summarizes, this structure "preserves the radical alterity of the mother and child . . . [and] offers a metaphor for exchanges in which both figures are protected from destructive fusion, while still fundamentally connected to one another" (Bollinger 2007, 330). Irigaray finds the placental economy useful for thinking about relations and intersubjectivity. The placenta as metaphor allows us to imagine a relation in which neither self nor other is subsumed by the other—it is a "mediating structure that permits each side of the intersubjective dyad to be simultaneously connected and separate, regardless of any implicit hierarchy in culture or biology" (Bollinger 2007, 330). Each side continuously negotiates its difference and supports the growth and health of the other. Significantly different from Beauvoir here, whose analysis of the pregnant body is one filled with images of aggression and attack, reflecting the "enforced maternity" thrust on her by patriarchy (Scarth 2004, 138), Irigaray's use of the placental economy gives us an enriched concept of intersubjectivity, which does not involve sacrifice of the subjectivity of the mother. It also gives us a different model of selfhood, which is not as individualistic as that which she sees offered by Beauvoir. Irigaray goes so far as to claim that embracing the "maternal creative dimension that is our birthright as women" (Irigaray 1993b, 18) is an integral step in developing a female subjectivity. As she states toward the end of the Introduction to part I of *Key Writings*, even sexual relations can create more than children: "Sexual relation could be a path to becoming more aware and attentive, above all to intersubjectivity, and to approaching each other instead of appropriating one another, through cultural or social bonds as well. Thanks to sexual love we might become fecund, not only physically, but also subjectively, spiritually" (Irigaray 2004, 5). So sexual relation becomes not only reproductive, "repetitions of Life," as Beauvoir might say, or even recreational, but intimately integrative.

IMPLICATIONS: MAKING MEANING OUT OF MATERNITY

Beauvoir argues, as we saw above, that women have been sold a bill of goods with regard to motherhood: "That the child is the ultimate end for woman is an affirmation worthy of an advertising slogan" (Beauvoir 2010, 567). Women who are not free, who live under the conditions that she describes in such a detailed manner in the chapter on motherhood, *cannot* choose motherhood with their eyes wide open, cannot possibly make a free choice regarding the maternal aspect of their being.

Beauvoir does believe that the concept of maternity needs to be rethought and that this would be better not only for women, but also for children. She presents what is for her, a way out of the double bind created by including maternity in woman's subjectivity, but does not take the route that Irigaray does of extending the notion of maternity as an integral part of woman's subjectivity, regardless of whether or not she gives birth. Rather, Beauvoir suggests distancing woman from maternity and making it more of society's responsibility, with a focus on creating the conditions necessary for maternity to become a free choice. Instead of being imprisoned by the all-consuming myth of motherhood: "It would obviously be better for the child if his mother were a complete person and not a mutilated one, a woman who finds in her work and her relations with the group a self-accomplishment she could not attain through his tyranny" (Beauvoir 2010, 568). Following from this statement, Beauvoir's gestures to this new meaning of maternity in the chapter on motherhood are largely practical—first of all, mothers should be able to go to work. And furthermore: "In a properly organized society where the child would in great part be taken charge of by the group, where the mother would be cared for and helped, motherhood would absolutely not be incompatible with women's work" (ibid.). Her (re)imagining follows from the harsh critique of the myth of maternity as all-fulfilling for woman when she states that "it is the woman who has the richest personal life who will give the most to her child and who will ask for the least, she who acquires real human values through effort and struggle will be the most fit to bring up children" (ibid.). In many ways, even what might seem obvious suggestions to us today are still progressive—indeed radical—were they actually to be implemented. On the one hand, we can see how Beauvoir's proposition supports woman, in order to attempt to get them out of the double bind where the woman with a career "has to choose between sterility, often experienced as a painful frustration, and burdens hardly compatible with a career" (Beauvoir 2010, 736). On the other hand, while she no longer has to choose between being woman and being mother once the social revolution Beauvoir proposes is realized, woman now ends up with a divided subjectivity. Children are clearly considered a burden and staying home with children in itself cannot, on Beauvoir's view, provide a rich, full life (Beauvoir 2010, 569). Even as late as 1989, while acknowledging that having "children can be a completely valid choice," she still maintains that it "is very dangerous today, because all the responsibility falls on the shoulders of the woman, because in general it's enslaved motherhood" (Simons 1989, 18).[6] On Beauvoir's proposed way out of the double bind then, woman has to be supported to work in the public world—her "maternal self" must be freed up so that she can have a productive, rich, full "other" self outside of what Beauvoir viewed as enforced maternity. Clearly it is woman's role outside the realm of motherhood that still seems more valued—maternity remains a burden or obstacle to her embodying her free subjectivity; the conditions for "free maternity" still, I would argue, exist only for a privileged few—and so, maternity in itself is not sufficient for becoming. Despite her assurance that "motherhood itself is not something negative or something inhuman" (Simons 1989, 18), there doesn't seem to be, in Beauvoir's view, any way to *integrate* maternity into woman's subjectivity. For this to be possible, the conditions that she discusses in *The Second Sex* would have to be fulfilled. As Scarth explains, Beauvoir

> argues for the conditions that would make "free maternity" or *maternité libre*, possible: choice and involvement in the public world. This is an argument both for maternity as an engagement or a project and for mothers as subjects. For Beauvoir free maternity is an engagement, an obligation and a responsibility, and an opening onto the future; a mother must have concrete opportunities to shape the world because she is taking on responsibility for the world her child will enter. (2004, 138)

Beauvoir's diagnosis is in many ways still absolutely accurate today. The myth of woman as Mother still exists and in much of North American society, at any rate. Women who manage to maintain their careers, have rich personal lives, or both even while they have children are often labeled bad or selfish mothers; and women who choose not to have children are still subject to the assumption that there is something wrong with them if they don't want children, that this choice is somehow not "natural"—the split between being mother and being woman or being "other than mother" still persists.[7] If, however, society acknowledges that women are free, autonomous beings, who, despite their biology do not necessarily have a biological imperative to have children, and that even if they have children that motherhood need not define them, or that having children is a valid choice equal to labor outside of the home, then we are free to imagine differently what motherhood in this new light might look like.

Beyond Beauvoir's more practical suggestions, where woman ultimately remains a divided subjectivity, however, I suggest that the philosophical seed we find in Beauvoir that inspires a radical (re)imagining of maternity is located in the discussion of the artist in "The Independent Woman" chapter of *The Second Sex*. Here Beauvoir holds up female artists as exceptional, not bound by the limitations normally placed on women, for they "seek to go beyond the very given they constitute" (Beauvoir 2010, 741); the female artist seems capable of embodying her transcendence and becomes someone "who gives meaning to her life by lending meaning to the world"

(Beauvoir 2010, 741). In one of the most powerful and lyrical sections of *The Second Sex*, Beauvoir goes on to explain that "for one to become a creator, it is not enough to be cultivated . . . ; culture must be apprehended through the free movement of a transcendence, the spirit with all its riches must project itself into an empty sky that is its to fill" (Beauvoir 2010, 748–49). Even though Beauvoir is referring here to only one group of women, I suggest taking this as inspiration that all women can become creators of their own subjectivity, that we can transcend the myth of motherhood and project a new meaning for maternity. It is through the notion of transcendence that woman would be able to integrate what in Beauvoir's view seems to be the two aspects of her being that Beauvoir's analysis leaves divided—with the movement of a transcendence a new culture not only of maternity but of woman could be founded. Surpassing herself as *either* "woman" or "mother," a new understanding of woman wherein maternity—in an expanded and enriched sense—can be "an engagement with the world" (Scarth, 138) could be created.

In Irigaray's work we see this project taken up and a nondivided subjectivity for woman created. In my analysis, Irigaray does give us a way out of the double bind through the integration of maternity into woman's subjectivity so that she is no longer forced to choose between being woman and being mother—regardless of whether or not she has children; regardless of whether she stays at home or goes to work. Irigaray does agree with Beauvoir's point that woman cannot find herself in motherhood in the way in which the patriarchal myth says she "should":

> Our tradition presents and represents the radiant glory of the mother, but rarely shows us a fulfilled woman. And it forces us to make murderous choices: either mother (given that a *boy* child is what makes us truly mothers) or woman (prostitute and property of the male). . . . She lacks an ideal that would be her goal or path in becoming. Woman scatters and becomes an agent of destruction and annihilation because she has no other of her own that she can become. (Irigaray 1993b, 63–64)

In order to not destroy herself or others, in order to avoid having a part of herself subsumed or annihilated by having to choose between being mother or woman, rather than reject the maternal body, Irigaray urges us to "speak the body," to not give it up, to neither deny our embodiment, nor to identify ourselves *only* as maternal bodies in a sense that would fix a definition of female subjectivity in place for once and for all, but to keep the body as "guardians of the flesh. We should not give up that role, but identify it as our own, by inviting men not to make us into body for their benefit, not to make us into guarantees that their body exists" (Irigaray 1993c, 16). As we have seen, Irigaray's discussion of the growth of woman's subjectivity includes the maternal dimension as integral to her being, but the maternal in her understanding is liberated from the crippling responsibility Beauvoir fears, because Irigaray bursts the borders of the meaning of maternity by using it as a metaphor. For Irigaray, a "woman's subjectivity must accommodate the dimensions of mother and lover as well as the union between the two" (Irigaray 1993b, 63). In other words, woman's subjectivity must be whole, she must not be forced to identify herself as one or the other, but always have the possibility of being both—and in front of her, open to her, as a becoming.

So what would this new sort of maternity look like if we bring Beauvoir and Irigaray together? Here, we can only begin to imagine it. If women are no longer forced to choose between being mothers and being women; if we transcend what patriarchy has foisted on woman, and (re)imagine maternity as an aspect of subjectivity that allows women to "lend meaning to the world," if it is something women could freely choose, then women could create all manner of change in the world—be it through their work, art, politics, writing, children, social change, and so on. In bursting these borders and including maternity as part of woman's subjectivity, linking it to creativity of making not only children but much more as well, we also create the possibility of motherhood itself being creative work. In reclaiming the body, keeping it as our own, integrating it into our subjectivity, woman can reinscribe the maternal body as a creative site—a site that produces, rather than just reproduces not only, or even necessarily, children, but much, much more. In (re)imagining maternity, it becomes something that we can celebrate, without fear of it becoming a prison—something that is valued, something we can share, and something that contributes to making women whole again; for we will not have to deny our creative maternal dimension even if we don't have children (whether by choice or by circumstance). For women who do choose to have children, those children would no longer bear the burden of being, as Beauvoir puts it, "the full extent of [their] mother's horizons" (Beauvoir 2010, 568). Children, we might imagine, will also be treated more and more as beings in whom we have to foster autonomy, and freedom rather than as the vessels of the thwarted dreams of their parents. Furthermore, by not having their creative maternal power frustrated—either through its being denied or limited to the realm of reproduction—but having their subjectivity and creative maternal power liberated, then women can share with men in the creation of a world, as their (women's) power would no longer be feared, but celebrated and shared as we recall Beauvoir projecting: "He would be liberated with their liberation" (Beauvoir 2010, 756).

Embracing—yet not being defined by—this creative power that is no longer limited to reproduction would mean that women could live, as both Beauvoir and Irigaray aspire—as complete women.

ACKNOWLEDGMENTS

I am grateful to Jennifer Hansen and Paul Forster for reading very early drafts of this chapter. My thanks go also to the anonymous reviewers for their comments and especially to the patient editors of this volume, Shannon Mussett and Bill Wilkerson, for their careful, generous readings and incisive comments on early drafts.

NOTES

1. For an analysis of power and maternity in Beauvoir see Smith 1986.
2. See Scarth, 115 for a more detailed analysis of how the myth of the Mother operates in Beauvoir.
3. See Smith 1986 for a more detailed analysis of how this project of creation is but an illusion.
4. See Bergoffen 2003 for a detailed discussion of the relationship between Irigaray and Beauvoir, and a critique of Irigaray's reading of Beauvoir.
5. *Between East and West* is a controversial work in Irigaray's corpus. It has been subject to much critique as she follows no rigorous comparative philosophy methodology, cites no Indian philosophers (let alone feminist Indian scholars), and yet claims to draw on the tradition of the "East." If one is unfamiliar with Asian philosophy, her work can be misleading as there is a tendency, I believe, in *Between East and West*, to romanticize the philosophies of the "East." However, as mentioned above, she also makes it clear that she is drawing on her own personal, embodied practice of yoga. For more on this, see Penelope Deutscher's "Between East and West and the Politics of Cultural 'Ingénuité': Irigaray on Cultural Difference" (*Theory, Culture, Society* 20(3):65–75).
6. Never mind the question left unanswered of who does the work of taking care of the children when women work. Today this work has become enslavement of a different kind. Immigrant workers—legal or illegal—bear the burden of much of the child care for women who work. Day-care providers—often women with years of experience raising children—find themselves needing to get certified as "Early Childhood Educators," thanks to the professionalization of what was has been traditionally considered woman's knowledge, so that they can look after other people's children for low wages. This demonstrates how child rearing is still not considered equal work or productive labor.
7. See, for example, Waldman 2004; Douglas and Michaels 2004, the title alone (*The Mommy Myth: The Idealization of Motherhood and How It Has Undermined All Women*), in fact, sums up Beauvoir's point of view, despite the fact that there is not one reference to Beauvoir or *The Second Sex* to be found in its index; Warner 2006; and I add a personal example—of myself, aware of the irony of still feeling vaguely guilty at having had to put my eight-month-old twins in respite daycare in order to (re)imagine maternity!

WORKS CITED

Beauvoir, Simone de. 1948. *The Ethics of Ambiguity*. Trans. Bernard Frechtman. New York: Philosophical Library.

———. 2010. *The Second Sex*. Trans. Sheila Malovany Chevallier, Constance Borde. New York: Knopf Doubleday.

Bergoffen, Debra. 2003. Failed Friendship, Forgotten Genealogies: Simone de Beauvoir and Luce Irigaray. *Bulletin de la Societe Americaine de Philosophie de Langue Francaise* Spring 13(21): 16–31.

Bollinger, Laurel. 2007. Placental Economy: Octavia Butler, Luce Irigaray, and Speculative Subjectivity. *Literature Interpretation Theory* 18:325–352.

Douglas, Susan and Meredith Michaels. 2004. *The Mommy Myth: The Idealization of Motherhood and How It Has Undermined All Women.* New York: Free Press.

Fell, Alison S. 2003. *Liberty, Equality, Maternity in Beauvoir, Leduc and Ernaux.* Oxford: Legenda.

Grosz, Elizabeth. 1994. *Volatile Bodies: Towards a Corporeal Feminism.* Bloomington: Indiana University Press.

Heinämaa, Sara. 2003. *Toward a Phenomenology of Difference: Husserl, Merleau-Ponty, Beauvoir.* Lanham, MD: Rowman and Littlefield.

Irigaray, Luce. 1985. *Speculum of the Other Woman.* Trans. Gillian C. Gill. Ithaca: Cornell University Press.

———. 1993a. *Je, Tu, Nous: Toward a Culture of Difference.* Trans. Alison Martin. New York: Routledge.

———. 1993b. *Sexes and Genealogies.* Trans. Gillian C. Gill. New York: Columbia University Press.

———. 1993c. *An Ethics of Sexual Difference.* Trans. Carolyn Burke and Gillian C. Gill. Ithaca, NY: Cornell University Press.

———. 2002. *Between East and West: From Singularity to Community.* Trans. Stephen Pluháček. New York: Columbia University Press.

———. 2004. *Luce Irigaray: Key Writings.* Ed. Luce Irigaray. London and New York: Continuum.

Jones, Rachel. 2011. *Irigaray (Key Contemporary Thinkers).* Cambridge: Polity.

McCarthy, Erin. 2010. *Ethics Embodied: Rethinking Selfhood Through Continental Japanese and Feminist Philosophies.* Lanham, MD: Lexington Books.

Moi, Toril. 1994. *Simone de Beauvoir: The Making of an Intellectual Woman.* Oxford and Cambridge: Blackwell.

Scarth, Fredrika. 2004. *The Other Within: Ethics, Politics, and the Body in Simone de Beauvoir.* Lanham, MD: Rowman and Littlefield.

Schwab, Gail. 2011. Sharing the World. By Luce Irigaray and Teaching. Ed. Luce Irigaray, with Mary Green; conversations Luce Irigaray, with Stephen Pluháček and Heidi Bostic, Judith Still, Michael Stone, Andrea Wheeler, Gillian Howie, Margaret R. Miles and Laine M. Harrington, Helen A. Fielding, Elizabeth Grosz, Michael Worton, and Birgitte H. Hidttun," *Metaphilosophy* 42(3):328–340.

Simons, Margaret A. 1989. Two Interviews with Simone de Beauvoir. *Hypatia* Winter 3(3).

Smith, Janet Farrell. 1986. Possessive Power. *Hypatia* Fall 1(2):103–120.

Veltman, Andrea. 2006. Transcendence and Immanence in Beauvoir's Ethics. In *The Philosophy of Simone de Beauvoir: Critical Essays*, 113–131. Ed. Margaret Simons. Bloomington: Hypatia and Indiana University Press.

Waldman, Ayelet. 2004. *Bad Mother: A Chronicle of Maternal Crimes, Minor Calamities, and Occasional Moments of Grace*. New York: Anchor Books.

Warner, Judith. 2006. *Perfect Madness: Motherhood in the Age of Anxiety*. New York: Riverhead Trade.

Zerilli, Linda. 1992. A Process Without a Subject: Simone de Beauvoir and Julia Kristeva on Maternity. *Signs: Journal of Women in Culture and Society* 18(1): 111–135.

Ambiguity and Precarious Life

Tracing Beauvoir's Legacy in the Work of Judith Butler

ANN V. MURPHY

The review of a new English translation of Simone de Beauvoir's *The Second Sex* that appeared in the *New York Times Book Review* (May 27, 2010) raised the question of Beauvoir's relevance today. Francine du Plessix Gray, while conceding that the book was "passionate," and "awesomely erudite," nonetheless dismissed the book as antiquated in terms of its contemporary relevance. She did so in quite strong terms:

> How does Beauvoir's book stand up more than a half century later? And how does this book compare to the previous one? I'm sorry to report that "The Second Sex," which I read with euphoric enthusiasm in my post-college years now strikes me as being in many ways dated. Written in an era in which a minority of women were employed, its arguments for female participation in the work force seem particularly outmoded. And Beauvoir's truly paranoid hostility toward the institutions of marriage and motherhood—another characteristic of early feminism—is so extreme as to be occasionally hilarious. (Gray 2010, 7)

She also wrote that "pessimism runs through *The Second Sex* like a poisonous river" (ibid.). Gray takes particular issue with the language that Beauvoir uses in her renderings of sex, menstruation, and childbirth, and finds Beauvoir's descriptions of the alienation that might accompany these experiences to be "paranoid," "extreme," and "occasionally hilarious." Indeed, Beauvoir's descriptions, according to Gray, are almost comically out of date. Further still, the claim for which Beauvoir is best known—that women are not born women, but become them—is dismissed as "preposterous." Gray's tone in this review vacillates between praise and disgust. For this reason, Gray's review of the new translation of *The Second Sex* is symptomatic of a tendency that has marked the reception of that work since it first appeared in 1949. As Tina Chanter has suggested, what seems to remain constant is "the apparent need to oscillate between denigration and idolatry when it comes to testifying to Beauvoir's contribution, role, and function" (Chanter 2000, 139). Chanter diagnoses this pattern with reference to certain reviews that emerged when *The Second Sex* was first published, but this same dynamic remains at play today, and is apparent in Gray's insistence that an "awesomely erudite" text is also "poisonous" and so antiquated as to be "hilarious."

Gray's review does not address the fact that *The Second Sex* is, among other things, a philosophical text.[1] The review is shocking for feminist philosophers to read, particularly given the excitement and anticipation that surrounded this first complete translation of a book whose effect on the evolution of feminist philosophy is difficult to overstate. At one point in the review, Gray goes so far as to claim that she prefers the first English translation of *The Second Sex*, because the second translation "doesn't begin to flow as nicely," even though the first translation has been widely indicted as truncated and misleading. But Gray seems completely disinterested in the content of Beauvoir's philosophy, preferring a translation that ignores the philosophical substance of Beauvoir's arguments in favor of rhetorical pleasantries. Gray's review is not only disheartening for its denigrating tone; it is outright dismissive of Beauvoir's philosophy, and of Beauvoir's status as a philosopher.

A certain resistance persists when it comes to taking Beauvoir seriously in relation to the Western philosophical canon, a canon that she has both adopted and changed, a canon to which many of us would insist she belongs as a philosopher in her own right. Beauvoir scholars have been arguing to this effect for decades now, and that is part of what is so alarming about the appearance of the review. In 2010 Beauvoir's work confronts a sexism that is still alive and well, as is revealed in an abiding refusal to take her seriously as a philosopher, or in all too familiar attempts to subordinate her philosophy to concerns about her appearance and her personal life. For instance, Gray notes that Beauvoir was "highly attractive to men" and that they were "central to her happiness" (Gray, 2010).[2] Indeed, Gray's review is vastly more attentive to Beauvoir's relationship with Sartre and her affair with Nelson Algren than to the substance of Beauvoir's thinking. Adding insult to injury is the fact that in April 2010 the *New York Times Magazine* published an online article and photographic essay—titled "Being and Frumpiness"—that was dedicated to an exploration of Beauvoir's fashion sense. The article contained a link to a nude photo of Beauvoir that was published in the French newsweekly *Le Nouvel Observateur* in 2008. Additionally, the *New York Times Magazine* piece comments extensively on Beauvoir's style— "touch of whimsy" in her "frumpy café ensembles," her "stately elegance," and her "remarkable beauty." Philosophically inclined readers also note that the title of the article is a play on the title of Sartre's book and not her own. To see Beauvoir's legacy subjected to such disrespect is discouraging, and it is made more so by the irony that it was Beauvoir, among others, who examined and criticized the reduction of women to their bodies and the concomitant inability to take them seriously as intellectuals. Hence the kind of indignity to which Beauvoir has recently been subjected in the contemporary media is an abiding effect of the very same sexism that she subjected to scrutiny in her own work.

This chapter argues once more for Beauvoir's importance and originality in reference to the Western philosophical canon. *The Second Sex* has received a disproportionate amount of attention in arguments that trace Beauvoir's influence on contemporary feminist theory. In contrast, this chapter is primarily concerned with her early philosophical writings. Other essays in this volume explore Beauvoir's engagement with major philosophical figures with whom she was in conversation. This chapter argues for Beauvoir's continuing relevance in reference to contemporary feminist theory by tracing the lines of connection between Beauvoir's early philosophical writings on ambiguity and Judith Butler's recent work on the themes of vulnerability and violence. This essay is especially concerned with Butler's work in her most recent text, *Frames of War* (2009).

LINES OF INHERITANCE

Much of the work done on the lines of inheritance that mark the relationship between Butler and Beauvoir has been preoccupied with the ways in which Butler's theory of gender performativity—as it was outlined in *Gender Trouble* (1990) and *Bodies that Matter* (1993)—finds some theoretical mooring in French existential phenomenology. In one of Butler's earliest essays, published in *Yale French Studies*, she credited Beauvoir as a forerunner in thinking on the sex/gender distinction (Butler 1986). While Beauvoir never embraced that exact language, her rendering of womanhood as a process and a becoming—as distinct from the realization of a natural, essential, or static sex—was heralded by Butler as an account whose promise lay in its ability to think of gender as an accomplishment and not a destiny. Hence, Beauvoir was able to avoid the pernicious tendencies that attend naturalistic accounts of sex to the degree that they pathologize those who resist what is considered to be the orthodox configuration of sex, gender, and desire. Butler applauds Beauvoir's account for the variability of gender that it allows, and is drawn to Beauvoir's account of becoming for its nuanced understanding of situated agency:

> I would like to show how Simone de Beauvoir's account of 'becoming' a gender reconciles the internal ambiguity of gender as both 'project' and 'construct.' When 'becoming' a gender is understood to be both choice and acculturation, then the usually oppositional relation between these terms is undermined. In keeping "become" ambiguous, Beauvoir formulates gender as a corporeal locus of cultural possibilities both received and innovated. Her theory of gender, then, entails a reinterpretation of the existential doctrine of choice whereby 'choosing' a gender is understood as the embodiment of possibilities within a network of deeply entrenched cultural norms. (Butler 1986, 37)

Butler applauds Beauvoir's refusal to see gender as natural, as well as her attempt to break with a Cartesian frame wherein the becoming of a gendered body is orchestrated by a consciousness that somehow precedes the process of embodied becoming itself: "Hence, we do not become our genders from a place prior to culture or to embodied life, but essentially within their terms. For Simone de Beauvoir at least, the Cartesian ghost is put to rest" (ibid., 39).

However, Butler later retracted some of her praise in *Gender Trouble*, where she persisted in her commendation of Beauvoir's claim that gender was a becoming, but expressed reservations regarding what she took to be Beauvoir's positing of a "doer behind the deed," or an agent that somehow prefigures the performance of one's gender. While Butler may have agreed with the variability of gender on Beauvoir's account, the rhetoric of volition and intent that pervades Beauvoir's existential descriptions of embodiment ultimately proves worrisome for Butler.[3]

In *Gender Trouble*, Butler's loyalties to Nietzsche and Foucault run too deep for her to embrace the kind of voluntarism that she understood to subtend the elaboration of the subject in French existential phenomenology. Nonetheless, insofar as Butler's account of the performativity of gender tends to accentuate the manner in which gender is the result of a socially constrained rearticulation of norms (as opposed to a natural given), it is indebted to two main tenets of existential phenomenology: first the desire to break with the idea of a sexual essence in favor of the idea of gender as an existential practice, and second the claim that gender identity is to some degree contingent on the recognition of others.[4] Indeed, there is no making sense of a performative account of gender apart from some understanding of the intersubjective and public dimension of gendered performance; nor is there any sense in which we can speak of the "reality" of certain identities without raising the question of recognition. Most recently, Butler's evocations of Beauvoir have been laudatory, as she has cited Beauvoir amicably in her discussions of transgender identity. As Butler has recently noted, there are certain thinkers in queer theory who have suggested that if one is not born, but rather becomes a woman, then becoming itself serves as the vehicle for the realization of all genders (Butler 2004b: 65).

While it is true that Beauvoir's rendering of agency at the ambiguous intertwining of self and other, transcendence and facticity, intention, and passivity, can be seen to reverberate in Butler's early discussions of gender performativity, I turn my focus here to Butler's most recent work, which has expanded its scope to consider not just the question of gender, but the question of the human—of what it means to be recognized as such, and of what moral commitments might follow in the wake of this recognition. Butler's work over the last decade has revolved around the themes of embodied vulnerability and dispossession, concerns that have increasingly been thematized in relation to the figure of "precariousness." In *Frames of War*, Butler distinguishes "precariousness" and "precarity," with precariousness signaling the universal ontological truism of the vulnerable body, its omnipresent availability to both violence and care. Precariousness is a constitutive feature of all life to the degree that it requires certain conditions in order to persist; in contrast, precarity "designates that politically induced condition in which certain populations suffer from failing social and economic networks of support and become differentially exposed to injury, violence and death" (Butler 2009; 25). Precarity and precariousness are surely intertwined, though precarity is meant to signal a politically charged inequity, while precariousness is understood as an ontological truism marking all forms of life. In what follows, I link Butler's idea of precariousness to Beauvoir's philosophy of ambiguity from the 1940s. I do not do so in an attempt to reduce Butler's recent work to Beauvoir's, but rather in an attempt to reveal how contemporary feminist and humanistic thinking continues to be symptomatic of certain tensions to which Beauvoir was keenly attuned.

I argue here for yet another way in which Butler's work echoes concerns that were first introduced by Beauvoir; if Beauvoir's claim that "one is not born, but rather becomes, a woman" seems prescient in hindsight, I argue that the elaboration of embodied ambiguity in Beauvoir's early philosophical writings demonstrates an equally as remarkable prescience in relation to Butler's recent thinking on corporeal vulnerability. Again, my aim is not to collapse the meaningful distinctions that abide between these two thinkers, nor is it to evade consideration of the ways in which historical context inform the work of each. Nonetheless, there are substantive lines of connection that are fruitful to explore when thinking the question of Beauvoir's contemporary relevance, and these are lines of inheritance that become more lucid as one turns to consider the late modern manifestations of what Beauvoir calls ambiguity. I have elsewhere argued that Beauvoir's early work is relevant to think of in relation to a host of contemporary feminist work being done on the theme of corporeal vulnerability by a diversity of feminist scholars (Murphy 2010). Indeed, the interest in the vulnerable body is a pervasive one in contemporary feminist philosophy, and does not belong to Butler alone. Nonetheless, I narrow my focus here to the particular consideration of Beauvoir's idea of ambiguity and its relationship to Butler's recent work on corporeal vulnerability in *Frames of War*.

THE AMBIGUITY OF "PRECARIOUSNESS"

Much of what binds the early Beauvoir to the recent Butler is that while they refuse to embrace a categorically nonviolent ethic, the work of both is infused with a spirit of nonviolence nonetheless. Stated otherwise, while neither Butler nor Beauvoir would argue for the possibility of a wholly nonviolent world, both would claim the minimization of violence and a resistance to oppression among their guiding aims. Beauvoir never understood ethics as a domain of inquiry that could ever be purged of violence; yet she persists in the belief that we must "resist oppression at any cost." Similarly, despite Butler's recent interest in an ethics of nonviolence, it remains the case that the state of vulnerability and dispossession to which Butler appeals is not one that prescribes an ethics of nonviolence, even as Butler is clearly interested in the cultivation of a less violent world.[5] I argue here that Butler's recent philosophy of vulnerability—couched in the language of dispossession and precariousness—is deeply resonant with Beauvoir's own thinking on the ambiguity that accompanies all human action to the degree that it is haunted, permanently, by the possibility of violence. For Butler and Beauvoir both, this is an ambiguity grounded in the fact that we are embodied subjects whose own freedom and existence is only defined as it encounters resistance. It is in the uneasy space that remains between an agenda that seeks to redress and minimize violence, and an awareness of the fact that violence is to some degree an existential ontological truism, that a concrete understanding of what it means to "assume" or "realize" ambiguity comes to the fore.

Both Butler and Beauvoir are interested in the dilemma that is posed to the embodied subject—vulnerable to others by definition—who must answer to the ethical provocation that lies in this vulnerability. I suggest that Beauvoir's account of ambiguity anticipates Butler's thinking in three significant ways: First, for both philosophers, the ontological fact of vulnerability, dispossession, and mutual exposure does not in and of itself yield a prescriptive ethics, much less one of nonviolence. Second, both precariousness and ambiguity are nonetheless productive figures in that they gesture toward the responsibilities that emerge from the recognition of embodied vulnerability. Finally, ambiguity and precariousness share a similar discursive status, to the degree that Butler argues that "precariousness itself cannot be properly recognized" (Butler 2009, 13), and a hallmark of Beauvoir's discourse on ambiguity is her similar attentiveness to the ways in which ambiguity as such is frequently the object of evasion, obfuscation, and denial. Hence, there is a way in which precariousness and ambiguity, as philosophical figures, are frequently objects of obfuscation and evasion; they signal a kind of dispossession in the other that provokes an uncomfortable reckoning with the realities of mutual exposure and the responsibilities that we must assume by virtue of this fact.

Vulnerability is one of the more pervasive themes in Butler's writing over the last decade, and considerations of vulnerability anchor many of her analyses in *Undoing Gender* (2004), *Precarious Life* (2004), and *Frames of War* (2009). In these texts, Butler stresses the simultaneous difficulty and necessity of thinking of corporeal vulnerability as the provocation for an ethics or a politics. Such an appeal is ambiguous by virtue of the fact that there is nothing in the acknowledgment that we are dispossessed and vulnerable before others that guarantees that this fundamental, ontological dispossession will be the locus of respect and not injury. For while it is surely true that my dispossession in the other, and the vulnerability I necessarily evince as an embodied being, *may* be met with nurture and care, there is an omnipresent risk that this dispossession may also be realized in scenes marked by neglect or abuse. This ambiguity is one that we are given over to at birth, dependent as we are for our survival on the care of others:

> I am referring to violence, vulnerability, and mourning but there is a more general conception of the human with which I am trying to work here, one in which we are, from the start, even prior to individuation itself, and, by virtue of bodily requirements, given over to some set of primary others: this conception means that we are vulnerable to those we are too

young to know and to judge, and hence, vulnerable to violence; but also vulnerable to another range of touch, a range that includes the eradication of our being at the one end, and the physical support for our lives at the other. (Butler 2004a, 31)

Here, the "range of touch" that Butler evokes is illustrative of the ethical ambiguity of the vulnerable body. Butler's engagement with the motif of vulnerability is not limited to a consideration of the vulnerability of infancy, but expands to consider the myriad ways in which vulnerability comes to be experienced over the course of a lifetime. In this sense, the primary vulnerability that Butler gestures toward in infancy forms the basis for her broader consideration of the ways in which interdependency can be thought in the adult world and the sphere of politics (Butler 2004a, 46). She shares with Beauvoir a specific interest in the phenomenology of vulnerability and of the radical ambiguity that phenomenological analyses of vulnerability lay bare. Phenomenologically, at least, there is evidence that the realization of vulnerability is not an experience that necessarily inspires an inclination toward nurture or hospitality; on the contrary, the experience of vulnerability opens to a broad spectrum of possible responses—everything from violence to empathy. Butler's claim that "the body is constitutively social and interdependent" calls for a situated ethics that is capable of negotiating the myriad ways in which these constitutive vulnerabilities are realized (Butler 2009, 31). In this sense, vulnerability and ambiguity are mutually constitutive, to the degree that vulnerability marks the ontology of an existent who is exposed to others by definition, and ambiguity signals the ontological fact of this exposure.

In *Precarious Life*, Butler is interested in thinking through the inevitable interdependency that individuals and communities bear in relation to each other. While she acknowledges the omnipresent potential for violence when it comes to how this interdependency is actualized, her work is nonetheless guided by the aspiration to arrest cycles of violence and work toward a less violent world. In this text, Butler's engagement with the motif of precarious life is framed by a concern with those modern forms of political violence that abuse the primary interdependency and mutual vulnerability we all evince as members of the global community. She is invested in thinking the idea of community otherwise:

> This way of imagining community affirms relationality not only as a descriptive or historical fact of our formation, but also as an ongoing normative dimension of our social and political lives, one in which we are compelled to take stock of our interdependence. According to this latter view, it would become incumbent on us to consider the place of violence in any such relation, for violence is, always, an exploitation of that primary tie, that primary tie in which we are, as bodies, outside ourselves and for the other. (Butler 2004a, 27)

In the more recent *Frames of War*, Butler returns to this problem via further exploration of the theme of precariousness. "Precariousness," on this more recent account, is the term that is intended to designate the vulnerability that all humans evince by virtue of their injurability, interdependency, and exposure to each other:

> Precariousness . . . implies exposure both to those we know and to those we do not know, a dependency on people we know, or barely know, or know not at all. Reciprocally, it implies being impinged upon by the exposure and dependency of others, most of whom remain anonymous. These are not necessarily relations of love or even of care, but constitutive obligations toward others, most of whom we cannot name and do not know, and who may or may not bear traits of familiarity to an established sense of who "we" are. (2009, 14)

What is of interest here is Butler's isolation of "constitutive obligations" that are suggested by the precariousness of life, and her willingness to distance these obligations from love and care. What shape, then, do these constitutive obligations take? How are we to recognize the most just and most ethical ways in which to respond to precariousness? When, if ever, does violence emerge as a legitimate option, and how are we to gage the legitimacy of the radically ambiguous range of responses that precariousness may solicit? What moral obligation is imposed by an ontology of universal and mutual exposure, particularly given the radically differential ways in which this exposure is realized?

Butler's response to these questions makes reference to the fact that precariousness is a generalized and anonymous condition to which each human being is given over by one's body. Concretely, precariousness may be realized in radically divergent ways, but it is nonetheless the case that precariousness is a figure that refers to a universal, incarnate vulnerability that each living being evinces in relation to every other:

> Over and against the existential concept of finitude that singularizes our relation to death and to life, precariousness underscores our radical substitutability and anonymity in relation both to certain socially facilitated modes of dying and death and to other socially conditioned modes of persisting and flourishing. (2009, 14)

The normative charge of this "radical substitutability" and "anonymity" does not refer to the condition of precariousness itself, but to the injustice of its wildly differential allocation. Butler is most concerned with those instances in which certain individuals and groups are left to bear intolerable kinds of suffering even as others are assured all manner of privilege and protection. Butler claims that the inequity that exists here imposes an obligation. This obligation relates to the injustice of the differential allocation of precariousness and vulnerability on a global scale, for in spite of the fact that precariousness is a universal and constitutive feature of all life, it is realized in scenes of grave inequity, and it is this inequity that Butler finds objectionable: "the injunction to think precariousness in terms of equality emerges precisely from the irrefutable generalizability of this condition. On this basis, one objects to the differential allocation of precariousness and grievability" (2009, 22). It is this inequity that generates the question of justice, accountability, and responsibility. Butler calls for greater attentiveness to this differential allocation of vulnerability, and the mechanisms that both generate and veil these inequities.

Butler's exploration of precariousness moves between the ontological and the ethical domains. In the past, Butler has claimed that while precariousness itself is not a normative or prescriptive figure, it nonetheless calls for an ethical response. More recently, Butler evinces greater willingness to think through what concrete measures might be called for by the recognition of the precariousness of all life. While Butler remains relatively agnostic regarding the concrete forms that this response might take, she nonetheless links the discourse on precariousness to a discourse on "normative commitments" and "rights": "The recognition of shared precariousness introduces strong normative commitments of equality and invites a more robust universalizing of rights that seeks to address basic human needs for food, shelter, and other conditions for persisting and flourishing" (2009, 29). Butler persists in thinking the strong moral obligations and normative commitments that follow on the recognition of precariousness, but crucially, she never divorces the thinking of precariousness from the possibility of violence. Indeed, she explicitly refrains from stating that the claim imposed by precariousness is fundamentally nonviolent. *Frames of War* begins with the concession that whatever obligation is imposed by precariousness, it is not one that seamlessly bends in the direction of nonviolence. "Of course, it does not follow that if one apprehends a life as precarious one will resolve to protect that life or secure the conditions for its persistence and flourishing" (2009, 2). Butler is clearly invested in a more egalitarian distribution of precariousness, but this normative aspiration never denies the reality, possibility, and even occasional legitimacy, of violence. In the next section, I argue that Butler shares this frustration with Beauvoir, who was among the first to think of ethics as concrete, contingent, and imperfect, and perhaps more vitally, understood violence as a constitutive feature of the human world, one with which no ethics could ever break.

AMBIGUITY AND VIOLENCE

Like Butler's account of precariousness, Beauvoir's account of ambiguity moves freely between two registers, the ontological and the ethical. At the heart of Beauvoir's theory of ambiguity was her understanding of the essential failure that marks human existence. Crucially, Beauvoir did not understand this failure as vicious, but rather took it to be the consequence of the fact that human freedom is only ever defined in scenes of constraint and frustration. The failure that marks human existence is a constitutive feature of an account that understands human action and intention to be realized in scenes of dispossession and resistance. One of the hallmarks of existentialism is the heralding of this failure as the mark of a subject whose existence was realized as the ambiguous intertwining of interiority and exteriority, self and world. For Beauvoir, agency, freedom, the will, and interiority only acquire their intelligibility as they collide with exteriority and a resisting world. This led Beauvoir to describe subjectivity as a *situation*, an ambiguous intertwining of human intention and the factical world, wherein each shapes the other. The relationship between interiority and exteriority, transcendence and immanence, freedom and facticity, activity and passivity, is radically indeterminate, such that each conditions the emergence or intelligibility of the other. This indeterminacy pervades every aspect of the subject's relation to the world, and it is one that no discourse can nullify or transcend. Moreover, this indeterminacy and ambiguity inform the existentialist understanding of human action as permanently haunted by failure, as intention collides with world and actions come to adopt unexpected significance. This pervasive ambiguity at the very heart of existentialist ontology informs Beauvoir's attempt to formulate an ethics in fundamental ways.

Because human intention is realized as an imperfect, concrete, and finite unfolding in the world, Beauvoir was resolute in thinking that ethical decisions must be made *without* recourse to a transcendent moral code that universally binds human subjects and guides them in ethical deliberation. In this sense, ethics are "ambiguous" precisely by virtue of the fact that there is no consolation to be found in the retreat to an abstract or transcendent morality. The ethics of ambiguity is an ethics of contingency and failure, and the ethics of ambiguity is a resolutely historical ethics. On Beauvoir's account, we are forbidden the consolations that come with a retreat to the abstract, the transcendent, or the universal, and instead must assume responsibility for the creation of particular moral values. Different values are solicited by different historical moments. Indeed, Beauvoir understood ethical choice not as an appeal *to* transcendent ahistorical values, but as the creation *of* value itself. This much is clear given her description of ethical choice:

> It is a wager as well as a decision; one bets on the chances and risks of the measure under consideration; but whether chances or risks must be assumed or not in the given circumstances must be decided without help, and in so doing one sets up values. (Beauvoir 1996, 148)

As noted above, this process whereby humans assign value to their world is one that is permanently menaced by the possibility of error and failure, with the consequence that ethics are always to some degree indeterminate. This ethical indeterminacy is a function of the ambiguity that lies at the heart of existentialist ontology. While Beauvoir frequently addresses the anguish that comes with assuming responsibility—particularly when there is no guarantee one is right—she is resolute in thinking that we have no choice but to embrace and assume the ambiguity that marks our existence. In the domain of ethics, the failure that marks the ambiguity of embodied life is not something to be transcended—indeed such attempts would be instances of bad faith—but instead embraced. This not only commits Beauvoir to an ethics that refuses the possibility of a universal moral law, it also commits her to a conception of ethics that never aspires to entirely break with the possibility of violence.

Ambiguity is above all a function of our corporeality, for the kind of indeterminacy that ambiguity signals is grounded in the metaphysics, ontology, and ethics of the finite existent. It is because we are embodied that our actions and intentions are frustrated and restricted. A kind of passivity, vulnerability, and subordination subtends all of our actions and frustrates our intentions. It is also as embodied that our actions are subject to a temporal dispersion and unfolding, such that we find our best intentions frustrated. The conception of ambiguity as marking a reflexive bond between interiority and exteriority, integrity and vulnerability informs a further elaboration of ambiguity that is important for thinking the relationship between Beauvoir and Butler, namely the notion that ambiguity accompanies all actions to the extent that there is no ethics that can entirely transcend the reality of violence. Following on Beauvoir's understanding of freedom as essentially agonistic (that is, freedom is realized only as it collides with others' freedom) is the further realization that ethics can never transcend the realities of violence that accompany this understanding of human action: "If man is waiting for a universal peace to establish his existence validly, he will wait indefinitely; there will never be any other future" (Beauvoir 1996, 119).

In the early essay "Pyrrhus and Cineas," Beauvoir addresses the inevitable violence that must inform the elaboration of an ethics. She writes there: "I am an instrument for some only by becoming an obstacle for others. It is impossible to serve them all" (Beauvoir 2004, 108/282). This blunt assessment of the nature of human freedom is one that refuses the possibility of an ethics of categorical benevolence or pacifism. Indeed, while Beauvoir never glorifies violence, she is not one to argue around its occasional necessity. There are times when one is entitled to take up arms against those who oppress. This possibility is described as a last resort, but it is one that is legitimate in Beauvoir's account. To the extent that failure marks the ontology of the human, so too does violence, which serves as "a mark of failure that nothing can offset" (ibid., 138/362). The possibility of violence is one that permanently haunts humanity because of the omnipresent reality of human failure, and again, for Beauvoir, this failure was not something to argue around or transcend; it was something to be realized and negotiated as best as possible. The possibility of failure permanently haunts human action, and with it the possibility of violence. "We are condemned to violence because man is divided and in conflict with himself" (ibid., 138/362).

In light of the above account, it is easy to see why Beauvoir might be accused of nihilism, and why many think of existentialism as a despairing philosophy. But in Beauvoir's eyes, this understanding of the relationship between ethics and violence was not pessimistic; it was simply the recognition of a difficult reality. Action on the behalf of some is by definition action against others; Beauvoir saw more virtue in an honest confrontation with the fact of human failure than she did in its evasion. The insistence on the mutual implication of individual freedoms leads to the "paradox that no action can be generated for man without its being immediately generated against men" (Beauvoir 1996, 99/143). Yet in *The Ethics of Ambiguity*, Beauvoir memorably claims that "every man needs the freedom of other men" (ibid., 71/102), and that "to will oneself free is also to will others free" (ibid., 73/104). In light of these claims, it is easy to read Beauvoir as advocating a world in which different freedoms and projects are all granted equal credence and respect, but this is not the case. Indeed, the realization of certain projects requires the resistance of others. Others' freedom is requisite for one's own because it is only in a concrete situation that freedom is realized, as it collides with the freedom of others in ways that can never entirely break with the possibility of violence. Human interests collide justifiably, and not all agendas can be embraced. "The bread that one eats is always the bread of another" (Beauvoir 2004, 107/281).

Her understanding of violence as an intractable dimension of human existence led Beauvoir to claim "violence is not an evil" (Beauvoir 2004, 138/362).[6] The existential rendering of freedom essentially disallows the possibility of a world in which varying conceptions of freedom are realized without violence. For this reason, Beauvoir is not preoccupied with an attempt to purge ethics of violence. Indeed, on her account, such an attempt is naive, dangerous, and doomed to fail. Her understanding of freedom forbids this possibility.

APPREHENDING AMBIGUITY AND PRECARIOUSNESS

In what remains of this chapter, I will highlight a few salient lines of connection between Beauvoir's early work on ambiguity and Butler's recent theorization of precariousness. The earlier discussion of precariousness indicated that while it is a discourse that aims for the realization of a more equitable allocation of vulnerability, it is not a discourse that can ever be divorced from the possibility of violence. It should be noted that while Beauvoir never argued for a categorical pacifism—indeed the very terms of her existentialism forbade her from doing so—she was nonetheless concerned with the injustice of oppression and inequity. While Beauvoir believed that freedoms were only realized in conflict, her philosophy as a whole is infused with a spirit of nonviolence and a concern for the minimization of abuse and oppression. It is true that she does not dismiss violence as a possibility; but she also insists on the possibility and necessity of solidarity. Beauvoir would not (and could not) argue against the possibility of violence, but she insisted that oppression must be resisted, and it is fair to say that Beauvoir aimed for the minimization of certain kinds of violence and the expansion of certain freedoms to populations that had been deprived of basic rights. Butler's "precariousness" is a similar figure. Beauvoir was resolute in thinking that the anguish that comes with rendering ethical judgment in a world where universal moral truths are nonexistent does not forgive responsibility, but rather obviates the urgency with which this responsibility must be assumed. Butler's recent thinking of precariousness is marked by the same commitment. Working toward a more equitable distribution of precariousness is not a project that can ever claim immunity to violence, though it may be one wherein there is a clear commitment to the lessening of violence. It is in this context that I suggest we read Butler's discourse on precariousness as a discourse on ambiguity; one that marshals a description of embodied vulnerability in the service of the elaboration of an ethics. Ambiguity indelibly marks existentialist ontology and ethics, and serves as the site of our specificity, dignity, and integrity. Indeed, Beauvoir's rendering of the deconstructive nature of the relation between ambiguity and integrity is particularly prescient, and it is the locus of one of the more powerful points of intersection between Beauvoir's early work and Butler's recent theorization of precariousness. Precariousness by definition signals a vulnerability, fragility, and passivity, but for precisely this reason it also serves as the locus of our integrity, and the concept around which one might begin to elaborate a humanism founded in response to the ambiguity we evince as embodied beings vulnerable to both abuse and care.

Another vital line of connection between Butler and Beauvoir is the preoccupation that both share with the way in which the discourses on precariousness and ambiguity can inspire attempts to conceal, or evade the ethical ambiguities that each of these concepts bears. For Beauvoir, the experience of ambiguity inspires the proliferation of discourses that attempt to conceal, explain away, or nullify ambiguity itself. In other words, the experience or realization of ambiguity operates in tandem with the various attempts at obfuscation. Beauvoir recognized that the truth of ambiguity is not one that settles easily: "This obvious truth, which is universally known, is, however, so bitter that the first concern of a doctrine of action is ordinarily to mask the element of failure that is involved in any undertaking" (Beauvoir 1996, 99).

Both thinkers argue that precariousness and ambiguity are more often than not signaled in discourses whose actual aim is their denial or evasion. Ambiguity and precariousness are not comfortable concepts to think about or to realize, in either their ontological or ethical dimensions, and Butler and Beauvoir were both attuned—in different ways—to various attempts that are made to conceal or nullify the disarming truths to which they call our attention. In Butler's case, this has been manifest in her concern to interrogate those kinds of violence that are motivated by the rejection of vulnerability and the attempt to shore up a mythic sovereignty at the level of both the individual and nation state. Butler is especially concerned with the tendency on the part of the United States to preempt violence against itself by waging violence against its others, "but the violence it fears is the violence it engenders" (2004a, 149). For Beauvoir's part, she understood that ambiguity as such was not something that was visible and intelligible apart from the various attempts that are made to evade or negate the bitter truths to which ambiguity attests. Beauvoir was specifically interested in the persistent desire—evinced by myriad ethical thinkers—to try to ground moral life in absolute certainty or universal truths.

Beauvoir's understanding of freedom informed her desire to distance herself from that agenda, but one of the more powerful dimensions of her account of ambiguity is the discussion of how late modern discourses on ambiguity are paradoxically marked by some attempt to evade or transcend ambiguity itself.

There is a striking resonance here with Butler's thinking of the ethical obligations that we might assume by virtue of some consideration of precariousness, for Butler insisted that precariousness as such is not capable of being recognized, so the moral claim that precariousness makes is not one that is accomplished in an act of recognition:

> Normatively construed, I am arguing that there ought to be a more inclusive and egalitarian way of recognizing precariousness, and that this should take the form of concrete social policy regarding issues such as shelter, work, food, medical care, and legal status. And yet, I am also insisting, in a way that might seem initially paradoxical, that precariousness itself cannot be properly recognized. (2009, 13)

Like ambiguity, precariousness is not readily apprehended as such; the object of recognition is rather the violence that is motivated by its differential allocation as well as the violence that is spawned when reckoning with one's own precarious life, and those of others, is injurious. Butler's recent claim that "precariousness itself cannot be properly recognized" echoes her earlier discussion—in *Precarious Life*—of the ways in which the recognition of vulnerability is complicated:

> A vulnerability must be perceived and recognized in order to come into play in an ethical encounter, and there is no guarantee that this will happen. Not only is there the possibility that a vulnerability will not be recognized and that it will be constituted as the "unrecognizable," but when a vulnerability *is* recognized, that recognition has the power to change the meaning and structure of vulnerability itself. (Butler 2004a, 43)

That both precariousness and ambiguity are easy targets for obfuscation is no accident; rather, the tendency to evade the vulnerabilities that are gestured toward by both precariousness and ambiguity proves to be a constitutive of each. Ambiguity and precariousness are both difficult to recognize in themselves; they are rather illuminated in complicated political, ethical, and social scenes, many of which are paradoxically motivated by a desire to conceal, evade, or explain away the ambiguities that reside there. I have argued here for the prescience of Beauvoir's thinking when it comes to the claim that ambiguity is often marked by attempts at obfuscation and denial. That is, while ambiguity may mark the human condition and those late modern discourses inspired to examine it, one does not recognize ambiguity itself so much as those discourses that attempt to evade it, obscure it, or somehow transcend it. Beauvoir encouraged vigilance in this regard, and this vigilance remains vital today. My claim is that this understanding of the discursive status of ambiguity anticipates Butler's recent figuring of precariousness to the degree that Butler has also insisted that precariousness as such cannot be the object of recognition. Instead, one is called to witness the precariousness of life as one navigates those political institutions and discourses that are so often bent on its denial. In that sense, ambiguity and precariousness share a kind of discursive symmetry, to the degree that neither is understood as a proper object of recognition; what are more visible, in both cases, are attempts at their denial and transcendence, many of which are marked by violence. Even more important is the fact that both Beauvoir and Butler understood the importance of grounding ethics in a respect for the body, for its vulnerabilities, and conversely its capacity to inflict violence. This sort of embodied ethic is by definition one that cannot offer the consolations that come with asserting categorical pacifism and benevolence in relation to an uncritical humanism. But both Butler, and Beauvoir before her, insist that this hesitation is one in which the very question of responsibility is born. The ambiguity and precariousness of life solicit a response, however imperfect and contingent such a response may be.

NOTES

1. This was a fact illumined by those who wrote opinion pieces in the *Times* subsequent to the appearance of Gray's review. The "Letters" section of the *New York Times Sunday Book Review* from June 13, 2010, contains two letters by Kari Weil and Marilyn Yalom, both of whom argued for Beauvoir's continuing philosophical relevance.
2. Gray's comments in this regard are illustrative of a tendency to evade the reality of Beauvoir's bisexuality. (See Simons, 1999.)
3. Ironically, while Butler goes to great lengths to distance herself from an account of gender as a voluntary performance by an autonomous subject, it was precisely this kind of humanistic voluntarism of which Butler herself was accused following the publication of *Gender Trouble*.
4. These similarities motivate Alan Schrift's argument that Butler is a "nouvelle existentialiste" to the degree that her performative account of gender draws heavily on the French existentialist understanding of the relationship between freedom and constraint.
5. See Catherine Mills, 2007, "Normative Violence, Vulnerability and Responsibility," *differences: a journal of feminist cultural studies* 18(2).
6. Indeed, Beauvoir's claim that "violence is not an evil" is one that demonstrates some foresight with regard to subsequent philosophical accounts in which there is a kind of ontological, transcendental (Derrida) or normative (Butler) violence at play in the very emergence of a world and the recognition of the other. These forms of violence are in themselves neither good nor bad; they are operative at a level apart from the abuses of force that would be intelligible in

the domains of ethics and politics. Arguably, in her early philosophical writings, Beauvoir was already attuned to the various forms that violence could assume.

WORKS CITED

Beauvoir, Simone de. 2010. *The Second Sex*. Trans. Constance Borde and Sheila Malovany Chevalier. New York: Alfred A. Knopf.
———. 1996. Ethics of Ambiguity. Trans. Bernard Frechtman. New York: Citadel. Carol Publishing Group Edition. Published in French as *pour un morale de l'ambiguïté: suivi de Pyrrhus et Cinéas*. Gallimard, 1948. English pagination preceding the French.
———. 2004. Pyrrhus and Cineas. In Simone de Beauvoir: Philosophical Writings. Ed. Margaret Simons. Chicago: University of Chicago Press. Published in French as *pour un morale de l'ambiguïté: suivi de Pyrrhus et Cinéas*. Gallimard, 1948. English pagination preceding the French.
Butler, Judith. 1986. Sex and Gender in Simone de Beauvoir's *Second Sex*. *Yale French Studies* 72:35–49.
———. 1987. Variations on Sex and Gender: Beauvoir, Wittig, and Foucault. In *Feminism as Critique*. Ed. Seyla Benhabib and Drucilla Cornell. Minneapolis: University of Minnesota Press, p. 130.
———. 1990. *Gender Trouble*. New York: Routledge.
———. 1993. *Bodies that Matter*. New York: Routledge.
———. 2004a. *Precarious Life: The Powers of Mourning and Violence*. New York: Verso.
———. 2004. *Undoing Gender*. New York: Routledge.
———. 2009. *Frames of War: When Is Life Grievable?* New York: Verso.
Chanter, Tina. 2000. Abjection and Ambiguity: Simone de Beauvoir's Legacy. In *Journal of Speculative Philosophy* 14(2): 2000.
Gray, Francis du Plessix. 2010. Dispatches from the Other. *The New York Times Book Review*. May 30.
Murphy, Ann V. 2010. "Violence Is Not an Evil:" Ambiguity and Violence in Beauvoir's Early Philosophical Writings. *philoSOPHIA: a journal of continental feminism* 1(1).
Schrift, Alan D. Spring 2001. Judith Butler: Une Nouvelle Existentialiste. *Philosophy Today* 45(1).
Simons, Margaret. 1999. *Beauvoir and the* Second Sex: *Feminism, Race and the Origins of Existentialism*. Oxford: Rowan and Littlefield.

True Philosophers

Beauvoir and bell

BELL HOOKS

Often in scholarly works focused on Simone de Beauvoir and Jean-Paul Sartre critics dedicated to separating truth from fiction insist on accurately identifying Beauvoir as a philosopher, refusing to simply lay claim to her self-chosen identity as writer. She insisted: "'I am a writer. . . . I have written novels, philosophy, social criticism, a play—and yet all people know about me is *The Second Sex*. Granted, I am pleased that that book has had such an impact, but I want people to remember that *I am a writer*! A feminist certainly, and I do not deny the importance of feminism in my life, but first of all *I am a writer*!" (Bair 1990, 543). One might add that Beauvoir did not deny the importance of philosophy in her life but it is all too obvious in studying her life and work that she seldom declared herself a philosopher. In her shadow self, in an interior landscape, she could live, learn, and write as the quintessential philosopher, always with no one else present to deny or affirm this status. Certainly the body of work she produced reveals her passion for logic, epistemology, metaphysics, aesthetics, and ethics. And she would add to these passions a later interest in psychology and sociology.

Even though Beauvoir entered the study of philosophy embracing a patriarchal standpoint, the uniqueness of her perspective was shaped by an organic, perhaps unconscious feminist understanding generated by her lived experienced, which represented an implicit challenge to patriarchal assumptions about intellectual practice. It seems absolutely fitting that contemporary feminist movement brought a global awareness to Beauvoir and an acknowledgment of her contribution to feminist politics as it pertained, not just to overall feminist movement, but in particular to that aspect of feminist struggle that directly related to the efforts of female thinkers to assert their commitment to intellectual practice on an equal footing with male counterparts. Certainly, Beauvoir's contribution laid the foundation for the emergence of feminist philosophy. What is most vital about feminist philosophy is that it makes use of all the tools in the philosophical tradition to challenge and disrupt patriarchal canons, offering a more comprehensive and truthful understanding of the nature of human experience. It is this holistic perspective that shaped Beauvoir's thinking from the onset of her intellectual practice.

Long before contemporary feminism embraced the concept of the personal being political, Beauvoir more often than not chose an exploration of the personal as her way to approach the philosophical. And in keeping with this merger she choose an outstanding white, male philosopher, Jean-Paul Sartre, to serve as her guide, her mentor, declaring of him that he was a "'marvelous trainer of intellects'" (Bair 1990, 143). With no concern for self-diminishment she could passionately assert throughout her life that: "'I was intelligent, certainly, but Sartre was a genius'" (ibid.). In retrospect, it makes sense that Beauvoir—seeking to make it in a male-dominated intellectual and literary world—not only boosted her entry into that world via her partnership with Sartre, but also made sure that she would not be seen by him or anyone else as a vicious competitor in their partnership by always pronouncing that he was the superior thinker, the intellectual genius. Obviously, it was important for Sartre that Beauvoir nurture his egoistic need to be seen as the "greatest" thinker—the true philosopher. In later years, philosophy professor Maurice de Gandillac talked about those early student years when the two young thinkers were competing against one another. He recalled that the jury hearing their exams gave first place to Sartre because of his "extraordinary self-possession," but "'everybody agreed that, of the two, she was the real philosopher'" (Bair 1990, 145). Despite her performance, Beauvoir never thought that it would be to her advantage to claim to be a philosopher, and certainly she was not eager to affirm the identity of "true philosopher," knowing that it would disturb the balance of her burgeoning intellectual and romantic partnership.

Always and consistently asserting her choice and her right to be a thinker, an intellectual, Beauvoir deliberately drew attention away from her philosophical thought and work by placing it in the context of her being a writer of "many different genres" (Bair 1990, 13). When feminist thinkers interrogated Beauvoir about her seeming allegiance to patriarchal intellectual regimes she responded: "'Women are wrong to accuse me of separating myself from them. If there is blame, it should be upon language, for we speak in the language of men. It is they who have given us our verbs and pronouns, and we who must do the best we can with them'" (Bair, 384). Even though Beauvoir advocated feminism openly toward the end of her career, she was earlier compelled to be an insurgent—dissident—undercover—feminist due to her dominant longing to be an intellectual.

It would be a mistake on the part of everyone who studies Beauvoir to assume she had absolutely no understanding of the obstacles facing her as a young female striving to enter academic and intellectual domains that were practically the sole terrain of patriarchal males. And even though she often suggested that she was accepted without sexist prejudice, this was never the case. She was always confronting sexism, and that was why it was utterly necessary for her to be partnered with a dominant male. Had it truly been the case that she was not subject to patriarchal devaluation, she would not have needed the endorsement of Sartre to join the circle of academic and intellectual male peers who engaged in philosophical discussions on a regular basis. We will never know the extent to which it was important for Beauvoir to be the only "chosen" female in the group, however, it is abundantly clear that she was socialized to accept patriarchal thinking, and when it suited her she embraced it. In *Memoirs of a Dutiful Daughter*, she shares that her papa declared with pride: "'Simone has a man's brain; she thinks like a man; she *is* a man'" (Beauvoir 1959, 121). Such judgments contributed to her thinking of herself as special, as different from other women precisely because she could speak and think in the language of men. Like many individual, exceptional women of her time, Beauvoir insisted: "'I've often said and it bears repeating . . . I never felt discrimination among men in my life, I refused to believe that discrimination existed for other women'" (Fullbrook 1994, 59). Armored by her denial of the reality of sexism-(clearly a survival strategy), it is not surprising that it is only as she no longer needed the endorsement of any male to affirm her rightful place as critical thinker, as intellectual, that she could acknowledge sexism's negative impact on her life.

Since patriarchy has no gender, Beauvoir could be as patriarchal as any male. And yet she needed to act as a feminist, however unconsciously, to assert her intellectual self. On the one hand, she courageously resisted her family and her sexist upbringing, choosing to be an intellectual, devoting herself first and foremost to the world of ideas, and on the other hand, accepting that her survival and triumph in that world would always, of necessity, require her to assume a secondary position. She might know herself to be, as her professors declared, the "real philosopher," but she would not allow that private understanding to intrude on her public performance as the lesser intellect in her partnership with Sartre.

Like many young females in the United States who were inspired by reading *The Second Sex* and the diverse memoirs at the onset of contemporary feminist movement (without knowing much about Beauvoir's disclaimers about her relationship to philosophy or Sartre and his intellectual practice), I was awed by Beauvoir's disciplined commitment to study, her independence of mind, and her relentless pursuit of new epistemologies. In my late teens I read Sartre and Beauvoir and saw them both as philosophers engaged in an intellectual partnership. In the racially segregated world of my growing up, the only time I heard the word "philosopher" was when I was mockingly called by that sobriquet when I was being deemed too "serious" about the world of ideas. Although I never told anyone, it gave me great pleasure to be called a philosopher, when I learned that the root meaning of the word was "lover of wisdom."

In African-American literary tradition from the past to the present day, one finds depictions of the philosopher. More often than not, "he" is the one who works with ideas, who posits a critical read on the universe. Most recently we see this character in Walter Mosely's fiction and his writing in the character of the philosophizing black professor who lives in what appears to be a ghetto underground, as well as in the works of lawyer and mystery novelist Andrew Voss. In these works, like many others, to hold the place of philosopher is the highest intellectual honor.

Raised in a southern, black, working-class home, ideas and idea-making were most definitely seen as the province of men, a place of patriarchal privilege where females were just never seen as even the potential equal of men. I was a fifties girl when *The Second Sex* was first published. And while I was raised to embrace the importance of education, to become a teacher, it would have been seen as nonsensical for me to talk about doing intellectual work, like Beauvoir (who soon usurped Emily Dickinson's place as my shadowy mentor) as I entered college classes and chose to declare myself a writer.

Guided by Sandra Lambert, a young professor who taught at the women's college in the Midwest that I attended for a year, I transferred to Stanford University—moving thousands of miles away from home against the will of my parents, in order to find a place where the female intellect was respected. She believed that I had within me an intense passion for learning that could serve as a steady foundation for intellectual work. At Stanford I entered a world where males were seen as worthy of the rubric "genius." I cannot remember any female gaining such recognition. Instead, I entered an academic scene where feminist thinking was waging war with outmoded sexist ideas about genius, creativity, and intellectual practice. Ironically, the segregated world of my upbringing had affirmed the importance of higher education for females and African-Americans more than anyone did in the predominately patriarchal world of college, both in my undergraduate and graduate years.

In the years before writing *The Second Sex*, Beauvoir had begun to think critically about issues of race. Her experience of race relations in the United States led her to the work of Gunnar Myrdal. Integrating thoughts about race with issues of gender, she began to see both issues with a new perspective. Meeting and befriending African-American writers like Richard Wright stimulated her inquiry. In her biography of Beauvoir, Deirdre Bair makes the observation: "The comparisons of blacks with women seemed obvious to her, especially the idea that men (more specifically, white men in United States) had succeeded in relegating both groups to positions of *alterité*, or 'otherness.' . . . Increasingly, the word 'other' became an important part of her vocabulary, so that when friends asked what she was writing she said as frequently as not, 'Just something about the other sex'" (Bair, 388–389). Writing *The Second Sex* moved Beauvoir into the domain of feminist discourse. Bair explains: "Everything began to coalesce with her decision to define groups of people as 'other' in relation to men. The next logical step seemed to be 'the need to define what these "others" were, then to study the historical situations which made such alterity possible in the first place, then to see what were the circumstances that made it legitimate'" (Bair 1990, 389). This was when she began to read history with a special eye to women's role in it and discovered there was none, for generally they were not mentioned at all. As late as 1982, Beauvoir explains that when she accepted the idea that women were seen as inferior to men, "'this was an extremely troubling discovery'" and it became the basis for her calling into question everything that has been written about women by men, deeming it all suspect (Bair 1990, 382). However, she was not ready to turn a critical eye to all that men had written about men.

Of course, reading Beauvoir in the late sixties, I did not see her through the lens of race. She was a powerful symbol to me of female efforts to gain freedom of thought and action. Her life, her work, was vital to my survival and personal growth, for she was the one female intellectual, thinker-writer who had lived fully the life of the mind as I longed to live it. Not only had she had made her home in the world of ideas without forsaking romance, having fun, and connecting with others in community, she did all this without compromising her passion for philosophical thinking. In college I read philosophy voraciously. I worked to apply the ideas of existentialism to the world I knew most intimately. And I did much of this work in the company of an older, black male writer and academic who served as concrete mentor, paving the way for me to enter a world of critical thinking that was often closed to females. With him I hoped to live the dream of intellectual partnership that Beauvoir had experienced.

Retrospectively I can see that my partner needed me to remain in a secondary role in relation to him. When I began to engage feminist ideas that moved me beyond the scope of his tutelage, issues of domination and power surfaced. Despite this breakdown in our bond, he had been for years the person who affirmed my intellectual endeavors, who listened to me as I worked with ideas. As we were parting, he actually stated that he wanted "the spotlight" to shine on him. When I suggested there was enough light for both of us, he disagreed. Again, I could easily see parallels between Beauvoir's experience and my own. Certainly, Sartre had been more than willing to allow her to share the spotlight as long as she remained in a secondary role. That never really changed. When publication of *The Second Sex* brought to Beauvoir a spotlight solely her own, the relationship between Sartre and Beauvoir began to change fundamentally. Prior to publication, it was Sartre's fascination with political theory and action that began to create a shift in their perspectives. Then in 1956, he began his affair with a young Algerian Jewish student who became the "secondary" helpmeet and no spotlight had to be shared, as she posed no threat of becoming primary. Years later, making her his "daughter" through legal adoption, this much younger female sycophant assumed a privileged position in his life that had not been accorded Beauvoir.

Despite this act of disloyalty, nothing changed the reality that at a historical moment when a female seeking to become an intellectual received little or no encouragement of support, Sartre gave all that and more to Beauvoir. He was, to use Toni Morrison's phrase from the novel *Beloved*, a "friend of her mind." After both their deaths, when letters and notes showed the myriad ways Beauvoir's philosophical thinking had shaped Sartre's work, it became all the more evident that he not only relied on her thinking to shape his work but that she accepted his borrowing from her because it was, perversely, the ultimate gesture of affirmation. No woman seeking to establish herself as an intellectual in Beauvoir's day could achieve that status without the support of prominent males endorsing her. Certainly, as a young black female striving to become an intellectual, I relied on the support of a male partner who affirmed my choice to think at a time when no one else offered consideration and praise. It was only as that relationship ended that I could see the ways my self-esteem was assaulted by his need to always be seen as the superior thinker.

Clearly, as Beauvoir moved closer to feminism, Sartre stayed wedded to the patriarchal logic that had always served as a foundation for his thinking about gender. In his life, Beauvoir was the exceptional woman, with whom he could share a lifetime of intellectual companionship long after romantic sexual engagement ended. Sadly, he was still willing to displace her by granting legal rights to his younger paramour, and he asserted her legal authority as his chosen kin and executor once he died. Being forced to surrender her privileged position by this displacement was a bitter blow from which Beauvoir never fully recovered. And yet, this experience helped her forge bonds of solidarity with women victimized by patriarchal thought and action.

In the wake of Sartre's death, feminist movement became a source of political resistance, much to Beauvoir's satisfaction. According to Bair: "All this activity gave her tremendous pleasure, and in the bleak years after Sartre's death, when her own health was often troublesome, speaking of her work on behalf of women seemed to bring zest to her voice and vitality to her countenance. These were truly her years of joyful participation in feminist affairs" (Bair 1990, 604). Although Beauvoir would continue until her death to tweak the truth of her partnership with Sartre—to maintain the myth that their lifelong partnership was built on a foundation of equality—scholars began to reveal a different picture after her death. Perhaps the most earth-shattering discovery was the extent to which Beauvoir, "the true philosopher," had influenced the thought and writing of Sartre (Fullbrook 1994). We will never know how many young women all over the world, irrespective of the gender of chosen partners, were utterly disillusioned as we were compelled by new scholarship to see a broader, truer picture of this lifelong affair. Even though I was troubled when I learned in my adult years that Beauvoir passively accepted Sartre's appropriation of her ideas without acknowledging the source, nothing can change the reading that shaped my own personal struggle to reconcile my longing to be a thinking female and an intellectual who also wanted to be loved. I needed the example of Beauvoir.

All during my girlhood years my patriarchal father had emphasized that no man wanted an educated thinking woman. Indeed, he would scold mama for allowing me to read and study and thus "ruining" my chances for marriage. When I announced to mama at sixteen that I would never marry, I asserted an independence of thought and action that would serve as the affirming foundation for future engagement with feminist philosophy. Even now it is difficult to find words that adequately name how frightened I was by my growing recognition that I wanted a different life than the one my parents had planned for me. Though not yet fully articulated, feminist resistance was the force that compelled me to cling to independence of mind, despite the threat of punishment and abandonment by my parents. Finding Beauvoir was akin to the experience of finding Rilke's *Letters to a Young Poet* during my suicidal teen years.

Simone de Beauvoir, as intellectual, philosopher, cultural critic, and as a politically radical leftist woman charted a path that was vital to me throughout the process of my intellectual growth. By the time of her death I had written memoirs, feminist theory, poetry, and cultural criticism. Again, Beauvoir as a writer of many different genres affirmed this process. Throughout her life, she faced sexism when it came to gaining recognition of her intellectual and political work. Understanding much of what she had endured, Bair still ended her powerful work with sentimental declarations:

> She had been an inspiration to many, the little girl with the mind of a man who turned the adversity of poverty into the good fortune of getting an education, becoming economically independent and taking charge of her own life. She lived that life on her own terms, prepared to defend her stances and decisions and willing to take whatever consequences came her way. (Bair 1990, 617–618)

Certainly, Beauvoir was as serious a critical thinker as her male peers, yet it disparages the scope of her thought and work even as a young scholar to suggest that having the "mind of a man" was the defining foundation. It was precisely her feminist consciousness that empowered her to move beyond the dictates of male thought and patriarchal boundaries.

Influenced by the life and writing of Beauvoir, it was still essential for me to move beyond her focus on woman as "other" to bring together a critical perspective for understanding female identity that began from the standpoint that female identity is shaped by gender, race, and class, and never solely by sex. While Beauvoir was interested in the issue of class as it relates to the construction of identity, like the vast majority of white intellectuals she considered race an issue that mainly impacted on the lives of people of color. And like many feminist thinkers in the United States studying the works of Fanon and other black thinkers, she appropriated many paradigms pertaining to race and applied them to gender. Even though Beauvoir read black women writers (primarily novelists) in the early 1980s, she did not address works of nonfiction by black women thinkers, even though black women thinkers have contributed much to the re-visioning of feminist theory and practice. Even today, racialized sexist hierarchies still overdetermine whether our work receives continued consideration.

Most contemporary white feminist philosophers, intellectuals, or both rarely give attention to the work of black women that does not focus on race. And anyone interested in the writing of black women philosophers must move outside canonical boundaries to find this work. Despite her long engagement with philosophical study, Angela Davis has little visibility as a philosopher. Even though I consider myself working as a feminist philosopher, that is not how I am viewed in most academic circles. In his unpublished work on the writing of bell hooks, philosopher Ron Scapp contends:

> To contemplate whether bell hooks is philosophical raises the question what does it mean to philosophize. If we use Socrates as a model of philosophizing then we know that to philosophize is to ask questions, and to critically engage the claims, positions, and values of others in dialogue. Clearly hooks does that. And if one raises objection that bell hooks does not have a system the way Hegel does we can simply reiterate that Socrates had no system. Socrates had passion, commitment, and questions. And hooks asks the question what is good, what is real, and what is it that we know. She does so in relation to race, class, and gender and so she is best understood as philosophizing about the dynamics and relationships that exist within a social and cultural context. What someone who is genuinely philosophical does is ask certain kinds of questions. Expressing a profound commitment to freedom, justice and love hooks' work should remind us that this is a philosophical position and a philosophical worldview. (Scapp 2011, 1)

These statements could easily be used to describe Simone de Beauvoir's intellectual practice. Beauvoir was attracted her to philosophy because it offered her a way to know; it legitimized her search for truth and her passion for justice.

That Beauvoir's work is to this day subject to interrogation that seeks to undermine the continued value of her intellectual practice reminds everyone that even after the awesome gains women have achieved through feminist political work, the female who seeks to claim intellectual work as her passion, calling, and vocation still encounters barriers continually constructed and maintained by sexist thinking. In her compelling study, *Simone de Beauvoir: The Making of an Intellectual Woman*, Toril Moi calls attention to the way in which Beauvoir's critics, on the left and the right, consistently attempt to diminish the power of her intellectual practice, her critical insights, and political visions by focusing on her persona (e.g., the April 21, 2010 *New York Times* piece, "Being and Frumpiness"), and by shallow critiques of her personality. Moi contends:

> As might be expected, a politically outspoken woman such as Beauvoir attracts much hostility from her opponents on the left as well as on the right. Paradoxically, however, politically motivated critiques of Beauvoir contain surprisingly little discussion of politics and much apparently pointless dwelling on her personality and private life. In fact such dwelling on her personality is best described as the politicized use of the sexist personality *topos*. The intended effect is to depoliticize her by presenting her political choices not as the outcome of careful reflection on the issues

at stake, but as the inexplicable *élans* of an overemotional or even hysterical woman. (Moi 1994, 81)

Much of what Moi highlights as attempts to diminish Beauvoir's intellectual contributions are strategies still deployed to devalue the work of feminist intellectuals to this day.

More often than not, those who previously asserted that it had no value appropriate the work of feminist intellectuals. Politically, it is evident that feminist political movement must insist that efforts to affirm the work of women intellectuals remain a central aspect of feminist struggle. Without such a focus I might not have had the opportunity to share reflections about the impact of Beauvoir's life and work on my intellectual development and process. Narrow-minded thinking, which sees any black female critical thinker as only useful when speaking on the subject of race, simply seeks to recolonize and dehumanize us. It is precisely to move against such colonization that leads feminist thinkers to always demand that we examine the ways interlocking systems of domination work in tandem to maintain systems of domination and exploitation. Simone de Beauvoir's life and work are a testament to the power of such resistance.

Our perspectives on gender fundamentally differ. Unlike Beauvoir, I never accepted any notion of male superiority; I embraced the gift of "genius" given to me even though I understood the sexist cultural devaluation of female thinkers. Believing myself to be the equal or better than male comrades with whom I shared ideas, I never accepted sexist notions that women could not be "great" writers or thinkers. And of course, while male mentors fundamentally shaped Beauvoir's thinking, females were my primary chosen guides as I worked to become an intellectual. Refusing to see feminism as solely about women's rights, there is the radical call to challenge and change patriarchy at the center of all my work. While Beauvoir separates issues of class, race, and gender—a perspective that distorts the true reality of human being—I continually insist that we cannot understand what it means to be female or male without critically examining interlocking systems of domination. And yet, without the intellectual practice of Simone de Beauvoir, I might never have fully realized my intellectual identity. As passionately as she followed Sartre, allowing him to be her guide, I have been fundamentally guided by her life and work. Moi gives voice to the homage all female intellectuals owe Beauvoir declaring: "Simone de Beauvoir now belongs to a past generation. Her pioneering example has opened the way for women to be taken seriously—and loved—as intellectuals and as women. . . . she still makes it easier for us to live our lives as we wish, without regard to patriarchal conventions" (Moi 1994, 256). Nowadays it is a common tendency to equate academic scholarship with intellectual work, even though they represent radically different vocations. Clearly females have achieved a level of equality with males in academe. No such parity exists in the world of intellectual work.

Indeed Beauvoir's example is precisely still so necessary because the obstacles she faced as she worked to be an intellectual woman must still be confronted. Hence the continuing effort on the part of established patriarchal thinkers, male and female, to discredit her writing. Yet these efforts will never change the reality that Beauvoir's life and work continues to inspire and affirm females who dare to choose the passion and discipline of intellectual labor. Whereas I was once most attracted to her intellectual partnership with Sartre, I am now seduced by the awareness that no matter what her relationship was to him, or any partner, the true constant in her life was thinking, working with ideas, and being a philosopher in the truest sense of the word.

WORKS CITED

Bair, Deirdre. 1990. *Simone de Beauvoir: A Biography.* New York: Summit Books.
Beauvoir, Simone de. 1959. *Memoirs of a Dutiful Daughter.* New York: Harper Collins Publishers.
Fullbrook, Edward and Kate. 1994. *Simone de Beauvoir and Jean-Paul Sartre: The Remaking of a Twentieth-Century Legend.* New York: Basic Books.
Moi, Toril. 1994. *Simone de Beauvoir: The Making of an Intellectual Woman.* Cambridge: Blackwell Publishers.
Scapp, Ron. 2011. Writing Philosophy: The Work of bell hooks. Unpublished Essay.

Contributors

DEBRA BERGOFFEN is emeritus professor of philosophy at George Mason University. She is the author of *The Philosophy of Simone de Beauvoir: Gendered Phenomenologies, Erotic Generosities* (State University of New York Press, 1997) and the editor of several anthologies. Her writings have focused on such figures as Simone de Beauvoir, Luce Irigaray, Jacques Lacan, Friedrich Nietzsche, and Jean Paul Sartre and deal with issues concerning the ethics and politics of gender and embodiment. She has just published a book on genocidal rape and human rights titled *Contesting the Politics of Genocidal Rape: Affirming the Dignity of the Vulnerable Body* (Routledge 2011).

SARA HEINÄMAA holds a senior lectureship in theoretical philosophy at the University of Helsinki, Finland; and at the moment, she works as Academy Research Fellow at the Helsinki Collegium for Advanced Studies, University of Helsinki (2008–2013). Her areas of specialization are phenomenology, existentialism, philosophy of mind, history of philosophy, and philosophical women's studies. Heinämaa also serves as the leader for the Academy of Finland research project, "European Rationality in the Break from Modernity," and the research community "Subjectivity, Historicity, and Communality," both located at the University of Helsinki. She has written numerous books and articles, as well as edited many collections. Some of her monographs include: *Toward a Phenomenology of Sexual Difference: Husserl, Merleau-Ponty, Beauvoir* (2003), and *Death, Birth and the Feminine: Essays in the Philosophy of Embodiment*, together with Robin May Schott, Vigdis Songe-Møller, and Sigridur Thorgeirsdottir (2010). Edited volumes include: *Edmund Husserl: Renewal and Humanity: Lectures and Essays*, edited by Sara Heinämaa (2006); *Simone de Beauvoir: "Must We Burn Sade" and Other Essays*, edited by Sara and Erika Heinämaa Ruonakoski (2007); *Consciousness: From Perception to Reflection*, edited by Sara Heinämaa, Vili Lähteenmäki, and Pauliina Remes (2007); *Psychology and Philosophy: Inquiries into the Soul from Late Scholasticism to Contemporary Thought*, edited by Sara Heinämaa and Martina Reuter (2008).

BELL HOOKS was most recently distinguished professor in residence at Berea College in Berea, Kentucky. She has served as a Professor of English at Yale University and a Distinguished Professor of English at City College and the Graduate Center of the City University of New York. Author of over thirty books, hooks is often identified as one of the nation's most influential women and leading "public intellectuals." Her work and writings cover a broad spectrum of topics on gender, race, class, culture, pedagogy, and the significance of media for contemporary American and African American cultures. Her corpus includes such works as: *Ain't I a Woman? Black Women and Feminism* (South End Press, 1981); *Feminist Theory from Margin to Center* (South End Press, 1984); *Black Looks: Race and Representation* (South End Press, 1992); *Teaching to Transgress: Education as the Practice of Freedom* (Routledge, 1994); *Reel to Real: Race, Sex, and Class at the Movies* (Routledge, 1996); and *All About Love* (HarperCollins, 2000).

WILLIAM L. MCBRIDE is Arthur G. Hansen distinguished professor of philosophy at Purdue University and President of the International Federation of Philosophical Societies (FISP). In addition to French philosophy, especially Sartre's, his research interests include social and political philosophy and philosophy in Eastern Europe. He was cofounder and first director of the North American Sartre Society, and is immediate past president of the North American Society for Social Philosophy. The four most recent of his 20 authored, edited, and co-edited books are *Philosophical Reflections on the Changes in Eastern Europe* (1999), *From Yugoslav Praxis to Global Pathos* (2001), *Calvin O. Schrag and the Task of Philosophy After Postmodernity* (2002), and *Social and Political Philosophy*, Volume 2 of the Istanbul World Congress Proceedings (2006). In addition, he has published well over 100 book chapters, articles, and critical reviews.

ERIN MCCARTHY is professor of philosophy at St. Lawrence University (Canton, NY), where she also teaches in the Asian Studies and Gender Studies Programs. She is the author of *Ethics Embodied* (Lexington Books, 2010), as well as several articles that have appeared in both French and English in journals and anthologies. With a background in phenomenology, existentialism, and Japanese philosophy, her current area of research, comparative feminist philosophy, combines these other areas with feminist philosophy. Her current project is a comparative feminist perspective on issues surrounding maternity.

ELAINE P. MILLER is associate professor of philosophy at Miami University, where she is also the director of the Graduate Program in Philosophy. She is the author of *The Vegetative Soul: From Philosophy of Nature to Subjectivity in the Feminine* (State University of New York Press, 2002), as well as numerous articles on Kant, Hegel, Nietzsche, Beauvoir, Irigaray, and Kristeva. She works on philosophical conceptions of nature and art and how they have influenced conceptions of subjectivity historically. She teaches courses in nineteenth-century philosophy, twentieth-century continental philosophy, existentialism, aesthetics, feminist theory, and environmental philosophy.

CONTRIBUTORS

SHANNON M. MUSSETT is associate professor of philosophy at Utah Valley University, where she is also the chair of the Department of Philosophy and Humanities. She is also the current secretary-treasurer for the Society for Phenomenology and Existential Philosophy. She specializes in nineteenth- and twentieth-century Continental philosophy, as well as feminist theory. Mussett has co-edited (with Sally J. Scholz) *The Contradictions of Freedom: Philosophical Essays on Simone de Beauvoir's 'Les Mandarins'* (State University of New York Press, 2006) as well as published numerous articles and chapters on Simone de Beauvoir and G. W. F. Hegel. She is currently working on developing a philosophy of entropy.

ANN V. MURPHY is associate professor of philosophy at Fordham University in New York. She is the author of *Violence and the Philosophical Imaginary* (SUNY Press, May 2012). Her interests are in the philosophy of gender, twentieth-century French philosophy, phenomenology, and political philosophy. Her essays have been published in journals such as *Continental Philosophy Review, Hypatia, Philosophy Today*, and *philoSOPHIA: a journal of continental feminism*.

SALLY J. SCHOLZ is professor of philosophy at Villanova University. Her research is in social and political philosophy and feminist theory. Her publications include the books *On de Beauvoir* (Wadsworth, 2000), *On Rousseau* (Wadsworth, 2001), *Political Solidarity* (Penn State Press, 2008), and *Feminism: A Beginner's Guide* (One World, 2010). She co-edited *Peacemaking: Lessons from the Past, Vision for the Future* (with Judith Presler) and *The Contradictions of Freedom: Philosophical Essays on Simone de Beauvoir's 'Les Mandarins'* (with Shannon M. Mussett). She has also published articles on violence against women, oppression, and just war theory among other topics. Scholz is currently faculty-in-residence at the Center for Peace and Justice Studies at Villanova, co-editor of the *Journal for Peace and Justice Studies*, and former editor of the *APA Newsletter on Feminism and Philosophy*.

MARGARET A. SIMONS is emeritus professor of philosophy at the University of Southern Illinois at Edwardsville. She is a founding editor of *Hypatia: A Journal of Feminist Philosophy* and a former codirector of the Society for Phenomenology and Existential Philosophy. Simons has published many articles and given over 100 professional paper presentations, many of which focus on the philosophy of Simone de Beauvoir. She is the author of *Beauvoir and* The Second Sex*: Feminism, Race and the Origins of Existentialism* (Rowman & Littlefield, 1999) and editor of *The Philosophy of Simone de Beauvoir: Critical Essays* (Indiana University Press, 2006). She co-edited (with Sylvie Le Bon de Beauvoir) Simone de Beauvoir's *Philosophical Writings* (University of Illinois Press, 2004), the first volume in a seven-volume series of Beauvoir's texts in English translation, and supported by grants from the National Endowment for the Humanities and the French Ministry of Culture, and published by the University of Illinois Press. The second volume in the Beauvoir Series, *Beauvoir's Diary of a Philosophy Student, Volume 1, 1926–27*, co-edited by Simons, Barbara Klaw, Sylvie Le Bon de Beauvoir, and Marybeth Timmermann, was published by the University of Illinois Press in 2006; and the third volume, *Beauvoir's Wartime Diary*, co-edited with Sylvie Le Bon de Beauvoir and translated by Anne Deing Cordero, was published by the University of Illinois Press in 2008. *Beauvoir's Political Writings* was published in 2012 by the University of Illinois Press.

GAIL WEISS is professor of philosophy and Human Sciences at The George Washington University. Her areas of specialization include phenomenology and existentialism, feminist theory, and philosophy of literature. She is the author of *Refiguring the Ordinary* (Indiana University Press, 2008) and *Body Images: Embodiment as Intercorporeality* (Routledge, 1999), editor of *Intertwinings: Interdisciplinary Encounters with Merleau-Ponty* (SUNY, 2008), and editor of *Feminist Interpretations of Maurice Merleau-Ponty* (Penn State Press, 2006), *Thinking the Limits of the Body* (State University of New York Press, 2003) and *Perspectives on Embodiment: The Intersections of Nature and Culture* (Routledge, 1999). She is currently completing a monograph titled, *Beauvoir's Ambiguities: Philosophy, Literature, and Feminism*, and has published numerous journal articles and book chapters on philosophical and feminist issues related to human embodiment.

WILLIAM S. WILKERSON is professor of philosophy at the University of Alabama in Huntsville. He writes and teaches in the areas of twentieth-century Continental thought and the philosophy of gender and sexuality. In addition to publishing many articles in such places as *Epoché, Continental Philosophy Review*, and the *Journal of the History of Philosophy*, he was co-editor, with Jeffrey Paris, of a collection of essays in social theory, *New Critical Theory: Essays on Liberation* (Rowman & Littlefield, 2001), and is the author of a book on sexual identity, titled *Ambiguity and Sexuality*, and published by Palgrave Macmillan (2007).

Index

1844 Manuscripts (Marx), 95, 99

A Note on Time, Eternity, and the Concept (Kojève), 105
a priori, 56, 59, 75, 83, 88
abortion rights, 135
Absolute, The, Beauvoir's view of, 4, 13n4, 18, 39, 111, 119–20; Hegel's 20, 118; and masculine self-conceptions, 179; and Plato, 23; and Sade, 83
absolute sovereignty 75, 80, 83, 84, 87
absurdity, 4, 6, 49, 68, 118, 154, 193
actualization, 103, 105, 106
aesthetic, 125, in Beauvoir and Plato, 16, 18, 22, 23, 31n6; in hooks' thought, 227, 238; and Merleau-Ponty, 176–177; in Rousseau's aesthetics, 43; women's bodies and, 142n7
Africa, 111
African-American, 229, 230, 238
age, 6, 7, 12, 47, 86, 113, 168
Age of Discretion, The (Beauvoir), 112
Algren, Nelson, 212
Aline et Valcour (Sade), 81
Allen, Beverly, 85
ambiguity, as desire, 177–183; as embodiment, 126, 221; and ethics, 65, 69, 75, 79, 87, 118; and gender, 213; and human existence, 2, 9, 18, 119, 219–20; and Merleau-Ponty, 11, 172–86; and perception, 173–77 187n5; and philosophy, 4, 5, 8, 18–20, 22; and precariousness, 12; 213, 215–17, 222–25, and violence, 219–22
ambiguous freedom, 82
America Day by Day (Beauvoir), 168

American Declaration of Independence, The, 86
Ancient Society (Morgan), 94
Aristotle, 15, 144n18
Arp, Kristana, 71n6, 72n14
art, in Beauvoir and Plato, 15–18, 20–23, 31n2, 33n19; Bergson's views on, 155; in Camus, 122n13; and childbirth, 200, Rousseau's views on, 43, 53n16; and work, 117, 206
Asia Minor, 111
Asian Philosophy, 201, 207n5
Aucassin et Nicolette, 112
Auschwitz, 80
authentic existence, 103, 178
authoritarianism, 5
autonomy, 184, 206; in Beauvoir's ethics, 9, 56, 67, 70; Kantian idea of, 58–59, 63, 71n11; and women's situation, 107

bad faith, Beauvoir's view of 7; and Beauvoir's ethics, 62, 65–68, 72n15, 221; and Bergson, 11, 153, 158, 161–66; and the desire to be, 180–82, 187n8; in *She Came to Stay,* 163–166; in *When Things of Spirit Come First,* 161–64
Bair, Deirdre, 17, 31n8, 56, 230, 232, 233
Bataille, Georges, 44, 45, 52n8, 81, 119
Bauer, Nancy, 41
becoming, in Bergson, 158; and Merleau-Ponty, 143n12; women's, 11, 139, 168, 191–94, 197–200, 204–06, 213, 214
"Being and Frumpiness", 212, 234
Being and Nothingness (Sartre), 60, 156, 178, 184

241

being-for-itself, 178–82, 184, 187n8, 188n8
being-for-others, 172, 179, 184
being-in-itself, 62, 178–82
Beloved (Morrison), 231
Benjamin, Jessica, 156
Bergoffen, Debra, 9, 31n6, 65, 71n6, 75, 76, 187n7, 207n4,
Bergson, Henri, 1, 10, 11, 71n12, 153–66, 168
Berkeley, George, 171
Bernard, Claude, 157
Between East and West (Irigaray), 201–02
Bible, the, 154, 166
Bibliothèque Nationale, 5, 153
Birth of Tragedy, The (Nietzsche), 15–17, 119
Bodies that Matter (Butler), 213
Bollinger, Laurel, 202
Boupacha case, the, 9, 79, 80
bourgeois, 93, 96
Breton, André, 161
Brownmiller, Susan, 85
Burnham, James, 96
Butler, Judith, 1, 11–12; as existentialist, 225n4; and gender, 225n3; and precariousness, 215–219, 221–25; relation to Beauvoir, 213–15; and repetition, 116, 211

Cahiers de jeunesse: 1926–1930, 153
Cahiers du Sud, 173
Camus, Albert , 116
Capital, Das (Marx), 94–95
capitalism, 97
Cartesian, 174, 184, 186, 213, 214
Casey, Edward S., 174
categorical, in morality, 57, 59, 62, 66–67, 69; and pacifism 221, 222, 225
categorical imperative, 55
Catholic Church, 7
Cervantes, Miguel de, 17
Chanter, Tina, 211, 212
childbirth, 133, 199, 200, 211
class, 7, 105; and Marx, 10, 93, 94, 96–99; and gender, 37, 41, 45, 47; and Sade, 77–79, 83; intersection with race and gender, 230, 233–35
class struggle, 93, 96–99
Claudel, Paul, 161

Cold War, the, 91, 96
collective, and the festival, 36, 39, 42, 44, 45, 50, 52n12; happiness, 60; and sovereign rights, 77–78, 85
Communism 91, 96, 97
Communist Manifesto, The (Marx) 93, 96
Communist Party, the 91, 93
Confessions (Rousseau), 37
consciousness, 7, 126, 131; Beauvoir's view of, 64–65, 68, 69, 107–108; and Bergson, 154–155, 158; embodied, 134; and gender, 196, 214, 233; non-positing, 175; of the other, 128, 156–158, 162–67; relation to self-consciousness, 105, 108, 179; revolutionary, 93
conventional self, 154
corporeal vulnerability, 12, 215, 216
Creative Evolution (Bergson), 165
Critique of Practical Reason (Kant), 57, 58, 63

daimon, 26
Damrosch, Leo, 43, 44, 50
Davis, Angela, 233
de Gandillac, Maurice 228
deep self, 11, 153, 155–56
Deleuze, Gilles, 5, 116, 121n12
democracy, 76
Derrida, Jacques, 116, 225n6
determinism, 93, 159
Deutscher, Penelope, 55, 70n12, 72n14, 72n20, 100n2, 120n4, 207n5, 116
devoir-être, 62, 64–69
Diary of a Philosophy Student: 1926–27 (Beauvoir), 153
Dickinson, Emily, 230
Dionysian, 119
disability studies, 186
Djamila Boupacha (Beauvoir), 79
Don Juan, 20
Dostoyevsky, Fyodor, 17, 83
Drieu La Rochelle, Pierre, 96
Du Bois, W.E.B., 82, 83
du Plessix Gray, Francine, 211
dualism, 186, 197

École *Normale*, 36, 91
embodiment, 10, 11, 83; and gender, 136, 193; and Irigaray, 205; and philosophy, 8,

16; in *She Came to Stay*, 164; in the work of Beauvoir and phenomenologists, 126–127, 129, 130, 133, 136, 141, 213–14
Emile (Rousseau), 37, 46, 49, 52n15
empirical determination, 58
Engels, Friedrich, 51n7, 93, 94, 98, 99, 100n10
Enlightenment, the, 37–38
epistemology, 227
equality, 44, 47, 49–50, 98, 109, 198, 219, 232, 235
equivocal couple, 138, 140
Eshelman, Matthew, 72n21
Essai sur les données immédiates de la conscience (Bergson) see *Time and Free Will*
essence, and existence, 17, 109, 180; and gender, 198, 214; Platonic, 20, 21, 192; of time, 179
ethical naturalism, 125
ethics, 1, 2, 35, 37, 125, 227; Beauvoir's, 6, 7, 9, 55–57, 61–70, 114, 118, 194, 219–22; in Beauvoir and Butler, 215–17, 223, 225–26; existentialist, 20; of the festival, 44–45, 50; Hegelian, 118; Irigaray's 197–99; Kantian, 57–59, 63; and Sade, 75–76
Ethics of Ambiguity, The (Beauvoir), 5; ambiguity in, 18, 174, 177–79; bad faith in, 187n5; Beauvoir's dislike of, 56–57; and the desire to be, 180–81; discussion of Nietzsche in, 103; discussion of Plato in, 23, 27; discussion of Rousseau in, 37; discussion of women's situation in, 46; ethical views of, 60–70, 114, 184; and existentialism, 4, 20; festivals in, 39–42, 44–46, 118; and freedom, 104, 222; and liberation 51n8; literature on, 71n6; oppression in, 116; relation to Marxism, 92–94, 96; and Sade, 75; science in 78–79; temporality in, 66–67, 111–12, 118; value theory in, 129; women's situation in, 194
Europe, 50, 97
existential ambiguity, 177
existential truth, 22
Existentialism, 17, 20, 104
existentialist ethics, 168n12, 194, 199
existential-phenomenology, 10, 126

Eye and Mind (Merleau-Ponty), 177, 185

Fanon, Frantz, 233
Faust, 20
Fell, Alison, 192
feminism, 99, 201, 211, 227, 228, 232, 235
feminist theory, 94, 108, 186, 213, 233
festival, 8, 35–50, 118–19
First Discourse (Rousseau), 37
Flaubert, Gustave, 17
Force of Circumstance (Beauvoir), 112
Forms, the, 15
Foucault, Michel, 56, 214
Frames of War (Butler), 213–16, 218, 219
France, 76, 96, 163, 192
free will, 59, 64
freedom, and ambiguity, 11, 178–79, 216, 224; and Beauvoir's ethics, 9, 55–57, 61–69, 75–76, 82–83, 88, 114–15, 219–22; Beauvoir's ontology of, 62–66; and Bergson, 10–11, 154, 157–59; and children, 206; and the festival, 8, 35–36, 37, 40, 42–46, 48–50; from oppression, 92; in hooks' life and thought, 231, 234; in immanence/transcendence distinction, 120n1, 121n10; in Kant, 57–60; in literature, 22, 30; in Marxism, 92–94, 95; in Merleau-Ponty, 176, 184; and the Other, 5–8, 55; and Plato, 23; in Sade, 75–76, 77–78, 79–82, 84; In Sartre, 188n9; in *The Second Sex*, 95; in *She Came to Stay*, 163–67; temporality of, 111–12, 117–19; and women's situation, 46, 48, 99, 118, 134, 193–96, 200
French Algerian War, 76, 80, 87
French Communist Party, the, 99
French Revolution, the, 76, 95
Freud, Sigmund, 36, 94, 98, 99, 121n8, 171
friendship, 24, 26, 68
Fullbrook, Edward and Kate Fullbrook, 31n2

Gass, W. H., 82, 86
gender, affect on one's self-conception, 187n4; Beauvoir's analysis of, 6–7, 10; in Beauvoir's life, 229; Butler's view of, 12, 41, 213–14, 225n3; importance to Beauvoir's thought, 8; in *The Second Sex*,

gender (*continued*)
230; hooks' view of, 12, 232–35; Irigaray's analysis of, 198–199; and festivals, 37, 45–48; and Marxism, 10, 98–100; and maternity, 200; and Sade, 76, 80; and war, 84; and work, 49
gender oppression, 80
gender performativity, 12, 213–14
Gender Trouble (Butler), 213, 214, 225n3
Geneva, 42, 43
genocide, 80, 83, 85, 86
Gestalt psychology, 174–75
God, 26, 60 83, 158, 179, 182, 201
Greeks, Ancient, 2, 17, 95, 110
Groundwork (Kant), 57, 63
Guattari, Pierre-Félix, 5
Gulag, the, 80

Hague, The, 86
Hegel, G.W.F. and the festival, 44, 45, 52n12; Kojève and, 105, 120n3; and recognition of the other, 68–69; relation to Marx, 92, 95; relationship to Beauvoir's thought, 4–5, 20, 70n1, 71n5, 98, 119, 122n14, 153, 178, 234; in twentieth century thought, 91; and women's labor, 104–06, 108–09; and work, 117–19
Heidegger, Martin, 6, 36, 65, 98, 126, 127, 193; and gender, 132; ontology of, 131
Heinämaa, Sara, 10, 32n12, 125, 126, 128–30, 133, 142n2, 147n33, 147n34, 192
history, Beauvoir's conception of, 5, 114; Beauvoir's relevance to, 12, 98; and class struggle in Marxist thought, 98–99; festivals and, 35, 39, 46, 50; Hegelian conception of, 118–19; Kojève's conception of, 105, Kristeva's conception of, 109; in *The Second Sex*, 41; validating war, 80; of Western philosophy, 1–2, 4; and women's situation, 99, 126, 195, 230
Holveck, Eleanore, 21
hooks, bell, 1, 12, 227, 234
human existence, ambiguity in, 2, 172, 174, 178–79, 183–84, 186, 187, 188n8, 219; captured by literature and biography, 6, 70; and embodiment, 127–29; and gender, 8, 10, 133–34; importance of self-other relations to, 6; in *Pyrrhus and Cineas*, 110; in relation to the good, 62; temporality and, 105, 119; as transcendence, 66; violence in 222; and work, 106
human freedom, 7, 9, 46, 60, 62, 92, 93, 117, 219, 221
human rights, 80, 83, 86–88
humanism, 6, 60, 92, 223, 225
Husserl, Edmund, 10, 36, 65, 125–28, 130, 131, 141, 153
Hutchings, Kimberly, 39

idealism, 97, 159, 161, 164
Ideas (Husserl), 127
immanence, distinction from transcendence, 120n1, 220; and festivals, 50; and women's situation, 10, 103–04, 109–10, 116–18, 139, 179, 187n8, 192–97, 200
India, 111
individual, the, freedom of, 5, 45, 134; and festivals, 50; relationship to the Other, 6, 119; relation to community, 8, 42; Rousseau and, 42; systematic thought and, 19, 37; moral tension in, 65; sovereignty of, 77–78, 223
individual freedom, 6, 51n9; and Bergson, 159; and ethics, 55, 60, 69, 75–76, 88, 167;
and Sade, 77–78
inequality, 7, 38, 40–43, 46–49, 103
Interahamwe, the, 84
interdependency, 12, 217, 218
International Criminal Court, 86
intersubjectivity, in Bergson, 11; and the couple, 140; and gender, 141; in Husserl, 142n5; and love in Irigaray, 202; in Merleau-Ponty and Beauvoir, 172, 183–186; and pregnancy, 145n24; in Sade, 9, 75
Introduction to the Study of Experimental Medicine (Bernard), 157
Irigaray, Luce, 1, 11, 82–83, 142n7, 143n12, 191–92, 197–203, 206
Islam, 96–7

Japanese philosophy, 201
Jaspers, Karl, 96
Jones, Rachel, 201

INDEX

Julie (Rousseau), 37, 44, 48
Juliette (Sade), 82

Kant, Immanuel, 1, 9, 55–70, 71n11, 92, 238
Key Writings (Irigaray), 202
Khrushchev, Nikita, 91
Kierkegaard, Søren, 19, 111, 112, 171, 178
Kojève, Alexandre, 45, 104–05, 106, 117
Korsgaard, Christine, 59
Kristeva, Julia, 104, 109, 139
Kruks, Sonia, 71n6

La pensée de droite, aujourd'hui (Beauvoir), 92, 96, 97
La vieillesse (Beauvoir), 168
Lacan, Jacques, 171
Lambert, Sandra, 230
Le Bon de Beauvoir, Sylvie, 153
Le Brun, Anne, 81, 82, 86
Le Doeuff, Michèle, 2, 3
Le Nouvel Observateur, 212
Leibniz, Gottfried Wilhelm, 15, 36
L'Encyclopédie, 38
Lenin, Vladimir, 93
Les Temps Modernes, 96
Letter to M. D'Alembert on the Theatre (Rousseau), 42–43, 47
Letters to a Young Poet (Rilke), 233
Levesque-Lopman, Louise, 137
Levinas, Emmanuel, 126, 147n34
Lévi-Strauss, Claude, 171
Library of Living Philosophers, the, 94
Lifeworld, 128, 130–31, 133, 141
L'invitée (Beauvoir), see *She Came to Stay*
literature, 1, 6, 16, 21–23, 117, 154, 160; and autobiography, 36, 56, 154; and Bergson, 156, 160–62; and existentialism, 32n10; feminist, 201; and philosophy, 8, 11, 17, 21–23, 29, 31, 32n14, 70, 101n11, 153; and Sade 75
"Literature and Metaphysics" (Beauvoir), 8, 15–23, 27, 29, 30, 31n7, 32n9, 168, 169n12
lived body, 136, 138–39, 141, 146n29, 193
lived experience, Beauvoir's discussion of, 179, 185, 227; and Bergson, 162; and Husserl, 32n12; in *Literature and Metaphysics*, 15, 17, 20–23; and Merleau-Ponty, 176, 178; in *The Second Sex*, 98, 129; ties to theoretical reflection, 27; Richard Wright, 168
Lives (Plutarch), 110
Locke, John, 171
logic, 227; of absurdity, 154; dialectical, 29; in Merleau-Ponty, 175; patriarchal, 232; of sovereignty, 77, 79, 80, 83, 86, 87
Lundgrin-Gothlin, Eva, 100n2

Machiavelli, Niccolò, 96
MacKinnon, Catharine, 85
Mandarins, the (Beauvoir), 51n4, 55, 61, 70, 72n15, 91, 100n1, 112, 147n34
Marcel, Gabriel, 17
marriage, 35, 108, 118, 162, 211, 232
Marx, Karl, 1, 4, 9–10, 36, 100n10; and Beauvoir, 91–100, 104–07, 120n4, 153
Marxism, 9–10, 91–92, 94–99
Marxists, 92–94, 100n8
master-slave dialectic, 69, 104–105
materialism, 93–94, 97, 99
materiality, 126, 131
maternity, 11, 107, 120n7, 191–93, 196, 199–206, 207n7
Matter and Memory (Bergson), 159, 164
Maulnier, Thierry, 96
McCarthy, Erin, 11, 191, 201
McBride, William L., 9, 91, 100n1, 100n9
Meditations, the (Descartes), 174
Memoirs of a Dutiful Daughter (Beauvoir), 2–3, 153, 186n1, 229
menstruation, 139, 143n 15, 145n26, 145n28, 193, 195, 211
Merleau-Ponty, Maurice, 36, 147n34, 181, 187n3, 187n4, 187n5; and Beauvoir, 134–36, 143n14, 145n22, 171–78, 183–86, 186n1, 193; and Heidegger, 65, 72n17; and Husserl, 126–28; and pregnancy, 142n12, 144n18; and Sartre, 131–32, 142n2, 142n3
metaphysics, 8, 15, 17, 19, 21, 27, 64, 221, 227
Metaphysics and the Novel (Merleau-Ponty), 173

Miller, Elaine P., 10, 103, 120n5
Moi, Toril, 2–4, 195–96, 199, 234–35
Monnerot, Jules, 96–7
Montaigu, Comtesse de, 44
Moral Idealism and Political Realism (Beauvoir), 70
moral, commitments, 214; conversion, 70n1; evil, 62; freedom, 66–68, 72n21; judgment, 57; law, 55, 58–61, 63, 67–68, 83, 221; obligation, 58–60, 63–64, 218–19; principle, 9, 58–59, 62; solipsism, 167; suicide, 157; truths, 222; values, 180, 220
Morgan, Lewis, 94
Morrison, Toni, 231
Mosely, Walter, 229
mother, 47, 113, 132, 136–41, 144n17, 144n18, 179, 192, 194–97, 199–206, 207n2; mother right, 51n7; mother-in-law, 77; motherhood, 107, 118, 145n22, 192, 194–96, 200, 207n7, 211
Murphy, Ann V., 11–12, 211, 215
Muslim, 80, 85
Mussett, Shannon M., 8, 13n4, 15
Must We Burn Sade (Beauvoir), 37, 75, 81–82
My Experience as a Writer (Beauvoir), 156
Myrdal, Gunnar, 230
myth, 16, 31n6, 53n18, 95, 232; literary, 20, 27; of maternity/motherhood, 11, 196, 199–200, 203–05, 207n2; in Plato, 8, 20, 28, 30; of woman, 95, 99, 153, 168

Nazi Occupation, the, 167
New York Times Book Review, 82, 211, 225n1, 234
New York Times Magazine, 212
Nietzsche, Friedrich, 10, 21–22, 31n4, 31n5, 83, 96, 121n9, 171; and Beauvoir, 103–04, 108–19, 121n12; and Butler, 214; on Plato, 15–18, 20, 29, 31n6, 33n19
nihilism, 64, 66–68, 115, 221
North America, 204
nursing, 132, 135–36

Oedipus complex, 37
On Redemption (Nietzsche), 110

On the Origin of Language (Rousseau), 38, 43
One Hundred and Twenty days of Sodom, the (Sade), 81
ontology, 35; of existent 217–18, 221; existentialist, 220; and freedom, 61
oppression, 5, 7, 12, 42, 50, 83, 104, 120n1, 186, 222; and class, 94; gender, 80; and Marx, 94; social, 41, 51n8; and violence, 215, 222; of women, 9–11, 46, 56, 76, 79, 94, 192–93
Origin of the Family, Private Property, and the State (Engels), 94, 99, 101n10
Other, the, 5, 35, 55–57, 66, 68, 105; and bad faith, 68; and Bergson, 153, 156; and freedom, 67, 69; in Marx, 95; obligation to, 71n6; women as, 76

Paris, 35, 39, 40, 51n4, 171
patriarchy, 192, 196, 199, 200, 202, 206, 229, 235
perceptual ambiguity, 172, 174, 177
Phaedo, the (Plato), 16, 31n3
Phaedrus, the (Plato), 8, 16, 23–24, 29–31, 31n3, 31n4, 32n10
phenomenology, 1, 10, 101n11, 133, 143n14, 178, 187n4, 217; French, 213–14; Husserlian, 126, 153
Phenomenology of Perception (Merleau-Ponty), 134, 136, 173–74, 176–78, 184
Phenomenology of Spirit (Hegel), 20, 52n12, 104, 153
Piaget, Jean, 171
Plato, 1, 4, 8, 15–18, 20, 23–30, 31n2, 32n10, 33n19, 62
Platonic dialogue, 8, 16, 18, 20, 22, 32n10
Plutarch, 110
poetry, 16–17, 52n16, 119, 233
politics, 1, 9, 35, 50, 62, 75–76, 206, 216, 226, 234; and Butler, 217; democratic, 44; feminist, 101n11, 227; and gender, 80, 84; Irigaray's, 207n5; and rape, 80; Sade's, 79, 82–83; of sovereignty, 79–80
Precarious Life (Butler), 216–17, 224
precariousness, 12, 214–16, 218–19, 222–25
pregnancy, 132–33, 135, 137–39, 141, 142n12, 143n15, 143n16, 144n17, 145n21, 145n24, 147n33, 193–96, 200

Prime of Life (Beauvoir), 3, 32n13, 160
proletariat, the, 93, 96
psychoanalysis, 37, 99, 202
psychology, 93, 155, 171, 227; Gestalt, 175
Pyrrhus and Cineas (Beauvoir), 5, 60, 67–70, 72n18, 104, 110, 113, 129, 160, 169n12, 221

queer theory, 214

race, 7, 79–80, 86, 169n13, 186, 230–31, 233–35
race studies, 186
racism, 114, 169n13
rape, 9, 75, 76, 79, 80, 83–85, 87, 144n17
rational law, 63, 65
religion, 49, 79, 96–97, 115, 154
Republic, the (Plato), 16
Review of the *Phenomenology of Perception* (Beauvoir), 173
Rilke, Rainer Maria, 233
Rorschach test, 81
Rousseau, Jean-Jacques, 1, 8–9, 35–50, 51n2, 51n3, 51n6, 51n7, 51n8, 52n15, 52n16
Rwanda, 83–86

Sade, Marquis de, 1, 9, 75–84, 87, 88
Salazar, António de Oliveira, 49
Sartre, Jean-Paul, 1, 10, 32n9, 32n14, 36, 45, 97, 100n7, 122n15, 126–27, 135, 141, 147n34, 178–79, 193; freedom and, 66, 72n21, 119; and Merleau-Ponty, 132, 142n2, 142n3; and Marx, 94, 98–99, 100n8; and Nietzsche, 31n6; relationship to Beauvoir, 2–3, 5–6, 63, 65, 142n8, 153, 156, 172, 181, 184, 187n8, 188n9, 212, 227–29, 231–32, 235–36
Satan, 106
Scapp, Ron, 234
Scarth, Fredrika, 193, 204
Scholz, Sally J., 8, 35, 51n2, 52n15
Schopenhauer, Arthur, 171
Schwab, Gail, 197
Search for a Method (Sartre), 98–99
Second Discourse (Rousseau) or *Discourse on the Origin of Inequality Among Mankind*, the, 38, 40–41, 43, 48, 51n5, 51n7, 53n17

Second Sex, The (Beauvoir), 7, 9, 10, 51n7, 53n18, 61, 70, 71n3, 72n15, 101n11, 113, 121n10, 121n11, 125, 129, 132, 187n8, 211–13, 227; and Bergson, 153; feminist views in, 229; Hegelian views in, 68–69; and immanence, 116–117; and the lesbian, 185; and Marx, 92, 94–95, 97–99; and Nietzsche, 31n6, 103, 108; and oppression, 56; and the Other, 157, 168, 179; and pregnancy/maternity, 136, 140, 192–93, 195, 200–01, 204–05, 207n7; and race, 230; and Rousseau, 36, 41, 45–47; and Sade, 75–76; and Sartre, 231; and Wollstonecraft, 52n14
Sexes and Genealogies (Irigaray), 199
sexism, 114, 212, 228–29, 233
She Came to Stay (Beauvoir), 11, 147n34, 156–57, 161–63, 173, 183
Simone de Beauvoir: The Making of an Intellectual Woman (Moi), 234
Simons, Margaret A., 10–11, 13n13, 31n7, 32n9, 70n1, 153, 156, 168n1, 168n5, 169n13, 204, 225n2
social construction, 36–37, 46, 129
Social Contract, The (Rousseau), 37, 44
social inequality, 38, 41–42, 47–48
social self, 11, 153, 155–57
sociology, 227
Socrates, 17, 24–30, 32n10, 32n17, 32n18, 234
solipsism, 70n1, 156–57, 160, 162–65, 167–68
Sorbonne, 91, 153, 171
sovereign, 23, 42, 75–76, 77–80, 83–84, 87, 164, 166, 183, 197; freedom, 78, 82–83, 88
Spengler, Oswald, 96
Spinoza, Baruch, 15
spirit, 20, 110, 179, 201, 205, 215; of gravity, 108, 110, 121n12
spontaneity, 6, 58, 63–64, 136, 158
Stalin, Joseph, 91
Stanford University, 230
state, the, 9, 47, 76–78
subject, the, 58–59, 63–65, 120n1, 129, 142n5, 178, 185, 198, 214, 220
subjective experience, 19, 153, 156

subjective idealism, 164
subjectivism, 162, 167
subjectivity, 15, 19, 105, 172, 220; in Marx, 92; in Merleau-Ponty, 185; in Sartre, 178–79, 184; in *She Came to Stay*, 183; women's, 107, 139, 141, 191–94, 196–206
surrealism, 161, 165
Symbolic Order, 197
Symposium, the (Plato), 16, 31n3
System (philosophical), 2–5, 7, 8, 19–23, 25–27, 29, 30–31, 36, 37, 79, 81, 98, 125, 160, 234
systematic (philosophy), 2, 4, 5, 8, 16, 18–21, 23, 32n12

teleology, 139
telos, 6
theology, 16
Thomas, Paul, 44, 51n8, 51n10
Thus Spoke Zarathustra (Nietzsche), 17, 104, 108, 114, 117
time, 10, 12, 20, 23, 32n10, 39, 60, 105, 114, 179; and the festival 40, 42, 45, 50; as frozen, 65; and morality, 59–60, 66; natural, 107; and Nietzsche, 103, 109–10; women's, 104, 116; and work, 107
time (leisure), 35, 38, 40–41, 45, 47, 53n17
Time and Free Will: An Essay on the Immediate Data of Consciousness (Bergson), 154–8, 167, 168n3
Toynbee, Arnold J., 96
transcendence, 66–67, 120n1, 121n10, 139, 179, 204–05, 220; and Bergson, 155–58, 164; and Butler, 214, 225; and childhood, 52n15; existential, 113; and festivals, 42, 45, 49–50; historical, 115, 119; and Nietzsche, 10, 103–104, 109, 112–13, 115–17, 120; and pregnancy/maternity, 11, 193–97; and repetition, 111–12
transgender identity, 214
Tutsi, the, 84–85
Twilight of the Idols (Nietzsche), 115

Undoing Gender (Butler), 216

United Nations, 86
United Nations Declaration of Human Rights, the, 86
United States, the, 91, 97, 223, 229, 230, 233
universal moral law, 58, 60, 221
universalism, 21

value-objects, 131
Van Gogh, Vincent, 111
Veltman, Andrea, 195, 197
Venice, 43, 44
Vintges, Karen, 32n11, 37, 56, 72n21,
violence, 12, 60, 83, 87–8, 165, 213–9, 221–6
Voss, Andrew, 229
vulnerability, 12, 76, 83, 186, 213–19, 221–24

war, 9, 35, 40, 55, 80, 84, 85–86, 114, 195, 230
Wartime Diary (Beauvoir), 70n1, 167
Weil, Simone, 171
Weis, Gail, 11, 171, 187n7,
Western philosophy, 1, 2, 8, 12, 197
What Can Literature Do? (Beauvoir), 168, 169n12
When Things of the Spirit Come First (Beauvoir), 11, 160–2
Wilkerson, William S., 9, 55, 71n9
will, the, 42, 58, 59, 61, 63–6, 103, 104, 115, 220, 230
Wittgenstein, Ludwig, 5, 98
Wollstonecraft, Mary, 46, 52n14
Woman Destroyed, The (*La Femme Rompue*) (Beauvoir), 161
Women's Time (Kristeva) 109
World War II, 35, 86, 96, 163

Yale French Studies, 81, 213
Young, Iris Marion, 130, 137, 142, 144, 187
Yugoslavia, 83–7

Zaza, 171
Zerilli, Linda, 193, 196

www.ingramcontent.com/pod-product-compliance
Ingram Content Group UK Ltd.
Pitfield, Milton Keynes, MK11 3LW, UK
UKHW041917140426
5217IPUK00013B/193

9 781438 444543